W9-ADJ-655

NEUROSES AND CHARACTER TYPES

NEUROSES AND CHARACTER TYPES

Clinical Psychoanalytic Studies

HELENE DEUTSCH

NEW YORK

INTERNATIONAL UNIVERSITIES PRESS

1965

PRINTED IN THE UNITED STATES OF AMERICA

Contents

v

CONTENTS vii

CONTENTS vii

CONTENTS vii

CONTENTS vii

CONTENTS vii

CONTENTS vii

CONTENTS vii

24. Psychoanalytic Therapy in the Light of Follow-up (1959) — 339
25. *Lord Jim* and Depression (1959) — 353
26. Frigidity in Women (1960) — 358
27. Acting Out in the Transference (1963) — 363

Bibliography — 375

Index — 378

Editor's Foreword

HELENE DEUTSCH'S *Psycho-Analysis of the Neuroses,* published over thirty years ago, has remained one of the most popular textbooks on the subject. For the many students it has served, its value has lain in the combination of vivid clinical description with lucid statements of the psychodynamic inferences required to account for the phenomena. The original volume seemed so fresh today that it was decided to retain it unaltered, and it now appears as Part One of this book. The later clinical papers, most of which have become as well known as the earlier ones, have been grouped chronologically in Part Two. We believe students will find this greatly enlarged edition as stimulating and useful as the original.

John D. Sutherland

Preface

In recent years I have frequently been approached by instructors and candidates of psychoanalytic Institutes as well as by psychiatrists interested in "dynamic psychiatry" with the idea of bringing out a new edition of *Psycho-Analysis of the Neuroses,* since the first edition was exhausted and difficult to obtain.

As the trend in psychoanalysis has recently become more theoretical and speculative, it seemed advisable to revise the book from the point of view of new theoretical concepts in analysis. On the other hand, the more clinical aspect of psychoanalysis has often seemed to me to be neglected. The idea of re-examining the old clinical material with more emphasis on the ego-psychological approach, therefore, seemed both attractive and necessary.

As I progressed in these efforts, I recognized by and large that to present a clear and objective clinical picture of cases observed analytically, it was not necessary to correct these observations or to change the interpretations given in the original edition of the book. I found instead that new formulations would only obscure the observations and that speculations, clever and interesting as they might be, would not increase our understanding of patients and their neurotic conflicts. Furthermore, since the book never attempted to deal with the therapeutic method of psychoanalysis and with its technique, it was not necessary or advisable to discuss the changes in technique, their value and differences, although in the thirty years which have passed since the book was first published it was to be expected that progress, especially in the field of therapy, had been achieved.

As my reluctance to revise the book grew, the demand for the book in its old form was increasing. This fact reinforced my impression that the merit of the book as an introduction to clinical work lay in its empirical aspect, which required no change. I was greatly relieved when the Publications Committee of the British Psycho-Analytical Society, the Hogarth Press (London), and the International Universities Press (New York) approached me with the proposition to publish an enlarged edition of the book, with the addition of my papers published after 1932, the year in which the first English translation had been brought out.

In keeping with the character of the original volume the additional articles are restricted to clinical ones (I appreciate highly the great poetic literary value of Don Quixote, nevertheless I consider the hero's psychological problems "clinical"). Two of the articles (published in nonpsychoanalytic magazines) are in the psychosomatic field, namely, "Psychiatric Component in Gynecology" and "Psychoanalytic Observations in Surgery." Some articles are perhaps more concerned with "ego-psychological" factors than others; for example, "A Discussion of Certain Forms of Resistance," "Some Forms of Emotional Disturbance and Their Relationship to Schizophrenia," "The Impostor," "Psychology of Manic-Depressive Conditions, Especially Chronic Hypomania," and "Don Quixote and Don Quixotism."

To those who are primarily dedicated to clinical work, each patient brings new insights and new data. The new papers continue the aim behind the previous publications, namely, to provide the reader with clinical experiences gained in psychoanalysis of patients and application of these experiences to psychological understanding in general. In this publication I again attempt to restrict the analytic material to direct observations without terminological confusion and fruitless speculations.

It is always depressing to be confronted with the fact that external and internal limitations permit us to communicate to others only a small sector of knowledge acquired in many years of observation. The value of such observations is that they can be utilized as a part of analytic research in general, as small stones for the great building.

Part I

Psychoanalysis of the Neuroses

Translated by

W. D. ROBSON-SCOTT

1

The Part of the Actual Conflict in the Formation of Neurosis

(1930)

LADIES AND GENTLEMEN—Instruction in psychoanalysis as a clinical discipline must differ essentially in its methods from all other forms of clinical instruction. The future doctor or therapist gains his practical education from the material available for him in the medical clinic; there he is able to study the disease in all its manifestations from direct observation of the patient himself. The future psychoanalyst, on the other hand, must gain his from direct observation of his own psychic life in his own analysis, and thus first experience empirically in himself what he wishes to understand later in others. Clinical demonstration, an important aid to medical education, can find no place in the education of the analyst.

These lectures will attempt to supply some sort of substitute for clinical demonstration. I shall describe to you some typical cases, adding thereto only such theoretical considerations as proceed inevitably from the case history.

All the cases I shall deal with here have been analyzed by me. I shall only here and there go into the technique of the treatment and the therapeutic process, and I shall assume in you a basic knowledge of the subject, much as the doctor at a clinic assumes a knowledge of pathological anatomy when he is discussing a case.

3

Psychoanalysis, as you know, emphasizes three etiological factors in tracing the origin of neurotic diseases: (1) *fixation* of the libido, (2) *regression,* and (3) the so-called current or *"actual" cause,* which may become through some frustration a decisive factor in the genesis of the illness.

To put this dynamically, we might compare the frustration to a wall against which a forward-moving mental force rebounds so that it is compelled to strive backward. This process of backward striving we call "regression," and this regression continues back to those deserted stations of former developments which exercise a peculiar power of attraction. This persistent power of attraction corresponds to "fixation." It is fixation, and neither the actual cause nor frustration, which is responsible for the type of neurosis, and thus it acquires the character of a *dispositional* factor.

Let me illustrate this more closely from three actual cases. All three are completely identical in the actual cause of the illness and in the type of frustration. In the clinical picture, on the other hand, in the structure of the neurosis, they are completely different.

We are concerned with three married women, each of whom fate has placed in a typical conflict situation. In danger of destroying their married life through a new love relationship, they are unable to find any other escape than that of neurotic illness. None of the three was in a position to resolve the actual conflict in a healthy, psychically normal way. Every attempt at a solution inevitably brought with it some form of renunciation. And to all three of them renunciation of the fulfillment of their love wishes seemed the only way out of the conflict. But the solution was not a satisfactory one; the frustration became intolerable and led to illness, i.e., the actual conflict was replaced by a neurosis. That these three women could find no other way out of their conflicts was due to their *neurotic disposition,* to the morbid tendency which comes to a head at the moment of frustration. What this neurotic disposition consists in, and why each of them found a completely different form of neurosis as an expression of her conflict, we shall now proceed to discover.

One of the three women becomes subject to typical hysterical attacks with *arc-de-cercle,* violent convulsions of the whole body, and typical defensive movements of the extremities. We learn from her analysis that the attack is a form of expression for crudely sexual fantasies relating to the renounced object which, shut off from consciousness, have found this path of gratification, and that the violent motor discharges signify both the fulfillment of the sexual wish and the defense against it.

The second patient expresses her conflict in a quite different neurotic form. She falls ill of agoraphobia, by which she is attacked every time she tries to leave her house, a symbol of her conjugal faithfulness. Her symptom literally blocks her path to freedom, and the patient prefers the loneliness of her home, free as it is from anxiety, to the tendencies which might well separate her from her home and family life. The anxiety, a symptom of her illness, becomes thus the guardian of her conjugal fidelity, and forces her to solve the conflict in this morbid fashion.

The third of these three women has the following morbid symptoms: she has the habit of opening and shutting her wardrobe over and over again from the fear that if she does not do this her husband will die. In the analysis it becomes clear that the act of opening the wardrobe corresponds to the wish to take out her clothes and pay her lover a visit, and that of shutting the wardrobe to the prohibition which prevents her carrying out this wish. At the same time the wardrobe serves as a symbolic representation of her genitals, which declare themselves ready to receive the loved object by the act of opening and defend themselves against this by the act of shutting. Among her other symptoms this lady has the following parting ceremonial, painful as it is both for herself and her husband: every time that he is about to leave the house she looks through his pockets to see that he has everything he needs with him. All the objects have to be pulled out of the pockets in a certain order and then put back again in the same order: keys, purse, cigarette case, handkerchief, etc., are all subjected to this procedure over and over again. And scarcely has her husband left the door but she calls him back again to go through the whole business once more.

In the course of her analysis it became clear that her sexual temptation had raised violent annihilation wishes against her husband. The unconscious wish for his death became especially intense one evening when he pulled his pocketknife out of his pocket while undressing. At this moment the latent wish was mobilized by an associative link with the knife. How the displacement onto other objects took place and what psychical mechanism the patient's wearisome activity corresponded to we shall learn in the further course of the discussion.

Let us consider in these three instances, identical in their actual cause, so varied in their manner of reaction, wherein the ground of this variety consists. All three women suffer from an inner conflict and each of them has her particular way, a specifically neurotic form, of resolving the conflict. The neurotic symptoms are indeed nothing else than unsuccessful attempts to solve the inner conflict. Why does each of these women choose so divergent a method of expressing the conflict in her symptoms? To answer this we must first investigate analytically the deeper causes of their illness; only in this way shall we discover why the three patients reacted so differently. Common to them all was the "actual cause" of their specific neurotic reactions.

We will now deal more closely with this "actual conflict." In the above examples we have seen how it led to a neurosis, and we have said that this neurosis represents an attempt, albeit a morbid one, to solve this conflict. Experience has taught us that inner neurotic conflicts arise when the libido is deprived of the possibility of finding an ego-syntonic gratification in the outer world, or when intolerable narcissistic injuries have prevented it from making satisfactory sublimations. In this case a situation has arisen in which we speak of illness from "external frustration."

The reaction of the individual to the external frustration may be a normal or a neurotic one. In either case he will find himself at the moment of frustration in an attitude of hostility to the frustrating reality.

We say in that case that the individual is placed in an actual conflict. This, however, cannot be described as neurotic so long as the person in question is in a position to solve this external conflict in a manner in keeping with reality. He might, for instance, adapt the outer world to his needs, or, where this is not possible, tolerate the frustration, i.e., renounce. He would then be free to look for new possibilities of gratification. It is only when these solutions are no longer possible, i.e., when the actual conflict with the outer world appears insoluble to the person concerned, that the "external frustration" becomes an internal one, and a vicious circle is set up. For the inability to resolve a real conflict was conditioned from the outset by internal motives. The external frustration in itself need not have any pathogenic effect; it is only when the external conflict transfers its scene of action from the outer world to the inner world that the inner conflict—the neurosis—arises. The ego disappointed in the outer world finds itself compelled to look for substitute gratifications, and thus enters upon the familiar path of regression. Hence what makes the reality-conditioned actual conflict a neurotic one is its subjective insolubility. But this insolubility is itself the expression of a neurotic attitude to the outer world and leads to the transformation of the real frustration into a neurotic conflict, which, however, need not necessarily lead to symptom formation. I need not enter more closely here into the forms these conflicts take. They either possess the mourning character of the unsurmounted external loss; or else they bear the stamp of an inner irresolution, the result of an undecided struggle between two psychic tendencies, e.g., between the two emotional currents of the ambivalent conflict or between an instinctual impulse and an internal prohibition, etc.

A typical example of a neurotic conflict is the impossibility of breaking loose from a no longer loved object, either from a neurotic inability to transfer to a new one, or conscious renunciation of a new one as a result of feelings of guilt toward the old one, etc. In such conflict situations analysis always reveals the repetition of an infantile prototype, covered over though it is by the actual situation.

In some cases the neurotic tendencies express themselves in a conflictual mode of reaction to the real world. In other cases it is clear that the external cause has taken on the part of an *agent provocateur*, which transforms an already chronically conflictual relationship to the outer world into a neurotic illness.

The neurotic symptom, that is to say, owes its existence to the same deep sources which gave rise to earlier difficulties in the adaptation to reality.

When a real conflict cannot be resolved in normal fashion, as a result of the inner incapacity for adaptation, the ego frequently makes convulsive efforts to find a compromise before committing the libido to still deeper paths of regression, and this solution will then bear a completely individual character. It is only when this does not succeed that the neurotic struggles ensue. I will try and make clear by an example what may perhaps appear somewhat obscure.

A patient began her analysis with the statement that there was nothing wrong with her and that she only came to me because her husband, whom she considered "nervous," had insisted on it. I had, however, already learned from her husband that an actual conflict had evoked neurotic difficulties in the patient, and this was substantiated in the analysis. After fifteen years of marriage the husband had fallen passionately in love with a niece who had just married into the family. In an evident desire to get rid of his guilt, and with regard to the platonic nature of his love, he had initiated his wife into the secret. On this the patient had entered into the role of her husband's "best friend," had suppressed every reaction in any way hostile, and tried by every means in her power to establish a friendly relationship with her new relative. The young woman seemed to her to be the most wonderful creature in the world, entirely occupied her yearning fantasies, and it was only when the lack of response on her part frustrated our patient's attempts at friendship that she encountered neurotic difficulties. It became clear in the further course of the analysis that her whole life she had had to fight against certain masculine tendencies, which she had at one point done her best to suppress on her husband's behalf. As a girl she had been both gifted and ambitious musically, and yet she had entirely given up her studies in this direction to become a good housewife, a sacrifice which she had made, as she always insisted, solely for the sake of her husband. After the disappointment she had now experienced she determined to put an end to this sacrifice, and began to study music anew, against which, to her surprise, no protest was made by her husband. At this she herself made further study impossible by indulging in an absolute furor of "housewifery," in which she forced herself to the most menial tasks and thus neurotically distorted the sacrifice she had formerly made to her husband. At the same time she lived in a state of perpetual strife with the servant girl, who could do nothing right in her eyes, so that, perpetually dissatisfied, she carried out all the household duties herself. Despite the most intense hatred for the unfortunate girl, whom she declared to be completely incompetent, she could not bring herself to the point of dismissing her. And when the girl finally left the house of her own accord, the same situation repeated itself with her successor.

It soon became clear in the analysis that her deeper reason for coming to me in particular lay in an unconscious relationship to me, which had existed, unknown to me, before ever the analysis began. Through certain circumstances she had transferred her affective attitude to her rival onto me and had come to be analyzed to win my love. Thus in her analysis she was able to live out the full force of her sadistic hate toward her rival, to recognize the secondary nature of her conflict with the servant girl, and subsequently to realize the neurotic basis of the conflict. Up to this point—this knowledge cost a year's analytic work—she had considered her real conflict to be completely settled and of no further importance, and imagined that she had long ago forgiven her husband for his infidelity. From this short sketch of the case it is possible to see how the actual conflict had grown from an "external" to an "internal" one.

Let us briefly complete our survey of the case. The patient found herself in a real actual conflict. The normal mode of reaction would have been: either to renounce the object and find a new one after a period of mourning, or else to enter into a struggle with her rival. But the first of these solutions the patient could not adopt, because, as the analysis showed, certain infantile attitudes, which she had continued to preserve, had the effect of binding the patient more strongly to the loved object in proportion as it withdrew from her. And the second possibility remained closed to her, because her aggressive vindictive tendencies were so intense that they had to be rejected and repressed.

But there was still one solution left, by adopting which the patient would have remained healthy, i.e., without neurosis. For the analysis revealed that she had been in similar actual conflicts several times before in her life, which she had always solved in the same way, by means of a compromise on the part of the ego—as I mentioned at the beginning. This compromise was: to renounce the heterosexual love object, but to force herself between the man and the woman and destroy the bond by taking homosexual possession of the woman. Thus had she tried to separate her parents in childhood, an action which masked itself in an excessive love for the mother. And this childhood situation was the source of the masculine tendencies which she had later sacrificed to her husband.

As this sole accessible solution of her present conflict had been rendered impossible by her rival's opposition, there was no alternative but neurosis. The hate tendencies against her rival she displaced onto the servant girl, the aggressions against her husband she transformed into masochism (menial domestic tasks), by means of which she sadistically tried to increase his guilt by the sacrifices which she went on demonstrating to him anew.

You can see from this instance how the actual conflict was replaced by the neurotic one without the patient herself being aware of the intolerability of the real conflict. And you can see too how the ego undertakes attempted solutions to protect itself from illness and that it is only when these fail that it succumbs to "insolubility," i.e., neurosis.

Our analytic knowledge of the human soul has taught us that every civilized person is really in a continuous state of *latent conflict,* with the real world on the one hand, and with his own inner forces on the other, since he has always frustrations to endure and inhibitions to overcome. The harmonious solution of these internal and external conflicts is the affair of his personality; and everyone has his characteristic, one might say characterological, manner of enduring and overcoming normal frustrations. The latent conflict will become an actual one only when the boundary of endurability for the person in question has been passed. This may happen either as a result of the extent of the frustration, or from some weakness of the ego, or because of some particular affinity between the frustration and the tendencies which have hitherto been successfully repressed. Here, too, the actual cause plays the part of the activating *agent provocateur*.

Thus the resulting conflict is constructed according to prototype. But, more than this, psychoanalysis is able to show us that many a conflict, similar to the actual one, has run like a thread through the life of the individual in a nonpathological rudimentary form. In many cases one gets the impression that the actual cause itself has arisen through an unconscious provocation and that the type of real frustration thus provoked is as specific for the individual in question as the type of conflict formation (e.g., in love conflicts). We have seen that the healthy person as well as the neurotic has the tendency to go on actualizing the once actual conflicts of his own childhood. In fact the action of the healthy man in this respect differs from that of the neurotic only in the fact that it is consonant with his ego and with reality; he brings up a family, forms clubs, "common ideals," etc.; in a word, he is continually creating his own conflicts in order to solve them. The neurotic, on the other hand, is unable to find a solution for the real conflict, and his ego gets into a condition which we have called the "actual conflict" of the neurotic. The affinity with the neurotic symptom, the dependence on the same dynamic factors, is shown too by the ease with which he can be grouped under one of the typical neurotic diseases, hysterical or obsessional as the case may be, without exhibiting, however, any actual symptoms of either.

It must be admitted that the question of the actual conflict has given rise to much lively discussion. Recently, for instance, Rank has reproached psychoanalysis with neglecting the actual conflict in favor of the historical past. Perhaps the best solution of the problem is to be found in Freud's words: "The actual conflict of the neurotic only becomes intelligible and soluble if one traces it back to the previous history of the patient and follows out the course which his libido took in the production of the illness." I hope that this pregnant definition of the actual conflict has been sufficiently illustrated by the example I gave you.

So long as a person's conflict is of a completely real character, he stands outside the scope of analytic interest. This begins as soon as the conflict has evoked neurotic reactions, as soon, therefore, as it has become intricately bound up with the whole neurotic personality, i.e., has undergone the transformation from a real to a neurotic conflict. Thus the question of the attitude to be taken by the analyst to his patients' actual conflicts really answers itself: the same as to all other psychic manifestations of the patient. The analyst must unmask the resistances wherever they can be discovered and must resist the patient's attempt to divert the attention of the analyst from unconscious processes to the plane of actuality.

If the actual conflict is manifest and plays a dominating role in the patient's mental life, he should be trained to turn his attention to the analysis of the unconscious sources of the conflict. If, on the other hand, it has been repressed and transferred to another sphere by symptoms or displacement (as in the case mentioned above), then it is of course essential to remove the unconscious resistances and unmask the actual conflict.

In two cases in particular is it necessary to submit the actual conflict to consistent investigation: (1) if the patient turns with alacrity to the infantile material and tries to divert the analyst's attention from the actual conflicts; (2) if the actual conflict and the transference neurosis, i.e., the neurotic relationship of the patient to the analyst, become merged in an intimate symbiosis, as a result of which the transference resistances unite under one standard with the unconscious resistances of the actual conflict against the analysis. I need only remind you of the behavior of the patient mentioned above, who transferred a large part of her actual conflict (the love frustration from her husband's lover) onto me; both of which, the actual conflict and the attempt to win my love, she sought to repress. To neglect the actual conflict in favor of infantile material in such a case would of course be a crude mistake on the part of the analyst.

It usually happens that with the formation of the transference neurosis the patient's interest is diverted from the whole conflict with the outer world onto the analysis or the relation to the analyst. With the solution of the transference neurosis the actual conflict sometimes disappears automatically, often indeed without being dealt with directly at all. Such cases supply convincing proof of the absolute connection between the actual conflict and deeper sources.

It sometimes happens that patients seek in the outer world outside the analysis a discharge for the feelings which the analysis has mobilized in them and which the analyst cannot gratify. They then realize in a manifest and actual form their neurotic transference wishes, thus creating a parallel in the outer world for the actual situation in the analysis. The obvious attraction which this course has for the patient when compared with the negative attitude of the analyst has the effect of turning the patient's interest from the cure, with consequent interference to the progress of the treatment. It happens, for instance, during analysis that patients form neurotic love relationships to obtain an actual substitute for the infantile wish fantasies which the transference has stirred in them. Such situations seriously endanger the course of the analysis. For the patient, as a rule, they soon bring actual conflicts in their train, which must of course be dealt with in the analysis.

If the patient suffers some real injury from the outer world which is accompanied by strong affective reactions, the analyst should modify his attitude accordingly. He will manifest his human interest and desire to help the patient even though he holds up the analytic situation for a period by so doing. Only when the loss reactions of the patient assume a neurotic character will he direct his attention more to these reactions and less to their occasion. There is hardly an event during the course of the analysis which will not gradually merge into the transference and the entirety of the analytic situation. The possibilities are countless and in most cases the analyst must rely on his knowledge and tact to show the patients the way to their inner conflicts. One cannot find a rule for everything.

SECTION I: HYSTERIA

2

Hysterical Fate Neurosis

(1930)

In our last lecture we considered the part played by the actual cause in the genesis of a neurotic condition, and we were able to see that the role of the actual conflict is only that of *agent provocateur*. In some cases indeed it is itself the result and product of a neurotic provocation. We also spoke of individuals whose existence is one long series of actual conflicts, called forth of course by their own attitude to life. In these chronic cases the actual conflicts acquire a specific character, for they are the reflection of an inner conflict which is forever seeking to express itself externally. But the opposite is true too: an external conflict will call forth different reactions according to the disposition of the individual in question. You remember the three patients I mentioned in Chapter 1, where one and the same cause provoked three completely different modes of reaction in three different forms of neurosis. It is clear that the causes of this difference did not lie in the actual traumatic experience, which was the same in each case. They lay in what may be described as "dispositional factors." Without going more closely into the meaning of this concept, I will confine myself here to the remark that what we call disposition can be traced back to two factors in the psyche: that which has been acquired from earliest infantile experience on the one hand, and an inborn constitutional predisposition on the other. The latter is accessible to analysis only in its results, whereas the former, the infantile experience, plays of

14

course an important part in the analysis. I do not intend to discuss the development of analytic knowledge of the infantile trauma here; I will merely mention that our understanding of the essence of neurosis starts from the discovery of the fundamental significance of the infantile trauma for the origin of the neurotic process (Breuer and Freud, 1895).

In the course of the years this discovery has been both widely developed and considerably modified. It is true, that is to say, that there are a number of cases in which a serious infantile experience, a so-called psychic trauma, not only provoked the neurosis, but actually caused it. In such cases one can say with more or less certainty that it is only the misfortune of having had the particular experience that has made the child ill. But with the overwhelming majority of patients it is easy enough to see that the so-called traumatic experiences of childhood have exactly the same significance as the actual conflicts of the adult. They had a traumatic effect because they could not be overcome—usually as a consequence of a predisposition in the child, which in some cases itself provoked the experiences. Indeed we are often able to establish a connection between the actual neurotic conflicts of the adult and these first traumatic experiences of the child. This connection is due either to a psychic experience of childhood which has not been mastered and which thus tends to repeat itself in later life, or to a particular predisposition which reacts neurotically to an accidental experience. If this predisposition remains unaltered in later life, it will mean that the individual tends to react to similar accidental experiences in the same neurotic way.

Our analytic experience has forced us to recognize this "dispositional factor." It became abundantly clear that many children were unable to overcome completely normal experiences in a normal way. One of our most important pieces of analytic insight, in fact, is the discovery that even the normal conditions of infantile life make demands which are by no means infrequently beyond the child's psychic powers. And the incapacity to deal with these difficulties can produce various pathological reactions. Our insight into the mental life of the child has taught us that he is really continually the victim of "actual conflicts," and that he quite regularly reacts to these conflicts in certain stages of his development by temporary anxiety states, the typical form of an infantile actual neurosis. He may nevertheless remain quite healthy, till some frustration in later life becomes intolerable and finally produces a neurotic illness. In this case analysis will enable us to establish a connection between the new neurosis and the infantile one. Moreover, it frequently turns out that the individual has only been relatively well in the interval.

In other cases the infantile neurosis has from the start the character of a lifelong psychic defect, in which case the neurosis has a specific form even in childhood; thus differing from the above-mentioned infantile anxiety states, which belong to no particular neurotic category. The type of neurosis rests in a constitutional factor, which can be recognized even in earliest infancy.

Before embarking on a theoretical consideration of these dispositional factors, I should like to discuss with you various forms of hysterical illness on the basis of analyses which I will describe to you. We shall then be in a position to draw theoretical conclusions with a greater degree of understanding.

I shall begin with the clinical picture of a patient, to which I will give the name of "hysterical fate neurosis." We shall be able to show that the patient, who was without symptoms and as unsuspicious as her friends and relatives of the pathological element in her fate, was nevertheless subject to the same difficulties and pathological fixations in her mental life as other people who suffer from severe hysterical symptoms.

The patient was twenty-five years of age and had made the long journey from overseas to Vienna in order to escape from the environment of her actual conflict and seek help for the emotional turmoil in which she found herself in psychoanalytic treatment. During the journey her turmoil had subsided, and when she came to consult me she gave the impression of a calm and self-possessed young lady without the slightest insight into her illness and, as she thought, in no further need of treatment. She was beautiful, cultured, and of wealthy family. Shortly before her departure she had made an unsuccessful attempt at suicide; a scarcely visible scar on her temple was all that remained of the revolver shot. She had made the attempt in a small hotel in her native town under circumstances which seemed to point, as she herself admitted, to some obsessional element in the situation. The motive for her suicide had indeed never been clear to her. Gradually, in this first interview, she began to see that there was something mysterious and apparently morbid in her life, something which convinced her that she was after all in need of analytic treatment.

It would take too long to describe the whole history of her case in detail. I will only give as much as is absolutely necessary to illustrate the typical features of a "fate neurosis."

She had an outwardly uneventful childhood, only troubled by the fact that inhibitions and inner difficulties prevented her from fulfilling her intense intellectual ambitions and her desire to go to the university and take up a profession. When still quite young she became engaged to a cousin, with whom she had a tender love relationship for several years. But she herself did not feel "fulfilled," as she expressed it, in this relationship. In her view her fiancé loved too much the "woman" in her, and left the intellectual tendencies, on which she laid so much stress, completely unsatisfied. She mentioned incidentally that despite his great love for her he had had polygamous tendencies, about which, however, she had never felt the slightest jealousy.

On one of her travels she made the acquaintance of an elderly man of high intellectual attainments in an important diplomatic position who awakened her interest. A friendly intellectual relationship developed, at first without erotic elements. The man's first wife was dead and his second marriage was, so thought my patient, a happy one. But when their friendly intimacy had grown closer the man confessed to her that his marriage was not a happy one and unable to compensate him for the loss of his first wife, whom he had loved passionately. This confession was too much for our patient's heart. To be loved as the dead woman had been loved! This sudden feeling was the beginning of a love relationship. She broke off her engagement, her new lover separated from his wife, and an apparently happy period set in for our patient.

Then a strange incident brought clouds into their relationship.

The lover was called away to his wife's sickbed. Our patient looked upon his departure as a natural act of humanity and made no sort of protest against the inevitable, taking advantage of his absence to go on a short trip. On the way she met a man whom she had known before, but for whom she had never felt the least interest, and to this completely indifferent object she gave herself without reservation. She became pregnant and an immediate marriage was decided on. Gradually, however, she altered her decision, interrupted her pregnancy, and returned to her lover with a remorseful confession of her guilt. Her relationship to him became as tender as before, he procured his separation from his wife, and the date of the wedding was settled. And then in the middle of the preparations the patient made the attempt at suicide, which meant for both the end of their relationship.

At times during the analysis a painful yearning for the loved one returned to her, though she felt completely convinced that she would never meet him again. In her description of it she would contrast this relationship with that toward her first love (her cousin). The second relationship was intellectually satisfying and a source of such great happiness just because her lover, himself so highly gifted, had so high an opinion of her own intellectual attainments. In contrast to her first lover, he made considerable intellectual and moral demands on her. But strangely enough it was just these demands, which she herself so deeply wished for, that became the cause of her unhappiness. She would go through nights of agony tortured by the feeling of her own inadequacy and inferiority. She had the impression of a dark mysterious shadow which was clouding her existence. The nearer she came to the fulfillment of her desires, just before the wedding, the deeper the shadow descended on her, driving her eventually to the attempted suicide, unmotivated as it seemed both to herself and others.

In her very first interview she had told me that the attempt had had nothing to do with unhappiness in her love affair. It is true that she had noticed at the time a certain estrangement and coolness in her lover, and had got the impression that she was about to make a hasty marriage which ought to be prevented. What had driven her to despair, however, was not these love conflicts, but the thought that in the event of their marriage being a failure she would be forced to continue in dependence on her tyrannical father. This it was which had seemed to her so intolerable.

The tragedy of her life did not consist in disappointments in love, but—as she herself quite consciously felt—in the fact that she was not in a position to free herself from her dependence on her father. For years she had attempted to win material independence by study and all manner of specialized work. But despite her manifold talents all her efforts had come to grief at the last moment owing to an inner inadequacy. In despair she used to say: "Why is it that I alone cannot do what every other woman in my country manages so easily and naturally?"

Let us turn for a moment to the family history of this young girl. She was the second youngest of a numerous family. The father was an exceptionally efficient man, stern, opinionated, and feared by those around him. The mother, who was despised by our patient, lived in slavish dependence on the father. This relationship between the parents roused disgust and protest in our patient. She herself, always a beautiful and talented child, had formerly been her father's favorite. Her only rival at that time was a brother four years younger than herself and of outstanding ability. This brother, whose gifts as a physicist had given rise to great hopes as to his future, died in his twentieth year. The patient herself was gifted in the same field, but, as already mentioned, was unable in consequence of her inhibitions to attain her aim of studying likewise.

Her childhood followed the typical development of a small girl. She loved her father, and, as even a superficial survey made clear, she possessed strongly negative, hostile tendencies toward her mother, which she herself attributed to the fact that her mother was stupid and uneducated and above all so slavishly devoted to her father.

For some time her infantile fantasies were feminine in character, and were satisfied by playing with dolls, and the analysis was able to reconstruct the normal oedipus attitude of the time, in which the wish to have a child was intensified by the birth of her small brother. And for a time she did actually find in the little boy some satisfaction for this wish.

Such an attitude in a little girl may be considered completely normal. Strong love relationship to the father, negative attitude to the mother, the unconscious wish to have a child from the father, in place of the mother—that is the regular oedipus attitude of the little girl, neither pathological nor even unfavorable. It is the later development of this attitude which is decisive for psychic health or illness.

Our patient's first psychic complication arose after the birth of the little brother, an actual conflict which had to be faced. A whole series of little frustrations and disappointments from her father, all of which she had faithfully preserved in her memory, served to represent this one great disappointment: the mother and not she had got the child.

A second source of disappointment weighed especially heavy on her psychic development: in the comparisons which she made between herself and her brother she could not help noticing that the little boy was better equipped somatically than she was. The feelings of inferiority and inhibitions, which had proved so great a hindrance to the attainment of her intellectual aims, owed their source to this attitude, which had persisted uncorrected in the unconscious. The jealousy of and aggression toward the little boy had evoked guilt reactions in her, which contributed in their turn to prevent her from entering into competition with her brother in later life. And this attitude of rivalry toward her brother was increased by the fact that he endangered her priority in the matter of their father's affection. The analysis made clear that the frustrations and disappointments of her childhood had led to strong aggressive reactions and vindictive tendencies toward the unfaithful father, the despised mother, and the little rival.

After the successful repression of these oedipal wishes this infantile relationship to the father expressed itself in a repudiation of her own femininity, which could be interpreted thus: "I refuse to play the part my mother played—to be passively and slavishly devoted to my father." Alongside this conscious revolt, however, arose an unconscious subjection to the father, from which she was never able to free herself; no answer was possible to her despairing question, "Why can't I be free and independent like other girls," because this answer lay hidden in her unconscious. But this was not the only form in which she expressed her inner dependence. The lack of satisfaction in her first love affair had been brought about by the fact that her lover, who was himself somewhat passive and in no way "tyrannical," had given her no opportunity of bringing herself into that repudiated but unconsciously desired relationship to the man, for which she had envied her mother as a little girl. For her unconscious libidinal desires this relationship of the woman to the man remained her only possibility of being "fulfilled" as a woman. The vehement protest against the mother's masochistic attitude was, it proved, really a protest against her own masochistic fixation. In the choice of her first lover she had indeed attempted to evade this unconscious urge. In this she did not succeed, and when a love situation mòre in accord with that between her father and mother presented itself she was driven to be almost compulsively unfaithful to him. One need only recall the situation in which her love for the second lover was stirred: so to be loved as the deceased wife had been loved.

To make clearer the meaning of this situation I will describe the following episode which came up during the analysis. When the patient was twelve years old she visited a bathing resort with her mother. Here a young colored native, a hawker, told her, strangely enough, his life story. He was already twice married, although only eighteen years old. He did not love his second wife, but his first, dead wife, he loved with unabated passion and could never forget her—except, perhaps, for her (my patient's) sake, whom he had so fortunately met that day. Would she—the little girl—consent to marry him? His first wife had left ·him a charming little child; would the little girl perhaps like to have a look at the child? Whereupon he gave her his address and she promised to pay him a visit. Then she wandered about for hours in the streets looking for the house, but the address proved to be false and she realized at last that she had been the victim of a hoax. This experience was a cruel mortification for her. But its peculiar identity with her last love affair rouses the suspicion that her own imagination had first played its part in helping the young native to invent this love story.

The same source was clearly responsible for another little episode which she experienced at the beginning of the analysis and which was all the more incomprehensible to the superficial observer as she was still strongly under the influence of her latest disappointments. Chance brought her into contact with a man who had just shortly before lost his wife and had in consequence fallen a victim to a melancholic depression. Regardless of her own conflicts the patient considered it her duty to save this man by her love and take the place of the deceased. The constant recurrence of such episodes in her life was certainly very remarkable.

Let us consider analytically the situation at the time of her second engagement. This man has not, like the first, been chosen as a contrast to the father, but on the basis of an unconsciously manufactured similarity. The inner urge to a satisfactory attainment of her goal leads her to make her choice not in accordance with the principle of escape, but of similarity. This choice would seem to be a favorable one, for it has been satisfactorily brought into line with her conscious demands. This man is, that is to say, active and imposing like her father, places her in a superior position over the first woman (which her father had not done), but—and that is perhaps her greatest triumph—he does not involve her in the humiliating role which her mother played, but puts her, on the contrary, on a pedestal, treats her as a comrade and makes the same demands of her which she had always made of herself (in order to stand in contrast to her mother). These demands she must strive to fulfill; strive, that is to say, to be intellectual and learned. But it is just these demands which give rise to the first, already neurotic, disturbance which had always rendered the fulfillment of these demands impossible to her. The motives of this inhibition became clear from the analysis. In the rivalry relationship to her brother she wished to attain what he had done, but was always forced to renounce this goal because of the inferiority feeling: "I'm only a girl." The old guilty feelings toward the brother, which had only been increased by his actual death, contributed their part, too, to this inhibition.

The chief motive of the inhibition, however, lay in the fact that despite the conscious protest against the nature of the mother's relation to the father she herself harbored in herself the unconscious infantile wish (which had betrayed itself in the compulsive repetition) to stand in precisely this relationship to the loved man. The distress which she experienced in her second love affair arose out of the conflict: "You love me in my pride and energy, and yet in my relation to you I can only be humble and devoted as my mother was to my father."

In her neurotic hesitation between this Scylla of conscious protest and the Charybdis of her unconscious masochistic attitude she provoked her lover's estrangement, and faced by the threatening difficulties of her marriage she sought to save herself by death. The statement she made in her first interview with me, "I will not be dependent on my father any longer," corresponded to a deeper truth than she herself could divine.

I should like here to produce some more material from the analysis to show still more clearly that our patient's fate was determined by a provocative compulsive acting out of an infantile fixation on the father.

A few weeks after the beginning of the treatment the father made objections to its continuance and refused to pay the fees any longer. I myself—being interested in the patient—suggested continuing the analysis gratuitously even against the father's will. The patient herself implored me to oppose the father's demand and to show him that the decision about the necessity of the analysis lay with me. It was clear that she wanted to see me in opposition to the father. (In contrast to the mother!) A dream which she had the night after this showed, however, that this reaction did not entirely correspond to her deeper attitude. It went as follows:

She is not in analysis with me, but with a Mrs. X——, who is a loathsome, tactless woman. This woman abuses me and advises her to leave me, for I only treated her for the sake of the money.

The analysis of the dream showed clearly that I myself was the loathsome, tactless woman who had come between her and her father to upset their relationship. And she, one and identical with the father, thinks exactly as he does and turns with him against the hostile interfering mother representative.

Yet another episode from the analysis. Once, when the patient was three years old, a glass object fell on her and wounded her on the head. Her father, summoned by her cries, rushed into the room in a state of desperate alarm. This was, as the patient explained, the happiest moment of her life. To see her father in pain, the desperate pathetic weakling instead of the stern tyrant, remained the almost conscious wish of her heart. In this wish she herself, his love for her, was the cause of his pain. The unconscious fantasy that drove her to attempt suicide had as its aim the repetition of this infantile scene (the wound in the head!). The object of her wish was this time the father and the lover in one.

As already mentioned, the patient herself never considered herself ill. All the failures of her life she attributed to her "ill luck," though, it is true, she did at times have the feeling that some "devil" was destroying her life. Whenever she was cheerful and happy she seemed to hear his voice: "It will turn out badly, just you wait and see; it'll be different from what you expect." And this gave her the feeling that there was something in her which inevitably interfered with her happiness. It ran through her life like an inscrutable decree of fate: she was capable of rousing love in others and feeling love herself, but all her love affairs ended in a cruel disappointment, in which she played sometimes an active, sometimes a more passive suffering part.

Possibly disappointment is the normal fate of *every* love relationship. But here too we must seek for the standard for *normal* or *pathological* in quantitative differences. The patient herself was only very occasionally aware of the morbid element in her existence; usually she attributed her unfortunate experiences more to the powers of the outer world than to her own inner forces.

As we have seen, one of our patient's typical experiences was to feel herself attracted by men who had already lost a loved wife, by mourning widowers whose mourning affected our patient like a love potion. The descriptions these men gave of their love for the dead woman were for our patient like the most passionate wooing of her own person. This form of love choice was determined by the fantasy: "So to be loved as the dead woman had been loved." It was for her a peculiar attraction to find someone whose love so far had belonged to another woman. The fact that the woman was already dead had the advantage that it was no longer necessary for her to become a murderess (in the sense of the unconscious death wishes) in fulfilling her wish. The situation was, so to speak, ready-made. Strangely enough, her unconscious feeling of guilt took no account of the real facts in the matter of her predecessor's death. The unconscious guilt was a bad partner in this inner business deal. It made itself independent and, as the analysis showed, behaved in relation to the patient's ego as if she herself were responsible for the woman's death. In all her dreams this guilt toward the "dead woman" made itself manifest.

Yet another unconscious motive played a very important part in her neurotic fate. The patient declared that she had never felt the least jealousy in any of her love affairs. Characteristic for this was her reaction to her lover's visit to his second (as she knew, unloved) wife's sickbed. Consciously our patient did not feel the slightest objection, but she nevertheless became rapidly engaged to another man and even deliberately pregnant in order thus compulsively to take an adequate revenge. It was only in the analysis that it was possible to recognize suppressed jealousy to be the motive of this neurotic behavior. That she did not permit herself this normal human reaction but preferred to react compulsively was conditioned by the fixation of her mental life in unsettled situations of infantile jealousy which she had repressed at the time and could experience only in unconscious repetition.

Our patient had developed yet another form of jealousy: the first lover (her cousin) had loved her with a sincere and faithful affection. Nevertheless, he did from time to time indulge his so-called polygamous tendencies, toward which our patient manifested the utmost tolerance and understanding. And yet at a time when she had already lost all interest in this lover and was at the happiest point of her relationship with his successor, it would happen that certain places or persons produced a distressing sensation of apparently unmotivated sadness in her. The analysis revealed the fact that it was usually a case of situations in which she had formerly had a real cause for jealousy when she had been engaged to the first lover and had been together with him in these particular places or company. It even happened that she would make feverish attempts, now it was all past and done with, to try and make certain whether and in what form he had been unfaithful to her at the time. He himself had actually no further significance for her, but a part of her infantile personality still clung to situations from which she was unable to free herself because the original reaction had never been properly dealt with. Of course, such displacements of affect, subsequent reactions, and compulsive repetition tendencies are common even to the healthy human mind; it is only their frequency and the degree of inner dependence they produce which entitles us to consider them neurotic.

The form of neurosis to which we ascribe a given neurotic reaction must depend on the same considerations we apply to the formation of a morbid symptom.

The center of our patient's analysis was her fixation on the father. We speak in such a case of a fixation of an infantile object and we know from our analytic experience that an object fixation of this sort is decisive for the genesis of hysteria. It is indeed possible for the object choice of later years to be determined by the prototype or the opposite of our first infantile erotic fixations, but only when the "taboo" has been removed, i.e., when the guilt with which the original objects were invested no longer applies to the new relationship, when the former *you may not* or *you cannot* has ceased to have its anachronistic effect, in short, when the infantile conditions of the object choice are freed from their disturbing inhibitions.

The fact that our patient made her object choice on the model of the father was not in itself neurotic, nor even her preference for widowers. All we can say is that a peculiar repetition tendency could be clearly traced in the course her life had taken.

Where are we then to find the neurotic element in a person's fate? Definite criteria we shall not be able to set up, any more than we can draw a definite line between health and disease in considering a complete personality. In dealing with the present case, for instance, the favorite method of social valuation will not lead us very far. The patient is on the whole a socially adapted being, i.e., she does not interfere with the interests of the community and gives expression to no sort of asocial tendencies.

It is merely that she lacks the capacity to attain a goal which is satisfactory to herself, and when we observe the course of her life analytically, we can see that her adult ego behaves exactly as her infantile ego did in relation to the infantile prototypes of her subsequent experiences. Even if we concede her predilection for widowers to be in itself unneurotic, the disappointment provoked by herself and experienced as a cruel "fate" must be considered a neurotic component of this choice. Just that element was taken from the infantile prototype which the adult ego should have been able, but was actually not in a position, to rectify. And therefore the disappointment which she had once experienced in relation to the father had to be repeated anachronistically in relation to the new object.

Here—in this case—the criterion of morbidity lies in the degree of individual unhappiness, which of course does not mean that whoever is unhappy is therefore neurotic. We have seen in this case that the later object choice, the result of infantile fixations, was accompanied by feelings of guilt the genesis of which was to be found in unsettled infantile conflicts. This guilt forced the patient to continual renunciations, penance reactions, and ultimately to attempt suicide.

These excessive guilt reactions, which were closely connected with the form of object choice, are the second criterion of morbidity in our patient's "fate neurosis."

When are we justified, then, in speaking of a fate neurosis? And is there any difference between a fate neurosis and a so-called neurotic character? I think there is a difference, even though it is only a quantitative one.

The fate neurosis is a form of suffering imposed on the ego apparently by the outer world with a recurrent regularity. The real motive of this fate lies, as we have seen, in a constant, insoluble, inner conflict.

We call this fate neurosis hysterical when it can be traced back to repressions which arose in that period of childhood in which infantile sexuality had reached that stage which corresponds most nearly to the genital sexual life of the adult. In such a case the libido does not regress to earlier stages of development; the unsuccessful repressions affect the choice of object and the conflicts which result from the infantile fixation on the object. Our patient was fixated on the father as infantile love object and all the experiences of her fate neurosis were the result of this fixation. If we wish to express what we have said in a formula, we should say, it is a fixation in the infantile-genital phase of libido development.

The distinction between the *fate neurosis* and the so-called *neurotic character* is a fluctuating one and cannot always be determined. The neurotic character exhibits more diffuse disharmonies in its relation to the outer world. These disharmonies are due to infantile traits which become attached to the adult personality; but they coincide to so large an extent with the whole ego organization that one is never in a position to trace the unsuccessful repression as clearly as in the fate neurosis. They are not, like a symptom or a typical fate formation, alien bodies organized against the ego in its entirety. They are components of a historical past, already assimilated by the ego, which give a definite character only to the complete personality.

In consequence of this symbiosis with the ego the neurotic character is not very accessible to analytic therapy. It is not here a question of alien forces opposing each other; and the influencing of what we call "character" will only be possible where excrescences of the neurotic symptom protrude, as it were, from the assimilated elements. And then along with the symptom the character mass from which it stands out will certainly be influenced too.

The fate neurosis seems more adapted for treatment, because the blows of fate are in this case conditioned by the same inner motives as neurotic symptoms. Indeed the suffering of the individual will be accessible to analytic therapy in so far as he himself recognizes it to be morbid.

3

Hysterical Conversion Symptoms: Pavor Nocturnus, Bed Wetting, Impotence

(1930)

LAST time we discussed a case of hysteria in which clinical symptoms were lacking—a "healthy patient," so to speak, healthy in the sense of being free from symptoms, but pathological in the whole structure of her personality and in the perpetual conflict with the outer world. This condition I called a "fate neurosis," and her fate as I described it to you was determined by the same infantile experiences and difficulties in development as we are accustomed to observe as etiological factors in the origin of other neurotic illnesses.

In the case histories of hysterical neurotics who do suffer from symptoms you will find exactly the same forces at work as we have seen with our last patient.

The case I am now going to describe to you is that of a young man of twenty-eight who came to be analyzed on account of interferences with his potency. It soon became clear that he suffered from a whole series of psychically determined physical symptoms which, however, he had always considered to be completely organic. The degree and character of his impotence varied very much. At times he was capable of erective potency, but with ejaculatio praecox; at other times a premature relaxation of the penis would occur, usually just before the emission. After some

29

months' analysis he attained complete potency, at the price, it is true, of a new symptom formation. For just as he was beginning to get better, a successful coitus had a very painful epilogue. He suffered thenceforward from bed wetting, which brought him, as one can imagine, into an extremely painful situation. The patient had to break off the analysis at this point for external reasons, but the symptom was spontaneously cured after a few weeks. The patient, however, knew as well as I that his analysis was not completed, and after about a year's interval he returned to the treatment, although his potency had left nothing to be desired the whole time.

Even by the end of the first phase of analysis it had been clear to him that his relation to me, which embraced many of his neurotic wishes and fantasies, played a great part in his mental life. During the analysis he had gradually brought everything under this group of fantasies, the center of which was my person, and had thus formed an intensive "transference neurosis," i.e., he had transferred all his infantile, symptom-formative attitudes onto me. The attainment of his potency was a mere result of the transference, due to the fact that all the anxieties and prohibitions which stood in the way of his relation to the female sex were concentrated on his relationship to me, as a result of which he was free to perform the physical act in a completely instinctual way with people to whom he was entirely indifferent, without tenderness or deeper psychological satisfaction. The only really satisfying element in the whole process was the narcissistic feeling: "I can do it." With the resumption of the analysis complete impotence set in again. It had clearly now become impossible for him to carry on this cleavage in his mental life any longer, and the act was again interfered with by anxieties and mental inhibitions. At the same time the patient began to masturbate excessively, which he had not done since puberty. At this point he told me, for the first time in the course of his analysis, of a habit he had had since early childhood. He could never go to sleep unless he had his hands under the pillow. And if it happened that his hands got free during sleep owing to the pillow being displaced or so forth, he used to wake up at once.

This habit clearly had something obsessional about it, and in order to understand it better, I intervened actively in the analytic situation. I advised him to try and sleep with his hands on the sheets for a change. The patient took my advice as a command and attempted to follow it. The first few nights, however, he went on sleeping involuntarily with his hands under the pillow. It was only by adopting countermeasures—by sleeping on a leather pillow which fitted close to the bed—that he succeeded in his resolve. But this had strange consequences. The same night, that is to say, he experienced a typical attack of pavor nocturnus, waking up with screams of fear. I already knew from the analysis that he had suffered for some time from these attacks as a child of five, and also that this symptom had been succeeded between his seventh and eighth year by nightly bed wetting, enuresis nocturna. I knew too that his childhood pavor nocturnus dated from a period in which he was at the height of his normal oedipus attitude and that the aim of his nocturnal cries was to persuade his mother to take him into her bed in order to protect him from his anxiety. I also knew that his infantile enuresis had begun just when he had succeeded in abandoning his onanism. The meaning of this is all so clear that we are probably justified in concluding that the enuresis too pursued the same disguised aim, the flight from his own cold wet bed into his mother's all too indulgent presence. And this may well rouse our suspicion that the freeing of his hands at the time of the treatment had mobilized something in our patient which had been active in his early childhood.

Such a command as this, to keep the hands under the pillow, occurs frequently in the sleep ceremonials of obsessional patients and is usually connected with unconscious prohibitions of onanism. It was thus obvious enough that the desire to protect himself from onanism played a part in our patient's obsessive act. It was indeed no mere chance that he should have told me of this habit just when he had begun to masturbate excessively again. It was clear then that his present pavor nocturnus must, like its infantile prototype, be connected with onanism.

Pavor nocturnus and enuresis nocturna are the two commonest neurotic symptoms of childhood. Pavor nocturnus is *par excellence* the most intense expression of that infantile anxiety which

lets us see the difficulties which even a normal child has to con-
tend with in his psychological development. Whether this form
of anxiety, which is typical for pavor nocturnus, has a specific
content is not clear. A sensation of anxiety when waking up from
an anxiety dream is a very common experience both with children and adults. But the convulsive utterance of a scream and a
typical motor inhibition, which can also affect speech and which
sometimes actually interferes in a most painful way with the utterance of the scream, would seem to correspond to some particular process. This desperate not-being-able-to-save-oneself owing to
the interference with one's freedom of movement seems to me to
be a specific factor in the anxiety reaction.

With our patient I was able to catch the reactivation of his
infantile symptom red-handed, so to speak. The dream which
preceded his last attack of pavor nocturnus was as follows: He is
lying in bed with a woman whose features seem to him familiar
but whom he cannot identify. He tries to have sexual intercourse
with the woman, but has the uncanny feeling that there is somebody in the next room who might be able to overhear him. At
the same time he has the uncomfortable sensation that the wall
in front of him is beginning to totter. He sees the wall growing
softer and slowly crumbling away, so that it threatens to crash
down on him. He tries to run away, but, as if paralyzed, finds he
cannot move his legs.

He awakes in a state of frightful dread, attempts to scream, but
cannot utter a sound; finally he becomes fully conscious and no-
tices that both his hands are lying on his erect penis. He brought
two series of associations to the dream. One led back to the childhood situation, in which he had overheard the nocturnal visits
which an elder brother used to pay his governess in the next
room. This overhearing of coitus had a stimulating effect on our
patient's fantasies and drove him to onanism. In the dream he
had reversed the situation, in that now he is overheard by others
experiencing what he himself had overheard in the original situation. He had clearly reacted to both situations in the same way.

The second series of associations led to the actual cause of the
dream. On the previous evening the patient, who lives in my
neighborhood, had gone past my windows. He stopped for a mo-

ment, and a thought, influenced by the transference situation, forced itself on him: "Who knows what she's doing at this moment! You bet she doesn't live as ascetically as I do!" This thought excited him very much sexually and he decided to find a prostitute. He wandered about, however, for some time in the streets and finally returned home without one.

It is clear that the occasion of the dream was a sexual wish directed toward me. The impossibility of realizing the wish led to the attempted wish fulfillment in the dream. The "unknown" woman was the forbidden, unattained woman. The experience in front of my window on the evening in question activated the infantile eavesdropping scene, which then served as dream material. Even in the manifest dream content there is inhibition of the sexual function. The intended pleasure is interfered with by the listener on the other side of the wall. This inhibition is a clear expression of the prohibition. In the course of the dream the inhibition is intensified into anxiety. The scene of this anxiety is displaced from the inner world to the outer; the danger lies now in the tottering wall which threatens to destroy him; and behind the wall lurks the punishing agency, the parental authority. The anxiety now assumes the form of a severe motor inhibition; the dreamer is unable to flee from the threatening danger. This element in the dream is a frequent and typical sensation of the so-called inhibition dream. The characteristic quality of such a dream is the throttling of the dreamer's intended action. And this throttling, as we know, is the result of an inner prohibition. What happens is that a tendency to action, which is completely harmless in the manifest dream content, cannot be carried through because behind it, as the dream analysis shows, lurks a proscribed and forbidden impulse of the dreamer's, which has formerly been repressed and is now once more rejected by the repressing agencies.

The impulses which were at work in our patient's case are revealed by the first part of the dream: the sexual act is interrupted by the forces which lurk behind the tottering wall. And the nature of the punishment is revealed, characteristically enough, by the form of the threat. The "crumbling away of the wall" is a typical form of projection of one's own body onto an object in the outer world, i.e., a castration threat in consequence of the forbidden and inhibited action.

Let us now analyze the above process a little more closely. The patient related that he had suffered from nocturnal anxiety states in childhood. At each attack he used to jump out of bed to seek refuge with his mother from the mysterious dangers that threatened him. We may assume that he pursues the same aim in the present situation.

At the beginning of the dream we have first the motor interference with the course of coitus. The subsequent motor innervation of the attempted flight is due to the same cause, for this was clearly just another expression of the former interrupted attempt at gratification (as once in the flight to the mother). The running in itself, as a motor act in the service of the threatened ego, has in fact taken on the sexual motor elements of the interrupted sexual act. And so the motor tendency, too, must be suppressed and inhibited like the sexual act itself. The inhibition of the sexual function is carried over into the inhibition of movement altogether. We can say that the patient's entire motility has become sexualized by taking on the elements of the interrupted sexual act. Thus the inhibition prevents the sexual aim being gratified, but nevertheless signifies a psychological gain. It intervenes, that is to say, to spare the patient the consequences of the intended action; for, as we have seen, the realization of this action is threatened with castration. The object of renouncing the motor action is to protect the patient from punishment. But in the dream this object is not attained, for the threat produces an intense anxiety state.

The patient wakes up, but the process which has been mobilized in the dream continues. We now have the third phase of the arrested action: he wants to scream and cannot—a typical sensation in the nightmare and a constant element in pavor nocturnus; and in our patient's case clearly a continuation of the throttled motor discharge tendency. Finally, however, the inhibition is overcome and he is able to utter the scream and so obtain relief.

In the analysis it became clear under what conditions this inhibition could be overcome—namely, when the motor action

acquires a new aim: he screams now, not to achieve the gratification of his inhibited sexual wishes, but to prevent their realization. At the moment of emitting the scream the patient attains
consciousness and finds his hands on his genital. The aim of the
scream, therefore, is to summon the aid of those forces which will
prevent the masturbation and its accompanying dangers. The
patient recollected that the pavor nocturnus of his childhood had
run precisely the same course. If the one form of anxiety state
proceeded without motor inhibitions and he was able to flee to
his mother's bed, the other form, i.e., the pavor nocturnus, ended
with the scream, the aim of which was to summon, not the com-
plaisant mother, but the forbidding father. The one form of
anxiety related to the libidinal longing for the mother, the fulfillment of which he still allowed himself. The other, the pavor
nocturnus, came in the long run from the same source, the longing for the mother; but this was confronted in its turn by a severe
punishment anxiety, which already bore the character of castration anxiety and inhibited the realization of the libidinal wish.
The result was ascetic renunciation. The motor inhibition was
released in the scream, the aim of which had become protection
from the consequences of the forbidden wishes instead of their
fulfillment.

The following night the patient had another dream. A monkey
has escaped from its cage in the Berlin Zoo and has raped and
murdered an old woman. The dreamer takes part in the pursuit
of the monkey. He is caught up in the general stampede—much
in the manner of an American film scene—but suffers from a
distressing feeling, as though he were the pursued instead of the
pursuer. Ultimately he succeeds in catching the fugitive—in the
dream it does not strike him as at all odd that he is no longer
a monkey but a man—and seizes the offender by the hand with a
feeling of triumphant joy.

He wakes up to find himself convulsively clutching one hand
with the other, by which action he shows that he himself was the
criminal in the dream. The monkey he associates with his observations of masturbating monkeys while studying in Berlin.
The infantile concept of parental coitus as a sadistic act makes
clear that he himself was the murderer. The analysis had indeed

already revealed the fact that at a certain period of his childhood —the period in which he suffered from pavor nocturnus—his onanistic fantasies were likewise sadistic in character. That the old lady in the dream was identical with me as the present representative of the mother became abundantly clear in the analysis of the dream. In the course of his associations the patient said jokingly that if I were really the person in question the motive of the murder could hardly be considered as sexual. For a few days before when paying his monthly fee he had had a "Raskolnikov fantasy" as he called it: it would be easy enough to murder me in my consulting room, which was fairly remote, pick up the money, and slink out unobserved. In this connection he recollected that the money arrangements at home had lain in the hands of his mother. In puberty, when the sexual bond with his mother had become intensified, he had reacted—in a way typical for young boys of this age—with hatred and inconsiderateness toward the mother, and there were continual unpleasant conflicts on the subject of money. The dream showed clearly to what an extent these conflicts had served the interests of his repressed libidinal tendencies.

Both these dreams were organically connected with his infantile pavor nocturnus. In the first dream the position of the hands beside the erect penis showed that the process corresponded with the struggle to suppress his onanism. In the second dream he awoke to find himself "clutching himself by the hand" in an attempt to ward off the criminal action. We must not forget that both dreams date from the time when my active interference had prevented him from hiding his hands under the pillow. It is easy to see that this habit was a result of his own masturbation prohibition. It was a defensive measure dating from the time of his infantile struggles against onanism. By withdrawing my protection I brought the patient into the original anxiety situation, and as a result of this the infantile symptom of that time, the pavor nocturnus, was also mobilized.

I have the impression that the analysis of the patient's reawakened pavor nocturnus has revealed something which may be taken as typical. Analytic observers have long known that children tend to suffer from pavor nocturnus at the time of their masturbatory conflicts. This fact is indeed so obvious that even nonanalytic observers have noticed it (e.g., Strohmayer, 1925, among others).

I will describe once more shortly the process we have discussed above. In the dream the wish-fulfilling tendencies are mobilized. The masturbatory tendencies connected with these repressed wishes are accompanied by physical innervations which are directed toward a motor discharge. In the dream, however, this discharge is subjected to a threat of punishment which produces an inhibition of the forbidden action (masturbation). This inhibition is extended to the whole motor system and the nightmare sensation of being unable to move, which is carried over into the waking state, corresponds to the suppression of the wish to masturbate. In some cases the effect of the punishment threat is continued in the state of half-sleep. One has seen terrified children reacting vividly in such cases as though they were in a hallucinatory condition; from their whole expression and their cry denoting "I won't do it again," it is easy enough to detect the punishment situation. The cry for help, which succeeds the end of the motor inhibition in pavor nocturnus, relates—as we have shown above—no longer to the satisfaction, but to the prevention, of masturbation. It was clear enough in our patient's case that the giving up of the preventive measure (hands under the pillow) had provoked the neurotic nocturnal procedure. The anxiety came to expression as soon as the precaution against it had been removed.

I have dealt in such detail with this mechanism of pavor nocturnus not only because it is one of the commonest forms of infantile neurosis, but also because the whole series of hysterical conversion symptoms from which our patient suffered had their origin in the same motor inhibitions which accompanied his pavor nocturnus. This is not to say that all the symptoms of our patient or of other similar sufferers are based on such a displacement process. It is only one form, one type of conversion symptom. But in general the action of a particular organ will always be interfered with when it is required to play some other part in addition to its usual role. There may be various motives for this new role cathexis. In our patient's case the motor inhibition was displaced from the sexual organ onto the whole motor system. And we shall have plenty of opportunity in further considering his case to speak of other displacements and injuries of organic functions which owe their origin to the functions acquiring another meaning in addition to their usual one.

You will remember that in the course of his analysis our patient developed yet another symptom which was due to the reactivation of an infantile symptom. I should like to deal with this in somewhat more detail and that for two reasons. First, it is a common infantile neurotic symptom, and secondly, it was the battle ground of his most important neurotic conflicts, which led to his illness and to the formation of other symptoms.

As you have already heard, the analysis made clear that his masturbatory activity was most intense in the phase of pavor nocturnus. At this period the onanistic fantasies had an exceptionally sadistic character. The struggle against these tendencies, which came to expression in the pavor nocturnus, ended in apparent victory. The patient ceased to masturbate, the pavor nocturnus disappeared, and a transformation took place in his personality which gave the decisive stamp to its later development. The aggressive little boy turned into a virtuous and kindly, somewhat subdued individual, "a perfect goody-goody," as he was known to his friends and acquaintances. But that this change did not represent a real overcoming of the tendencies in the sense of a healthy development was proved by the fact that just at this time the enuresis nocturna set in. It is true that something happened at this time which we may consider as an actual cause or "actual conflict." It is hard to say whether the lack of such a traumatic experience would have prevented the neurosis. But I have the impression, and with our patient the impression is particularly strong, that the experience, which we will discuss shortly, had the effect it did because of the patient's inherent predisposition. We will now consider the genesis of the new symptom from two points of view: first, the attitude of the little boy after he had given up his masturbation; secondly, his reaction to the traumatic experience.

Our analytic experience shows us that such violent struggles against masturbation or such severe guilt reactions as we have

here do not always end in the mere renunciation of onanism.
Such an excess of guilt is usually followed by a self-punishment,
especially when the libidinal tendencies have so sadistic a character. It may have various consequences. The anxiety may simply
be released by the guilt reactions, so that apart from the renunciation of the pleasure functions which produce the anxiety a
personality arises which is ever inclined to inner prohibitions
and asceticism, but which is free from anxiety and actually
healthy. Or instead of the renunciations we may have self-punishment, which will express itself in the formation of new symptoms.
This is what happened in our patient's case. With the renunciation of the sadistic functions of his sexual organ he had taken
upon himself the castration threatened in the anxiety states of the
pavor nocturnus, and this came to expression in the enuresis nocturna. The analysis showed that he behaved at that time in this
symptom as if he no longer had a penis. But even in this self-
punishment the little boy's unconscious had not given up the
primal force of the human psyche, the pursuit of the pleasure
principle. Together with the self-punishment process, with the
renunciation and repression of his sadistic tendencies, a transformation had taken place in the claims of his libido. He was no
longer the aggressive little man wanting to commit "sexual murder" on his mother; he now wanted, like the mother, to be loved
and have intercourse with the father. Such a transformation is
usually the combined result of several causes. Our patient, for
instance, remembered in the analysis that his onanistic activity
had not been confined to the sexual organ, but had included the
whole area of the perineum and the anus. In addition to this,
chronic constipation, worms (from which he had suffered for
years), frequent irrigations, etc., had so increased the excitability
of that region that it ultimately became invested with fantasies
which gave it the character of a passive female organ, as frequently happens in the mental life of male patients and in the
activities of perverts. The renunciation of his male organ, the
"self-castration" as self-punishment, did not betoken the renunciation of the pursuit of pleasure. The male-aggressive tendencies
gave way to female-passive ones, with strong cathexis of the anal
zone as a new pleasure organ. At the same time a transformation

came over his character, and the naughty boy grew into a "perfect goody-goody." It was at this time that the traumatic experience we are about to speak of took place.

When he was eight years old a little sister was born and our patient showed a particularly strong interest in all her cleansing and washing operations. In this connection the analysis was able to catch him out in an odd slip of memory. For a long time he obstinately maintained that the enuresis had not by any means appeared for the first time in his later childhood. On the contrary, he felt able to state with the utmost positiveness that he had never, from birth to puberty, given up the habit. By day, it is true, he had succeeded from a sense of shame in restraining himself, but at night he had never been able to do anything against it. But apart from the mother's objective confirmation of the fact, it became abundantly clear in the analysis that the enuresis had originated at the time of his sister's birth and represented an imitation of, and identification with, her. Another mistaken idea confirmed this fact further. Until puberty our patient had imagined that the bladder processes in the female sex were not subject to voluntary innervation. He thought that the urine flowed out of itself as soon as the bladder was full, and that in consequence women had to go to the lavatory much more frequently than men. It is true that he corrected this view later, but it proved to have been a very superficial correction. To be a woman—like his mother or little sister—meant for his unconscious, at the time of his infantile enuresis, to have a hole out of which urine flowed spontaneously "like a waterfall." Curiously enough, his interest in waterfalls expressed itself also in his sublimations: as an engineer he was particularly interested in his student days in the application of water power.

Whether his sister's birth and the identification with her would have resulted in such female urethral fantasies if the transformation to a passive attitude, expressed in the "self-castration" and the presence of urethral-anal tendencies, had not already taken place, is very hard to say. I should like to add that another determinant was contained in the symptom of enuresis: a female birth fantasy, the center of which was the identification with the mother, and a vague idea of amniotic liquor, which is universally present in human birth fantasies.[1] Here, too, it is difficult to decide whether the actual pregnancy and confinement of the mother had mobilized a release of his female fantasies in this direction. In any case the feminine relation to the father remained from now on an important element in our patient's mental life, and as you will see from what I have to say later on, a whole series of his hysterical symptoms originated in the same source.

I would remark in general that enuresis nocturna always appears to originate in the way it did with our patient. I have found this myself in several cases, and other analysts have confirmed me in this view.

To return to our patient. You will remember that in addition to other interferences with his potency he suffered from ejaculatio praecox. Abraham (1917) has pointed out that with patients suffering from ejaculatio praecox there is usually a close connection between ejaculation and urination. He found that these patients had experienced strong sensations of pleasure in childhood from the emptying of the bladder, that they had been difficult to train to cleanliness, and that they had suffered from bed wetting. He refers to the pleasure gained from the passive act of allowing the urine to flow and the fact that the libido of these patients entirely lacked masculine activity. He was also struck by the fact that in these patients "there frequently exists . . . a particular erotogenic state of the perineum and posterior part of the scrotum. These parts correspond developmentally to the introitus vaginae and its surrounding parts."

Thus Abraham too establishes a connection between ejaculatio praecox and urination on the one hand, and the feminine-passive attitude on the other. The derivation of enuresis nocturna from the passive-feminine components of instinctual life does not, however, appear to have been clear to him. I shall be able to give you

---

[1] In the enuresis of female patients exactly the same unconscious ideas are present as in the case of the man. The penis is looked upon as a sort of tap, and bed wetting is one of the reactions to the discovery of the anatomical difference between the sexes. Here, too, birth fantasies play of course a large part.

still further confirmations of my views on this point from our investigation of the same patient.

You remember that our patient reacted to the first successful coitus after the recovery of his potency by reverting to his infantile symptom of bed wetting. The analysis showed that the apparently successful coitus had left unsatisfied something in his fantasy life, and that something was the feminine component, which at that period he was not yet able to exclude from his sexual life. And this component he gratified subsequently in the symptom.

I do not intend to enter here into a more detailed consideration of ejaculatio praecox. It is much more complicated than you would gather from what I have said about it so far. It may accompany any neurosis, and only analysis can decide whether its character in any given case is more obsessional or hysterical.

The patient in question had reached the genital stage of libido development and then afterward renounced it, regressively, in part. His neurotic conversion symptoms have a completely hysterical character, and we shall now proceed to analyze them in detail.

4

Hysterical Conversion Symptoms: Paralysis, Speech Defects, Gluttony

(1930)

You will remember that I directed your attention in the last lecture to two symptoms which arose during the patient's treatment or which were provoked by it and which formed a bridge to the manifestations of his infantile neurosis.

I tried to show you in what sources of anxiety his infantile pavor nocturnus originated; and hope I succeeded in making clear from this case that the so-called "anxiety paralysis," i.e., the impossibility of fleeing from the apparently external danger, was due to the same mechanisms which condition the motor inhibitions of hysterical conversion. It is a question here of the transformation of a purely psychic process into a physical mode of expression.

It was the transference of the forbidden sexual fantasy onto the act of masturbation which stirred the internal prohibition. The suppression of the sexual act led by displacement to the inhibition of the rest of the motor apparatus. We often find such manifestations of repressed onanism in analysis, sometimes as disturbances in the motor, and sometimes in the vasomotor, sphere. I have often seen cases in which the patient's hand would swell up and become red whenever his associations led him to memories of repressed masturbation. Such a symptom represented a kind

43

of shame reaction like, say, blushing, and contained also a self-betrayal, a self-reproach in face of the analyst.

I recollect a case of paralysis of the right arm, in which the immediate cause was clearly the nonabreaction of an affect. The patient was a student in a technical school, and during a dispute with his mathematics teacher the chalk suddenly dropped out of his hand and he was unable to write any more. The paralysis of the arm continued for many months, and the making conscious of the fact that the cause of the conversion was his rage against the equally feared and hated teacher did not lead to therapeutic success. Under hypnosis the patient abreacted with the strongest emotional outbursts the fury which he had really experienced but suppressed at the time. The short analysis which accompanied the hypnotic treatment revealed, too, the infantile experiences which had predisposed him to this mode of reaction. But neither this nor his understanding of the peculiar part played by his teacher as a transference object for the parental authority was able to effect more than a temporary improvement. It was only when the pertinacity of the symptom and its inaccessibility to all therapeutic measures made a real psychoanalytic treatment essential that it was possible to show that the scene with the teacher had become connected by devious routes with onanism prohibitions on the father's part, against which the patient had reacted with violent aggression accompanied in its turn by severe guilt. The analysis was then able to unmask the paralysis of the arm, which had followed from the opposition to the teacher, as the expression of a sort of "self-castration" of the rebellious organ.

A certain similarity between the genesis of this symptom and that of our other patient's enuresis may serve to redirect our attention to a further consideration of his case. You remember that he acquired this symptom after he had given up his actively onanistic desires. The aim of the new symptom, which had arisen out of anxiety, was to protect him from the direct anxiety experience. But though it represented the renunciation of one form of pleasure gratification, it served at the same time the satisfaction of other pleasure tendencies. This transformation was of such a nature that active genital tendencies were given up under the pressure of the guilt, and—as a result of the castration accepted in his fantasy life—feminine urethral and anal tendencies were intensified and came to expression in the symptom of enuresis.

The patient retained the habit of nocturnal bed wetting till puberty, i.e., till the time when he began to masturbate again after a long interval, and also at a relatively precocious age to indulge in sexual intercourse without any manifestations of inhibition. Till his eighteenth year he remained completely potent, with a tendency, however, to depressions and the formation of conversion symptoms.

Thus about his eighth year and for several years afterward he suffered from a defect of speech of the nature of aphonia; later on from a kind of intermittent limping, then from persistent constipation, heartburn, dryness in the mouth, and vomiting. He was in fact a chronic case, went from one specialist to the other, visited spas and health resorts, and either got better for short periods or else exchanged one symptom for the other. None of the medical examinations succeeded in finding any sort of organic change in the patient. All his symptoms could be described simply as "psychogenic."

Such a state of things left no doubt of the fact that it was a question of conversion symptoms, i.e., that a psychic process had been transferred onto physical sensations. Such a transference, or conversion, can of course affect a healthy as well as an organically morbid part of the body. One can indeed speak of a "compliance of the organ" as the cause or occasion of the psychic process being established in the physical sphere, when certain changes in the organ, which are not in themselves morbid, give harborage to a psychic process in search, so to speak, of a home.

But our patient's case gave no cause to assume such a "compliance" in his symptom formations. When the psychic difficulties were removed the physical symptoms disappeared without leaving any trace of this compliance in the organic functions. Some of these symptoms disappeared, in fact, without it being quite clear why they had availed themselves of the organ in question.

One often reads in case histories of a conversion symptom disappearing immediately after its psychic determinants have been cleared up in the analysis. My experience leads me to conclude that this immediate disappearance of a symptom is the result of autosuggestion, as though the patient said to himself: "Now I know what the symptom means, so it must of course disappear." The conversion symptom certainly has its specific determinants, but they are so intimately and inextricably bound up with the neurotic conflicts in their entirety that the symptom can be really cleared up only when all the mental conflicts have finally been unraveled as a result of the completed analytic treatment. As regards the treatment of conversion symptoms we can lay it down as an axiom that the *symptom* is easy to get rid of, but the *neurosis* difficult.

All our patient's conversion symptoms, the most varied organ cathexes, could be traced back to a common source. We may say, in fact, that his pavor nocturnus and enuresis nocturna, his earliest infantile symptoms, formed the first links in the continuous chain of his conversion symptoms. And the fact that specific organs were made to represent a specific content was, as you will see, variously but always purely psychically determined.

Let us go over once more the course taken by our patient's neurosis, paying a certain regard to the chronological sequence.

His earliest infantile anxiety comes from a specific source and has only one aim, the fulfillment of which relieves him of this anxiety. It is, that is to say, the expression of a longing for the mother, and at first the effort to attain this aim meets with no particular obstacle. Uninhibited the little boy makes for his mother's bed and there, completely free from anxiety, he quietly goes to sleep by her side. In this phase he does not yet seem to have entered into the fateful rivalry relationship with the father. The frequent aim of infantile anxiety, to interfere with the mysterious relationship of the parents to each other by one's presence in the bedroom, seems still to have been in the background at this period.

It is only when the longing for the mother has become involved in the struggles of the oedipus complex and the vague instinctual demands are no longer satisfied by her mere proximity that the psychic process becomes more complicated and the settling of these unconscious instinctual claims more difficult.

During the time in which the pavor nocturnus appears the

wish for the mother has already acquired a distinctly genital character. The urge toward masturbatory discharge and its suppression were clearly recollected in the analysis and had, as the dream I reported to you showed, been reactivated in the transference.

The original course of the development of the anxiety has thus become more complicated. For the old longing-anxiety and the temptation to gain freedom from it through the fulfillment of the libidinal wishes have been recognized as incompatible with reality and already rejected by the ego. And this has given rise to the conflict which comes to expression for the first time in the attacks of pavor nocturnus—a conflict whose development we can easily follow in the subsequent symptom formations.

Let us observe this process somewhat more closely. Instead of the former motor action, in which he sprang from his bed and ran to seek refuge with his mother, we find this activity has been stifled and succeeded by onanistic fantasies. The renunciation of the actual relationship with the mother was the result of the intensified instinctual claims, an intensification which clearly had the effect of mobilizing the repudiating and repressing forces of the ego. But this renunciation of the mother is only an apparent one, for what he had formerly been allowed to gratify has now been introverted, i.e., it has been transferred to his inner life, to his unconscious fantasy activity. The character of this we have already learned: these fantasies were the expression of his sadistic tendencies, and the transference dream we investigated led us back to the infantile situation which marked the starting point of his neurosis. In this situation we saw the little boy struggling against his masturbatory activity. Now the suppression of masturbation as a result of a prohibition either from the outer world or from one's own will is a conscious act which can on occasion succeed quite easily. The difficulty occurs when those instincts which have been rejected by the conscious personality and deprived of the outlet of masturbation lead to inner tensions. These latter clamor with elemental force for some means of discharge and find this in the neurotic symptoms. In the dream mentioned above and in the conflicts our patient had to fight through in his nocturnal attacks we were able to observe clearly enough the tensions resulting from the suppression of the masturbatory fantasies and the process of neurosis formation.

The primary, very intensive fixation on the mother now acquires in a particular phase of development an aggressive genital-sexual character. He had the opportunity to overhear his elder brother having intercourse with the governess, which experience had the effect of stimulating his own instinctual claims still more. In his fantasies he transferred the situation he had overheard to the scene of his own longings, his mother's bedroom. But the longing for the mother as well as his masturbatory activity were subject to a prohibition. And the dream allows us to see in the clearest possible form the author of the prohibition and the content of the threat of punishment. That stern power "behind the wall," whose role the little boy assumes in his own aggressive fantasies, reveals itself in the analysis as the representative (via the elder brother, etc.) of the original paternal authority from whom the threat of punishment for the forbidden wishes proceeds. The father himself is the wall standing between him and the mother, which threatens to fall on him and crush him to death. In the "crumbling wall" we saw a clear symbol of the castration threat, which opposes his instinctual tendencies and forces him to suppress his masturbatory wish.

The inhibition of the masturbation might be considered as a successful act of repression if it included the fantasies and the instinctual claims as well, especially at a time when the child's ego is not yet capable of overcoming it in any other way but by repression. But in our patient's case we were able to watch the failure of the repression, a failure which expressed itself in his nocturnal attacks. In these attacks, along with the motor inner-vation which served the repudiated instinct, other innerva-tions too, unconnected with the instincts, are subject to the inhibiting process. They are involved in "this, and successful re-pression, i.e., freedom from anxiety, is no longer possible. We shall be able to follow this unsuccessful repression in the patient's subsequent neurotic symptoms, and we shall see that he has set up in his own psyche a representative, so to speak, of that paternal authority which threatened his unconscious infantile wishes. Moreover, at a time when his adult personality has freed itself from the external dependence on the father, this representative continues with the greatest tyranny to threaten him anachronistically with the same menace as it had done at a time when the immaturity of his ego and hence the inability to control his instincts might seem to have justified the prohibitions.

You will be able to observe over and over again with this patient that all his symptoms had the one aim of ridding him of his anxiety. But conditions were attached to this freedom from anxiety which he was only able to fulfill in his symptoms and inhibitions. The question inevitably arises: what was the anxiety which the patient sought to protect himself from in his symptoms? From the anxiety proceeding from an instinctual danger or from the anxiety in face of the forbidding and threatening powers? You will soon see that the answer to this question is not difficult. On one occasion the ego shrinks from some instinctual force and seeks for measures to protect it from this anxiety. On another occasion it develops fear of punishment under the pressure of guilt and submits to inhibitions and renunciations in order to escape this punishment. And finally it forms symptoms which are themselves of a punishing nature. But in reality it is impossible to differentiate too sharply between these various states.

When the ego becomes aware of the instinctual danger it reacts to this awareness with anxiety. And this anxiety is a signal for the formation of countercurrents whose business is to inhibit the unconscious instinctual tendencies and thus free the ego from anxiety. The inhibiting influences proceed from the superego and remain as unconscious as the instinctual tendencies themselves. We shall encounter them in various forms: as conscience anxiety (superego anxiety)—in which case they inhibit the instinct, but do not get rid of the anxiety—as neurotic guilt reactions; and, above all, as symptoms, which have the character of anticathexes, i.e., measures designed to protect the ego from the unconscious instinctual dangers.

Now let us return to our patient's pavor nocturnus. The instincts of which we have spoken, have been repudiated by the forbidding powers. In his infantile attacks these powers are still partly in the outer world, i.e., the onanism prohibition and the castration threat connected with it are still part of his educational environment. But they are already partially internalized, in that the threat of punishment has become a function of his own sense of guilt. It appears that we tend altogether to overestimate the significance of the actual threat from the outer world in the genesis of castration anxiety. In some cases it is difficult to avoid the impression that those forces of the outer world which were formerly concerned in the formation of moral agencies are simply projections of the already internalized castration anxiety which arose under the pressure of the sense of guilt. Our patient, for instance, never met with the slightest gesture from his father which could be interpreted as a castration threat. On the contrary, his father's kind and gentle disposition only made him feel more guilty about his own intensely sadistic aggressive impulses; as a result his own severe superego punished him with anxiety and transferred the punishing function to the father in his dreams and masochistic fantasies.

You will remember our view of the motor inhibition in the pavor nocturnus. The first object of repudiation was the masturbatory fantasies, or their motor discharge. This was followed by the inhibition of the entire motor system. But at this point the process, from the point of view of release from anxiety, may be regarded as having proved a failure, for the inhibition is accompanied by the development of intense anxiety. It is as though the first stage of the process, the inhibition, represented an unsuccessful attempt at escape, in which the fear of punishment is carried over into the act of inhibition itself. The scene of danger is then transferred from the inner to the outer world. The motor inhibition produces in turn the distressing sensation of being unable to flee from an actual danger (the collapsing wall). At the end of the whole process the instinctual wish ·is clearly given up and with it the inhibition is overcome. The liberating anxiety scream re-establishes contact with the obstructing, but no longer punishing, outer world.

From immediate observations of pavor nocturnus one cannot avoid the impression that the object of the child's nocturnal screams is to avoid, with the help of the outer world, something which is already subject to an inhibition, i.e., the masturbatory impulse, but which can ultimately be removed only through assistance from the powers of the outer world.

But in this case the interference with the faculty of speech as a part phenomenon of the entire motor inhibition was due to other motives too. The cry for the indulgent mother was no longer permitted at this period and so the interference had a definitely ascetic character. Even in his childhood—and later too—the patient's speech difficulties acquired the significance of an independent symptom.

We have already mentioned that in his eighth year the patient suffered from aphonia and that this complaint occurred spasmodically later on in life too. The analysis revealed that his faculty of speech was always interfered with in those situations in which particular repressed impulses tried to avail themselves of the organs of speech in their effort to break through.

At the time of his little sister's birth our patient's aggressive-sexual instincts had already been extensively repressed. This process of repression had been inaugurated by the pavor nocturnus, and by the time he developed enuresis nocturna his former sadistic personality had been completely transmogrified. The outcome of the repression conflicts was the transformation of his aggressive tendencies into masochistic-passive ones, and, as we have learned, in the symptom of enuresis itself he renounced his male organ and identified himself with the once desired mother as well as with the aggressively envied sister. This identification with the female objects had very serious consequences for his whole psychic development. For it did not remain partial and confined to isolated symptom formations, as is frequently the case with hysterical conversion symptoms. As you will see, a whole number of his symptoms did indeed correspond to such partial identifications, but they arose on the basis of a general attitude, which brought with it the diversion of the libido from the masculine role.

But despite this transformation process he had not at the time of his sister's birth wholly given up his libidinal attitude to the mother. For even though his actively directed wishes were subject to repression, he had tried to win his mother for himself by another method. The little boy clearly wanted to beat his one-time enemy at his own game. But his earlier attempt to do this with the father, by trying to take his place as the aggressive little man, had suffered a sudden check through the neurotic anxiety attacks. We have seen that he defended himself against the consequences of his guilt-laden period by renouncing the masculine role and transforming his sadistic tendencies into masochistic ones. I have already drawn your attention to the fact that this transformation not only took place under the pressure of the sense of guilt, but that earlier phases of development (particularly the urethral and anal) had predisposed him toward it by offering him certain surrogate gratifications. It was as though memories of former pleasurable sensations were awakened by his castration anxieties and internal threats of punishment, which promised him some compensation and encouraged him to renounce the pleasure which he obtained from the threatened organ.

And now in the new situation created by the birth of his sister he attempted to identify himself with the new rival to his mother's love as he had done before with his father. Even the bed wetting had been partly determined by this identification, but, as you have seen, this motive alone was not enough to account for the symptom. For the eight-year-old boy would certainly have indignantly repudiated any attempt at such an emasculating identification, if his masculinity had not already suffered attack from other causes. The identification with his sister in the bed wetting was only a sort of consolation prize for the masculinity which had already been masochistically surrendered owing to the sense of guilt.

A similar fate overtook his "masculine" voice. The first inhibition of speech, as we can clearly see, related to his active cry for the mother. But now the newborn child seemed to show him another way of gaining possession of the mother. For he noticed the fact that her inarticulate cries always succeeded in calling forth the mother's tender care. And not only was his jealousy aroused by this spectacle of maternal tenderness; he also felt himself violently interfered with in his night's rest and all the habits pertaining to an only child. And so he attempted to adopt the same measures as the little sister, and in the transition phase between being a wild, aggressive scamp and a good little boy he did in fact become a perpetual nagging nuisance who was continually trying to monopolize the attention of those around him. It was only when he discovered that this method did not work that he relapsed into silence—in the most literal sense of the word, for when he got up one morning he found himself unable to utter a sound. This inhibition followed directly on his failure to compete with his sister on the same lines. Just as in the rivalry with the father he had ended by renouncing the male organ and had expressed this renunciation in a symptom (enuresis), so now he gave up the crying and replaced it by a symptom which represented a sort of "negative" to his former attitude (as with enuresis and active masturbation).

We can analytically pursue this analogy in the formation of the symptoms still further. The motive which led to the psychic self-castration was the intense sense of guilt, the strength of which was in proportion to the aggressiveness of his original tendencies. The same forces were active in this case. The rivalry with his sister was accompanied by an aggressive rage against which he attempted to defend himself by identification. When this attempt failed he increased this rage, and his aggression against the little squaller took the form of wishing the little devil would shut up forever. In the language of dreams such a state of "being dumb" often serves to represent "being dead." Finally the masochistic turning against himself brought with it the loss of his own speech, exactly like the loss of the male organ in the symptom of bed wetting.

We have seen that the renunciation of the male function of the genital organ opened up new possibilities of gratification, and that through the reactivation of former erotogenic pleasure zones. The speech inhibition, too, brought the patient new compensations, and not only in what we call the "epinosic gain," i.e., that he was now paid more attention. For here, too, the speech organs, and especially the mouth, had acquired an erotogenic significance, and the doctors and parents contributed to this source of unconscious gratification by their treatment of the organ in question. Moreover, the identification with the sister had assisted in reactivating his oral erotism. For in the nutritive process the little girl had attained that intimate union with the mother which was now denied to him. But the success and intensity of this identification in the cathexis of the oral zone were possible only because the patient had already repressed the male-genital tendencies, and in the subsequent transformation of his libido had recathected all those zones which had corresponded to his passive-feminine wishes.

Thus the "compliance of the organ" in symptom formation of which we have spoken really means the cathexis of organs which are predisposed to this by the nature of their past development.

The surrender of a higher stage of libido development is always accompanied by regressive cathexes of former pleasure organs—either those in which the pleasure function has displayed in the past a particular intensity or those which appear specially suited to the newly arisen but anachronistic aims. In our patient's case the anal, urethral, and oral organs proved the best adapted to his passive-feminine tendencies. The identification with the little sister had of course played its part in this result too. Thus the inhibition of speech was variously determined: it represented on the one hand a reactive expression of the identification with the sister, in which the act of crying was replaced by the inability to speak; but also, and more important, it signified a masochistic deflection of the aggression from the sister onto his own ego. This led to an ascetic renunciation of the function of speech, since the speech organ had to serve unconscious tendencies which had been repudiated by the ego. The harmless ego-syntonic function of the organ was drawn into the process, much as the repudiation of a single specific motor innervation in the pavor nocturnus had brought with it the inhibition of the entire motility, even though this was in some measure guiltless; or again, as in the case of the technical school student mentioned above, where the sublimated and completely ego-syntonic function of writing had to be renounced, because other functions of the arm had been rejected by the ego.

But not all our patient's neurotic troubles had the ascetic character of inhibition, i.e., renunciation of the function. Without going further than the oral symptoms, I would remind you of the gluttony which used to alternate later on in our patient's life with loss of appetite, dyspepsia, heartburn, and vomiting.

This gluttony recurred in a certain phase of the treatment, which showed that in the chaos of his fantasies it was not only the passive impulses which had invested the oral organs, but that deeply repressed tendencies of a very infantile actively aggressive character had found their way there too. In this period immediately after the analytic hour the patient was compulsively driven by a distressing feeling of hunger to visit a restaurant in my neighborhood where he would greedily devour several helpings of particularly pungently flavored food.

This phenomenon appeared at a time when he had begun to protest against his passive role in the analysis. The analysis, he felt, made him "soft and effeminate," and such a relationship to a woman was intensely humiliating for him as man. But after eating highly seasoned food he always felt as if his body was being strengthened by fresh masculine forces.

The unconscious impulses which came to expression in this gluttony symptom had a very active and aggressive character. But as a result of the repression of his genital libido his aggressive wishes in relation to me were not even now permitted to take a masculine-genital form. The only form his active protest could assume was this very infantile wish of devouring the desired object. And as reality and the patient's judgment on the one hand and the unconsciousness of the wish on the other hand prevented any direct gratification on the object itself, the patient had to content himself with highly seasoned foods as the only way of satisfying his cannibalistic wishes.

In contrast to the inhibitions described above, in which a function of the ego (e.g., speech) had to be renounced owing to its connection with unconscious tendencies, the gluttony has exactly the opposite meaning. Here too a function of the ego (nutrition) is made to serve unconscious libidinal tendencies. But instead of being inhibited it acquires the character of a superfunction. It is only the purposelessness and futility of the excessive eating that point to the unconscious aims that underlie it. Similarly neurotic greed, often to be met with in hysterical women, can never be assuaged by nutrition, because this hunger is the expression of other unconscious wishes which are destined to remain unsatisfied. A classic example of the overdetermined nature of this pleasure in eating is to be found in pregnant women. The deeper meaning of such neurotic greed has found its expression in literature. In Balzac's novel *Two Women,* in describing a pregnant woman's passion for rotten oranges, he intuitively recognizes the cannibalistic nature of the fantasies directed against the child in her body.

5

Hysterical Conversion Symptoms: Fits, Trance States

(1930)

W<small>E</small> will now turn our attention to another symptom of the same patient we have been dealing with hitherto, a symptom which recurred from time to time during the long years of his psychic suffering. I have already mentioned this symptom and called it "intermittent limping." In the course of the years it acquired a more chronic character and was diagnosed by the doctors as rheumatism, for lack of a better word. As you may imagine, the symptom defied all the antirheumatic cures, and yet it was one of the first to be given up by the patient in the analysis, though I must confess that the genesis of the symptom was never quite cleared up.

With conversion symptoms, especially, it is usually possible to reconstruct the so-called "traumatic" situations which first gave rise to the symptom in question. We shall find that the symptom itself will regularly follow one of two courses. It will either remain intact, i.e., the psychic excitation which expressed itself in the symptom remains and sends out permanent innervations which maintain the symptom (this applies chiefly to symptoms in the sphere of motility, paralyses and contractures); or the symptom (and this is especially true of symptoms of a sensory nature) recurs intermittently and under particular conditions, whose

57

associative connection with pathogenic situations can be traced in the analysis. A typical and common intermittent symptom is, for instance, hysterical vomiting, which will recur on particular occasions as an expression of repulsion and disgust; and then there are a whole series of symptoms which have taken over the role of defense mechanisms and occur only in situations of danger.

Thus one of my female patients used to suffer from malodorous outbreaks of sweat when dancing, so making what was for others a completely innocent pastime into an impossibility. For this ascetic and repressed girl the physical proximity of the man, involved in the act of dancing, was obviously by no means innocent, and so she was forced to defend herself against her own fantasies by this unpleasant symptom. In other situations in which she felt in any way endangered she would develop other physical symptoms which all served to keep those around her at a distance.

Our patient's limping—the genesis of which, as I have said, was never completely cleared up—also represented a defense mechanism against certain psychic impulses. When the symptom first appeared, in puberty, the patient was exceptionally ambitious. This ambition, however, came into conflict with other tendencies. You will remember that he had exhibited strong passive-feminine traits in his childhood. Now in puberty his libido was already completely homosexual; the object of his affection was always one of his school companions, and usually his closest rival in his ambitious aims. In all those situations in which his rivalry with this companion was to be put to the test, as in examinations for instance, he began to limp, and at the same time an inhibition of speech set in, which the patient himself referred to as a "limping of the tongue." The analysis showed that both symptoms were the result of his passive-masochistic attitude to the loved object. Despite his conscious effort to defeat his rival, the unconscious urge to yield to his companion, which availed itself of the symptoms in question, always got the upper hand. The genesis of this passive-masochistic attitude became clear to us in our consideration of his enuresis nocturna.

With the repression of his active-genital impulses his whole libidinal relation to the world became feminine-masochistic, and so a great part of his symptoms was simply an expression of the gratification of, or defense against, these tendencies. The development of his personality as well as the formation of the symptoms took place on the one hand under the pressure of the punishing and forbidding agency (masochistic reactions, ascetic renunciations in the symptoms, etc.), but at the same time they served as a means of gratifying the libidinal impulses. It is of course difficult to draw the line between these instinctual gratifications and the masochistic reactions of the sense of guilt, for in the wish fulfillments both work in the same direction.

We have seen that some of our patient's symptoms were rooted in the identification with his sister and mother. When he was twenty-two years old his mother died of cancer of the stomach, and after this event the tendency to identify himself with her underwent an extraordinary intensification as expressed in the form his symptoms took.

The numerous gastric symptoms he produced had originally nothing to do with his mother's illness, although they too represented an identification with her. His pregnancy fantasies, for instance, had exactly the same content and intensity as we are used to find in hysterical women and girls: from obstipation to vomiting, tensions in the pit of the stomach, etc., the whole gamut of pregnancy reactions was to be found in him. Even his ever-recurring desire to be X-rayed proved in the analysis to be directed toward the fulfillment of two infantile fantasies: the injection of the probe represented the fantasy of oral impregnation, while the X-ray photograph was to satisfy his infantile curiosity as to what happened in the stomach.

After the mother's death the identification with her took on an uncanny character. Originally the symptoms proceeding from this identification merely had the significance of a feminine relationship to the father. This was the case with the enuresis and pregnancy symptoms, etc. They acted as interpreters to his unconscious libidinal wishes and contributed in large measure to their gratification.

The mother's death increased his unconscious sense of guilt toward her. In a case like our patient's, where an inversion of the oedipus complex has taken place, the sense of guilt toward the parents tends to acquire another direction and character too. This inversion first found expression in a masochistic attitude to the father and had as its goal the satisfaction and appeasement of the little boy's sense of guilt in relation to him. But the desire to play the mother's part in the relation of the parents to each other inevitably brought with it the desire to get rid of the once-loved mother. Moreover, this desertion of the mother—even though it happened under the pressure of the love prohibition —was accompanied by a large measure of self-accusation over his own faithlessness, and so the actual death of the mother in-evitably mobilized in him severe pangs of conscience. These led our patient to an identification with the mother in her sufferings: he must die as she had done. This idea had the effect of produc-ing in him the same gastric states as his mother had suffered from. The digestive organ, menaced as it was by the sense of guilt, was continually in the forefront of his attention, and the narcis-sistic care he expended on it took on the character of a hypo-chondriacal anxiety.

This increased awareness was a reaction to an anxiety signal which had arisen through the threat from his guilt-laden con-science. But he did not stop at this hypochondriacal anxiety; under the influence of the self-punishment he actually produced in himself those symptoms from which the mother had suffered, from pains to a high degree of emaciation. Whereas the former identification symptoms were means of unconscious gratification, these latter were clearly the result of punishments proceeding from the superego.

I should like to take this opportunity to say a few words about hypochondriacal anxiety in hysterical patients. I have often been able to observe that the formation of a conversion symptom is preceded by a hypochondriacal anxiety about the organ in ques-tion. It is as though the "erotization" of an organ at the same time increases its narcissistic, ego-libidinal cathexis and so evokes the hypochondriacal anxiety. When the libidinal cathexis is dis-placed from the repressed genital onto some other part of the body, as in hysteria, the castration anxiety would seem to undergo the same displacement and then find expression in the hypo-chondriacal anxiety. This remark only applies to those forms of hypochondriacal anxiety which have a transitory character and are succeeded by the formation of conversion symptoms. If the symptoms once become manifest, then the hypochondriacal anxiety is, typically enough, given up and the symptom succeeds in releasing the anxiety tension.

Our patient's last-named symptoms already had the character of self-punishments. It is noteworthy that he was really free from anxiety during the whole period between his infantile neurosis, i.e., the severe attacks of pavor nocturnus, and the beginning of the anxiety tension evoked by his hypochondriacal apprehensions. His only complaint was a slight feeling of oppression which followed him like a shadow; moreover, he experienced a sensation as if he was living in a cloud, which somehow prevented him from really enjoying life. This oppression, this "cloud," as he expressed it, was really a vague diffused anxiety, which had to be intensified by the analysis before its motives could be made conscious. All his symptoms were aimed at freeing him from anxiety and did in fact succeed in doing so, apart from this vague uncanny feeling. The task of the analysis consisted in temporarily undoing this achievement on the part of the symptoms by making conscious the repressed impulses and reactivating infantile attitudes in the transference. My proposal that he should stop hiding his hands under the pillow was meant as just such an attack on his freedom from anxiety. You will remember my description of the severe outbreak of anxiety, which had hitherto been so successfully controlled, and how this occasion enabled us to see its source and deal with it in the analysis.

A large part of his symptoms pursued the same goal as the hiding of the hands under the pillow: namely, the attainment of freedom from anxiety. But whereas the hiding of the hands amounted to a simple renunciation, the symptoms aimed simultaneously at gratification and release from the sense of guilt, i.e., from the punishment anxiety. This, however, could only be attained through a complicated process of repression, displacement, recathexis, etc. The libidinal cathexis of the genital was displaced from the threatened organ onto other parts of the body, those, namely, in which a predisposition (in the psychic sense) was present. This recathexis was accompanied by an inhibition of the organ's normal function. You have there the relatively simple process by which inhibition takes the place of anxiety. In this process of displacement the organ which originally has the cathexis, the genital itself, may react in various ways. There are cases, for instance, in which the entire castration anxiety as well as the inhibitions resulting from it and the measures to overcome it are transferred to other organs, while the sexual organ itself enjoys an undiminished potency.

In other cases, again, the inhibition directly affects the sexual organ, and the neurotic conflicts which result from the repression of genital wishes assume the simple form of a renunciation of its function. When the neurotic process is confined to this renunciation, it is usually accompanied by diffused disturbances, such as depressions, inferiority feelings, fluctuating anxiety, disinclination to work, etc.

With the formation of conversion symptoms we are used to speak of a "genitalization of the organs," for in hysteria we know that the libido has first reached the genital stage before being subjected to repression. But as a result of this repression regressive tendencies may come to expression in various ways. Physical organs which had temporarily, and quite normally, served so-called pregenital libidinal gratifications in infancy may reacquire their original cathexis through this regression; but in this case they have usually acquired an excessive cathexis, for constitutional or other reasons, before the genital development (e.g., the intensification of the oral cathexis from too long or too short suckling, or of the anal cathexis from too frequent enemas, etc.).

Traumatic experiences in infancy also play a large part in the choice of organs. With our patient, for instance, the sister's birth and his jealousy of and identification with her were of great significance.

A fifteen-year-old girl, whose analytic case history I will deal with subsequently, is a very good example of the significance of the traumatic, provoking experience. Her neurosis had broken out in puberty in the form of severe fits and twilight states. These symptoms had been preceded by a phase in which she suffered from difficulties in feeding, so serious that they threatened to bring about a physical collapse. Her sufferings began with severe tonsillitis, which compelled the patient—so that she should be looked after properly—not only to move into the mother's room, but actually to sleep in the same bed with her. This situation, as well as, probably, the patient's exclusion from actual life and the resultant tendency to introversion and increase of fantasy activity, had mobilized the so far latent neurosis.

The reactivation of the infantile reactions in this case was, as we shall see, brought about through the similarity between the actual situation and a similar situation in the past which had clearly not been completely surmounted. This reactivation is the easier for us to understand as the patient was at this time in early puberty, and we know from experience that it is quite normal for such reactivations of infantile traits to occur in this period. In her case, as in that of our first patient, the traumatic infantile experience consisted in the birth of a sister, which took place in her sixth year. Hitherto our patient had slept in the same bed with her mother, but now she had to make way for the little intruder. At this time she was seized by a violent jealousy of the intimate oral relationship between the suckling child and the mother, an "oral envy" so to speak. This was made clear from several infantile memories she produced from this period, which all had something to do with taking or giving food. For instance, in the most desperate period of the war—the family lived in the war area—she had stolen food from her mother's storeroom and given it away to complete strangers.

Her first neurotic trouble (in connection with the tonsillitis), the difficulty in taking her food, could be described as a simple inhibition. It was here clearly a question of the repression of the reactivated oral wish. The patient refused nourishment on the simple ground: I cannot eat. It proceeded, however, to become more than a simple inhibition. Apart from the "epinosic advantage" which she gained through the increased tenderness and attention of those around her, she indirectly succeeded in obtaining the gratification which she appeared to renounce in her refusal of nourishment, in that so much care and love were expended on the process of feeding, her mother preparing special dishes for her, etc. Characteristically she refused with the utmost disgust to drink milk directly, but on the other hand the medicines her doctor ordered she insisted on taking with milk. But according to a religious ritual which the family rigidly adhered to, the taking of milk after meals was strictly forbidden. It was —according to the Bible—only allowed to the sick. Thus she was in the triumphant position of being the only member of the family able to enjoy the "milk forbidden by the fathers."

But although this difficulty in nourishment owed its origin to the reactivation of infantile jealousy toward the little sister, other mental conflicts were involved in it too. Above all, an important part, as we shall see later, was played by the motive of revenge against the father, who, like her little sister, was a rival for her mother's love.

This patient's case had shown us how an inhibited and interrupted action can find satisfaction in other ways. It is as if the unconscious tendencies misled the forbidding powers by the act of renunciation, i.e., by the abstention from the direct means of gratification, which they then nevertheless achieve by other and indirect ways. It is, however, typical for the hysterical conversion symptoms that they serve simultaneously the forbidding tendencies and the tendencies seeking gratification. In our former patient's case, for instance, we saw how his aphonia proceeded from a prohibition, a suppression of the aggression, and yet how it fulfilled at the same time his libidinal demands. His gluttony was a direct expression of his oral aggression, but it was allowed only under the pretext that it was an intensified gratification of the ego function of hunger.

When we compare conversion hysteria with other forms of neurosis we shall see that it represents the most successful solution of the neurotic conflict, especially when it is a question of symptoms which have become chronic and which thus make it possible for the patient's ego and actual circumstances of life to be adapted to his altered physical state. Conversion hysteria is able to exploit to the best effect the "epinosic gain" and the "flight into illness." Especially the former of these is benefited by the respect shown to physical suffering in contrast to the distrust and bewilderment which psychic symptoms provoke. Even the patient himself often has a considerable degree of insight into the alterations of his physical state. How frequently do we find obsessional neurotics who regard themselves merely as "eccentrics," and sufferers from anxiety who spend their whole time trying to rationalize it! But the symptoms of the conversion hysteric are so crass and obvious that he is enabled to withdraw from all those life tasks which are too much for him.

The great achievement of the conversion symptom is the fact that it leads to freedom from anxiety. In this form of symptom formation the affect of the mental conflict is completely and successfully repressed or converted. As we have seen, the ideational content explains the choice of organs and the whole nature of the symptom.

With some symptoms it is easy enough to tell which affect has been converted, e.g., with vomiting nausea, with blushing shame, with inhibition rage (as in the case of our patient's aphonia); the same is true of symptoms which have taken over the role of liberator from anxiety, i.e., those which represent a direct conversion of the anxiety affect.

But as we know that every suppressed affect is capable of being transformed into anxiety—in so far as it represents a danger for the ego—its transference from the psychic onto the physical sphere means in the long run a release from the threatening anxiety experience. A phenomenon which we can very frequently observe in analysis signifies the reverse of this process, namely, the appearance of anxiety when an attempt is made to give up the conversion.

Perhaps we can make this process clearer from the following comparison: A burglar, who represents the repudiated impulse, has been shut into a locked and bolted room. The danger he signifies for the ego in the next room—let us take the case of a young girl—is similar to that which the girl would feel in her fear of burglars. We know from our analyses how typical this fear of burglars is in young girls. It corresponds to the inner instinctual danger; the burglar is merely a disguise for the man who she wishes to gratify her unconscious erotic wishes. As long as the door is locked the ego remains free from anxiety. If we substitute the conversion symptom for the room in which the danger signified by the direct wish fulfillment is locked up, we can understand that when it fails in its task—i.e., when the bolt, which equals the part played by the symptom, gives way—the danger for the ego is increased and the ego has to react to this danger with anxiety. But this danger—and that is the most important point in our comparison—threatens from two sides: from the burglar (ravisher) as well as from the side of the powers who forbid the ego the fulfillment of the dangerous wish. If we carry the comparison further and imagine there to be another room occupied by the parents, who keep a strict watch over their daughter's morals and severely condemn the relationship with the burglar (ravisher), then it is easy to see why the failure of the bolt, of the symptom, exposes the ego to danger from two sides, from the wish impulse (burglar) and from the superego authority (parents).

This comparison leads us to the following consideration: Would the girl have been afraid of the fulfillment of her instinctual wishes, of the "burglar," if she had not been aware of the presence of her forbidding parents? We assume that this would not have been the case, and conclude from this that the anxiety in face of the libidinal danger arises only when some power in the outer or inner world raises a protest against the libidinal wishes. Thus this anxiety relates not so much to the instinctual demand as to the consequences that might follow from its direct gratification. The ego—in our case of the young girl—feels afraid of the agency which has assumed the role of the parents, renounces in consequence the instinctual gratification, condemns the libidinal wishes, and either locks them up in the unconscious by means of repression, or, where this is not successful, resorts to compromises which find expression in symptoms. If we imagine this fear of the parents transferred to the inner world, we see that this anxiety, which leads either to repression or symptom formation, relates to the inner representative of the forbidding powers, the superego.

You have seen that the symptom formations not only represent substitute gratifications, but that they clearly betray the unconscious influence of the superego. Mere renunciation of direct gratification is never enough for the superego, as it might be with indulgent parents. The superego is able to detect the impulse, even when it appears in the disguised form of a substitute gratification. So in most symptoms we can recognize beside the disguised gratification an equally disguised repudiation or punishment. This was particularly clear in our patient's enuresis. It was certainly due to the punishing effect of the superego that the sadistic tendencies were transformed into masochistic ones, thus enabling the libidinal wish fulfillment to conform to the demands of the superego. Alexander (1927) even goes so far as to hold that the superego must first be bribed, so to speak, by the suffering, before it will allow instinctual gratification in the symptom, a point of view which may be true of many cases, but which cannot be accepted as universally valid.

From direct analytic observation it is at any rate possible to lay down that the more sadistic the repressed tendency, the severer is the superego, the stronger the sense of guilt, and the greater the part played by the punishing tendencies in the formation of the symptoms. In the course of our discussions we shall be able to observe this "aggression against aggression" at its clearest in those forms of neurosis in which the libido has regressed to a stage in which its tendencies are still very sadistic and its relations to the object very ambivalent.

In conversion hysteria the symptoms are able to maintain both libidinal and punishing elements just because the repressed impulse is anchored in the genital stage of development, where the sadistic components are weakest and the ambivalent conflict least pronounced. This does not mean of course that the sense of guilt plays no part in hysteria. But from the cases we have been discussing you have been able to see that the reactions of the sense of guilt remain just as repressed and unconscious as the libidinal claims (in contrast to other forms of neurosis, such as obsessional neurosis, for instance).

In connection with the case history of the fifteen-year-old girl which I referred to when discussing oral disturbances, I should like here to mention that her neurosis did not remain confined to particular conversion symptoms. The fantasy life of this sexually mature girl attained a peculiar intensity at the time of her feverish illness, and the affectivity which had been increased by the introversion was unable to find any sufficient possibility of discharge, whether direct or indirect.

I ought really to describe to you at this point all the normal processes of puberty, in order to show that our patient's symptoms were merely distortions of these processes, merely displacements of the inner disposition of forces, in the sense of an intensification of the instinctual demands along with a simultaneous increase of inhibitions, which are in any case normally present in puberty. We know that regressive forces play an important part in puberty; i.e., the more the way of sublimation and normal substitute gratifications are closed, the more must the tendency to reactivate the infantile be increased.

I will not here go into the question of the value of early sexual experiences in puberty. It seems to me very questionable; and I have known cases of the severest neurotic conflicts in young people, with whom the actual sexual gratification completely failed to prevent the reactivation of the infantile. On the contrary, their sexual freedom intensified the tendency to repeat the unsettled infantile conflicts, which completely colored the actual experiences. Perhaps the attainment of sexual maturity must be succeeded by a phase of inner conflict before a psychic assimilation of the actual gratification is possible. One must apparently be equipped in exactly the same way *for* the attainment of the goal as *against* the frustration, as far as the settlement of the infantile difficulties is concerned.

Moreover, our little patient's environment was such that any attempt at actual gratification would have evoked so much conscious guilt that it would perhaps have made as great a demand on her psychic equilibrium as the defense against the instinctual claims itself.

For a long time after her illness the girl, who had formerly taken so lively and active a part in everything, was unable to find any new contact with real life. She reacted to every attempt to enjoy things as before with a depression and excitement which gradually developed into typical hysterical convulsions. What soonest became clear to her in the analysis, and what, as she had to admit, had not been completely hidden from her before, was the fact that she harbored within her a violent rage, which she suppressed, until finally the inability to control it provoked the motor discharge of the seizure.

Her illness gradually assumed the form of one of those major hysterias accompanied by fits which one does not often meet with in analytic practice, and which seem to be growing ever rarer even in clinics and sanitariums. Symptoms and so-called character neuroses clearly enjoy more favor in the neurotic choice. Nowadays major seizures, trance states, absences, etc., are made to serve philosophies of life, telepathic phenomena, and spiritist materializations, and this seems to diminish the patient's desire for treatment or even cure.

What happened during the seizures was always covered by complete amnesia, and so we, the patient and myself, had to rely on the information of those who were in a position to observe them. During the treatment the patient lived in a sanitarium far from her home; thus I was able to form a picture of what went on in the seizures from the reports of the doctor of the institute. My first impression was that the seizures were reactions to frustrations, however trifling, especially when these frustrations proceeded from a particular doctor in the institute.

For external reasons the analysis had to be broken off after a few months, before we were able to penetrate to the very bottom of the infantile experiences. Nevertheless the making conscious of her puberty conflicts had succeeded in restoring the girl to health, at any rate for the time being.

After the patient had become fully conscious of the fact that the seizures were really expressions of outbreaks of rage, the question inevitably arose: against whom was this rage aimed and what was the cause of it? The patient was very soon ready to admit that the rage was directed against her father. All her accusations against him and all rationalizations of her rage took as their ground his neglect of the family and his brutality to her mother. It was not so easy to get her to see that the "neglect" was identical with "refusal of love," and that the word "brutality" was an expression of the patient's view of parental coitus and the mother's numerous confinements. You remember that the tonsillitis was accompanied by a reactivation of oral longing for the mother, and that the analysis was able to show that in all the reactions which followed the illness the girl had become quite a little child dependent on the mother. The patient was conscious of her hatred of her father and the warmth of her love for her mother; what she did not realize was that this represented a complete inversion of the real emotional relationship. This inversion was really a return to a state of feeling which had formerly actually been present—namely, a primary, excessive love for the mother and a furious protest against the interfering father. These emotions, however, had undergone a transformation and the final result was a reaction to the normal oedipus relationship.

Moreover, the suspicion was justified that during the war the little girl had really been witness of violations, which formed an actual kernel for the violation fantasy in her puberty. At any rate the concept of the sexual act as an act of violation was peculiarly noticeable in her wishes and defense mechanisms.

That the convulsions procured her the motor discharge of an attack of rage was not difficult to prove; and that they represented coitus as well as the defense against it, and also a dramatization of the act of birth, became clear in the course of the analysis. The rage affect and these wish fantasies were connected with the affective protest: not the mother, but she herself should be violated by the father and give birth to a child. What was behind our patient's seizures was merely the intensification of typical puberty fantasies, their motor discharge, and dramatic representation.

This case supplies a ready answer to the question: what are the quantitative or qualitative factors which smooth the way to a motor dramatization of such typical fantasies? Here it was unmistakably an intensely violent aggression against the frustrating environment. In its outward pressure this aggression was bound by other energies, which were able to avail themselves of the same methods in their effort at realization as the rage affect. The hysterical fit is perhaps the best demonstration of such a combination of destructive tendencies and libidinal impulses, a symbiosis which hysteria with its genital impulses toward the sexual act and birth seems best able to bring about. Coitus is after all the best reservoir for the man's aggression and the woman's masochism, and the act of birth, a fight between life and death, is an orgy of destruction on behalf of the new life. Anyone who has acquired analytic insight into the mental processes of the woman in her procreative functions will know of these paradoxes of life.

In our patient one could see clearly how the discharge of rage and the instinctual claims coincided in one single act. They were both different expressions of a libidinal wish directed toward the father: the rage as a reaction to the frustration, the sexual discharge as a result of unconscious fantasies, both contained in the neurotic seizures.

The trance states only went to confirm this reconstruction of the hysterical fit. They were merely better organized representations of the same wishes and emotions which were released and satisfied in the fits, only they were reduced to their component parts and formed into ordered actions.

These states lasted for days and even weeks on end and were succeeded by complete amnesia. This amnesia could be removed in part, and for the rest the analysis had to rely on the material supplied by those who had the patient under observation. The states took three different forms:

(1) Scenes of rage with hallucinatory and illusory persons, accompanied by hitting and screaming and rolling on the ground to the point of exhaustion.

(2) Performances of dancing, declaiming, or singing, all before an imaginary public.

(3) Scenes of remorse with bitter reproaches and weeping, where the patient would beg for forgiveness.

It is interesting that—according to her brother's testimony—she produced things in these states which were inaccessible to her in normal life. She would speak, for instance, in a language which she had learned from her nurse in infancy but had long forgotten. The analysis revealed that she lived through situations in these states which had occurred at that period and that the reactivation of those situations brought with it this revival of the long-forgotten language.

The people who formed the subject of her hallucinations were in reality for the most part strange and indifferent objects to her, but they were connected by association with certain persons against whom, as the analysis showed, these affects were really directed. The analysis revealed the individual scenes as screen memories, and unmasked the theatrical performances as realizations of fantasies in which the patient had seen herself as the future dancer, actress, or coquette. The audience, numerous as it was, gradually dwindled to one man, in whom we were finally able to recognize the father. These fantasies constituted one of the stumbling blocks to our patient's education. For one of the goals of the prolonged trance states was to keep her from study and prevent the fulfillment of the conscious wish—which had met with the father's approval—to go to a university after passing her matriculation. This state of things reduced her to despair and constituted the greatest part of her suffering. But behind the word "study" lay concealed the fantasy of "freedom," of the narcissistic gratifications of a film star, of admirers and lovers, in short of a mode of life in complete contrast to her own family milieu. It was an embellishment of the "prostitute fantasy" which ultimately led by devious routes to one single man, the father. The object of the trance states was to prevent the fulfillment of these wishes by keeping her from study, but they brought her instead disguised gratifications, not only of these wishes, but of many others.

In the last type of seizure she was able to recognize the element of self-punishment; for that matter a large part of her waking fantasies contained aggressions both against herself and others. Thus during the analysis, for instance, she reacted to her mother's written leave to go on a mountain expedition with the greatest indignation, reproaching her for being so little concerned about her safety. Instead of enjoying the scenery, she occupied herself during the expedition with fantasies of falling down precipices and lying at the bottom with shattered limbs. What a splendid combination of revenge and self-punishment!

Under the protection of unconsciousness she was enabled to give an otherwise forbidden satisfaction both to her aggressive and libidinal wishes, under the pretext that she herself was not the subject of the experience, for she refused to admit her identity and split herself off from the "other" self through amnesia.

If conversion hysteria works out its conflicts on the patient's body itself and is thus able to make a compromise between the fulfilling and forbidding tendencies in the symptom, and the hysterical seizure is able to discharge the libidinal and destructive impulses in one single act, then the trance states also serve both the instinctual claims and the demands of conscience under the disguise of screen actions, and the protection afforded by the clouding of consciousness and the subsequent amnesia.

6

Anxiety States: Diffused Anxiety—A Case of Cat Phobia

(1930)

THE hysterical neuroses we have just been considering were distinguished by their freedom from anxiety, and I have tried to show you what forces this fettering of the anxiety was due to. In the one case it was the renunciation of the unconscious instinctual claim which guaranteed the freedom from anxiety (inhibited states); another time it was a favorable compromise between the permitting and forbidding tendencies, which came to expression in the conversion symptom; in yet another case we were able to recognize in the symptoms direct acts of punishment, which anticipated one of their inner motivations through the anxiety, which was itself a punishment (e.g., our patient's cancer symptoms after the mother's death).

We will now turn our attention to a case in which the unfettered anxiety controls the clinical picture. The patient I am going to speak about is particularly instructive for two reasons. On the one hand she is overwhelmed by anxiety feelings which are diffused in their nature, attached to no particular ideas, and not amenable to phobic precautionary measures. But on the other hand, under certain conditions, which are felt as a danger and have to be avoided in order to escape the anxiety, her anxiety feelings are intensified and do acquire a more specific character. This part of her anxiety avails itself of a mechanism which we

74

call phobia and which evolves protective measures for removing the anxiety. We shall learn from our patient's case how this phobic defense measure arose, and especially from what motives the patient, who had been for all practical purposes healthy up to a given moment, suddenly became subject to anxiety states.

I should like to remind you of the case of the young girl whose hysteria—free from symptoms as it was—we called a "fate neurosis." You remember that the course of that "healthy patient's" life had acquired a particular character through the compulsive repetition tendency of the unsettled infantile conflicts, which brought with it ever more tragic complications and disappointments. Similarly this patient, whom I am going to speak to you about, was a "fate neurotic," for her life too was a continuous compulsive repetition of certain situations. She too had failed to see anything morbid or abnormal in the course of her destiny. In fact her conscious attitude to life—unlike that of our former patient—was one of complete acquiescence in her destiny. She felt herself in no way harshly treated or persecuted by hostile forces and had no desire to alter anything about her external life. She came to be analyzed on account of certain anxiety states which had made their appearance in the last few years. She suffered from an almost continuous feeling of oppression; and in addition to this diffused anxiety, she began to be subject to more definite forms of anxiety, e.g., dread of heights, ships, and cats. These anxieties were really only intensifications of a continuous anxiety state, even though the most recent of her symptoms, the dread of cats, had the character of an animal phobia.

Till her marriage in her twentieth year the patient had been entirely free of symptoms. Her marriage was not really unhappy, and it was only the childlessness of the union that gave her cause for depression. After three years of marriage the husband died, and from now on she shared her home with a married girl friend, seeking consolation for her loneliness in her profession (she was a chemist) and in sublimated relationships to women. For the last few years she had lived in a *ménage à trois*, i.e., she had a relationship with her friend's husband. The prelude to this relationship was the warm, but in no way consciously sexual relationship with the girl friend. The intimacy of this relationship had led the

girl to speak of her married life and the lack of satisfaction it provided for herself and her husband. By this confidence the friend
had made our patient a partner, so to speak, of her sexual life, and
consciously or unconsciously arranged matters in such a way that
a sexual relationship took place between our patient and her
husband. But the most important thing about this triangular
relationship was that, through mutual confidences and the media-
tion of a third person, i.e., the husband, the two women were
enabled to satisfy their unconscious homosexuality. They never
indulged in a consciously homosexual relationship, nor, she
alleged, was the harmony of this triangular relationship ever
disturbed by jealousy.

When I said at the start that the patient's life was an example
of a fate neurosis, I was referring to the fact that our patient's entire psychic life, from earliest childhood to the love relationships
of later years, represented such a triangular constellation as I
have described. But it was only in her last experience that this
erotic condition of the triangular relationship acquired a real
nature. Hitherto these triangular friendships had always been
platonic.

In the analysis the patient had a memory of being pulled out
of bed by her mother when she was three years old, because the
mother was tortured with anxiety about the absent father. The
patient could still picture the mother's anxious face before her,
and remembered how they had lain in bed hugging each other
and waiting for the father's return. When I pointed out in the
analysis that it was somewhat odd that the mother should have
wakened her little child to protect herself from her own anxiety,
and suggested that the situation had really been reversed—i.e.,
that the little girl had herself waited in longing for the father
and had sought the mother's help in her anxiety—the patient
was gradually able to see that the basis for her later love triangle
had already been laid in this bedroom scene. Very early in life
she had sought to flee from her excessive love for the father and
had found help with the mother, to whom she clung now with
an overcompensated affection for the rest of her life. When she
was four years old the mother gave birth to a little girl, and on
this occasion, as she vaguely remembered, the patient received

a present from the father. What it was she could no longer recall; she remembered only that she was discontented with it and therefore very angry with the father. This memory was almost naïve in its obviousness, for a present, as analysts know, is a very frequent and familiar symbol for a child. She was discontented that the mother, and not she, had got the child from the father. This trauma gave rise to strong aggressive reactions against the mother and the newborn child.

But such mental situations are typical, and burden most girls with the severest sense of guilt for the rest of their lives. Just as the active castration and the death wish against the rival father form the center of the little boy's sense of guilt, so with the little girl the death wish is directed against the pregnant mother and newborn child. And just as the little boy lives under the pressure of this sense of guilt in a state of castration anxiety or else expresses this in some form of self-punishment (compare our first patient's enuresis), so the girl often condemns herself to permanent—psychically conditioned—childlessness or to death fears during pregnancy and all manner of renunciations in her own motherhood. Sometimes the original wish for a child remains attached to the child of the "other woman," and is satisfied there, i.e., she renounces the wish to have a child of her own and expresses the longing for the other woman's child in various forms. Thus she may become a teacher or governess or else affectionate aunt, ever in the center of some family circle, bringing up a child who prefers her to its own mother. Or she will take under her special protection the child of some friend to whom she stands in particularly tender relationship. Such situations, in which the woman has renounced a child of her own in order to take away the child from another woman, often bring with them the most intense sense of guilt. And then even the other woman's child must be self-torturingly, masochistically given up.

This first triangular constellation, in which our patient waited in longing for the father and then remained bound in overcompensated love to the mother, was succeeded some years later by a similar situation, in which the triangle consisted of her elder brother, herself, and the little sister. Every tender approach of the brother's to the younger sister met with her violent jealousy and attempted opposition. But that did not prevent her allying herself with the sister—united by the penis envy of the other sex—against the brother. The analysis brought up a mass of memories connected with these common fantasies—castration wishes—of the two girls directed against the brother.

Another triangular situation was easily to be recognized in a beating fantasy which the patient retained for many years. The content of this fantasy was as follows: The brother is beaten by a third person and she looks on in a state of tense excitation. The brother is naked; he has no penis; his buttocks, on the other hand, are particularly prominent. The meaning of this fantasy is that the beaten child was the patient herself, who was punished in this way for the brother's castration. The patient's masochism, so clear in this fantasy, found permanent expression in a self-torturing element in her character. These guilt reactions were the result of the mother-child murder fantasy and the castration wish against the brother.

The next triangular situation was of the same nature—this time with two fellow schoolgirls—in which one was beaten by the other for some naughty action, while the third looked on. This beating had to be repeated over and over again, for it was accompanied by fully conscious genital pleasure sensations, for which the patient then had to punish herself.

This "triangular formation" proceeded from that compulsive repetition tendency which characterizes the fate neurosis. In her most recent experience the patient was called into the bedroom by her friend. Thus she was not herself the intruder, but was invited by the other person. This time it was not a trick of memory as in the infantile experience, but the patient's unconscious, which so arranged the situation that she could spare herself the reproach of having been the intruder, although she had herself provoked her friend's invitation. In the present situation she found fulfillment of her infantile wish, to be loved by the man who belonged to another woman. And in this case she was able to elude the superego and appease the sense of guilt by, so to speak, purchasing this wish with a simultaneous renunciation; for she leaves the man his rightful wife and suffers every day the

painful renunciation in the other's favor, thus being enabled
to possess him in common without feeling guilt.

But the most important thing about this remarkable relationship was the satisfaction of the deep-buried unconscious homosexual impulse; the tender form in which it came to expression
was indeed responsible for initiating the triangular relationship,
for it was only by the path of homosexuality that the approach
to the man was made possible.

This combined love relationship proved to be particularly
favorable and releasing for the patient. A whole series of impulses
hostile to the ego could hereby be mastered and satisfied. Thus
she was able to assuage the murderous jealousy which filled her
mental life, and to express as well as overcompensate the hatred
against the rival. She was indeed for several years quite satisfied
in this relationship and, as we have said already, practically
speaking, healthy, though she was, it is true, always to a certain
extent predisposed to anxiety. Nevertheless the major anxiety
hysteria first began in the setting of this last triangular experience.

For her friend's marriage had not been childless. Even before
the patient had joined the *ménage* two sons and a daughter had
been born. For the patient it was a matter of course, for reasons
which I have mentioned, that not she, but her friend should
have children. She herself was condemned to childlessness, but
loved her friend's children with a self-sacrificing affection. Now
while she was having the relationship to the husband the friend
again became pregnant and gave birth to a daughter. And this
birth reawakened all those reactions in our patient's psyche
which she had experienced at the time of her little sister's birth.
The other, and not she, had got the "present." Everything which
had so far been held in balance by successful repression on the
one hand and by reaction formations and disguised acts of peni-
tence on the other now broke down. The aggressive tendencies,
the repressed pregnancy fantasies, and the overcompensating
homosexual relation to the friend—all hitherto contained and
satisfied in the mitigated form of the "fate neurosis"—received
through this new frustration a shock which the patient's ego did
not seem to get over.

Soon after the child's birth, but quite unconscious of the connection, the patient began to suffer from fears and anxieties of various kinds. She gladly took charge of the child, but frequently felt afraid that she or someone else might let the child fall. The harmony of the home was not disturbed, but the patient's condition assumed more and more the nature of an anxiety hysteria. At first she was only occasionally subject to anxiety feelings, but gradually the intervals in which she remained relatively free from anxiety grew ever shorter. As I mentioned above, this chronic anxiety expressed itself at times in the intensified form of intolerable anxiety attacks; once on a mountain expedition, on board ship, and finally and especially on seeing cats.

It would take up too much time if we were to go into all the determinants of these particular anxieties. At the center of her dread of heights and water was a pregnancy fantasy. You remember the development of our patient's attitude to the female procreative functions. She was forced to renounce the child, but the repressed pregnancy fantasy remained a permanent part of her unconscious mental life and determined indeed the course of her life.

Even during her friend's pregnancy the patient began to suffer from feelings of anxiety, which she ascribed to her care and solicitude on her friend's behalf. But then the child's birth mobilized a whole series of once-repressed reactions. The sadistic impulse, which had once related to the mother and newborn sister, was now directed against her friend and her friend's child. Her own pregnancy fantasies, which came to expression in oppressions, lack of breath, palpitations, dizziness, as in a real pregnancy, had the effect of making the patient herself the object of her sadistic impulses. This inversion is a very common phenomenon and often leads to distressing anxiety states in pregnant women. I have often been able to observe how young women resist conception or artificially interrupt their pregnancy, because they are tortured by a presentiment that they are going to die in childbirth. The analysis of such fears shows that this anxiety proceeds from the threat that the infantile death wish against the pregnant mother might now be masochistically realized in their own person, now identified with her. Moreover, experience shows that the little girl's aggressive wishes need not necessarily relate to a real pregnancy in the mother; the suspicion in fantasy is alone enough to give rise to such impulses.

Our patient, however, had experienced the real pregnancy of the mother, and now in her fortieth year this traumatic reaction of her childhood was intensively revived. The anxiety feelings in her fantasied pregnancy were death fears lest she should herself suffer that death to which she had once condemned the mother in her unconscious hate impulses.

I shall come to speak later of cases of agoraphobia in which the anxiety proceeded from the turning of a sadistic impulse against the ego. But I should like to mention here that the patient I am talking of showed the same mental mechanism as in these cases. She identified herself in her wishes with the pregnant mother—or friend, as the case may be—and hence her severe superego threatened her with that form of punishment which she had directed in her sadistic wishes against the mother. This part of her anxiety related to the danger with which her superego menaced her, and the intensity of the anxiety corresponded to the amount of her sense of guilt. The pregnancy conflict was also particularly increased by the patient's age, which exposed her to the real danger that the neurotic renunciation of the child would become permanent, for biological reasons. In her childhood it had been too "early"; now it threatened to become too "late." Her anxiety feelings at this period became especially acute during menstruation, though she had always, it is true, been particularly irritable and difficult at such times. She was conscious of some vague feeling of reproach against the mother in this connection. She thought her mother had not instructed her sufficiently about the process of menstruation, and this had had serious consequences for her. What exactly these bad consequences consisted in she could never quite explain. It remained for the analysis to convince her that menstruation and birth processes were so closely connected in her unconscious that the old reproach against the mother's pregnancy was revived by it every time.

Another important source of her anxiety was revealed by the form of the transference. In her resistances the patient fought for a long time against the sexual fantasies which related to my person. Soon a large part of her anxiety was concerned with this relationship to me, and as she recognized herself the extent to which I had begun to take the part of her girl friend in her life, she asked me one day reproachfully whether she had come to me "merely to exchange one illness for the other." And in reality since the child's birth her love for her friend had grown into a sort of illness. The tender care which was expended on the little girl had reawakened in her the same jealous impulses as she had suffered from at the time of her sister's birth; and as then, this happened just at the time when the erotic demands on the mother—or the friend—had reached their highest pitch through the overcompensation of the aggressive hate against the rival. For in our patient's unconscious two enemies stood ranged against each other: the aggressive hatred and the overcompensating love, both repressed and both productive of anxiety. And the more the love tried to win the upper hand, the severer grew the sense of guilt against the increasing hate.

The analysis was able to throw a particularly interesting light on the meaning of our patient's cat phobia. In the sense of the old fairy-tale symbol, in which the cat is always the companion and double of the wicked witch, the animal represented the patient's own wicked feelings against the woman. The witch herself, the counterpart of the good fairy, represents the "wicked mother" for all of us and serves to embody our own wicked attitude in these primordial ambivalence conflicts. And to this she owes her immortality in the fairy tale.

Our patient's phobia had the same meaning as the fairy tales. The anxiety she felt related to the danger with which the "wicked woman" within her threatened her. But this danger from her own emotional attitude consisted not only in the guilt-producing aggression against the woman; it was also conditioned by her former life, in which these aggressions had already played a part. But they had been repressed and transformed into an overcompensating love for the mother, which had in its turn been transferred to the friend. Now this love, as we learned from the fantasy life of our patient, had a masochistic character—the desire to be maltreated by the friend—and betrayed thereby its derivation from the original aggressive tendency. Thus as well as fearing to be punished for her death wishes directed against the friend, the patient was afraid at the same time of her libidinal relation to her, for the masochistic character of this relationship constituted a serious danger. She attempted to escape these dangers by transferring them onto the symbolized animal. The cat became the representative of both her dangerous ambivalent impulses toward the woman. By avoiding the animal she tried to escape the internal dangers that threatened her. This is indeed usually the goal of the phobic mechanism. But our patient could not reach this goal, for the mechanism only managed to absorb a part of her diffused anxiety; the greater part was not to be disposed of through phobic anticathexes. Why this should be so we cannot say with certainty.

It would seem that phobia in general differs from true hysteria in its closer relationship to the obsessional neurosis and that the formation of a well-consolidated phobic system presupposes more of those forces which play their part in the genesis of obsessional symptoms. But we will go into this question more deeply in our further discussion of phobia and obsessional neurosis.

Still less can one answer the question as to why anxiety hysteria should be unable to guarantee freedom from anxiety by the formation of conversion symptoms. Perhaps this is partly due to the strength of the sadistic component of the libido, which provokes in its turn a greater severity on the part of the superego, so that the latter will not allow the wish-fulfilling instinctual tendencies to find expression in conversion symptoms.

This intermediate position of the phobias between obsessional neurosis and hysteria can frequently be observed in those cases which exhibit a combination of phobic anxieties with conversion symptoms and hysterical seizures, and in those in which obsessional symptoms go hand in hand with those of a phobic nature. And among those patients who suffer from phobias there are some who, in their personality as a whole, have a definitely hysterical, and others again who have a more obsessional, character. But we will return to this question later.

7

A Case of Hen Phobia

(1930)

I SHOULD like to describe to you a case of phobia in which the phobic anxiety related to an animal which is seldom the subject of animal phobias. Dogs, horses, and cats are the most frequent depositories of phobic anxiety. Sometimes the anxiety relates to large, fierce animals which occur in fairy tales and stir the child's fears. Sometimes, too, small creeping beasts or spiders, snakes, etc., produce an uncanny sensation, which may in certain circumstances develop into severe anxiety.

Our patient suffered for years from a hen phobia. This was particularly painful for him, for, born and brought up in the country, he was so handicapped by his phobia in his profession of farmer that he was literally forced to leave his enemy in possession of the field and seek refuge himself in the city to find some other outlet for his anxiety.

When he came to me to be analyzed he was already, practically speaking, cured of his phobia. The young man—he was then twenty years old—had come at the insistence of his family, who had discovered that he was a manifest homosexual and demanded that he should attempt to get rid of his perversion by analytic treatment. The patient himself was not at all agreed on the point. He was indeed quite content with his homosexuality and took care to emphasize the aggressive masculine element in his relation to men, although his whole personality bore a pronouncedly soft and feminine character. The objects of his affection were always fashionable young men who belonged, according to his own description, to the same type as himself. This type of object choice we call narcissistic, i.e., one loves in the other person what is like oneself.

This object choice was indeed somewhat striking, for it was obvious from the first stage of the analysis that the roots of his homosexuality lay in a fixation on a brother ten years older than himself. It was only when the analysis had succeeded in unraveling the intricate threads of his psychic life that the meaning of this paradox grew clear.

The patient had no recollection of having been ill in the first six years of his life. It was only in the latency period that the first neurotic difficulties made their appearance, and then as a reaction to a traumatic experience. I should like here once more to stress the point that such traumatic experiences may well be the occasion for the outbreak of a neurosis, but they are extremely seldom the ultimate and only cause of the illness. In the analysis they serve as signposts, landmarks, or stepladders to deeper unconscious sources, to which they owe their operation and sometimes, too, their origin.

Our patient's traumatic experience formed, as it were, the stereotype for his later puberty neurosis as well as for his perversion, and in discussing this extremely interesting and instructive case I shall use this experience as my basis of operations. For this experience provided the stepping stone in the analysis not only to the later stages of the patient's development, but also to that period of his childhood which was buried in amnesia. The analysis almost always shows that the pathogenic effect of such experiences—whether they have been subjected to amnesia or not —is solely due to the fact that they have fallen on soil that has been well prepared for them.

My patient's experience had never really been subjected to amnesia, but its deeper significance for the development of his psychic life had remained hidden from him. It needed the analysis to re-establish the connection between the apparently harmless experience and his later neurotic difficulties.

One hot summer day the little seven-year-old boy was playing with his grown-up brother in the farmyard of the house where he had been born and brought up. He was playing at something on the ground in a squatting, stooping position, when his big brother suddenly leaped on him from behind, held him fast round the middle, and shouted out, "I'm the cock and you're the hen."

It was clearly a case of a playful sexual attack on the part of the brother. It developed into a tussle between them, for our little friend refused to be a hen at any price. Nevertheless he had to give way to the stronger brother, who went on holding him clasped in the same position, and in a paroxysm of rage and tears he screamed out, "But I won't be a hen!"

From now on the little boy began to be considerably restricted in his freedom of movement. He felt himself compelled to give all hens a wide berth, which was none too easy of accomplishment in the precincts of a farm. At this time it was not yet the fear of hens as such which drove him to this measure, but the fear of his big brother's sadistic attacks, for every time a hen came into sight he used to tease the little boy by shouting out, "That's you!"

This original avoidance of the brother's taunts gradually developed into an avoidance of hens, with whom he had always hitherto been on singularly good terms. His fear indeed soon grew into a regular hen phobia. Every time he wanted to leave his room someone had to be got to shut the hens into their coops and keep watch for any hens that might come into sight. It was only when all these precautionary measures had been observed that the little boy would timorously venture to leave the house. Even then he would look anxiously in every direction to make quite sure that no frightful fiend in the shape of a hen came into his range of vision. If he did by any chance see a hen he would have a violent attack of anxiety. For some two years he was afflicted by this restriction of his freedom, after which the phobia completely disappeared. The analysis revealed the fact that this release coincided with the departure of the brother, who left home at this time to pursue his studies.

In puberty our patient was particularly difficult to manage, and after an unpleasant incident with his French governess he was sent away to school, where he lived with one of the masters, to whom he was very attached. When he returned home for his holidays after some months, he succumbed once again—after an interval of some six years—to the hen phobia so that he hardly dared to leave his room. The phobia, however, gradually lost its strength; he became again, practically speaking, healthy, only he lost all interest in the female sex and developed, as you have heard, into a manifest homosexual.

Let us turn somewhat more closely to his infantile history before the traumatic experience. He was much younger than his three brothers and sisters, and definitely his "mother's darling." He clung to his mother's apron strings and accompanied her in all her doings. It turned out that hens had already played an important part in his fantasies long before the experience with his brother. His mother used to pay particular attention to the henhouse, and the little boy took a lively share in these activities, was delighted at every newly laid egg, and used to be particularly interested in the way his mother felt the hens to see whether they were laying properly. He himself loved to be felt over by the mother, and would often ask her in fun when he was being washed, etc., whether she would feel him with her finger to see if he was going to lay an egg. At first this pleasure in being touched related to the genital, but gradually—perhaps in connection with the feeling of the hens—he displaced these sensations further back. He manipulated with his fingers in the anus, kept back his feces or else laid beautifully formed fecal eggs in every corner of the room and was highly astonished that his mother did not welcome this love gift with the same pleasure as in the case of the hens. In these games he played a double role: on the one hand he was the mother, touching and manipulating with the finger; on the other hand he was the hen, being felt and laying the egg. This anal game had been largely hidden by amnesia and came to consciousness again only in the course of the analysis.

This was followed by a phase in which the educative influence of his environment seemed to have been crowned with success. The little boy abandoned these dirty habits, became extremely clean, and gave the impression of having given up anal pleasures altogether. He began to play more with his genital onanistically,

and one might have concluded that he had developed successfully from the anal to the genital phase. The analysis, however,
showed that the onanism only signified an attempt to get anal
sensations in another way. In his onanistic manipulations he so
managed things that instead of pressing with the finger from
behind, he pressed the penis against the perineum from in front
and thus obtained anal sensations. His fantasies remained centered on the mother, whom he endowed in his imagination with
a penis: in this game his own penis was one of the mother's organs, just as his finger in the earlier fantasy had really belonged
to her. In this phase his attitude was, it is true, passively anal,
but the object choice was heterosexual. It was the experience with
the brother that signified a turning point in the object choice. In
this experience his passive-anal attitude—which in itself denoted
a predisposition toward homosexuality—was already homosex-
ually directed, in that the brother had taken the place of the
mother. For the game with the brother had fully activated his
passive homosexual predisposition. The analysis showed that
even before this experience, when watching the cock leaping the
hen he had identified himself with the hen, and the reason for
the violence of his protest against his brother's act in the cock-
and-hen game was his conscious repudiation of the unconsciously
desired passive role. The scene with the brother signified for him
the sexual act between the cock and the hen, i.e., between his
brother and himself, and his scream, "I won't be a hen!" meant
really "I repudiate my passive-homosexual wish." The hen phobia, as the analysis showed, was only a further development of
this repudiating tendency.

I should like to mention here yet another point from this experience with the brother. The patient related in the analysis,
though not as yet connecting it with this experience, that he had
a zone round about his waist in which he was so ticklish that even
when trying on a suit or when it was approached in any way at
all he used to collapse into fits of uncontrollable laughter, and
formerly when schoolfellows had tried to tickle him in this part
he had often actually fainted from laughter. In the analysis it
was possible to relate this oversensitiveness to the scene with the
brother. For in that fateful situation the brother had clasped him

from behind round that part of the body which belonged to this ticklish zone. As we have already seen, this embrace had brought with it a fulfillment of the patient's passive libidinal wishes. But this fulfillment awoke simultaneously a violent repudiation of the passive tendencies. The laughter was an expression of the gratification, or the memory of the pleasurable element in that experience, but it was a laughter which had been turned to pain by the revulsion, an already repudiated, somewhat melancholy merriness.

As far as our patient could remember, the experience with the brother had not been accompanied by the tickling sensation, but in the place where he had been embraced our patient retained a physical recollection which sought expression, every time that it was refreshed by later contacts, in a pleasurable discharge, i.e., in laughter, which called forth simultaneously the defense, as in the original cry, "I won't be a hen!"

In the conflict with his brother he had been the vanquished one, and the later fainting fits which accompanied the tickling were a repetition of his own passive surrender after his attempts at defense had failed. We know that in his relation to his mother he had experienced strong pleasure sensations when being touched by her. This pleasure in being touched in one whose skin erotism was obviously strongly developed had also extended to the other parts of the body which came specially under the mother's care in the process of cleansing, etc.—under the chin, the armpits, and the heels. In our patient's case this sensitiveness to being touched was probably displaced from these parts of the body onto that zone which played a part in the experience with the brother, corresponding to the fate of his libido, which turned from the mother to the brother.

I have the impression that this form of skin excitability with the peculiar affective reactions which were so strongly developed in our patient's case has the same origin in all forms of ticklishness. It is indeed a striking fact that the typically ticklish regions are those which are especially affected by the cleansing process in infancy. It would seem as though these regions remain subject to pleasurable, and later, repressed, recollections of these infantile experiences of skin erotism. The ticklishness is then the reactivation of the pleasure and the repudiation simultaneously.

Let us return to our patient. The scene with the brother signified for him a homosexual seduction, an experience for which he had long been fully prepared in his unconscious fantasies. His resistance represented his repudiation of this wish fulfillment, the repudiation of his own passive homosexuality, which manifested itself in the hen phobia.

In order to investigate this whole process more closely, we will recall the two classic case histories of animal phobias, the horse phobia of Little Hans (Freud, 1909b) and the wolf phobia from the "History of an Infantile Neurosis" (Freud, 1918).

Little Hans had repressed the hostile impulse against the father and had displaced his aggressive tendencies from the father onto a suitable animal object, from which he then lived in fear of revenge, i.e., an aggression against his own little person. With him the anxiety was a warning signal in face of the inner dangers, an anxiety the content of which was, "If you want to kill the rival father, you will be castrated by him," and the castration danger was expressed in the threat, "You will be bitten by the horse." It is characteristic that this threatening danger was displaced onto the outer world.

The little Wolf Man likewise projected his inner danger onto the outer world. But with him the danger lay in the passive-homosexual relationship to the father (contained in the unconscious wish to be eaten up by the father). With him, too, the inner danger was displaced onto an animal. Even though the process in the little Wolf Man's case is more complicated, it is, as Freud says, here too a question of castration anxiety. What Little Hans fears as revenge and punishment, namely castration, is for the Wolf Man a precondition of the gratification he unconsciously desires. For in order to be loved by the father as the mother is, one must sacrifice one's male genital.

And how is it with our patient's hen phobia? He too, like Little Hans and the Wolf Man, displaces the inner danger onto the outer world. But the projection mechanism functions differently with him. He splits off that part of his personality which represents his passive homosexual attitude to the brother; the hen, with which he had already identified himself in the past, corresponds to this part of himself, which has been split off and projected outward. The hen is for him a sort of mirror of his feminine tendency; every time he looks in this mirror, i.e., every time he sees a hen, he is afflicted by fear of his own instinctual tendencies, which must lead to the same result as in the case of Little Hans and the Wolf Man: namely, castration.

We must remember that his primary anality brought with it a predisposition toward passive homosexuality, and the brother's attack from behind merely mobilized and confirmed this predisposition. The fear of hens characteristically disappeared as soon as the brother had left the home—a proof that the real danger for his passive libidinal wishes lay in his relations with the brother.

During puberty the following incident occurred: his brother entered into a relationship with the French governess. Our patient too solicited her favors, but was rejected as too young. Far from accepting this rebuff, he fell upon the governess from behind in a fit of fury and tried to violate her in this position. After a tremendous family scene it was decided to send the boy away from home.

These experiences in puberty point to an earlier rivalry relationship to the brother. Probably the mother played a part in this rivalry; and the analysis revealed points which suggested that he had connected his observations of cocks and hens in his fantasy life with his mother and father. One also got the impression that the little man had not been able to tolerate the rebuff on the part of the mother, and for this reason had carried through the process of inversion into the feminine. Probably the speed and ease with which this process was effected was due to his strongly anal predisposition thereto. But this normal oedipal attitude remained only an assumption based on certain facts that pointed that way; the analysis was not able to supply any positive evidence in this direction. In the analysis the mother relationship appeared only in the following very unmasculine form: on the one hand, he identified himself with her, on the other he wished to be gratified by her in an anal way. From this point he developed straight into the brother relationship, without the father playing any more immediate part in the analysis.

The experience with the governess was decisive for his further development. The frustration he had met with on the part of the woman intensified his homosexual tendencies. He returned to school, apparently sublimated and without neurotic difficulties, but his whole behavior clearly betrayed passive tendencies.

On a visit home in his seventeenth year he again fell a victim to his hen phobia, whereupon he sought refuge again in the town. On the day of his return he made the acquaintance of a nice-looking young man, to whom he behaved in a markedly aggressive fashion, telling him (also homosexual) of homosexual experiences which he had never had, and finally actively seducing him. From this moment on he had a whole series of analogous homosexual experiences, in which he always played the part of active seducer.

The explanation of this sudden change in his attitude was that he had formerly timorously repressed all homosexual impulses out of fear of his own passivity, and had preferred to set up phobic mechanisms rather than suffer the break-through of these impulses. But the fettered homosexual libido was able to come to expression under one condition, and this condition was that he must take the active part in his homosexuality and not the passive one. By doing this he attained two goals: first, he was able to maintain his activity, had no need to give up his manliness or to renounce his male genital; and secondly, by choosing a narcissistic object, i.e., by forming love relationships with young people like himself, he was at the same time able to enjoy the experience passively, in that he identified himself with the others.

But what finally released his homosexuality was the fact that he had discovered on his last visit home that his brother was a manifest homosexual. The realization of this fact occasioned indeed the revival of his phobia. Simultaneously, however, immediately after his return to town and under the influence of this realization, he relinquished the fear of his own homosexuality and—identifying himself with his brother—became actively homosexual, and so was able to say to himself, "I need no longer be afraid of my brother's attack, for I am myself the attacker."

The therapeutic prospects for such an analysis, in which the patient has accepted his perversion in a full sense of his mental health and has come to be treated only at his family's request, are extraordinarily unfavorable, but surprisingly enough *this* analysis ended with the patient's becoming heterosexual, and if the information I hear from time to time about him is correct and the external conditions of his existence can be accepted as indicative, his heterosexuality has been permanent.

The solution of the therapeutic task was so interesting in this case that I cannot refrain from describing it to you shortly.

The patient came to be analyzed in a state of intense self-satisfaction. He was the type of narcissistically feminine young man with small capacity for love, for whom a relationship with a similar object was the only possible form of love relationship. At the beginning of the analysis he professed to be "violently" in love with a young actor. This actor, a typically narcissistic object choice, was the embodiment of all those qualities which the patient would have liked to find in himself. He himself wanted to be an actor; his friend *was* one. His friend was tender like a woman and noble like a man, ready for every sacrifice, and yet in full possession of his personality, etc. At the same time the patient bestowed as much admiration on his own person, and was as vain and self-satisfied as if he had actually possessed all these qualities he professed to find in his friend.

In the analysis his narcissistic self-glorification was a little shattered. Whereupon he ran away from the analysis, but soon began writing despairing letters begging me to take him on again, for he was at his wit's end to know what to do. He celebrated his return with the following dream:

He turns out the light by his bed to go to sleep. At the same moment he feels a pressure at his neck, a choking in his throat; a heavy form embraces his body, tries to crush his chest; he defends himself, they close their teeth on each other in the struggle, fall onto the floor, and continue there the process of pulling, hitting, scratching, throttling, etc. He succeeds in reaching the electric light switch, and turns it on just in time to see a dark-clothed female figure flit by, and realizes that this was his opponent. He feels his strength deserting him and knows that he is going to die. He recognizes in his opponent a young male acquaintance of his. He says: "I have committed suicide," and thinks to himself, "I don't deserve any better." At the same time he knows that the other has murdered him, and yet he declares that he has committed suicide. Finally he thinks to himself, "How noble of me to take the blame on myself!" and wakes up.

In its analytic interpretation the whole tussle in the dream reminds one of E. T. A. Hoffman's *Elixiere des Teufels,* where the two sides of the ego, Medardus and Viktorin, struggle wildly with each other. The patient saw the analogy, and correctly diagnosed the female figure in the dream as myself, the cause of his conflicts in the analysis. To the "young man" he associated a meeting with an acquaintance the day before, whom he knew to be a sadistic-aggressive homosexual who tortured and exploited his victims. The patient despised him wholeheartedly and avoided his company. In the course of conversation the "young man" told him that things were not going well with him; he suffered from depressions and anxieties. At this, two thoughts crossed the patient's mind: first, "You don't deserve any better"; secondly, "Like me."

These associations showed clearly his own identification with the young man. Whereas he had so far put himself on a level with his love partners, who corresponded to his conscious ego ideal, and had felt himself to be like them in his narcissistic self-admiration, the dream revealed his deeper, repressed identification—coming to the surface under the influence of the analysis—with the evil, sadistic, aggressive elements. In the dream he discharges his whole furious aggression against his attacker, against the sadistic partner, who is at the same time his double, his repressed and overcompensated ego.

The apparently clear and transparent picture of his passive attitude here becomes somewhat confused. His phobia, as we understood it, proves to be the final product of a very complicated process. His feminine attitude, it is true, was very early and dispositionally determined (anal relationship to the mother, etc.), but the final result was reached by way of a furious hatred of his opponent, the powerful father or brother (the woman in the case of the dream). In this struggle he had to admit himself the weaker (cock-and-hen conflict) and the original hater was transformed into the powerless lover.

The dream, however, showed clearly that this conflict between himself and the "other" continued to be acted out within him. The "other" in him, who mishandles and finally murders him, is the sadistic part of his personality, which at the same time sits in judgment over him, condemning him, on the ground that he "doesn't deserve any better," to suicide.

We see here the despotic tyranny of this inner criticism and may rightly assume that it ultimately represents the execution of justice against the ego on the part of the aggression. The resulting masochistic attitude, however, became a danger for the ego, for, like the original feminine-libidinal wish, it brought with it the threat of the loss of masculinity. The defense against this danger we have already recognized in the phobia; but we now see that the flight into the phobia also related to the punishment, which again involved the danger of castration. In fact, the punishment and the fulfillment of the feminine-libidinal wishes both have the same fateful consequences and have therefore to be repudiated by the ego, as happened in the phobic mechanism.

In the course of time our patient solved his inner conflict through a series of apparently successful compromises, and compensated his psychic emasculation by a self-glorifying narcissism. But the analysis reactivates the conflict in its deepest and ultimate sources. His inner peace is disturbed, the narcissistic protective wall collapses, and so the therapeutic process has its chance.

Let us recall the patient who suffered from a cat phobia. In her case a hostile impulse, intensified to a death wish, against her girl friend was repressed and displaced onto a suitable animal object. Every encounter with a cat mobilized the old hatred in the patient, and at the same time the reaction to this hatred; a threat, namely, on the part of the superego and thereby a danger for the ego, represented by the cat, which now assumed the role of the punishing mother. But we saw too that the projection object, the cat, was at the same time the representative of the homosexual, positive-libidinal impulse, and that the whole process clearly signified a compromise between this impulse and the punishing agency. This compromise would seem to be a favorable one for the ego, for it possesses in the phobic symptom a warning signal to protect it against anxiety. It is as if a severe preceptor were to threaten a child with punishment in order to arouse anxiety, but were to promise him at the same time not to punish him, provided he refrained from doing some particular thing.

In the case of our last patient the hen phobia was the direct projection of a libidinal tendency, or of the danger of castration which was attached to the fulfillment of the libidinal wish. But here too the phobia was really the final product of a struggle against certain aggressive impulses.

Both these cases seem to confirm the view that in contrast to hysterical conversion symptoms the phobia is characterized by a stronger regressive tendency in the sense of sadistic-aggressive impulses. Hence the superego behaves more severely and brings the ego into those dangerous situations which can be projected in the phobia and thus take on the character of an external danger and so be avoided. But it does not behave so implacably as in the obsessional neurosis, for provided that certain avoidance measures are observed the phobia is able to grant the ego freedom from anxiety and symptoms, whereas the constant inexorable pressure of the sense of guilt in the obsessional neurosis leads to a continuous series of precautionary measures, defensive struggles, etc. We will return later to this comparison between the phobia and the obsessional neurosis.

8

Agoraphobia
(1928)

THE cases I am about to discuss all conform to a quite definite type of illness. They are people who develop intense anxiety states when left alone in the street. They become subject to all the phenomena of anxiety: palpitations, trembling, and especially the feeling that they are going to collapse and meet with some irreparable disaster. Their anxiety is a real death anxiety and their phobic fear is, "I am suddenly going to die." They are suddenly seized by the thought that they are going to succumb on the spot to debility, a heart attack, or paralytic stroke, or some other catastrophe. Frequently the anxiety is centered on the idea of being run over, train or motor accidents, etc. It is typical of these states that they completely disappear or are considerably alleviated when the patient has someone to accompany him. Sometimes the mere sight of his home in the distance restores his sense of security. The companion must usually fulfill certain conditions, such as that some sort of tender relationship must exist between him and the patient. Many sufferers from agoraphobia insist on the company of a particular person. Others are less exacting and are content with anyone who is likely to be able to render "immediate assistance." There are some rich patients who are happy only when they have their doctor by them with the saving injection syringe.

97

As there appeared to be nothing very specific about the choice of companion, this aspect of the matter was neglected in favor of the patients' assertion that it is merely a question of obtaining assistance in general. But in the three cases I am going to discuss here the significance of the particular companion seems to be of importance and to throw a certain light on the essence of this form of phobia.

One of these cases was entrusted to me several years ago by a colleague on his departure from Vienna. The patient was a young girl with typical agoraphobic symptoms. Every time she went out without her parents she was attacked by violent anxiety of the sort described above. Her companion had to be either her father or her mother. According to her, the first attack occurred on an occasion when she had seen a man collapse on the street in an epileptic fit. Henceforth she was unable to recover from the shock of what she had seen, the less so as she was constantly getting to hear of sudden deaths. In this connection she seemed to be peculiarly unfortunate, for she was always encountering ambulances or funerals and was ever being reminded anew through these "experiences" of the possibility of her own death. It is indeed remarkable how often sufferers from agoraphobia are surprised by these apparently chance traumatic encounters. This is due of course to their always being on the lookout for such things, which others pass by unnoticed, so that they are able to maintain the impression that they have particular ill-luck in this respect.

From the previous history of our patient I should mention that about the time of her falling ill, i.e., about a year before the beginning of the treatment, she entered into an erotic relationship with a young man, which was sanctioned by the bourgeois morality of her parents as long as it remained a "platonic love."

In her treatment with the first analyst her condition had considerably improved. It was obviously a case of a "transference success," the meaning of which became clear in the course of the analysis. The kind and understanding treatment, which served in the first part of her analysis as a substitute gratification for her unconscious relationship to the father, had the effect of enabling her to come to the analysis unaccompanied and to move freely within a wide radius of the analyst's house. The fantasy, in the sense of love fulfillment, which now related to the analyst, served as protection against the anxiety and took the place of a companion.

Soon after the departure of her first analyst, Dr. X——, a new displacement of the anxiety intervened with an unexpected content: something might happen to Dr. X—— on his travels, he might have a heart attack, for instance. For a time her anxiety about his person replaced that about herself. But this was only temporary; soon the old anxiety about herself recovered its former prominence.

What was the decisive factor in our patient's agoraphobia?

I should like first to stress the fact that the departure of the analyst was felt as a disappointment in love and called forth a sadistic reaction, which was, however, repudiated and transformed into anxious solicitude. Her anxiety corresponded to a typical hysterical reaction formation. The fact that the anxiety related first to her own person and then to the frustrating object (the analyst) makes it probable that some sort of bridge can be found between the two.

The patient's analysis grouped itself round two traumatic experiences, the first in infancy, the second in puberty. The infantile experience was the actual overhearing of parental coitus, from which she gained the impression that her father was throttling and torturing her mother. The experience in puberty was a severe seizure which her father had after a bath, in which he collapsed completely as if dead, so that he had to spend some considerable time in a sanitarium.

All the patient's puberty fantasies were a revival of that infantile eavesdropping situation. They were feminine-masochistic in character, and in addition to the normal contents—violation, degradation to the rank of prostitute, etc.—they had some particularly violent traits, i.e., a red-hot iron rod is stuck into her genitals, or she bears a child and bursts into pieces in the process.

In all these masochistic fantasies, which had arisen around the eavesdropping scene, the patient had identified herself with her mother. The oedipus complex ended with the fixation of this identification and of the death wish against the mother attached thereto, which had a particularly aggressive character. The later experience—the father's sudden seizure—which occurred during her puberty conflicts, had revived the memory of the infantile experience and mobilized the hitherto repressed reactions against the father. These reactions culminated in a death wish against the father. The content of this wish was, "If you don't love me as you then loved my mother, may you die!" The father's convulsions and loss of consciousness were the associative link with that first infantile scene. The repudiated death wish against the father corresponded to the regressive reactivation of the infantile wish to "castrate" the father.

The outbreak of the neurosis followed upon an actual sexual attack on the part of her lover. In the first instance, therefore, her parents' protection "on the streets," i.e., outside her home, related to a danger founded in reality. But this did not exhaust their part as companions. For as soon as the patient got into the temptation situation (i.e., outside the protection of her home), her otherwise well-repressed instinctual impulses were immediately mobilized.

As we have already seen, these impulses were definitely masochistic in character. The infantile mother relationship, maintained by the fixation, to which the patient regressed, depended, as we know, on a masochistic identification with the mother. And this identification had the effect of turning the aggression directed toward the mother against her own ego, thus constituting the greatest danger for it.

The aggressive tendencies against the frustrating father had shown themselves particularly clearly in the transference relationship to Dr. X——. But the analyst's friendliness and the hope of his love had modified her aggression, and this in its turn seemed to have made the patient free from anxiety. But the frustration brought about by his departure had remobilized the entire sadistic revenge attitude and given the anxiety a content more nearly related to its unconscious origin. The form of death, that is to say, to which the analyst was condemned, corresponded exactly to the impression the patient had gained of her father's seizure, and also, be it noted, to the fate she feared for herself in her agoraphobia.

The whole well-repressed content was mobilized only under

particular conditions. When her parents were not present, the street, which was for her a partly real and partly symbolical "temptation situation," became such a condition. We can now understand why the anxiety in face of the inner dangers was diminished when she took her parents with her. The apparent protection from the external dangers of the street was only an obvious rationalization for the unconscious dangers of her inner life. The presence of the parents protected her not only from the fulfillment of the forbidden sexual wishes, but also from the aggression against the forbidding parents, which was intensified in the situation of sexual temptation and seemed clearly to be compensated and modified by their presence and tender solicitude. At the same time the danger of death which the intensification of the aggression had brought the ego, which was masochistically identified with the mother, had been lessened and the anxiety had been alleviated.

The second patient I have to talk about was a lower-middle-class woman, some forty years old, the mother of three children, and hitherto, practically speaking, healthy. The eldest daughter, a girl of seventeen, was brought up by the mother in the strictest rules of bourgeois morality, and had begun to be interested in men and love and all the things that are of most importance for a girl of her age. The mother felt upset by this fact, and though she pretended to be sympathetic, actually she spied continually on her daughter, consumed with curiosity about her harmless love life, and learned from her diary, which she came across "by chance," that she was just beginning a relationship with a man in whom the mother felt a certain interest.

This was the signal for the mother's neurosis. Her whole conscious and unconscious fantasy activity represented a reactivation of her puberty. This already elderly woman began to have all those fantasies of defloration, violation, and prostitution which are typical of puberty and which were all dangers which she, the loving mother, should have been fearing for her daughter. In these forbidden and repudiated wish impulses the patient had indeed identified herself with her daughter. At the same time the daughter had become the hated rival against whom the patient's entire revenge reaction, which had once related to her own mother and now related to her daughter, was directed. She felt almost consciously that her daughter was standing in the way of her happiness as her mother had once done in her own childhood. She used to say that she had been quite differently brought up by her mother from "modern" girls. She was never allowed to go out unprotected and her whole love life was strictly controlled. This same situation of control she repeats now in her agoraphobia. Tortured by death fears as she is, she can no longer go out alone. The only possible companion is the daughter, but in reality this condition can seldom be fulfilled, so that she is more or less confined to the house.

It is easy enough to understand the meaning of this situation. The daughter must see to it that the mother does not succumb to her instinctual impulses, those impulses, namely, in which she is identified with her daughter. In addition to her other instinctual dangers, the patient is exposed to the aggressive death wish against the rival, which rages against the ego owing to the identification which has taken place. In this situation the mother is at the same time enabled to keep watch over the daughter, who is threatened by dangers not only from her awakening sexuality, which the mother must protect, but also from the unconscious aggressive impulses of the mother. Thus the daughter, as protecting agency, has taken on the role of the superego, the forbidding and threatening protection, which had once been in the hands of the patient's own mother. We have here a process analogous to that of the former case: the companion becomes the "protected protector." The circumstance that the object of the identification, against which the aggression is directed, assumes the role of protective companion and performs its office as a loving and not as a threatening agency enables the death anxiety to disappear. The identification process on the one hand, and the death threat against the ego on the other, are both transitory in their nature and bound to the temptation situation represented by being out of doors. It is worth noting that the patient's anxiety originally related only to a particular section of the way, a path alongside a hedge, behind which she had often seen men relieving themselves. I mention this, because I have the impression that exhibitionistic tendencies play an important subsidiary part in the determination of these street dangers. But I shall come back to this point in my next case history.

In this third case history we have to deal with a twenty-seven-year-old woman who had been married for three years. She was the middle one of three children. In her earliest childhood her relation to her brother, who was two years older than herself, was one of peculiar jealousy (penis envy), and her relation to her two-years-younger sister one of strong oral envy. Both relationships were heavily charged with aggression and guilt. When she was four and a half her brother died of appendicitis. This death confirmed in her the severest sense of guilt, all the more owing to the decisive events connected with it. The most important of these was the disappointment she experienced at her mother's hands, for, instead of winning her through her brother's death, she lost her. For the mother, consumed by grief, withdrew from the family, lived alone in an attic, and thus brought the daughter into a situation which, though certainly desired by her, was nevertheless dangerous. For she now slept in bed beside the father and was able to a large extent to realize her oedipal fantasies. And when the mother tried to resume family life after a year, the little girl was already exhibiting the neurotic reactions to these incidents. And then in the latency period further neurotic difficulties occurred: fear of thunder and earthquakes and all manner of small conversion symptoms, which the analysis revealed to be pregnancy fantasies. Even in the prepuberty period she had heard of women who go on the streets at night and do something "dreadful," and could not be persuaded in consequence to leave the house after dark. Her ideas about these women combined with depreciatory fantasies about her mother, and made her, the mother, into a prostitute.

Two memories from the latency period played a large part in the analysis. The first related to an anxiety attack in the street on her way to ask forgiveness, at her mother's instance, of a lady from whose garden she had stolen fruit. She angrily obeyed her mother's command, but was unable to carry it out, because she was overcome halfway with palpitations and trembling. She realized herself that this represented suppressed hatred against the two women.

The other memory was connected with a story called *The Watcher in the Tower:* The lighthouse is kept by a woman, who lives there alone with her little daughter. One day the little girl finds her mother lying dead on the ground at the top of the tower. She has died suddenly of a heart attack in the middle of discharging her duties. The gallant child coolly takes over her mother's task and heroically saves the ships in danger.

Since reading this story she had been overcome by the most violent anxiety every time her mother left the house, and had waited by the window or door till she returned. The patient explained characteristically: "I don't know whether I really felt anxious about myself or my mother." The content of this anxiety can be guessed from the content of the story, in which the little girl takes the mother's place. But with the patient the mother's death is the condition for an unconscious wish fulfillment.

The part which the patient seeks to play in her identification with the mother is subject to the same depreciation and humiliation of her own person as she had attributed to the mother. The fulfillment of these unconscious wishes would turn the patient into a prostitute exactly as she had done to her mother in her fantasy.

You remember the infantile situation which was certainly the traumatic basis of her neurosis. The little girl had been deserted by her mother, a trauma in the sense of the loss of the object. The mother had surrendered to her the place beside the father, i.e., she exposed her to the danger of her unconscious wishes—which culminated in the identification with the mother—being fulfilled.

When the mother returned to the family, the little girl was already firmly fixed in the rivalry relationship; but it was possible for her to maintain her position only under one condition: if, as in the case of the watcher in the tower, the mother were to die (the analogy is strengthened by the scene in the two situations: attic—tower). Whenever in later life the patient found herself in situations in which her repressed libidinal tendencies—with her, too, masochistic in character—could be realized, she would call for her mother; not only to prevent the realization of her wishes, but also so that the death wish which had been directed against the protecting, or disturbing mother, should not be realized against herself. The anxiety signal in her agoraphobia revealed itself in the analysis as the old call for the mother.

Let us return to her case history. Even in her schooldays she had a sentimental love relationship with a schoolboy friend. When she was eighteen years old she became acquainted with her future husband, who made a strong sexual impression on her and asked for her hand. But the domestic atmosphere of her childhood was incredibly bigoted. After her son's death the mother had adopted an obviously neurotically toned asceticism, and her own renunciation was accompanied by an extremely severe moral attitude, which invested everything sexual with the strictest prohibition. The patient now found herself in a conflict, for her platonic relations with her first friend, for which she had received her mother's sanction, were of course disturbed by her feelings for her future husband. It was impressed on her that one must remain true to one's first "ideal" love. The patient felt unable to decide either way. The relationship to her future husband was clearly prohibited, even externally, for he was an atheist, in contrast to the pious mother. The conflict thereupon assumed a neurotic character and the patient set about to try and find some way out of it. She became possessed of the idea that she would bring about the first friend's death by breaking off relations with him, i.e., she desired to get rid of the disturber of her wishes, as she had once desired to get rid of her brother. She underwent the same operation (obviously in an attempt to discharge the sense of guilt prophylactically) as her brother had died from. And in this way she was enabled to make a decision: she broke off relations with the friend and became happily engaged to her future husband. At this point the agoraphobia broke out. As she was on her way one Sunday to visit a friend of her mother's (the patient lived far from her home) in order to tell her of her release, she was suddenly disturbed by the thought, "What will she think of my behavior?" Lost in thought she turned into a rather quiet street, where she was suddenly overwhelmed by anxiety: "Now I am going to collapse helplessly." Unable to proceed further, she sent word to the friend she was going to visit, in whose company she was able to finish her journey.

What had happened? The breach with her first friend had heavily charged her sense of guilt and evoked the memory of her brother's death. By this breach she had made it possible to gratify her sexual wishes, just as she had been enabled by the death of her brother to sleep beside the father. All her wishes now acquired an infantile character and were accompanied by severe prohibitions. As then, the mother withdrew her love and left her to face the sexual danger. As then, the death wish against the mother was activated. And just as she used to wait for the mother in the first infantile neurotic situation, so now she was unable to proceed without the mother's protection and the discharge of the murderous sense of guilt against her. Hence she had to have this friend, as mother imago, to accompany her.

The neurosis developed into a typical agoraphobia. On the advice of her doctors she married, but her condition grew worse and worse. The one thing she gained was that her husband, whom she tortured and fettered to herself by her symptoms, was able to act as the accompanying person. Soon coitus was attended by severe anxiety states and vaginitis.

In the analysis she developed a strong "transference neurosis," which enabled me to gain considerable insight into her illness from her relationship to my person.

The first phase was occupied by a "negative transference": refusal to be cured by me and distrust of my tolerance. How could I be an analyst when I allowed my own daughter, as she imagined in her fantasies, no sexual freedom? Every gesture of mine she construed as a prohibition, and hesitated between absolute protest and slavish obedience. She always accepted my interpretations without a cavil, but it would often happen, when she was about to tell, for instance, some particularly confirmatory dream, that she would begin to laugh and be unable to stop doing so for a quarter of an hour on end. It was clear that her apparent acceptance was accompanied by a contemptuous mistrust.

When I gave her a piece of advice, for example, to consult a woman doctor, she became overwhelmed by compulsive doubt, felt she had to obey and yet could not bring herself to go. One day I exhorted her to walk to my consulting room instead of taking, as she usually did, a taxi. She took one, nevertheless, on the way, but this time, contrary to custom, she was attacked by the most intense anxiety in the taxi, and the content of the anxiety was that she would now be punished with death for having transgressed my command. On the stairs she was possessed of the feeling that something had happened to me. During this analytic hour she had for the first time an anxiety seizure, which gradually developed into a typical, tonic-clonic hysterical seizure. She collapsed on the floor. At the end of the seizure she knelt down before me and said, "Forgive me." When I asked her what I had to forgive her for, she said, "This rage." She had seen for herself that the seizure was a discharge of rage.

On this day she went away completely free of anxiety for the first time in seven years. I should mention that this was the first hysterical seizure she had ever had.

She spent the next few days, too, almost without anxiety. This was due to the fact that she had found a ceremonial centering about my person. When walking in the streets she used to try and keep beside women in whom she could find some resemblance to me. If the person in question appeared to be "delicate" she would avoid her, for she might "collapse." Or else she would wait for hours in the neighborhood of my house, remaining free from anxiety the while. She used a visiting card of mine as a sort of talisman, as a part of myself. Similarly she invested the landlady I had recommended to her with a part of the transference. She would go about with this lady, though with a certain feeling of uneasiness, for she feared that the landlady might collapse on the street. As far as her anxiety was concerned, the way to my house was divided into two halves. The first half was productive of anxiety; in the middle there was a "hole" which intensified the anxiety, and after this she was safe.

With the increase of the positive transference went an increase of anxiety, lest I might refuse to see her any more if I got to know of everything about her. Then she brought up fantasies in which I did all the things which she was forbidden to do. She fantasied, for instance, that I had mysterious relations with men, that I undressed naked before my male patients; and one day she confessed to me under strong resistance that she had the idea that I masturbated during the analytic hour. All these accusations were a mirror of her own wish fantasies, and established an identity between us through a common guilt motive. But she also saw me in quite another light, as a hypermoral and self-castigating person, an image that corresponded to her own ascetic ego ideal. This splitting of my person was the equivalent of the double image she had once had of her mother; and with this double image she had identified herself, on the one hand in all the forbidden sexual acts she had imputed to the mother, and on the other hand, in the mother's severe prohibitions, which had been taken over by her superego. Even the vindictive death wish against me was, as the analysis showed, the signal of revolt against the mother, and was thus transformed into the death threat against her own ego.

This identification between me and the mother was illustrated particularly clearly in a characteristic dream:

The patient is lying on a hard trestle, her feet toward the fireplace, which is a mixture between a stove and a gas fire. The trestle consists of two chairs which have slipped apart, so that a part of her back hangs, as it were, in the air. On the floor beneath this part of her back is a burning candle. She has to keep raising herself in the middle to prevent getting burned. The dream is accompanied by palpitations and anxiety.

The associations to this dream led back to that danger situation in which she had found herself when her mother had left her to sleep beside her father. She recollected that her father, who was obviously an obsessional neurotic, used to look under the bed with a candle before going to sleep. The movements she carried out in the dream were a repetition of the typical *arc de cercle*, which she had produced in her seizure in the analytic hour. The fireplace by her feet represented a condensation between the stove in my consulting room and the kitchen fire at home. At her mother's wish she used to cook the breakfast at this fire, during which procedure she had an intense fear of mice which sometimes crept out of the holes under the hearth.

Onanistic impulses are also recognizable in the movements of the dream, and the guilt for these impulses as well as for the fantasies about the father she ascribed to the mother, who had brought her into these situations, just as I had done recently by making her fantasies conscious.

In another dream she is lying beside her mother in bed, watching her masturbating. She tries to stop her, and wakes up in a state of anxiety. The identification here between the dreamer and her mother on the one hand, and between me and the mother on the other hand, becomes clear when we remember the act of masturbation which she attributed to me.

As the anxiety tension in her relationship to me diminished, the patient summoned up more courage to impart her sexual fantasies. They were throughout of a genital-feminine, strongly masochistic character, and the active and passive birth fantasies, related thereto, had a far-reaching significance for her agoraphobia. The hysterical seizures she produced in the analytic hour enabled me to probe the content of this agoraphobia.

They would occur, for example, when she was reproducing anxiety dreams, or would even themselves have the character of a dream, and after the seizure was over the patient was always able to describe the content of the fantasies which had accompanied it. They proved to be representations of birth situations. For instance, she dreamed that she was in a dark cellar, being pursued by a woman; she is seized by frightful dread, for she can find no escape from the cellar. Suddenly she finds that blood is flowing from a hole in her head; an ambulance arrives, takes her away, and—she is saved.

Her associations showed beyond a shadow of doubt that this was a representation of her own birth.

In another dream, in telling which she also had a seizure, she saw herself standing by a window; she wonders why she is afraid to jump out of it. Then she throws a little doll out onto the street and is promptly seized by an intense feeling of anxiety that she is going to die. The violent convulsions of her whole body, which occurred in the seizure, were attempts to ward off this anxiety. This dream, too, was a clear example of birth symbolism.

Of peculiar interest in this patient's case was the gradual transformation of the phobia into a hysteria with seizures. With the improvement in her relationship to me and the mitigation of the destructive function of the superego went a diminution of the anxiety. And yet every time impulses connected with the mother relationship were released in the analysis the patient had a hysterical seizure, though these were characteristically confined to the analytic hour.

These seizures represented situations of a definitely genital character (masturbation, coitus, birth, delivery). The patient felt that she could allow herself these seizures in my presence, for even though they were accompanied by a "sensation of dying," she knew that she had nothing to fear if I was there. But outside in the streets she felt that she needed the anxiety, as though it would act as a warning signal in face of danger. I think we may accept the patient's interpretation. So long as the aggressive tendencies of her superego threaten her with death, the wish impulses must be suppressed by severe prohibitions. But where the tension between ego and superego (i.e., in the analytic situation between her and me) is lessened, the permitting forces can find expression and she can allow herself the symbolic representation of her repressed instinctual wishes in the seizure. To sum up, I think we may say that by the adjustment of her aggressive tendencies in the analysis, the severity of her superego was diminished, the genital tendencies were able to find expression, and instead of the inhibiting anxiety the motor discharge in the hysterical seizure was made possible.

We see in this case the transformation of one form of neurosis into another, the change from phobia to hysteria with seizures. In this connection I should like to discuss another case, in which an anxiety hysteria changed to an obsessional neurosis. The patient was a girl of twenty years, the only child of rich parents, whose father, however, had obviously little interest for family life and was more like a guest in the home than a parent. From the very beginning the mother, who was extremely neurotic, had bestowed the full measure of her unsatisfied love on the child. The infantile mother-child relationship had been successfully maintained to such an extent that at the time of her treatment the eighteen-year-old girl still slept with her mother and used to suck her breast or finger regularly before going to sleep. The analysis revolved chiefly around this mother relationship and attempted to dissolve the morbid mother fixation through a mother trans-ference. During the whole treatment the father had only one sig-nificance: that of a highly unwelcome intruder who threatened from time to time to come between the patient and her mother. In any case the oedipus complex had culminated in confirming the mother fixation.

The mother told me that the patient refused to leave her side from her earliest childhood, and that she had in consequence really been her slave ever since her birth. Her morbid traits, how-ever, had appeared only in puberty. The daughter had begun then to suffer from anxiety states when the mother left the house, giving as her reason that something might happen to the mother —"She might, for instance, be run over." She would wait for her mother by the window with an expression of intense anxiety on her face, and would light up with relief when she saw her mother return home again alive.

It is obvious to anyone trained in analysis that this hypersen-sitive anxiety had the character of an overcompensation and must be considered as a hysterical reaction formation. The anxiety sensations and the ideas about the mother's death in the street are reminiscent of the cases of agoraphobia discussed above, in which the appearance and disappearance of anxiety seem to be dependent on the absence or presence of particular people or their representatives. And yet the cathexis in this case was of a different nature. The anxiety is the same, but the death danger relates to the object, whereas in the agoraphobia it related to the ego itself. As far as the content is concerned, the agora-phobic patient we last discussed suffered from an anxiety phase which was exactly the same as in the present case.

Our patient's first neurotic manifestations were hysterical in character. The anxiety related to the threatened loss of object, and the ambivalence toward this object came clearly to expression in the content of the anxiety, i.e., that something terrible would happen to the mother.

The first hysterical phase of her neurosis was succeeded—as we shall see—by a transformation into an obsessional neurosis. In the analysis one could clearly trace the regressive reactivation of the anal-sadistic tendencies after successful genital repression.

But before this happened another symptom formation of a hysterical character occurred. The patient could not go out without her mother, because in the interval something terrible might happen to the mother (at the hands of the father, as the analysis showed). The only difference between the new symptom and the old one was the change of scene. Now the patient was outside, and the mother at home. The content was the same: fear of the loss of object and revenge against the object. This anxiety about the mother was again nothing else than a loss anxiety, i.e., she was afraid that the mother might give her love to the father in her absence. The hate tendencies against the mother proceeded on the one hand from the disappointment reaction, and on the other hand certainly from the normal oedipus complex, even though it had been very much covered over by impulses of the opposite attitude.

This symptom too is closely related to agoraphobia. The patient is unable to go out alone for fear that something might happen to the mother in the interval. The close relationship lies in the fact that this patient too is attacked by anxiety when she is deprived of her companion—the mother. Only the content is different: it is not she but the person whose companionship she desires who is threatened by the dreadful fate.

Thus far the patient's symptoms show a certain affinity with the clinical picture of agoraphobia. In what follows a transformation takes place, which on the one hand increases this affinity, but on the other hand diminishes it. The patient is unable to go out without her mother, but in contrast to her former state she is also tortured by the most violent anxiety when she is in her presence. She holds her mother in a convulsive embrace, continually worried lest something might happen to her. And finally the hitherto inhibited impulse comes to expression in a compulsive form: she becomes afraid lest *she* should throw her mother under a tram or a motor car. This obsessional fear is accompanied by the obsessional impulse really to push her mother to destruction.

Thus in this case too we see the transformation from one form of neurosis into another, in which the same content—the aggressive impulse—remains repressed in the first form and an anticathexis in the reaction formation of overanxious tenderness is all that comes to the surface. The anxiety springs from two tendencies which merge into each other: the one is the continuation of the early infantile relationship and corresponds to the danger of object loss, the other is a warning signal against the sadistic impulse and demands a further overcompensation through tenderness. The presence of the object is the condition for the freedom from anxiety—which constitutes the neurotic symptom in our case, so long as it has a hysterical character.

We assume that in the further course of the neurosis sadistic impulses, hitherto repressed, have broken through as a result of regressive processes. The anticathexis through overanxious love is obviously no more in a position to prevent the pressure of these impulses. They appear in a compulsive form as a temptation to murder, and the patient protects herself from the evil deed by means of precautionary measures which themselves correspond to the content of the deed.

In this case the neurotic mechanism is closely related to phobic anxiety in that we have here a very marked tendency to anxiety which is always pressing for precautionary measures, and the slightest attempt to neglect these leads to the development of intense anxiety.

The obsessional neurosis, on the contrary, is usually able to obtain a wide measure of freedom from anxiety through symptom formations. The obsessional impulses and their anticathexes are alike removed from the original content, and the whole neurotic structure would seem to be far better organized than in this case. And yet the feeling of inner compulsion and the anxiety about carrying out the obsessionally urgent impulse here are definitely obsessionally neurotic in character. As we have seen, the regression to the anal-sadistic phase was the motive for the transformation of the symptoms in this case.

In our last case of agoraphobia, on the other hand, the symptom transformation occurred as a result of the diminution of the hate tendencies and of the severity of the superego through the favorable conditions of the transference.

From the above material we can explain the relationship of agoraphobia to hysteria on the one hand, and to obsessional neurosis on the other hand, as follows. We know from Freud that phobia, in view of its connection with the genital phase, is to be reckoned as a form of hysteria. In my opinion we are here dealing with people in whom the ambivalence conflict is acuter, the sadistic impulses stronger, than is usual in the genital phase. The fact that the genital phase has been reached and maintained prevents the actual formation of obsessional symptoms; but the anal-sadistic phase is still able to exercise an attraction which may provoke a regressive relapse and produce a transformation of the hysterical neurosis into an obsessional illness (as in the case we have just discussed) or else a fluctuation of symptoms.

Under certain conditions repressed impulses will be mobilized and the relationship to the tenderly loved object will be regressively degraded to the formerly existing and fixated identification. As a result of this identification the aggressive impulses mobilized under the same conditions, which are directed against this identified object, are turned against the ego in a way to threaten its very existence.

When we come to discuss melancholia you will observe a similar process. There the object is introjected and the ego suffers the fate of the object at the hands of the destructive instinct: the death threat and its anxiety reaction in the threatened ego. The difference is that in agoraphobia the identification takes place on a higher stage of libidinal development and is thus temporary and capable of adjustment. It occurs only under certain conditions and can be removed by the presence of the approving and loving object. This is also true of the aggressive tendency which, involving the ego in mortal danger, can yet be adjusted successfully by the presence and protection of the object.

I consider this identification with the object of the hostile tendencies to be the characteristic element in agoraphobia. The sense of guilt is able to be satisfied by the fact that in the "turning against the ego" the latter itself experiences the death threat. But the tension between the ego and the threatening agencies in the superego will be released only when the presence of the protecting object confirms the fact that the object is not in danger and has not deserted the ego.

In our last case we were able to follow in the transference the genesis of this tension between ego and superego. It revolved round two identifications: the one related to the degraded object, and the danger-bringing impulses formed the bridge of identification: "I am like you, my instinctual wishes make me like you." The other identification related to the severe prohibiting object— the ascetic mother—whose severity, however, was called forth only by the temptation situation in the street.

I was also able to observe strong exhibitionistic tendencies as an important subsidiary element. My last patient, I should like to add, was much freer from anxiety in the street when she shut her eyes. And of central importance was the passive and active birth fantasy, for which the being-away-from-home and out-in-the-world had an important symbolic significance.

The confinement anxiety as an element of the feminine-masochistic fantasy is a direct legacy of the castration anxiety, and it was just the cases of agoraphobia which enabled me to see clearly what seems to me characteristic of the development of the female libido in general. The renunciation of the wish for a penis is directly succeeded by the vague desire for a painful sort of violation, and hence the castration wish and its immediate successor, the defloration or confinement wish, acquire the same meaning in the woman's unconscious. The unvanquished castration anxiety is transformed into neurotic defloration or confinement anxiety. In the analysis of agoraphobes this transformation process can be clearly seen. Moreover, I have the impression that the feminine-masochistic birth fantasy plays the same role in the case of *male* agoraphobes too.

Whether these cases supply a complete answer to the question why the anxiety occurs only in the street, I do not know. There is of course always a predisposition toward anxiety, which breaks out under certain conditions attached to the street. Freud found these conditions to lie on the one hand in the loss of the protective cover of the home, and on the other hand in the temptations of the street. This temptation occurs where the love life is degraded by regressive factors to prostitution; this is especially conditioned by the masochistic tendencies which were clear enough in the cases I have discussed. The street likewise offers a peculiar danger to the exhibitionistic impulses, which were strongly represented in the cases analyzed by me.

A further important determining factor was the active and passive birth fantasy. Moreover, the strongly libidinal significance of the legs and the act of walking, which Abraham (1913) has drawn attention to, certainly played a part too.

If we compare all these cases of phobia we shall find their common ground to lie in the fact that the inner danger is projected outward and attached to a situation or a particular object. In the animal phobia a suitable animal is chosen to incorporate the danger, and in the agoraphobia a part of the universe. The ego is thereby enabled to substitute a real, and so avoidable, danger for an unconscious and so unavoidable danger. Moreover, by the fulfillment of certain conditions the ego is able to obtain freedom from anxiety. With the animal phobia these consist in mere avoidance; with agoraphobia it was the presence of the object of an averted aggression which permitted the aggression to become attached to a libidinal impulse and thus diminished the anxiety-productive dangers for the ego.

9

Obsessional Ceremonial and Obsessional Acts

(1930)

THE patient I am going to talk about today was a pious Catholic school mistress, who at the time of her analysis had tried to find escape from the world, becoming a novice in a convent. The impression she made when one saw her might have misled one to diagnose her as a case of catatonic stupor. She lay motionless in bed, her legs pressed together and her hands held rigidly away from her body; whenever anyone attempted to approach her, her face took on an anxiously tense expression. Her rigid attitude relaxed only when it was a question of defending herself against anyone touching her or her bed. Her food had to be pushed over to her, and not given her by hand, and even her nearest relatives had to perform certain cleansing operations before approaching her. After contact had been established, I soon learned that the rigid attitude, the restriction of her relation to the outer world, was conditioned by one single thought: her body must not be touched, for it might thereby be polluted. "Dirt" meant, particularly, sexual things, with which the whole world was polluted. Her mother had, for instance, bought something in a shop which had, of course, been touched by the shop assistant: "Who knows whether he himself had not had to do with sexual things, or perhaps shaken hands with someone who had come directly or indirectly in contact with sexuality?" This was the sort of dread from which she constantly suffered.

117

The condition in which I found the patient was the result of a gradual development of several years; the ascetic final stage, so to speak, of restrictions of her freedom of movement. At first these restrictions were merely obsessional cleansing operations and all manner of obsessional ceremonials of the character of commands, prohibitions, etc. Later she used to employ all sorts of safety measures in her intercourse with her immediate environment, and made it a condition of further intercourse that those around her should change their clothes or have a bath, etc., before approaching her, and finally she had hoped to be able to escape the filth of the sexually polluted world behind the walls of the convent. But here too the visits of the priest, the excretory processes of the nuns as well as her own, brought with them the same dangers, from which she had finally saved herself by the condition of rigidity I have described to you.

Out of her analysis, which lasted three years, I will briefly discuss only what seems to me necessary to understand the psychic mechanisms of such an illness.

The first things I learned about the patient's childhood—which her mother had also told me independently—stood in crass contrast to her later cleanliness compulsion. Up to her twelfth year the patient had expressed all sorts of tendencies which betrayed a strongly anal and sadistic disposition. She suffered from chronic constipation, spent hours of her time in the lavatory, liked to besmear the walls, went about mostly unwashed, and had, as she herself admitted, strong, conscious pleasure sensations when defecating, and felt the greatest interest in her stool, etc. She was a naughty child, tortured her younger brothers and sisters, enjoyed pulling the wings off flies, found it difficult to get on with her playmates; in short, in her mother's words, she was "naughtier than the naughtiest boy." After her twelfth year a complete alteration in her character, with which I will deal later, set in.

Before discussing this I must point out that we are not always able to see so clearly the origin of the later reactions in the case history. Usually tendencies like those of our patient are repressed much more early and made gradually unrecognizable by reaction formations, so that these primary and original attitudes can only be revealed by analysis.

Our patient's neurosis broke out in her seventeenth year, and yet the analysis showed that the first traces of her later illness led back to childhood. Even in her tenth year she began, although herself dirty and still occupied with her cloacal habits, to be at the same time extraordinarily pedantic in tidying up. She would not allow a speck of dust on the floor, picked up every scrap of paper she could see, and took the greatest care not to let any drop on the ground. In this connection she expected to be praised by her mother for her care and cleanliness, and felt unhappy when her mother did not do so. Moreover, she transferred this solicitude onto her elder brother. She would feel anxious lest he might possibly "have dropped something," or she would go over all his things to see if everything was in order. These first signs of the neurosis were recognized as such neither by the patient nor by her friends. For us they already constitute a proof of the repression which had taken place. The pedantic care in tidying up is an obvious reaction formation against the dirty habits which she had indulged in in the lavatory; the urge toward cleanliness served to suppress her pleasure in dirt. Her meticulous behavior and the desire to be praised by her mother perhaps already indicate a very unsatisfactory relationship with the mother and reveal themselves as the first reaction of the sense of guilt.

Her solicitude about her brother could be traced back to certain common experiences of which she had the following memory. One night when she was a little girl she woke up with feelings of anxiety and oppression and felt her some-years-older brother lying on her in her bed. The patient indignantly blamed her mother for this experience, because she had not paid more attention to the children. Surprisingly enough, the patient was able to be convinced in the analysis that she had completely distorted and displaced this infantile experience in her memory. It was not the elder brother who had seduced her, but on the contrary the younger brother—who had been entrusted to her care—whom she had seduced. And the reproach against the mother had also quite another aim. At a much earlier age the mother had, it is true, forbidden something which had been covered in oblivion. This prohibition had related to the little girl's onanistic games, and the reproach against the mother had been reactivated and introjected by this new forbidden act, the active seduction of the brother, i.e., the old self-reproach about the onanism combined with the sense of guilt proceeding from the seduction of the brother. The reproach against the mother that she had "paid too little attention" really meant the opposite, namely, that she had paid too much attention at that time to the onanism, which she had forbidden. But the aim of this unjustified reproach was to liberate the patient from the self-reproach. The analysis was able to show the patient many situations in which she had employed this mechanism of getting rid of her own sense of guilt by putting the blame on her mother.

The first infantile symptoms (dirty habits, etc.) disappeared, the patient remained apparently healthy, but showed a typical change of character. She became extraordinarily cleanly, conscientious, pedantically exact in all she did, hypersensitive toward her family, extremely truth-loving, ready to renounce all worldly pleasures out of sympathy and love for others, correct' and reliable, with a trace of asceticism—in a word, the little devil had become an angel incarnate.

Such a change of character represents a typical phase in the life of an obsessional neurotic. It is a character formation which arises from reactions against repressed anal and sadistic impulses. It sometimes happens that the neurosis stops here, without proceeding to symptom formations; the individual remains healthy, socially indeed of great value, and only the analyst is able to recognize in him the disguised obsessional neurotic. The capacity for love, the free mobility of the libido in such people is, to be sure, not very rich or plentiful, because a large part of their mental energies are occupied in maintaining the tension of the reaction formation, in order to prevent the break-through of the repressed material.

With our patient, however, the process went beyond this stage. When she was sixteen years old her father died. The patient then became peculiarly active. At home she assumed the father's role, took on herself the care of her younger brothers and sisters and pursued this goal with the greatest energy. At the same time she tried to withdraw the children from their mother: she wanted to take over the mother's role, too, in relation to the children. Thus she hoped to emerge as victor from the old fight for the father against the mother, originating in the oedipus complex, and to be the mother to his children. She behaved as if she were hypersensitively concerned for the mother and gradually separated her from the children, apparently only from solicitude for her health. In actual fact she assumed the management of the house and at the same time lavished the most tender, motherly care on the children. In pursuance of this devotion she felt the wish to find a father for the children. But it must be no ordinary father. Hence she became engaged to her rich chief, although she was apparently very attracted by a young though poor colleague of hers.

At this point the neurotic symptoms broke out. The first of these was a sleep ceremonial: she had to get up several times during the night to see whether all the six children were asleep, whether they were tucked in and had no fever. The aim of this ceremonial, an obvious death wish, compensated by hypertenderness, against the children, was to enable her to fulfill her unconscious wish to marry her poor lover.

One can see here the stupendous accomplishment of the ambivalent conflict: she voluntarily sacrifices her happiness to her brothers and sisters—indeed one might say she forces this sacrifice on them—in order to be able to develop an unconscious hatred toward them which goes to the length of actual death wishes. In order to ward these off she invents the sleep ceremonial.

The fight against her own sadistic impulses proceeded further and led to the formation of new symptoms. Every evening she had to count over all the little objects in the house and hide them in her bed, so that she herself was forced to lie in bed crouched up in the most uncomfortable position because there was so little room left for her.

The analysis soon made it clear to the patient that the little objects really represented her little brothers and sisters. With excessive solicitude she counted the objects, i.e., the brothers and sisters, to make certain that they were still there. In this displacement onto trivial objects she does exactly what she had formerly done directly to the children in her tender anxiety about their sleep. Such a displacement from the original object onto a trivial object is very characteristic of the obsessional neurosis.

In this displacement ceremonial the negative, aggressive attitude to the brothers and sisters—which was intensified to a death wish—also found satisfaction. The act of hiding the objects under the bedclothes is a symbolical burial, and the subsequent ceremonial represents an atonement for the crime. In this ceremonial the little objects had to be pulled out of their hiding place and washed and handled with particular care, as if to undo the guilt-laden act she had just perpetrated.

I should like to draw your attention to the double meaning of the symptom formation, which is particularly clear in this case. The one obsessional act serves to satisfy an unconscious tendency; the other signifies a protection against this, a revocation and annulment of it. The endlessness of such obsessional proceedings follows from the fact that the ambivalent conflict of the obsessional neurotic, i.e., the fight between his positive and negative impulses, can never come to an end, and hence ever new reactions of the sense of guilt require new protective measures to cope with charges of the aggressive tendencies.

The sacrifice our patient wanted to make to her brothers and sisters naturally did not take place. The engagement was broken off. Her symptoms increased to such an extent that she got into a position of the most painful dependence on them. Some of these symptoms were so clear in their structure that they deserve to be mentioned. She suffered, for instance, from a severe *délire de toucher,* touching compulsion, which was indeed the cause of her severe catatonic situation in the bed. At first she carried out a touching ceremonial: every object had to be touched so many times in a particular sequence; then she had to wash her hands the same number of times; then the touching began all over again and was followed by the washing, etc., until she finally went to bed, where she found peace only when the blanket was tucked in tight all round her body.

In this touching compulsion she gave expression to the wish to touch her own genital, repeating thus an action which had been forbidden by her mother in infancy. Another equally repressed "wish to touch," which found a compulsive and displaced expression, related to the brother's genital, in the recollection of the attempted seduction I mentioned above.

In another determinant the touching compulsion represents the wish to "lay hands on" the loved person of her environment: in the transferred sense, in destroying them. The realization of this wish is subject to the compulsion, because it is inhibited by the opposite tendency, i.e., the prohibition. But by being displaced onto indifferent objects this wish was nevertheless able to find a compulsive expression.

The washing compulsion was also determined by more than one cause. First she cleans her hands in an actual sense after the contaminating symbolical touching of the genital. And secondly, this compulsion acquires a metaphorical meaning, in that she "washes her hands in innocence."

In this exhausting struggle between "wishing to touch" and "not being allowed to touch" the prohibition ultimately gained the upper hand. There was nothing she was allowed to touch, for, as we heard at the start, everything might have been polluted with sexual products, with stool and urine, and all such "loathsome things." At first this prohibition related only to the objects of her immediate environment, but later it extended to everything, until her freedom of movement was so restricted that she was no longer able to stir a limb, and arrived at that condition in which we first became acquainted with her.

The prohibition extended to everything connected with the excretory processes, i.e., feces and urine. Everything in the world could have some indirect connection with these things—which meant that the prohibition included the whole world. The origin of this prohibition in the protective measure against those wish tendencies which aimed at reactivating the infantile pleasure in anal things is clear, but it is no less clear that the compulsion extends to the measure itself.

Other determinants of this touching compulsion led back to "misdeeds" of her childhood which had heavily loaded her unconscious sense of guilt. These "misdeeds" had by no means disappeared from her consciousness. But the patient had no idea that they had left behind any guilt reactions in her, nor, therefore, that they came to expression in her obsessional acts. Such a separation of a conscious content from its affective element is likewise very characteristic of the obsessional neurosis.

Her touching anxiety, for instance, had for some time the character of a syphilis phobia. Between the content of the compulsion and the infantile experiences a very tragic bridge has been established by more recent actual complications. The patient's younger brother, of whose seduction by the little girl we have spoken, had acquired, when she was already quite grown up, a luetic infection, and had committed suicide from remorse about it. In the patient a connection was established between this actual event and her infantile experiences: at first she had the compulsive idea that she too had syphilis and her brother had "somehow" got his syphilis through her fault, but she was unconscious of the connection between her sense of guilt toward the brother and those infantile situations. She thought that she might have got syphilis from masturbating, for she remembered that her mother had once told her that one can become blind from rubbing the eyes with the hand after touching the genital. Afterward she had heard that syphilitics often become blind. She had been unconscious of the fact that the mother's remarks were a prohibition of onanism, but the connection between her sense of guilt about the onanism and her syphilis phobia on the one hand, and between the self-accusation that she was responsible for her brother's illness and the active seduction of the little boy on the other hand was made quite clear in the analysis. Thus her touching anxiety had the following meaning: there was nothing she was allowed to touch, for otherwise her dirty, i.e., onanistically contaminated, fingers would infect the whole world with syphilis, just as she had once infected her brother, and thus been responsible for his death. But it also represented the unconscious prohibition: not to attack her brother's genital as she had done on that occasion in infancy.

In this touching compulsion we can observe two things particularly clearly: first, that the idea of contamination had an anal origin and that the repressed anal tendencies, despite the strong reaction formations (pedantry, meticulous cleanliness, etc.) of which we have spoken as being the qualities of the second period of her childhood, then led to the neurotic formations; they then continued in the genital phase, so that the genital sexuality also acquired the character of dirt and contamination. Secondly, we can see how the old anal and onanistic tendencies came to expression, and how a mechanism arose from their prohibition which then in its turn became a compulsion (prohibition of touching and washing compulsion).

I should like here to describe some more interesting episodes from the patient's illness. When she was some eighteen years old, her mother fell hopelessly ill of consumption. Night after night the patient sat up attending to her. After the mother's death she developed an intensive brooding compulsion: would she ever meet her mother again? Was she quite sure that she had not given her mother the wrong medicine, which might have poisoned her? The origin of the compulsion is not difficult to recognize.

In connection with her mother's death she started a new obsessional ceremonial, the analytic interpretation of which is particularly interesting. This ceremonial caused the patient to suffer for several weeks from insomnia, which could only be overcome by taking heavy drugs in a sanitarium. The content of the ceremonial was as follows: after going through a short sleep ceremonial, which had for years now been a complete matter of course to her—something like a prayer one repeats automatically —the patient would go to bed. But she would have to get up again at once and see whether the door was really shut, and repeat this several times till she could ultimately bring herself to the decision to lie down again. She had, however, to repeat the compulsion, this process of looking to see whether the door was really shut, punctually once every hour.

This ceremonial proved—like every other—to be severally determined: it was the repetition of her eavesdroppings at the door of her parents' bedroom, but it was also to make sure that she was undisturbed in the pursuance of her masturbatory wishes.

But this sleeplessness proceeded, above all, from her solicitude for her mother's illness, a solicitude which had gone to uncanny lengths in its zeal. She had felt herself bound to carry out all the doctor's instructions with the most painful exactitude, and had considered it a dangerous sin of omission if she did not give the prescribed medicine "according to instructions" punctually to the minute day and night. In order to ensure this meticulous punctuality she kept awake the whole time during her mother's illness. For she was subject to her own tyrannical command: "If you don't do this, mother will die." It is not difficult to guess the wishes which lay at the root of this exactitude.

After the mother's death she continued this compulsive action in another form. It was easy to show that her mother's death had not extinguished her former hostility against her and that she still had to continue the defensive measures against the old hatred and so even after her death remain faithful to her self-imposed command not to go to sleep.

Another reason for this was her fear of waking up the next day and finding that she could not open her eyes, i.e., of becoming blind. You remember that the idea of going blind was connected with onanism and the mother's threat: "If you put your hand there you'll go blind." Thus the prohibition of sleep meant: "You mustn't go to sleep for then you might masturbate." Here again a prohibition which once came directly from the mother and was then introjected has acquired the character of a compulsion. All these prohibitions and commands were masochistically intensified by the patient, and in time she became completely their slave and her life a veritable hell.

She restricted her existence in yet another peculiarly complicated way. She would suffer no clock in her room (a frequent phenomenon with obsessional neurotics), for she could not bear the ticking sound, but she was driven by the compulsion—as at the time of her mother's illness—to keep looking at the time in order to miss nothing: "Otherwise some accident might happen." Thus she so arranged matters that she could hear a church clock striking from her room. The attempt to get someone else to relieve her every now and then from the hourly watch came to grief, because the patient had the compulsion that she had to follow intently the breathing of her sleeping companion lest it might perhaps stop, and adapt her own breathing to the rhythm of the other. The explanation of this symptom was as follows: in the last days of her mother's illness the doctor had felt her pulse, sounded her, and said: "It's missing beats; it won't last much longer." The patient listened now to see that her sleeping companion's breathing did not stop, as a defense against the wish that it should stop. The old death wish against the mother she now turns masochistically against herself as a self-punishment. "If her evil wish were to be realized, her own breath might stop at the same time." And hence she must adapt her breathing to that of her companion.

You have heard the condition and the relation to the outer world the patient had got into through her neurosis. The analysis freed her from her sufferings, but it did not succeed in giving her the enjoyment of life or in liberating her repressed sexuality. Under the condition of asceticism—she now finally took the veil —she was able to remain, for all practical purposes, healthy. Religion meant for her successful sublimation. It clearly provided her with a possible way of getting rid of her sense of guilt. The prayers and penances became a substitute for the apparently "nonsensical" obsessional ceremonials. In the new world which she had chosen and made for herself in the convent, she could feel herself "adapted to reality." She herself was completely satisfied with the result of her analysis. And the analyst? He too must at times be content with having found a *modus vivendi* for his patients equal to their capacity for adaptation.

If we recapitulate shortly our patient's case history, her complicated path of suffering, we find the following scheme: in the first period of her childhood manifest anal-sadistic tendencies; in the so-called latency period strong reaction formations in her character (pedantry, overconscientiousness, etc.), but even in this phase indications of obsessional symptoms, which at first looked like mere slight distortions of these characteristics: the urge toward cleanliness in reaction to the "dirt" of the first phase, the excessive solicitude about the brother in reaction to her active seduction, and the exaggeratedly tender wooing of the mother as a result of the suppression of hostile impulses.

We have been able to establish connections between this reactive phase with the first sign of the infantile neurosis and the later illness, and we have been able to observe that the reaction formation in the character traits is no longer sufficient to suppress the original proscribed tendencies, and that the patient must now employ much more complicated mechanisms to overcome the severe inner conflicts. The outbreak of the illness, the formation of the symptoms, is just the moment in which these complicated mechanisms have to come into play.

The first infantile phase, in which we learned to know the patient as an anal-sadistic child, must be considered as dispositionally determined. But what was the cause of the reaction formation which set in in her tenth year? Under the influence of education on the one hand, and the developmental tendencies in the ego on the other hand, the ego began to be discontented even with the troublesome aggressive and contaminatory instinctual expressions, sought to defend itself against these through repression, and built up a reaction formation as a bulwark against the surging or repudiated impulses. In this case it is fairly easy to guess why this repression set in just at this particular period of her life. For it was at this time that the fateful seduction of the brother took place. This event, which, strangely enough, had remained within her memory without the slightest conscious self-reproach, had nevertheless evoked strong feelings of guilt in the unconscious. We can observe the consequences of the unconscious sense of guilt—which had arisen as a result of this act—both in the first reaction formation of childhood and in the later morbid symptoms. Up to her tenth year the patient's inner censor had been particularly mild in its régime, and the little girl had been able to indulge with a complete lack of inhibition her anal-sadistic instincts for a surprisingly long time. But the seduction of the brother was clearly the last straw, and from now on the critical agency abandoned its tolerant attitude. Once having abandoned it, it seemed to have directed its attention even to the misdeeds of the past, for we suddenly find repressions and reaction formations appearing all along the line; the once repressed onanism, the aggressive tendencies against the mother and brothers and sisters, the dirty habits—all this tale of long ago becomes subject to feelings of guilt which call for expiation. For some time she was indeed successful in restoring a psychic balance by the reaction formations.

In puberty, after the father's death, the neurosis erupted in the form of symptoms. The patient reacted to the father's death with a deep but not morbid type of mourning. She tried to identify herself with the deceased, i.e., to take over his role in the family. Another loss reaction is discernible in the reactivation of the oedipal attitude. For toward her brothers and sisters she also assumed the maternal role and sought to find them a father surrogate by marrying her chief. All this acquired the character of a masochistic sacrifice, obviously with the unconscious aim of depriving the superego of a motive for punishment. This sacrifice inaugurated the vicious circle of her neurotic conflicts. Following upon this masochistic sacrifice, and probably also upon the loss of the love object (renunciation of the lover), the old sadistic impulses broke through and turned against the objects which the sacrifice had related to. These sadistic attacks assumed symbolic and obsessional forms. The now severe superego thereupon became active, and gave rise to the struggle between the libidinal impulses, which sought to find expression in harmless but endless actions, and the forbidding powers, which undertook equally endless counteractions. One might say that all the forbidden and all the forbidding spirits were up in arms. Sometimes the one and sometimes the other got the upper hand. All those misdeeds, whether realized or merely imagined—the onanism, the murderous impulses, etc.—sought satisfaction in symbolic acts. But all the counterimpulses in the psyche protested with equal vigor in symbolic attempts at revocation. We have only to remember the endless procedure of burying the small objects and the subsequent cleaning and counting, etc.

What was particularly striking was the fact that all the aggressive and obsessional impulses were directed against those objects which were undeniably and unmistakably the subject of love, i.e., the positive element in her emotional life. All her tender and positive impulses were exposed to a continuous and endless conflict with her sadistic impulses.

Just as we ascribed her anal-sadistic impulses to a constitutional factor, so this conflict between love and hate represented a constitutional ambivalence, i.e., love and hate were simultaneously and inseparably directed toward the same object. With this kind of disposition the sadistic aggression has the character of a libidinal urge which serves not only the hate but the love also.

But we were also able to see that the patient reacted to every aggressive impulse with a defensive or leveling counteraction, and we recognize this to be an expression of the sense of guilt, of the superego. In the symptom formations we saw how the patient's ego stood as it were between two fires: on the one hand the unconscious impulse against the objects of the outer world, with a definitely aggressive sadistic character; and on the other hand a particularly strong reaction on the part of the superego—also aggressive and directed immediately against the ego—which inevitably forced the ego to take counteractions.

But even before her illness, in the phase of characterological reaction formations, we met this same sense of guilt and were able to pursue its development in the course of the illness and its expression in the obsessional defensive measures. The later development of the neurosis was such that in obsessional oscillations between instinctual satisfaction and prohibition the ascetic tendencies got more and more the upper hand, until finally, quite independently of the superego, the symptoms corresponded more to the prohibition, as a result of which the patient's whole life acquired a masochistic character.

If the patient attempted either spontaneously or on my advice to suppress the obsessional acts, she produced thereby a severe oppressive condition, which gradually developed into anxiety. This clearly shows that the aim of her obsessional acts must have been to ward off a danger productive of anxiety. Thus the symptoms had here the same task as the phobic avoidance, i.e., they provided release from an inner danger. But what the phobia can accomplish with the aid of the projection mechanism is here brought about by the imposition of prohibition, by commands and by an active revocation, a wishing-to-make-undone of what has already been symbolically accomplished or intended.

In the phobia the anxiety affect occupies the center of the suffering, and the neurosis deals with this affect by appearing to make it relate to a danger in the outer world, and yet this danger to the ego really proceeds from the representative of the inner authority, from the superego. The anxiety itself is the result of an inner threat on the part of this power, a successful warning for the ego, successful in the sense of the freedom from anxiety it provides, though this freedom is dependent on the observation of a particular condition. This condition is: instinctual renunciation. The phobic representative in the outer world, which has to be avoided, thus unites in itself both the instinctual tendency and the forbidding power. The formula runs: "If you shun the instinct you will escape the punishing authority." We cannot avoid the impression that here too the severity of the superego applied particularly to the aggressive impulses, and in the peculiar strength of these impulses we were able to recognize the dynamic source for the development of intensive anxiety.

In our obsessional-neurotic patient, as we have seen, her wearisome symbolic operations brought her ego one advantage: the continuous freedom from anxiety. In this respect the obsessional neurosis proved to be more successful than the phobia. But we did not get the impression that this freedom from anxiety was due to any less severe an attitude on the part of the superego. On the contrary, the pressure exerted by the superego, the continuous and unrelenting action of the sense of guilt, compelled the harassed ego in its defensive mechanism to adapt or subject itself ever more completely to these powers.

In some of our patient's symptoms the repudiated tendencies (mostly of an aggressive character) were displaced onto trivial objects only to be counteracted at the instance of the sense of guilt. Gradually the symptoms began to acquire predominantly the character of gratifications of the sense of guilt, of acts of penance, without the instinct coming to expression even in the most remote form of substitute action. The ego was indeed completely at the mercy of the superego; it became aware of the sense of guilt and was ruled and tyrannized by it. By following exactly the development of the symptoms we were able to see that the sense of guilt was not diminished even when the ego had renounced all instinctual gratifications and substitute formations.

There are cases of obsessional neurosis in which the sense of guilt behaves less insistently as well as those in which it completely dominates and continually occupies the patient's consciousness. There are, for instance, patients who are forced by their sense of guilt actually to provide themselves with some sort of guard to prevent a murderous action, or to be constantly reassured by those around them that they have not actually committed it. When they are not under observation they become desperate lest they have done something "terrible." One of my patients who suffered from the obsessional idea that she might have put poison in her child's food once actually intended under the pressure of the sense of guilt to inform the police that she had poisoned her child.

In all these cases we see the unrelenting severity of the superego. In discussing other forms of neurosis, too, we have seen the effect of the sense of guilt, but nowhere else did it stand so undisguised and imperious in the center of the psychic life. On the basis of our clinical experiences we can say that the more aggressive these suppressed wish impulses are the more severe is the superego, a fact which I have already expressed in the formula: "Aggression against aggression."

Such observations have led Freud to assume that it is the same aggression whether it is attached to the libidinal impulses in the form of sadism or whether, when these are suppressed, it is incorporated in the superego and made the expression of its severity. It is a fact that the instinctual tendencies of the obsessional neurosis are sadistic in character. Hence we can account for the strength of the sense of guilt and the aggressions of the superego in Freud's sense from the fact that when the libidinal sadistic impulse is suppressed the aggression, thereby made free, becomes attached to the superego, and instead of being directed to the outer world is now consumed in the inner life.

This view follows the same lines as the scientific studies developed by Freud in 1920. In these he assumes two kinds of instincts: the sexual instincts and the destructive instincts, which are interwoven. Every separation of the two kinds of instincts, every "instinctual defusion," brings with it the release of the destructive tendencies, which are then either directed against the outer world in the form of aggressions or else introjected, i.e., they turn against the ego as if it were an object of the outer world, so that instead of sadism (outward) we have masochism (inward).

This inversion is a reaction of the sense of guilt to the outward-striving aggressions, the throttling of which leads to a vicious circle, for by becoming attached to the superego they make this itself sadistic, through which a fresh intensification of the inner tension of the sense of guilt takes place.

The higher the stage of libidinal development the more thorough is the mixture of the two forms of instinct. In discussing hysteria—which corresponds to the genital stage of development —we have seen that the ambivalent conflict, i.e., the fight between positive and aggressive negative tendencies, does not play nearly so large a part as in the obsessional neurosis, and that here the sense of guilt seems to be less and the superego gentler.

Our understanding of the effects of regression is increased by our knowledge that the intensification of the ambivalence, the increase of the sadistic components as a result of regressive processes, is connected with the decomposition of the instincts, for the separation of the destructive instincts from the libidinal goes parallel with these regressions. This enables us to understand, too, why the severity of the superego appears to go hand in hand with the depth of the regression.

With regard to the phobia I might perhaps add that the instinctual decomposition is clearly more extensive there than in conversion hysteria, and consequently the superego is more severe and the danger to the ego greater. Nevertheless the libidinal impulses seem to have effected a compromise with the aggression of the superego in the projected object, so that the sense of guilt does not rage so relentlessly against the ego as in the obsessional neurosis.

10

Obsessional Ideas

(1930)

In contrast to the case I discussed in the last chapter, the analysis of the obsessional neurosis I shall deal with today is very simple in its structure, can be easily and completely reconstructed, and ended, as I will say in advance, with a complete cure after a relatively short treatment.

The patient, a young woman of twenty-eight, came to be analyzed for one single symptom: one single obsessional idea. One might say that in this case the neurosis was, so to speak, nipped in the bud by the analysis, and the inner conflict was successfully readjusted before the suffering could take on a permanent form. The patient related that she had been engaged up to the previous year, but through her fiancé's fault the engagement had proved a failure and was broken off at his desire. It had been of many years' standing, for he had kept putting off the actual marriage. Recently she had been more insistent in her demands that he should come to a definite decision, and this had already led to differences of opinion between them in which the fiancé became clearly ever more subject to the influence of his mother, who opposed the marriage.

Two years before—i.e., one year before the breach—the obsessional idea appeared in an acute form. One day the patient woke up with the feeling that she had dreamed her fiancé had died.

The rest of the dream she could not remember, nor was she even certain whether it really had been a dream or "something like a dream."

She then proceeded to reproach herself most vehemently for this dream or "not-dream," as if she had done something very wicked by dreaming it. Then came the idea that this dream memory would always pursue her and never leave her in peace; she would never be able to be happy again. It is clear from this that the reproach was due to an inner perception of the repressed material, that the dream was intuitively recognized as a wish fulfillment and therefore productive of the self-reproach.

Not much interpretation is necessary. This dream represented the break-through of the death wish against the lover under the most naïve disguise: "The dream will pursue me," i.e., "I will never get rid of this wish, for it is too strong in me; I shall always have to reproach myself for it and never be able to feel free from guilt."

Apart from these self-reproaches there was very little to discover in this obsessional neurosis; few symptoms, and thus little opportunity to deal with them analytically. Looking back one could find no real obsessional ideas in her early years. Only between her sixth and seventh year (i.e., at the age when the obsessional neurosis is most liable to break out) she suffered from a very intense anxiety, which was obviously neurotic, about her father, who was suffering from some slight indisposition. This anxiety points to a death wish against the father, caused presumably by the erotic disappointment she had suffered at his hands. This assumption was confirmed later. You will notice the analogy with the actual symptom: the death wish representing the sadistic reaction to the erotic disappointment.

It turned out that even before the outbreak of her illness the patient had experienced some signs of what was to come, which she had not, however, felt to be morbid. She suffered from a violent but unfounded jealousy toward her fiancé, which always related to a certain type of woman in no way corresponding to his actual preference. Simultaneously with this obviously pathological jealousy she was affected by a strong erotic wave, the manifestations of which amounted to obsessional ideas: the patient could not help thinking continuously of sexual matters, mentally undressed every man she saw, fantasied coitus with them, became as though possessed with compulsive ideas of the male genital, which she continually saw in her mind's eye. Soon afterward she became subject to the obsessional idea which brought her to be analyzed.

The first weeks of the analysis passed very monotonously— little material, no dreams, few ideas. Suddenly the situation altered entirely. The patient, whose transference had hitherto been scarcely observable, fell violently in love with me. She produced the most intense homosexual erotic fantasies, which were soon replaced by an equally intense hate against me. This was succeeded finally by a death wish against me in the same form as in the first symptom: she "might have a dream" that I had died.

This acute outbreak of the transference had come about through a mere chance. The patient had seen into my bedroom through a door which happened to be open. The position of the beds had reminded her of her parents' bedroom, and the rapidly established identification between me and her mother had immediately led to the transference.

The wave of the transference and obsession, however, soon receded. A new obsessional idea appeared. She became afraid to stay alone in the house with her father (for some years a widower for the second time) lest he might sexually abuse her. Finally she only felt safe at the time of menstruation. Then she transferred the content of the first obsessional idea completely onto the father: she "might have a dream that he had died."

That is the whole history of her obsessional neurosis. From these few symptoms and the transference, it was possible to make a complete reconstruction of the infantile events which lay behind it. Let us return to the starting point of her neurosis. The patient experiences a frustration from an actual love object. The circumstances of the frustration situation repeat the oedipus situation with photographic accuracy: the fight for the lover between her and her mother. Here it is *his* mother who interferes with the relationship and forbids the marriage. The patient is defeated and the hyperintense hate tendencies against the man, who had chosen in the mother's favor, prove stronger than the love impulses. The death wish erupts from the unconscious and is transformed after its repression into a reactive anxiety about her lover, which acquires the character of an obsessional idea (dream) and as such becomes conscious. The fact that this idea remained impervious to all reasonable arguments was due to its true content being unconscious.

The patient's childhood had been a peculiarly difficult one. In her fourth year, i.e., at an age which we consider to be the "heyday of the oedipus complex," when her mother had been dead two years, she was faced with the problem of a young step-mother. The fight for her father's love was hereby made very much more difficult. And just as in the present situation, she was defeated by the mother. The hatred for her stepmother and the furious intensity of the rivalry had remained completely conscious in her memory; it was only the sexual wishes, the libidinal content of this rivalry conflict, which were hidden from her. The reactivation of the infantile situation had stirred the old extreme hatred against the father, which was conditioned by the young woman's sadistic constitution, and which was now displaced onto her present lover, who had also frustrated her.

This frustration, the "actual conflict," became transformed into a neurotic conflict. The disappointed libido regressed to the anal-sadistic phase, and this regression, as we know, inevitably brings with it strong aggressive reactions. The *agent provocateur* in this transformation of the real conflict into a neurotic one was pro-vided by the fact that the specific disappointing situation was a repetition of that infantile frustration which had clearly not yet been settled. The mobilization of the hate against the lover was accompanied by a turning from the heterosexual to the homo-sexual object. This homosexual attitude first came to expression in the morbid jealousy, which appeared fairly suddenly. At the same time this homosexuality was violently repudiated and the patient sought help by a flight into heterosexuality, which had a pathological-compulsive character. The aim of the obsessional ideas of the male genital was to suppress the homosexual fantasy. One might say that the intensity of the compulsive thought about the male genital was really conditioned only by the repudiation of the thought of the female genital. The patient was in the middle of this struggle against the sadistic and homosexual tendencies when she came to be analyzed.

By seeing into my bedroom she was able to establish a rapid identification between me and her stepmother, which provided her with the motive for a violent transference neurosis with its accompanying content. The patient's ambivalence, which was in any case particularly deeply rooted in her constitution, was uncannily intensified by the actual conditions of her life. The patient had, that is to say, two mothers: a living one whom she hated and a dead one whom she loved. After the disappointment at the hands of the father she directed her whole yearnings to the dead mother. Indeed her relationship to women was ultimately built up on her hatred for her stepmother and her love for her dead mother. After the frustration from the man the homosexual relationship was intensified and found its first expression in a morbid jealousy. This ambivalent relationship to the woman could be effectively lived out, and then successfully dealt with, in the transference.

The last act of the neurosis—the erotic obsessional ideas with regard to the father, the anxiety lest he should maltreat her sexually, which were the expression of her own wishes, and the hatred in the form of the death wish (expressed in the obsessional idea: "He might die")—was also chronologically the starting point of the neurosis. The simple structure of this neurosis might be expressed in the following scheme: excessive love for the father transformed into hatred as a result of the frustration; hatred toward the stepmother, longing for the dead mother; both ambivalent tendencies united in the homosexual relationship to the woman; eruption of the homosexual impulses at the renewed frustration from a heterosexual object, with sadistic revenge impulses against the latter as a repetition of the disappointment experienced at the hands of the father; and finally a return to the father with the love and hate tendencies which had originally been directed against him; in this last phase the analysis and also the therapeutic process terminated.

You will observe—and that is the real reason why I have described this case to you—how the patient repeated the whole history of her unconscious mental life in the reversed order of her symptoms, until in her last symptom she had reached the starting point of her repressed conflicts.

After six months' treatment the patient left the analysis cured of her symptoms, but—we must add—without having essentially altered her character. But it was difficult to keep her in the analysis after her symptoms had disappeared. As far as one can prophesy at all, we may venture the prognosis that she will probably remain healthy for all practical purposes, but as a result of her aggressive tendencies and her ambivalent attitude, so deeply rooted in her constitution, she will certainly frequently find herself in serious conflicts.

In considering the case once more from the theoretical standpoint, let us start from that psychic experience of the patient which we called "inner perception." The knowledge that the neurotic symptoms represent a compromise between the forbidding and the libidinal tendencies is one of the oldest and most elementary principles of psychoanalysis. The symptom serves the gratification of the instincts at the same time as the repudiating ascetic impulse. With our first obsessional neurotic patient —the nun—we were able to recognize in every single symptom the operation of these mutually opposed forces. The dichronous nature of the symptom formation so typical of the obsessional neurosis was particularly clear in this connection. This is due to the fact that the prohibited instinctual tendency and the forbidding mechanism take place *one after the other* (e.g., first the burying of the objects and then the careful guardianship over them). The relentless nature of the struggle is explained by the fact that the sadistic impulse concealed in the instinctual wish is repudiated by an equally cruel and sadistic superego. Another reason for this implacability is to be found in the severe ambivalent conflict, as a result of which every positive wish impulse is accompanied by intense hatred, and these two components of the object relationship, the positive and the negative, face each other like two opponents in an undecided fight. Moreover, this ambivalent conflict is, so to speak, constitutionally determined, for the more remote the phase of libidinal development it belongs to the more violent it is. In the obsessional neurosis the severity of the ambivalent conflict is conditioned by the disturbance of the libidinal development in the anal-sadistic phase to which the patient has regressed.

Not all obsessional neuroses are alike in this respect. There are some cases in which the struggle takes place more in the intellectual life—e.g., brooding compulsion, etc.—and others in which the obsession is expressed more in the motor sphere, i.e., in action. Our first patient belongs, on the whole, to the second type, whereas the last one suffered more from obsessional ideas.

The clinical picture of obsessional neurosis can be extraordinarily varied, but despite this variety the same typical mechanisms are, as psychoanalysis has been able to show, always present. In all these various clinical pictures the personality of the obsessional neurotic is so identical—individual character traits and peculiarities always coming from the same source—that one can really only speak of quantitative or formal differences. Thus obsessional acts and obsessional ideas are only formally different, for the amount of psychic energy necessary for the motor discharge in the obsessional action is no greater than for the energy cathexis of the thinking process in an obsessional-neurotic brooder. We shall see, moreover, that obsessional-neurotic character traits derive from the same forces of energy.

In discussing the reaction formations in the latency period of our first patient we have heard how meticulous she could be in her cleanliness, how scrupulous in her morality, and how loving in her sympathy. But we have not yet concerned ourselves with certain of her characteristics which also belong to the permanent inventory of the obsessional neurosis, i.e., superstition, distrust, doubt. I think it is worth while to say a few words on this subject.

Very characteristic for the obsessional neurotic are his reports about all those peculiar and uncanny happenings which seem to pursue him. If he thinks of somebody, then the person in question promptly appears; if he feels affectionately toward somebody, then the person in question is sure to die in consequence; if he utters a curse on someone, then this is realized in the most terrible form. All these events are described by these unhappy people to prove the "omnipotence" of their wishes—especially the bad ones—and their thoughts. This behavior has its psychological motivation in the fact that through the severance of the inner connections between the repressed unconscious wish impulses and the sense of guilt which attaches to these impulses a tension arises in the ego for which a rationalization is eagerly sought. Thus where it is not possible to ward off the sense of guilt through character traits which we have learned to recognize as reaction formations, we find along with the symptoms or even without their formation expressions of the sense of guilt which are characteristic of the personality of the obsessional neurotic.

Thus despite what is sometimes a very high intellectual level, and in full consciousness of the absurdity of his behavior, the obsessional neurotic can be so influenced by blind superstition in his relation to the outer world that he is continually dominated by it in all his actions. The cause of this lies partly in the fact that the patient attains to a certain inner perception of his unconscious impulses and through the strength of his aggressive tendencies becomes liable to overestimate psychic processes in relation to reality, and partly in the fact that the warning voice of his sense of guilt makes him responsible for the results of his wishes in the outer world. This superstitious belief of the obsessional neurotic that his thoughts find their realization in the outer world has a certain affinity with the projection mechanism of the paranoiac, who projects the inner perception of a psychic process onto the outer world, onto his persecutor.

And this has brought us back to our patient. You remember that the patient's dream memory and the fear that the dream might be realized also corresponded to an inner perception of the repressed material. The repressed impulse was the sadistic revenge against the lover. The inner perception was the representative of the sense of guilt, which had assumed the part of the inner persecutor. Why the patient's illness stopped at this stage, why the impulse did not find expression in an obsessional act, or why the sense of guilt did not lead to obsessional preventive and punishing mechanisms, is hard to say. In any case her neurosis proceeded from the same sources as the numerous symptom formations of our first patient.

Another typical character trait of the obsessional neurotic is distrust. In this case the suppressed hate impulses are displaced onto the outer world. The individual behaves as if the hostility did not lie in him, but as if it was directed against him from without. Here, too, the effect of the sense of guilt seems to be that its victim can only expect bad from others.

Another obsessional neurotic patient of mine showed this sort of projection very clearly in her symptoms. She was obsessed by the thought that she was an object of envy to her younger sister. Her life was filled with protective measures against this envy. She dared not please anyone, have nice clothes, or betray any sort of accomplishment, lest she should provoke it. She could not love anyone, become engaged or have children—in a word, she must give up everything which seemed to her worth having in life, for otherwise she might rouse her sister's envy. At the same time she had to utter all sort of magic words, perform certain tasks, carry out wearisome obsessional activities, all in order to paralyze the effect of this envy.

Again it is her own hatred and envy of the sister which has turned so cruelly against herself. She attempts to project outward the inner perception of these feelings, and she behaves as though they would flow in the reverse direction from her sister to her. Thus in order to save herself from the sense of guilt and the self-punishing tendency, she leads a life of complete renunciation of all she desires and subjects her whole existence to a masochistic punishment ceremonial.

One of the most typical, and for the analyst most disagreeable symptoms of the obsessional neurotic is doubt. It is the greatest foe of the therapeutic process, for every positive result of the treatment falls a victim to this most obstinate of all symptoms. "Is it really so? Did I tell that correctly? Did I really dream that? Can that be of any use to me?"—and so on *ad infinitum*.

This doubt is the expression of the ambivalent conflict, of the inner uncertainty, "Do I love or hate?" This is transferred from this original question, which lies at the base of every relationship of the obsessional neurotic, onto every psychic action by displacement, and becomes attached not only to expressions of emotion, but also to the thinking process.

Between the doubt and the feeling of inner compulsion, which expresses itself in the symptoms, an intimate connection exists. The source of both is the inner indecision, which can produce the feeling of doubt as well as an uncanny state of tension which calls for discharge. But this discharge tendency is confronted by an equally strong inhibition as a result of the undecided fight between love and hate. Every resolution, every psychic action is inhibited by being displaced onto something else. And if one of the inhibited resolutions does finally come to the point of decision, it will then be compulsively carried out with the greatest expenditure of energy and will thus form the basis of the symptoms.

We have still to deal with another essential component of the inner uncertainty of the obsessional neurotic. In the analysis of our last patient we recognized a strongly homosexual component in her libido. Experience has taught us that this unconscious homosexuality often plays an important part both in male and female obsessional neurotics. Thus the inner indecision is not confined to the ambivalent problem, "Do I love or hate?" but relates also to the choice of object, "Do I love the man or the woman?" Freud has shown us in *The Ego and the Id* (1923) to what an extent the constitutional bisexuality of man is responsible for the fact that the ambivalent conflict has rendered the oedipus complex so much more complicated than we had at first assumed, that in fact the "boy has not merely an ambivalent attitude towards his father and an affectionate object-choice towards his mother, but at the same time he also behaves like a girl and displays an affectionate feminine attitude to his father and a corresponding jealousy and hostility towards his mother" (vice versa, of course, in the case of the girl). When this normal complication is accompanied by an intensification of the sadistic tendencies and therewith an increase of the ambivalent conflict, a far-reaching inability to re-establish the heterosexual object choice may be the result.

Apart from this inner indecision of the obsessional neurotic, from the incapacity to give his libido a definite direction, to decide whether he should love the man or the woman, there are other factors which drive the libido in the direction of homosexuality. Thus on the one hand the anal disposition of the obsessional neurotic encourages a passive relationship to the man in the sense of passive homosexuality, while on the other hand the strong instinct for mastery encourages an aggressive relationship to the man, which also has a libidinal character. In the female obsessional neurotic the fixation in the sadistic phase has the effect of intensifying the active impulses in the woman and thus strengthening her masculinity complex. This is especially obvious with female obsessional neurotics whose neurosis has come to a stop at the stage of character formation.

In the anal-sadistic phase the coitus fantasies of children also have a sadistic character. In their fantasies of this, as they imagine, cruel act, children of both sexes identify themselves with both partners, with the passive and the active; they then carry on this double identification into their later life, especially when—as is the case in the obsessional neurosis—the libido is fixated on the sadistic phase. This double identification also plays its part in strengthening the homosexual tendencies.

To return once more to our patient, you remember that her symptom had directly taken on the character of an "inner perception," and was derived from libidinal impulses as well as the sense of guilt. In contrast to phobic patients she had felt the danger to be an inner one, without making the attempt to displace her fear of the impulse or its consequences onto an external danger.

We have seen clearly how this perception of the impulse arose from the reaction of the superego under the pressure of the sense of guilt (Freud: "The superego knows more than the ego about the id"), and how the superego gave expression to the full measure of its severity in the verbal threat: she would never be happy again, "because she had had this dream."

From what we know of her history before her acute illness we may assume that the patient would certainly have formed obsessional symptoms in the course of time if the progress of her sufferings had not been arrested by the psychoanalytic treatment.

SECTION IV: MELANCHOLIA

11

Melancholic and Depressive States
(1930)

IT lies outside the province of these lectures to discuss psychotic
states. But I cannot omit some consideration of one of the so-
called "narcissistic neuroses," namely, melancholic depression,
for this throws light on much that is necessary for the understanding of neurosis.

The patient we will turn to for this purpose was at the time
of her treatment fifty years old, formerly a very talented and, in
her own country, very well-known authoress. Naturally fond of
work and society, in the last few years her whole personality had
undergone a complete change. She shut herself off more and more
from people; though she continued in her profession for some
time, till an acute attack some three years before had made her
condition so much worse that she had to go into a sanitarium.
There the illness made rapid progress. For about a year the
patient had been in a deep depression, which was periodically
interrupted by severe anxiety attacks and almost delirious excitations. All her fears revolved round one single thought, to
which she clung obstinately, although she was able to see herself
at times the absurdity of her *idée fixe*. Despite this occasional insight, however, she remained attached with varying degrees of
affect to the thought: she would be thrown into the street un-
clothed as she lay in bed, and would there, lonely and deserted,
have to suffer a terrible death. Sometimes she gave expression to
this thought with complete apathy, sometimes she would beg that

145

it should happen "sooner rather than later," another time she would scream for help in the intensest delirious anxiety: "They're coming, they're coming! Don't let them take me! Have pity on me!" From time to time she would insist that she did not deserve anything else and one did well to punish her so cruelly. If one went into this self-accusation, she could bring forward nothing more serious than the most trivial, common-or-garden shortcomings.

It was only very slowly and gradually and without real analysis that one was able to get nearer her psychic life and acquire a tolerable degree of insight into her condition. From the disordered material she gave me I will select only what is important for the understanding of her case.

She felt she could say with certainty that her illness had begun with the loss of a little dog, which was for her the most precious thing she possessed. She never found it again, and thereupon fell into a depression which gradually led to a severe melancholia.

Even before this the patient had suffered for several years on end from obsessional symptoms, which were her secret and about which not even her immediate friends had any knowledge. As a child she appears to have been psychically healthy; at any rate we did not succeed in discovering any early symptoms, though the whole character of the patient bore the typical stamp of reaction formations, as we have seen them in our obsessional neurotic patients.

An intense jealousy against a very beautiful and talented sister eight years younger than herself had remained in her conscious memory. But the hatred and death wish against the sister were afterward deeply buried beneath the reactive feeling of the tenderest and most solicitous sisterly love. This change occurred after the mother's death—in the patient's twelfth year—when she took over the mother's part in her relation to her so much younger sister. Indeed one gets the impression that this overcompensating feeling toward the sister enabled her to remain free from guilt in relation to the dead mother. Be that as it may, we have here yet another example of what we have so often met before: the patient is now ready to sacrifice everything for the sake of the sister whom she had formerly so deeply hated.

In her eighteenth year, as mentioned above, she fell ill of obsessional-neurotic symptoms with typical obsessional ceremonials. She had to repeat everything she did a certain number of times; otherwise, as the inner voice threatened, "something would happen to the loved sister." In this fear the original evil intention against the sister comes to very clear expression. It is obvious that the masochistic love which entirely dominates her consciousness allows only the other thought to become conscious in the form of this fear. This overcompensation, however, has not entirely succeeded in appeasing the sense of guilt, for the omniscient superego knows all about what is repressed and insists on the obsessional ceremonials to ward off the evil wishes. Why she fell ill precisely in her eighteenth year has never been clear to me. Let it suffice that the insight we have got into the illness has shown us so much of the sadistic tendencies that we can say from our experience from what dispositions the neurosis arose and to what inner mechanisms it owed its origin.

When the patient was twenty-one years old the father died, and the difficult financial position in which she and her sister found themselves forced her to take up a profession and work hard. This meant that she had finally to renounce her ambitious fantasies for the future, namely, to become a great writer, and in the wearisome labor of a typist to take upon herself a conscious though very willing sacrifice for the sake of her younger sister. She now surrounded her charge with the most tender solicitude, and in the hard struggle for existence she was, for all practical purposes, cured of obsessional-neurotic symptoms.

We can only explain this spontaneous cure on the assumption that the difficulties of life and her self-sacrificing renunciation had brought with them so much masochistic gratification that her aggressive impulses against the sister could be satisfied in thus being turned against herself. All the emotions which are now directed toward the sister have been, one might say, purified, freed from the negative components of the ambivalent conflict. Her narcissism, once deeply hurt by the sister, now manages to find —even if indirectly—satisfaction. The patient gives up the struggle, but tries to realize through the sister everything she had dreamed of and not been able to attain for herself. A narcissistic identification of this sort often occurs in the relationship of parents to their children; in our patient's case it arose on an already morbid basis, as a defense mechanism, which might guarantee psychic health for a certain period but was bound to end in disaster.

For several years the two sisters lived in complete retirement, the elder entirely immersed in her masochistic sacrifice, the younger occupied with fairly futile and worthless attempts at authorship, and both of them waiting for the great day on which the world would recognize the "genius" of the younger one. This mutually dependent existence was unexpectedly interrupted by the marriage of the younger sister. With a certain lack both of gratitude and consideration she deserted her elder sister to go and live abroad with her husband. The patient bore the parting with quiet dignity, even appeared to be pleased at the sister's happiness, and remained behind alone. Henceforth she went her way somewhat neglected and retiring, in company with a little dog which she had acquired after her sister's departure. One day, about a year and a half after this, the dog got lost. The patient spared neither pains nor trouble to find it again, but in vain. It was at this point that the severe depression set in.

This temporal coincidence left no room for doubt that the depression was a result of the loss of the animal. Even the patient was quite clear on the point; though she had to admit that the extent of her grief seemed even to her to be somewhat incompatible with the occasion for it.

It not seldom happens that the outbreak of depressive states is brought about by an apparently trivial loss, a change of abode or something similar. These events are merely the immediate and welcome occasion for the break-through of deeper, more significant, and hitherto suppressed reactions. The condition for the mobilization of those reactions lies in the character of loss.

Our patient's dog was only a surrogate object for the lost sister; its disappearance mobilized the full force of the grief which the patient had hidden within herself after the loss of the sister.

In the further course of the treatment the patient's so reason-

able attitude at the separation from the sister was soon succeeded by bitter reproach against the ungrateful one, by the
return of the most intensive sadistic vindictiveness against the
once-hated, afterward loved, and finally so faithless sister.

What had this sister done to her? For the sake of a strange man
she had betrayed her self-sacrificing love and ruthlessly left her to
a life of loneliness. This was the thanks she got for having
reached the little orphan a helping hand at the time when she
was completely helpless. The clearer the picture of her own loss
became in the analysis, the louder grew her reproaches against
the sister until they took the form of wishing her to be thrown
out into the street, where she would have landed in any case if
she had not had mercy on her.

By pursuing our patient's psychic development we are able to
form a consecutive scheme of what went on within her. First,
hatred and aggression against her sister; defense against these impulses through obsessional-neurotic mechanisms; afterward successful overcompensation of the hate through love and tenderness;
satisfaction for the narcissistic injuries through identification
with the sister; and finally, transformation of the aggressions into
a masochistically satisfying self-sacrifice for her—a brilliant accomplishment, an excellent piece of management in the psychic
household.

After the disappointment at the hands of the sister this psychic
arrangement is not given up; it is only added to by new quanti-
ties of aggressive impulses, until the patient becomes seriously ill.
The identification is maintained, as well as the masochistic turning against the ego. The punishment to which she had doomed
the sister, of being "thrown out into the street," in order that she
should meet with a miserable end there, we hear the patient demanding with monotonous regularity, no longer, however, as a
threat against the sister but against herself, sometimes imploring
it to be carried out, and at other times defending herself against
it with the most violent anxiety. Now we understand whom this
punishment relates to and why the patient declared in her most
severe self-accusations, "I don't deserve anything else." The
crimes she had attributed to herself were indeed quite trivial, but

her sister's act had "not deserved anything else" than to be visited with the severest punishment.

Deserted by the sister, the patient remained lonely and without a love object. She could not indeed find a new object for her affections, for the conditions of her fixation on the sister had taken from her every possibility of forming a transference onto new objects. She remained bound to the sister. The psychic energies, which are no longer capable of a positive readjustment of this relationship, suffer the following fate: the withdrawn libido retires to positions which were already prepared by the far-reaching identification with the sister. Instead of flowing into the outer world the stream of libidinal energy now flows back into the inner world and narcissistically invests the ego itself. The narcissistic identification with the sister, which was formerly used to the sister's advantage, is intensified, and all the aggressions and murderous hate tendencies against the sister are now directed against her own ego.

You remember the case of agoraphobia we discussed. The patient in question remained free from anxiety in the street when she was accompanied by her mother or a mother substitute. We were able to see that as a result of a process of identification the aggressions which had been directed against the mother became a danger for her own person. There it had been a case of a hysterical identification, which related to particular psychic actions and ideas and admitted of readjustment. But with the very severe case we are dealing with at present the identification had quite another character. It involved a surrender of the object in the outer world; the object was already completely incorporated in the identified ego, so that all the feelings and ideas relating to the object were now directed toward the ego itself.

In the earlier periods of her life the patient had still possessed the inner possibility of controlling her sadistic impulses by reaction formations (hypertenderness, etc.). At that time she was able to inhibit and bribe the punishing, destructive forces of the conscience partly through protective measures (obsessional symptoms) and partly through masochistic sacrifices.

But the sister's treacherous behavior brought about a collapse of this psychic structure, which had so far been maintained and held together by her love. Now she had nothing left but rage, hate, and destruction. Her only alternatives were either to discharge her entire aggression outward against the sister, or to master it and suffer in herself the consequences of this suppression. For we know that an aggression inhibited in this way places itself at the disposal of the energies of the superego and can thus be directed inward against the ego itself.

In the last phase of her psychic sufferings our patient went through a mental process which is typical of melancholia and brings with it a peculiar intensification of the destructive impulses.

The identification with the loved sister had taken place before the outbreak of the melancholic depression. In this way the patient was able to find compensation for various renunciations. It was only after the final loss of the sister that this identification brought with it serious results for the patient and awoke severe reactions in the form of a melancholic state. For the loss of the object was followed not only by a reawakening of the sadistic aggressions, with which we are already familiar from the period of her obsessional-neurotic symptoms, but also by a new regressive process. This led to a still more deeply buried phase, in which the aggressions are still more murderous, the ambivalence still more destructive. In this primitive suckling phase, which was now reactivated, the child's relation to the outer world is established through the nourishing mother's breast, and for this phase the cannibalistic incorporation of the object by the mouth is characteristic.

After the final loss of the loved object our patient sinks into this oral phase of development. Hence the identification of the sister now becomes synonymous with the "incorporation," i.e., with the complete disappearance of the boundaries between her own ego and that of the other. The "instinctual decomposition," which this new regressive process brings with it, releases still more destructive forces to be turned against the ego. In this "identified" role the ego is humiliated and insulted and persecuted by the severest punishments and sadistic cruelties.

Thus we see that the cruel repudiation and severe self-accusations of melancholia, which originally related to the object, still remain in force, and it is only the scene of action which has been altered. The ego now appears to be split into two parts. The one part contains the introjected object, while the other part repudiates this identified ego, raging against it and punishing it. This part, which has now drawn the aggressions to itself, corresponds to that inner critical agency which we have already learned to know as the superego.

We have observed that the lower the phase of libidinal development, i.e., the deeper the regression into the infantile, the less firm is the link between the destructive tendencies and the libidinal, the more extensive the instinctual decomposition, and the stronger the aggression in the superego.

In the obsessional neurosis this decomposition, i.e., the releasing of the destructive tendencies, is not so extensive as in melancholia. In the former the relation to the object is maintained and the destructive impulses themselves are still libidinal in nature. Love turns to aggression, but in this aggression there lies a libidinal component which preserves the love object. We have seen, it is true, that even in the obsessional neurosis the instinctual decomposition comes to expression in the excessive severity of the superego.

In melancholia the instinctual decomposition has much more serious consequences for the ego than in the obsessional neurosis, for in the latter the superego demands the strict observance of the protective measures through which it manages to stave off the destruction.

The process of the "introjection" of the object so typical of melancholia was very clear in our patient's case. For even before the outbreak of the psychosis the identification with the sister had acquired great importance. Indeed, we can pursue still further this "internalization" of the original relationship between the patient and her sister, i.e., its displacement from reality onto the psychic processes.

In a certain phase of her existence the patient had solved the original ambivalence conflict with the sister to such an extent that after the parents' death she had offered herself as their representative to the sister, and thus established a parent-child relationship which enabled her to become for all practical purposes healthy. We tried to explain this therapeutic process through the masochistic sacrifice on the one hand, and through the successful overcompensation of her feelings to her sister on the other hand. But we shall be able to grasp the deeper psychological technique of this process only from its subsequent failure and development in her later illness. Through her maternal relationship to the sister the patient clearly succeeded in diminishing the former tension between the psychic agencies, which was already observable in the obsessional-neurotic symptoms, by love. She achieved this by herself taking over the role of the educative power and making it gentle, just, and forgiving. In this function she had to a certain extent made herself an example for her own superego, and so was now able to bring about that it should treat her as indulgently as she treated her sister. This process was a successful reversal of what had preceded it, when the aggression against the sister had then turned against her own ego. In the therapeutic process the destructive tendencies seem once more to be bound by love so that the placated conscience can allow itself a certain indulgence. After the disappointment at the hands of the sister the patient gave up her indulgent parental role and simultaneously introjected this relationship into the inner world of her psyche. But that which had formerly seemed to be appeased by love, and consciously and actively directed to an object in the outer world, now turned, at this retreat from the real world, insulted, angry, relentless, and above all unconscious, against the ego itself.

We are here witnesses of a historically chronological process. The superego arose, in the first place, from the identification with the parents, as the inner representative of the original authority in the outer world. In the later relationship to the sister a part of this "internalization" was again projected outward into the actual world; in this way the operation of the superego, which was at this point particularly severe, could be modified. After the disappointment from the sister this projection suffered a new introversion, i.e., the withdrawal into the psychic representative of what had originally been the parental authority, which she had later herself wielded and wielded indulgently, with regard to the sister. But this inner agency had now ceased to be indulgent and turned its full severity against the patient's ego.

With this the introjection was extended to the object-libidinal relationships—for these were subject to the identification, the oral "incorporation"—as well as to the authoritative part of the relation to the outer world. In the latter the patient had herself taken over the part of the parents. This reproduction of the parental relationship had finally acquired a thoroughly castigating character; by its introversion the punishing-destructive forces in the superego could find expression.

The mother-child relationship between her and her sister now played its part within her, no longer mildly and indulgently as formerly, but as the expression of the highest tension between the suffering ego and the raging superego.

In the patient's self-reproaches we heard the voice of the accusing and threatening superego. Another time the passively suffering part of the ego seemed to come to the fore and gave expression to its violent fear of punishment, and then again we heard the attempts to ward off the punishment by imploring for mercy and promising to be good, exactly like a child who has been punished or threatened. But in unbroken monotony we always heard *two* voices, which indicated a mighty struggle deep in the unconscious between the narcissistic ego love and the destructive ego annihilation.

In discussing the fate of the libido we recognized in the regression to the oral phase and the introjection of the object connected with it a process typical of melancholia. The case we have just been dealing with is a classic example of this. Whether this is true for all cases of melancholic depression one cannot say with complete certainty. In the long run the essence of the melancholic clinical picture is the cleft between the ego and the superego and the murderous struggle between the two psychic systems which this gives rise to. There are without a doubt cases of melancholic depression in which an unusual severity on the part of the superego is alone enough to cause it to rage sporadically and perhaps even periodically against the ego, to make it impossible for them to exist harmoniously beside each other, and to demand payment from the mishandled ego.

Another case of mine throws a very interesting light on this point. In conscious hatred against her mother this patient had turned her whole life into one long protest against her. One may say that every gesture of her life betokened a vindictive triumph against the mother. Her love life, her intellectual interests, her choice of profession, in short, the whole content of her existence, had been built up on this undying hostility. From time to time she suffered from severe depressions, which signified an obedient surrender to the mother, a renunciation of the values which had been erected against her, a penance for the constant transgressions of the maternal commands. On each occasion the depressions were succeeded by a period of peculiar intensification of joy in life, efficiency in her work, and capacity for love. The very intensity of this mood arouses our suspicions, and its connection with the old mother relationship is shown by the peculiar intensity with which the aforementioned life forms directed against the mother appear in it. In this case the depression seems to be succeeded by a slightly manic "triumph" in which the ego throws off the domination of the punishing conscience or else manages to persuade it to be specially tolerant for a period after having submitted to its castigation.

The processes of normal psychic life seem indeed to be of a similar nature. The periodic changes of mood, to which most people are subject, probably correspond in a modified form to the periodicity of manic-depressive insanity, with the continuous alternation between the dependence on the superego and the triumph of overcoming it. It is perhaps one of the deepest necessities of civilized man to throttle so much aggression within himself that its accumulation in the superego from time to time begins to exert pressure on the ego, whereupon the latter, cowed and threatened, reacts by diminishing its positive relations to existence, i.e., sinks into a more or less acute depression. Then the tension seems gradually to relax and is succeeded either by a throwing off of the pressure and a happy feeling of inner release (hypomanic states even in normal life), or else by a state of quiet composure, the sign of the harmonious reconciliation within.

Hysterical depressions may occur as the result of a real object loss, in which case they represent the pathological reaction to this loss. And, as we have seen, melancholia also may arise from a real loss. The mode of reaction corresponds to the dispositional factor. With hysteria the actual loss may evoke a return to an object which has been surrendered in childhood but retained in the unconscious, and in this case the pathological depression takes place outside the realm of the real conflict under the sign of regressive processes and infantile fixations.

We were able to observe such hysterical depressions in the patient whose sufferings we described as a "fate neurosis." All her life she had been unconsciously mourning for her father, whom she had never given up as love object. Every new erotic experience was doomed to end with the renewal of the old reaction to loss.

The "loss" can also have a more narcissistic content. A typical example of this is the menstrual depressions, which are an expression of a loss reaction in the sense of castration or unconsciously fantasied pregnancy. In this category one should include too the frequently very severe climacteric depressions in both sexes in reaction to the diminishing "femininity" or "masculinity."

It is often difficult to draw the line between a melancholic and a neurotic (hysterical) depression. In his paper on "The Problem of Melancholia" Rado (1927) maintains the view that neurotic depression is based on the same mechanisms as melancholic depression. Within the category of depression there are certainly several types of illness and also fluctuating transitional phases between these various types. The determining factors are the depth of the regression, the inner fate of the object relationship, and the extent of the process of decomposition, i.e., the release of the destructive tendencies. In the course of our discussions we have often been able to observe how dependent are the severity and the form of neurotic suffering on these last-mentioned factors.

Part II

Clinical Papers

12

A Two-Year-Old Boy's First Love
Comes to Grief
(1919)

R UDI was just two when his nurse left him. Because of his mother's heavy professional schedule and because of the pressure of external events, this nurse had been a mother surrogate to little Rudi for two years. It was she who from the beginning served all his autoerotic needs; it was she who fed him, assisted him with his excretory functions, and fulfilled his wishes. Consequently, in his first object choice Rudi disregarded his mother. Indeed, the nurse well knew how to make little Rudi's object choice even more exclusive, for she did not allow anyone else to perform the tasks of love.

On the surface, the relationship between Rudi and his nurse did not appear to be too tender. His mother's wish not to spoil the child was quite in keeping with the views and temperament of his nurse. She cared for Rudi with great devotion and yet with a certain detachment. He responded with a similar attitude: there were no demonstrations of tenderness, no kisses, no embraces. Any show of tenderness by his mother was received by Rudi with an air of stolid endurance.

First published as "Der erste Liebeskummer eines 2-jährigen Knaben" in the *Internationale Zeitschrift für Psychoanalyse*, 5:111-115, 1919. English translation in *Dynamic Psychopathology in Childhood*, ed. L. Jessner and E. Pavenstedt. New York: Grune & Stratton, 1959.

The nurse left the home without saying good-by to the little boy who had been in her care. A young and lively nursemaid took her place, assuming the role of playmate and friend. The child was delighted with her. He brought out all his toys to show his "new friend." He let her sing to him, show him pictures, and did not want to let her out of his sight. The whole transition appeared to be much easier than one would have thought. True, the child was so caught up in his play that he did "forget" several times to mention his toilet needs, and when he did ask to go, he refused help from anyone but his mother.

At mealtime his manner was somewhat distant, but he did accept food from the new nurse. At bedtime he asked for his mother, and let her undress him and put him to bed without protest. After an hour or two he awoke, which was unusual, and wept aloud. His despair grew when the nurse attempted to calm him. Crying, Rudi asked for his mother and would not let her go during that whole sleepless night. This behavior was strange indeed, for ordinarily Rudi had quite decidedly warded off his mother and asked only for his "La" (Paula, the name of the first nurse). During the night Rudi put his arms around his mother, asked her to lie down beside him, kissed her, and called her many tender names. Every few minutes he reassured himself by asking, "Mommy, are you there?" Toward morning he fell asleep for a short time. When he awoke he remained quietly in bed without a sound. His little misdeed made itself known only by the odor: Rudi had soiled his bed, although this had not happened for a year. This ambitious little boy, who normally showed signs of the greatest repugnance and remorse when he occasionally wet his pants, now remained quite indifferent when his misdemeanor was discovered. There was no sign of affect, neither triumph nor remorse; it was as if this were an everyday event.

Rudi then let himself be dressed without resistance and played happily and cheerfully with the new nurse, but he absolutely refused any offer of food. With every attempt to offer him something to eat, his face took on an expression of extreme despair such as had never been seen in him before. He was neither angry nor obstinate; on the contrary, to the nurse he made tender gestures with his hands as if to console her for his behavior. His mother finally succeeded in getting him to eat a little, although Rudi, who had called for her in despair when the nurse attempted to feed him, let his mother feed him only with the greatest resistance.

Rudi, who had been fully toilet trained, now wet and soiled his pants. When attempts were made to "catch" him and put him on the potty, he would let go of a few drops of urine, only to wet his pants a few minutes later. Sometimes he would announce his need to go, but when the nursemaid hastened to help him he would say, "Oh no, Rudi goes wee wee only for Mommy."

Until now, Rudi had shown great obstinacy in withholding his excretory products. He had clearly enjoyed retaining his always constipated stool and waiting until the last moment to urinate. Now he relinquished this source of pleasure. His feces, which were found in his bed or in his pants, were now ideally soft, a state of affairs no medical or dietary measures had been able to produce. It was as if he were protesting, "I have something. I have something precious, but it is a gift. It is only for my loved one." Now that his love object was gone, he would not yield his most highly prized and love-laden possession. Occasionally, he offered it to the substitute closest at hand: "Only for Mommy."

Rudi's need for demonstrations of tenderness increased during the following days. He embraced and kissed everyone around him. He talked to his dolls with expressions of tenderness he had learned from his mother: "My sweet, lovely bunny," etc. He even lavished expressions of tenderness upon all inanimate objects, as if he were seeking an outlet for his newly freed love.

The name of the lost one was never mentioned in all this time. Rudi often made a slip in addressing the new nurse, but always corrected himself ("La . . . Rosa, please : . . ," etc.). When the nurse, now somewhat more certain of her success, asked him, "Are you going to cry when Rosa goes away?" Rudi answered, "No, but Rudi would like to cry when Paula goes away."

During the nights that followed, his behavior remained the same. His mother had to stay with him, to assure him of her love, to cuddle him. At times Rudi would look with a horrified expression at the nurse's bed. When the latter was requested to put out the light beside her bed and did so, Rudi said, "The light went out by itself." When told that Rosa put it out, he insisted, "Oh, no, it went out by itself."

On the third day, the mother gathered her courage and asked him, "Where is Paula?" Rudi answered with an air of the greatest indifference, "She went to the tailor" (where Paula had been in the habit of going on her brief outings).

On the fifth day, Rudi no longer wet and soiled but still would allow no one but his mother to help him with toilet functions. Only when his mother was away did he permit the nurse to help him. At this time he also began to sleep normally again.

His refusal of food, however, persisted. When attempts were made to feed him, he would turn his head away, press his lips together, and begin to cry bitterly. In a pitiful voice, as if pleading for help, he would cry "Mama, Lina, Mama, Lina" (Lina was the cook and was greatly liked by Rudi). When one of them hastened to his side, Rudi calmed down, ate a few spoonfuls, only to return to his former despair. He still did not mention the name of his beloved.

Attempts to withhold food until Rudi got hungry did not succeed. On the days when he refused food, Rudi had been in the habit of stilling his hunger with snacks which had been cut up for him and which he ate without help. Forcing fluids upon him turned into a long drawn-out ritual. On the sixth day of his mourning, Rudi was given nothing to eat in the morning. He was taken for a walk and returned with a good appetite. At lunch he wolfed down his soup quite greedily. But for the rest of the meal, which consisted (as did all meals during this period) of his favorite foods, he returned to his former behavior. His hitherto good mood once more turned into despair, and he pushed his food away.

On the ninth day of separation Rudi returned to reality. He seemed to be his old self once more, but there was a change in his personality. In a sense, he had become socialized; he was more tender and more in need of tenderness. His erotic needs appeared to be greater and he showed a greater interest in people around him, treating them with a certain respect and considerateness. He was tender toward his dolls, animals, and other toys, and at every opportunity would ask: "What is that?" "What is it called?" The poems which were recited to him he learned by heart avidly. He loved his new nurse tenderly, but not with the same intensity and single-mindedness as his former nurse. His sleeping, eating, and toilet habits had returned to normal, except that his constipation had given place to regular bowel movements.

For the psychoanalyst, Rudi's little misdemeanors during the nine days described above serve to confirm facts with which we have long been familiar. It is the particularly clear-cut and unequivocal nature of his behavior which made this episode from his life seem worth reporting.

We know that infantile autoerotic sexuality obtains its satisfaction through the organic needs of the child's own body, that is, in eating and excretory activities. For the infant, the satisfaction of hunger becomes at the same time the first means of deriving pleasure from his own body. Strong feelings of pleasure are also obtained from the elimination of urine and feces. Children learn to give up the pleasure derived from excretory functions in order to gain the sympathy and praise which those in charge of their training offer them as a reward. From the moment that this exchange has taken place, a great value is placed upon the child's libidinized excretory activities, and his excremental products become a cherished gift to the chosen love object. Little Rudi appears to have valued his excretory products very highly. He was as grudging in his gifts to his beloved as he was sparing of his tenderness: this is evidenced by his constipation as well as by his urinary habits.

Upon the loss of his love object, Rudi no longer denied himself the pleasure derived from excretory functions which educative measures had previously compelled him to give up. When he lost the object for whose sake he had relinquished these pleasures, he indulged in them without restraint. And, further, he would not yield this precious gift unless a substitute object was present. At times his mother seemed to him worthy of this gift, apparently because she reminded him of his former libidinal tie: "I will do it only for Mommy." It was only when his libido was freed for new object cathexes that Rudi was able to give up a form of libidinal gratification which he had already abandoned once before. Together with the change in the nature of his object relationships, there was a change in his excretory functions: when Rudi became an affectionate child, lavish with his tenderness, his constipation ceased and his urinary needs were announced on time.

In his eating habits, Rudi expressed the cannibalistic phase of his pregenital sexual development. Eating remained closely connected with sexuality, but his sexual drive from here on, like his excretory functions, was object-directed. This was evidenced by the fact that he would eat only to please his love object. Upon the loss of his object, his sexual drives won out over his hunger, and it was only when new object relations were formed that both functions were served harmoniously.

It is not quite clear why the decathexis of that portion of the libido connected with the oral stage took place at a slower rate. We do not know whether this was due to Rudi's individual predisposition or whether it is the norm. It is possible that there is some connection between this behavior and the fact that Rudi was not given to expressing his affection by kisses.

Little Rudi overcame his first bitter disappointment in a period of nine days. The completion of this task represented a major step in his adjustment to his external environment. We do not know how this first great accomplishment will influence the future of his psychic functions, the vicissitudes of his life, and his further strivings. As analysts, however, we cannot help but engage in some conjectures.

13

Homosexuality in Women

(1932)

THE following remarks on homosexuality in women are based on findings in eleven cases which I have analyzed more or less thoroughly. At the outset I wish specially to emphasize that on the physical side none of these eleven cases of manifest homosexuality gave the impression of a constitutional modification of physiological characteristics in the direction of masculinity. It was true that my patients showed signs of an unusually strong bisexual disposition, but these signs referred solely to the preliminary phases of what in its later development would be termed masculinity. Those phases appear, however, to have no physical correlate, or at any rate none which can be observed, for, as I have said, none of these patients displayed any physical signs of virility. Anatomically and physiologically we should have described them as "feminine." At the same time I do not wish to deny that other homosexual types exist in which the genital

---

The material in this paper consists of observations collected during a period of many years prior to 1931 when it was intended to be read at the International Psycho-Analytical Congress, which did not in fact take place. In the meantime there appeared a paper by Freud entitled "Female Sexuality" (1931), in which he discussed the *normal* sexual development of girls. What finally decided me to publish my observations in 1932 (*Internationale Zeitschrift für Psychoanalyse*, 18:219-241, 1932; English: *Psychoanalytic Quarterly*, 1:484-510, 1932 and *International Journal of Psycho-Analysis*, 14:34-56, 1933) was the fact that in many points they bear on this paper of Freud's.

165

stands in contradistinction to the rest of the psychic and physical personality (secondary sex characteristics, etc.). I only say that *my* material did not include any such.

The first case of homosexuality which I analyzed dates from about twelve years ago. It was a case of inversion, manifest but not actively practiced. The patient was perfectly aware that her capacity for love and her sexual fantasies were confined to her own sex; she also experienced quite unmistakable sexual excitations when embracing and kissing certain women with whom she was in love. Her attitude to them was monogamous and faithful, but at the same time only platonic, even when she knew of a similar perverse inclination in the women in question. One could not really say that she was attracted by any particular type; in any case the women were not "masculine" and the patient herself belonged to the fair, "feminine" type. She was by no means hostile to men; she had many men friends and did not object to being admired and courted by men. Feelings of sympathy had led her to marry a man who in appearance was markedly "masculine" and she had had several children, for whom her feeling was not passionate, but yet maternal.

She could not explain why her homosexuality did not take a more active and urgent form; she only knew that her inhibitions were too strong, and rationalized them on grounds of social timidity, her duty to her family, and her dread of "bondage." She could trace her love for women back to puberty, when it began in the manner typical of that time of life and had reference to teachers and other persons in authority. I cannot remember whether these persons were characterized by any special severity; at any rate the patient was governed by two feelings—on the one hand a sense of security, and on the other a dread of the woman in question. She had never really fallen in love with a man; she was at first attracted to her husband because she regarded him as a particularly active and masculine person. At the very outset of their married life she found herself disappointed, as she told me, for precisely in that respect her husband did not come up to her expectations. Above all, he was lacking in sexual passion and activity and, in other ways also, he failed her most when she looked for activity from him.

The patient came to analysis because of her neurotic difficulties. For years she had suffered from fits of depression and from feelings of anxiety with a definite content. These related to women in her employment, toward whom she had not the courage to adopt a suitable attitude of authority. Her requirements were indeed exacting and she worried when they were not fulfilled, but she was incapable of giving an order, not to mention a reproof. In just those situations where this was necessary she was seized with shyness and anxiety in relation to the other woman. Especially when there was a change in her household staff and she had to prepare for the advent of a strange woman, her anxiety and mental conflict redoubled. It was in such situations that she quite consciously blamed her husband for not protecting and supporting her actively enough.

In the last few years the attacks of depression had become more and more frequent and were accompanied by suicidal impulses. On quite a number of occasions the patient had made unsuccessful attempts to commit suicide; the last of these brought her to death's door. It happened that a physician who was an intimate friend of mine was called in, and he was able subsequently to assure me of the seriousness of this attempt.

For months the patient's analysis centered in the castration complex. At that time—twelve years ago—the assumption of a castration complex in women was not yet such a matter of course as it is today. My attention was, however, so much arrested by the material which pointed in this direction that I was inclined to regard that complex as the nucleus of her neurosis and of her perversion. Her penis envy was so overwhelming that it even manifested itself in her relation to her little sons, whose penes she cut off in her dreams and fantasies. Although the patient's sadistic tendencies were particularly strong, her conscious personality was rather of a reactive character. That is to say, she was affectionate and yielding, with unmistakable obsessional traits in the form of marked "propriety" and correctness. The transference to me was very strong and was of the type in which for a long time nothing appears in the patient's consciousness or behavior but tenderness, admiration, and a sense of security. She felt as happy as if at last she had found a loving, understanding mother who gave her all that her own mother had denied her. For her mother had been a woman of a severe, cold nature whom the patient had all her life quite consciously hated. After her mother's death—which occurred some years before the analysis —she fell into a deep depression and it was during this period that she made one of her attempts at suicide.

During the analysis, several fits of depression succeeded one another at short intervals. They were always accompanied by characteristic dreams and they revealed certain definite material. At that time, twelve years ago, I made a short communication to the Vienna Psycho-Analytical Society on the subject of these dreams, in a paper on dreams of returning to the womb and suicidal ideas. I need not go into the dreams in detail here; it will be sufficient for me to say that they contained nearly all the known symbolism relating to the mother's body: there were dreams of dark holes and openings into which the patient crept, dreams of cosy dark places which seemed to her known and familiar and where she lingered with a sense of rest and deliverance. These dreams began to occur during a period when the patient, oppressed by a conscious longing for death, constantly declared that, but for her relation with me and the confidence she had in me, no power on earth could prevent her from committing suicide. A remarkable point about the dreams was that, again and again, one particular dream picture appeared: the patient saw herself wrapped up like a baby in swaddling clothes or a binder. Her associations showed that two dim memories were emerging in these dreams. One had reference to a scene after her last attempt to commit suicide by poisoning: she woke up out of deep unconsciousness, still strapped to a stretcher, and saw the physician bending over her with a kindly smile. She was conscious that he had saved her life (as was actually the case), and she thought: "Yes, this time; but all the same you cannot really help me."

Another series of associations led to the memory of a dangerous operation undergone by her mother. The patient remembered having seen her mother wrapped up as she herself was later and carried on a stretcher to the operating theater.

This recollection opened the way analytically to a murderous hatred for her mother which had hitherto been repressed but now became the focal point of the analysis. After about eight months of work, childhood memories emerged which proved to be the center both of the neurosis and of the perversion. These memories went back to her fourth, fifth, and sixth years, at which period the patient practiced masturbation in a way which was noticeable, at any rate to her mother. It was impossible to determine whether this masturbation actually went beyond the normal and, further, what was the content of the fantasies which no doubt accompanied it. Anyhow, what happened, according to the patient, was that her mother, not knowing what else to do, resorted to the following plan: she tied the child's hands and feet, strapped her to the cot, stood beside it and said: *"Now go on with your games!"* This produced a twofold reaction in the little girl. On the one hand it evoked a feeling of furious anger with her mother, for which, bound as she was, she could find no motor discharge. On the other hand it gave rise to a violent sexual excitement which, in spite of her mother's presence or perhaps in defiance of her, she tried to gratify by rubbing her buttocks against the mattress.

To the child's mind the most terrible thing about this scene was that her father, whom her mother summoned, remained a passive witness of it and did not try to help his little daughter whom he loved tenderly.

Let me still relate how that recollection was recovered analytically. This was made possible by a dream of the patient's, in which she saw herself sitting behind the bars in a police station, having been accused of some sort of sexual misconduct. Apparently she had been brought in from the street under suspicion of being a prostitute. The police inspector, a kindly man, stood on the other side of the bars, without helping her. Here we have in fact an almost direct repetition of the situation in her childhood.

After this scene in childhood the patient gave up masturbation and therewith repressed her sexuality for a long time. What she repressed at the same time was her hatred for her mother, which in real life she never again betrayed in the same degree.

I do not regard the childhood scene with the mother as trau-

matic in the sense that it produced the subsequent psychic attitude of the patient. It merely brought together in concentrated
form all those trends which determined her whole sexual life.
The reproach against her mother that she had forbidden masturbation would certainly have arisen in her mind even *without*
this scene. The reaction of hatred toward her mother was perceptible also in other situations of childhood and was in accordance with the patient's sadistic constitution. The same was true
of her reproach against her father for failing to protect her from
her mother. But this scene brought all these trends to the boiling
point, so to speak, and thus became the prototype of later
occurrences.

From that time on, every sexual excitation became associated
with the mother's prohibition and with the most violent aggressive impulses against her. These were opposed by the patient's
whole psychic personality: reaction to these hate impulses took
the form of a strong sense of guilt toward her mother, which
caused the hate to be transformed into a libidinal, masochistic
attitude. This was why the patient replied to the direct question
why she had so far not formed any homosexual tie by saying
that she dreaded bondage. What she really dreaded was the masochistic attachment to her mother. This explains, too, why she had
a dread of her women servants and reproached her husband with
not protecting her properly.

Although, as the analysis went on, an excessively strong penis
envy manifested itself, it was not the central point of the patient's personality; neither her character nor her attitude toward
men indicated that she belonged to the type of woman who has
a "masculinity complex." It is true that this does not seem to have
always been the case, for analysis revealed phases, both in her
childhood (before the time of the fateful experiences described)
and also at puberty, in which unmistakable signs could be detected of a very marked development of activity, with a masculine
bias. Especially at puberty she manifested quite plainly interests
which were rather unusual in a girl of her period and social
sphere. She succeeded brilliantly in sublimating this element of
masculinity, and it remained sublimated all her life. But it
seems that a considerable part of it remained as a burden on

her mental economy, as was plainly shown in dreams and certain symptoms, in a sense of inferiority, etc.

I was greatly tempted to assume that it was just the patient's homosexuality which served to express her masculinity. But precisely here she did not fulfill my analytic expectations and thus I was confronted with a problem which I could not solve till years later.

But to preserve some sort of chronological order in recording my experiences I must for the moment discontinue my theoretical reflections on this case.

After we had worked through the above piece of analysis (that is to say, after eight months) the patient's father appeared, really for the first time, on the stage of the analytic play. With him came all the impulses belonging to the oedipus complex, beginning with the vehement reproach, which the patient had never been able to get over, that he had not been active enough in his love for his daughter. I would especially emphasize that it was already clear to me at that time that the patient's hatred of her mother and libidinal desire for her were much older than the oedipus complex.

I hoped that with the resuscitation of the father relation— above all, through the renewed animation and correction of *this* relation—the outlook for the patient's libidinal future would become more favorable. I therefore sent her to an analyst of the fatherly type. Unfortunately the transference never went beyond respect and sympathy, and after a short time the patient broke off the analysis. About a year later I met her and saw before me a blooming, radiant woman. She told me that the fits of depression had altogether vanished. The desire for death, which in her perpetual nostalgia had always been with her, now seemed very remote. At last she had found happiness in an extraordinarily blissful and uninhibited sexual relation with another woman. The patient, who was very intelligent and well versed in analysis, informed me that her homosexual relation took the form of a perfectly conscious mother-and-child situation, in which sometimes the one and sometimes the other played the part of mother. It was, so to speak, a drama in which the actors doubled their parts. In their homosexual caresses they derived gratification, especially from the oral zone and the external genital organs. In this relation there was no sign of a "masculine-feminine" opposition of roles, but the antithesis between active and passive played an essential part. One received the impression that what made the situation so happy was precisely the possibility of playing *both* parts.

The result of the analysis was clear. All that had so plainly emerged in the analytic transference situation had now been dissociated from the person of the woman analyst and carried over to other women. Wishes frustrated in analysis could be fulfilled in relation to these new objects. Obviously, with the overcoming of her hostility to the woman analyst the patient had also overcome her anxiety, so that, in place of these two feelings (anxiety and hostility) which produced the neurotic symptoms, she was able to form a positive libidinal relation with a woman. But first her infantile mortifications at the hand of the mother substitute had to be wiped out by sexual gratification. The analytic treatment had not led to a further and more favorable resolution of the mother fixation, that is to say, to the renunciation of homosexuality and a turning toward men.

Here I will pause and postpone theoretical discussion till after I have cited others of the cases I have analyzed.

I must just add that, since the analysis, this patient has made no further attempt at suicide, but that I have heard that recently the old difficulties with women servants have begun again. I conjecture that there has been some trouble in the love relation and that this has probably led to a neurotic reaction. At all events there is no longer any question of such fits of depression as occurred before the analysis.

In the course of the last three years I have analyzed several cases of homosexuality in women, in which the perversion was more manifest than in the case already discussed, and where the analysis began, so to speak, where our patient left off. All the women in question stood in a mother-and-child relation to their homosexual love object and more or less consciously recognized this fact. In all the cases the forms of sexual gratification were the same: sleeping in close mutual embrace, sucking one another's nipples, mutual genital and, above all, anal masturbation, and cunnilingus, mainly in the form of sucking, practiced intensively by both parties. Here again the double role of each partner must be specially stressed.

One of these patients divided her twofold role between two objects. One would be a little girl, quite young and helpless, who assumed the part of the child, while the other would be some older, very active and authoritative woman, in relation to whom the patient herself played the part of the helpless girl. The latter relation generally began as follows: the patient, who was herself very active and ambitious in her work, entered into a sublimated relation with the other woman. For a short time her attitude was one of almost imperceptible rivalry, which became conscious only in the analysis. Then she began to fail in her own performance, in a manner which was clearly neurotic, and to drop into a subordinate position in relation to her friend. For example, after they had begun to prepare a technical work together, the upshot was that the patient (who was perhaps in fact the more gifted of the two) merely acted as secretary when the book came to be written. If, when they were engaged on any such joint task any sexual intimacy developed, the role of the active seducer was always left to the other woman.

I am selecting from this patient's life history and analysis only such material as I require for the confirmation of the theoretical conclusions which I shall suggest later.

The patient was one of a very numerous family; she had several sisters and two brothers, only one of whom, four years her senior, played a part in her life history. When the patient was nine months old and still being fed by her mother, a younger sister was born, who became her rival for the mother's breast. In earliest childhood the patient developed all sorts of oral symptoms from which we were able to reconstruct a situation which may be described as one of "oral envy." For a long time her relation to this sister remained one of rivalry; even in childhood she let her take precedence—obviously by way of overcompensation. Thus she mentioned in analysis that as quite a small child she had heard that, when there was so little difference of age between two sisters and so great a resemblance as between her and her sister, only one of them would marry and have children. She left it to her sister to achieve this feminine success and already at puberty, when her parents were divorced, soon after the birth of the youngest child, she gave up her father to her sister and remained with her mother.

Very early in childhood the patient showed reaction formations against her aggressive tendencies which, prior to the birth of the next sister (when she herself was six years old), took shapes suggestive of an obsessional neurosis, though this never actually developed. At all events, during her mother's pregnancy at this time the patient reproached herself most bitterly for not feeling the same goodwill toward her and toward the coming child as did her sister Erna, who, she was convinced, prayed every evening for the welfare of both.

Analysis revealed very strong aggressive impulses against the mother,[1] especially in her pregnant state, and against the newborn child. The patient's life and whole character were, as we discovered, shaped under the pressure of efforts to amend her murderous thoughts against mother and child.

On the next two occasions when her mother was pregnant (she again gave birth to girls) the same reaction was repeated and it was only when the youngest sister was born (the patient, as I have said, being then twelve years old) that the psychic situation changed. She had always remembered the father of her early days as a very mysterious, strange, and powerful man, who inspired anxiety and timidity, but now the patient's attitude toward him gradually underwent a change. He developed heart trouble which finally forced him to give up his work, and this involved his family in financial difficulties. This fact acted on the patient as an incentive to assume the role of the father herself and to indulge in fantasies in which she adorned high positions and was the breadwinner for the family. Later, by means of hard work, she actually translated these fantasies into reality.

In spite of this identification with the father and although she

[1] Melanie Klein's observations show very illuminatingly what blood-thirsty impulses of aggression enter into the child's relation to the mother, especially when mobilized by a real experience (e.g., the birth of a brother or sister). The great value of these observations is that they were made in direct contact with children.

envied her brother his masculinity, her attitude, at the time when her youngest sister was born, was no longer one of rivalry, as it had been in the case of the other sisters. On the contrary, she fancied herself exceedingly in the role of a little mother and wanted to have the baby all to herself. From the point of view of her oedipus complex she was already behaving in this situation exactly like a normal little girl. Analysis showed that she had been able to achieve this positive oedipus attitude only when she had dared to bring her father nearer to herself out of his over-whelming inaccessibility, and had thus been able to master her acute dread of the fulfillment of her masochistic sexual desires.

My experience has convinced me that this change of object, i.e., the turning of the libido away from the mother and toward the father, is more difficult in proportion as more aggressive and sadistic tendencies are predominant in a girl. This is not only because her active tendencies are an impediment, but also be-cause precisely in such cases the change-over to the passive role must inevitably take on a peculiarly masochistic character, where-upon the ego must reject it as dangerous.

It is true that the patient had attained to the normal oedipus situation (as the history of her puberty plainly showed), but in so doing she derived from the relation of rivalry with her mother fresh food for her old preoedipal aggressive impulses against her. With this was associated a burden of guilt which could be light-ened only by new overcompensation, by renouncing the father, and remaining finally arrested in the mother fixation.

If we want to formulate in a succinct way the psychological basis of this relation we can put it as follows: "I do not hate you; on the contrary, I love you. It is not true that you refuse me the breast and give it instead to my youngest [i.e., one might say "preoedipal"] sister; you give it to me, and there is no need for me to kill you and the baby. It is not true that I have killed the baby, for I myself am the baby whom you love and nurse." This fundamental attitude toward her mother was reflected not only in the form of direct oral gratification, as described earlier, in the patient's homosexual intercourse with the young girl, but also in her submissive, passive attitude, as mentioned above, to the older woman whom she loved.

It would appear that the homosexuality thus formulated has as yet nothing to do with the oedipus situation; it is a continuation of the preoedipal situation and a reaction to it.

Nevertheless, in the nature of the patient's relation to the young girl we not only see the reflection of the *active* side of the original mother-child relation, as exemplified in the typical identification of herself with the nursing mother, but we note already unmistakable indications of a fresh influence, namely, that of the oedipus situation. The young girl always represented the patient's youngest sister, toward whom all her life long she actually assumed, by way of sublimation, the role of mother; while the unsublimated homosexual impulse was directed toward a strange young girl as love object. At one time she was the mother giving the breast to her child (by the father) and at another the child who was suckled. In this sexual experience she was able to transform her hatred of her mother into love, for she was granted her mother's breast; at the same time she could be the mother in her function of actively giving and so convert the aggressive impulses against her mother into activity.

I will now relate some dreams from the analysis of this patient, selecting from a large quantity of material those which serve at once by their *manifest* content to confirm what I have just said.

In one dream, the patient saw herself in the street with her youngest sister. She herself was pregnant. She was hurrying to reach a house which she saw before her. In the middle of the front of this house was a deep bay window which stood open. This was her mother's room, and she wanted to reach it to give birth to the child there. She had a feeling of great anxiety lest she should lose the child in the street, i.e., lest a miscarriage should occur before she reached the house. She told her sister about this anxiety and then actually had a miscarriage in the street.

The real situation in the patient's life made it very easy to understand the dream. On the previous day she had had a visit from a little friend, who lived in another town and had not seen her since the beginning of her analysis. This girl was her homosexual love object, of which her youngest sister was the prototype. The patient slept with her that night, holding her tightly embraced in her arms. Before the sexual tension found its discharge she was disturbed by an uncomfortable feeling that, if she gratified her homosexual desires, the analysis might suffer. She therefore sent the little girl away from her bed (lost her, so to speak, out of her arms), so as not to spoil her relation with me. It is plain that her pregnancy in the dream (i.e., the state in which she had the child with her, within her) stood for the actual sexual embrace. The longing felt in her dream for her pregnant mother, manifesting itself in a fantasy of the mother's womb as symbolized by the deep bay window, is extraordinarily clear, as is the simultaneous identification with the mother and with the child *in utero*. In addition, it happened that, in this same analytic hour, the patient remembered for the first time that her mother had had a miscarriage when she herself was about three and a half. This was the very period of childhood in which she had been so strongly attached to her mother and had reacted to the latter's pregnancy with such an extraordinary aggressiveness.

The other element in the dream, "I was walking with my youngest sister," also expresses the situation before she went to sleep and means: "I have my beloved by my side." This dream situation reveals a fact which I had arrived at analytically, namely, that her sexual relation to her friend contained also the fulfillment of the oedipal wish, for the new little daughter belonged not to the mother but to the patient herself. In the dream situation: "to reach the mother and give birth to the child," or, "not to reach the mother and to lose the child," we have a remarkably clear indication of the identification of mother and child or giving birth and being born. The situation is connected with the preoedipal mother relation belonging to the very period when the mother's miscarriage occurred. The blending and overlaying of this situation with the oedipal wishes also seems to be clear here.

I will give only a fragment of a second dream. The patient dreamed that she was lying on a sofa when a figure approached and tried to expose her. She endeavored to scream and woke up crying out: "My God, Frau Doctor!" On waking she noticed that she had her hand between her thighs.

A series of associations to this dream led to a subject which occupied her in real life at this stage of the analysis, namely, that of masturbation. For a long time the patient had refrained from this practice for fear of having to tell me about it. Lately she had begun to allow herself to masturbate (although not without inhibitions), under the impression that I had nothing against it. The exclamation: "My God!" was intended for me and meant that I ought to save her from the danger of punishment, i.e., either prevent her masturbating or allow it. This interpretation followed from associations, some of which led back to an experience of her childhood. She had once touched an electric switch when her hand was damp and had been caught in a circuit so that she could not pull her hand away. At her cry for help ("My God!") her mother had rushed to her and was also caught in the circuit, but thus weakened its action so that the patient was able to free her hand. She had been saved by her mother. In the dream, I (like her mother) was to save her from what she had touched, i.e., from the consequences of her transgression of the prohibition. I was to do this by letting myself be drawn into the circuit of her excitation, embracing her, and gratifying her desires.

I have quoted this fragment of the dream to illustrate that other important component part of her homosexuality by which the struggle with masturbation is resolved in that seemingly favorable way by her mother's intervention, i.e., her expressed sanction.

In another dream, a tall strong woman whom she took for her mother, although the latter was not really so tall and strong, was overwhelmed with grief because Erna (the younger sister, next to the patient in age) was dead. Her father was standing by. She herself was feeling very cheerful because she was going away with her father to enjoy herself. But a glance at her mother showed her that it would not do; she must stay with her because she was in such trouble.

The interpretation of this dream is self-evident. The patient could not gratify her oedipal wishes, she could not be gay and happy with a man, because her sense of guilt toward her mother, whose child she had killed, bound her to her mother and forced her into homosexuality.

Here is a short fragment of another long and illuminating dream. She saw herself in analysis with Miss Anna Freud, who was dressed as a man. In the dream this was explained on the ground that it was necessary for her to change her analyst. She thought that, with me, what she had to do was to produce free associations, but that with Miss Freud it would be a matter of actual experience.

On the evening before the dream the patient had been taken by some friends to a lecture in the hall belonging to the Psycho-Analytical Society, at which Miss Freud and I were present. In association with the dream she now told me that, when she was thinking of being analyzed, Miss Freud and I had been recommended to her. From the descriptions of us both she had formed the picture that Miss Freud represented the mother ideal, that she would be motherly to *all* children and ready to help them if they asked her, whereas my maternal feelings would, she imagined, be chiefly confined to my own children (would be, so to speak, sexualized). She remembered, too, that she had meant to write to us both before choosing, and it now occurred to her for the first time that she had asked for my address only.

On the evening before the dream she had had an opportunity of comparing the two of us. She thought that her idea of us was quite true and—how glad she was that she was doing analysis with me! This protestation seemed rather suspicious to me and I pointed out to her that the dream seemed to contradict it. It had struck me that the patient, who had gone to the lecture in order to see a certain analyst there, had not said a word about him, although he was sitting next to Miss Freud. Moreover, we had not yet interpreted the circumstance of Miss Freud's appearing in the dream in men's clothes.

Some days later she dreamed that I was sitting *opposite* her, instead of behind her as I always did, and that I had a cigar in my hand. She thought: "The ash on that cigar is so long that in a minute it will drop." Her first association to the cigar was: "Only men smoke them."

My being turned by the patient into a man reminded me that

she had done the same with Miss Freud in the previous dream, and it struck me that, from where the patient sat during the lecture, she must, if she looked at Miss Freud, have seen simultaneously a photograph of Professor Freud with a cigar in his hand, which was hanging on the wall. A similar photograph is on the writing table in my consulting room. I now took the photograph and showed it to her and she confirmed that this was the position in which I held my hand with the cigar in the dream.

Further analysis showed that the desire of her heart had been to be analyzed by Professor Freud, but that this wish, which sprang from her deep longing for the great man, for her father, had been repressed, and that Miss Freud had also been drawn into the repression. As I have already said, the patient had indeed also repressed her meeting with the analyst of whom I spoke and the impression made upon her by Professor Freud's photograph. The repressed material then broke through, as I have described, when she turned me and Miss Freud into men.

This mode of reappearance of her father in her dreams proved that her turning to women represented also a flight from men. The analysis showed from what sources these flight tendencies were derived: a sense of guilt toward her mother and dread of disappointment and frustration.

Taking a rapid survey of this case we see that the first period of the patient's life was passed under somewhat unusual conditions. Her mother nursed her and a younger sister at the same time, and when the patient had to give up the breast to the latter she developed—with a certain justification—a strong oral envy. Her reaction to her mother's pregnancy in her third year was one of violent hostility and jealousy of the coming child. The dream of the miscarriage illustrates the little girl's mental state at that period and her strong wish herself to take the baby's place in the mother's womb.

This dream was, however, overlaid with recollections of a later period (her twelfth year) and revealed in her identification with her mother her desire to have the child herself. This wish already indicates the oedipal attitude, the development of which, apparently late and slow but nonetheless powerful, we were able to trace during her analysis.

It is difficult to say whether the longing of her early infantile period (a longing which she never mastered) to be the sole possessor of her mother and to be nursed and tended by her had the effect of inhibiting the patient's normal libidinal development; or whether the further vicissitudes of her sexual life were determined by difficulties arising out of the oedipus complex and familiar to us from other cases. I have tried to show, in studying her dreams, that her return to her mother did not imply the renunciation of her longing for her father and that her relation to him was one of perpetual, terrified flight, which forced her to repress her feminine attitude toward men.

From this material I should now like to draw certain theoretical conclusions which seem to me personally to be important for the understanding of feminine sexuality in general and of feminine homosexuality in particular.

It has often been said that our knowledge of *feminine* sexuality extends only so far as this is identical in childhood with that of *males*. It is not until *puberty,* when the woman really becomes a woman biologically, that the situation grows clearer and easier to grasp. Freud has thrown considerable light on the processes of the early period, in a paper entitled: "Some Psychical Consequences of the Anatomical Distinction between the Sexes" (1925), in which he states that in girls the oedipus complex does not establish itself until after the phallic phase. I have spoken elsewhere (1925) of a "swing toward passivity" in girls, at the center of which lies the desire for an anal child by the father. Already at that time I pointed out that this swing toward passivity is really a regressive process, the regression being to a phase *before* the phallic organization, which is identical in boys and girls. In my view we have been too much absorbed by the processes in the phallic phase and by its various manifestations and vicissitudes, with the result that we have treated somewhat cavalierly the phase in which the swing toward passivity takes place. We content ourselves with establishing that the desire for the penis is exchanged for the desire for a child, and that it is then the task of the normal psychic forces in the little girl to secure her adjustment, without injury, to this fresh frustration. I think that no one who has made clinical observations will dispute the fact that the strength of the desire for a child depends entirely on the strength of the earlier desire for the penis which it has replaced. So that one may say: the stronger the wish for the penis, the stronger the subsequent wish for a child. The harder the little girl has found it to endure the frustration of her desire for the penis the more aggressive will be her reaction to the frustration of her desire for a child. Here we have a vicious circle, which so often puzzles us in analyses, as we repeatedly find that the most ardent, most feminine wish for a child occurs precisely in those women whose psychic struggles over their castration complex or penis envy have been the most severe.

Let us suppose, however, that a little girl has managed to develop in a tolerably normal way as far as the oedipus complex and has abandoned all hope of the penis, so that everything is ready for the conversion of her phallic activity into passivity. She is ready, that is to say, to receive an anal child from her father. Now it does yet not follow that she is in a position to master the fresh disappointment, i.e., the frustration of her wish for a child. We must keep the scheme of her libidinal development before us and not forget that when this swing toward passivity takes place a number of *active* forces also come to life and raise their heads again, so to speak, with the recathexis of pregenital tendencies. In the normal psychic economy they no doubt find their appointed place, for the mother's part in relation to her child is *active*, a fact sufficiently illustrated by the way in which little girls play with their dolls.

But what happens when a little girl, first, shrinks from the masochistic peril associated with the swing toward passivity and, secondly, is unable to bear the real frustration of her wish for a child, while she is convinced of the fruitlessness of her wish for the penis? Let us visualize the situation of a child who has lost the narcissistic stimulus of her unrealizable wish for the penis and who through frustration, disappointment, or fear feels rejected by her father, so that she finds herself alone with her libido, which she can sublimate only to a small extent. What will she do? She will act like all living creatures in situations of danger; she will flee to the place where she once felt secure and enjoyed protection and gratification, i.e., to her mother.

It is true that she has experienced frustrations at her mother's hands also, but all these frustrations were preceded some time by gratification, for the mother who frustrates and who is hated was once the mother who granted desires.

There can be no doubt that, even in the phallic phase, the mother accords some gratification to the child's sexual instinct when she is attending to the girl's bodily needs. But apparently at this period the instinctual claims are more imperative and cannot be so extensively gratified through their dependence on the functions which subserve the ego as in previous phases. We must bear in mind also the undisguised nature of the phallic sexual aims, the readiness with which they manifest themselves and the mother's shrinking back when she perceives the wishes betrayed by the child. We know from the analysis of mothers that the more any unconscious recollections of their own masturbation in childhood are mobilized by similar activities in their children, the greater is their horror of these activities. And further, the more the mother in an unconscious role of seducer has herself excited the child, the severer will be the frustrations which the child now suffers. The subsequent *direct* prohibition of masturbation, the forcible interference with the child's activities in that direction, fan the flame of her hostility to her mother who inflicts the frustration. Together with phallic masturbation, there comes also the *affective* discovery in the little girl of her anatomical "defect."

We already know that the responsibility for her lack of a penis is laid by her at her mother's door. Hence the sadistic impulses of the phallic phase come to be directed against the mother and probably give the signal for the change of object, while by this sadistic turning toward the mother the passive-masochistic attitude toward the father is facilitated. This is the result of what I have called the "thrust toward passivity." Undoubtedly, not all the little girl's aggressive impulses are drawn off into the masochistic-passive attitude. A large amount of aggression is turned upon her father when he inflicts the disappointment, while another part remains attached to the mother in the relationship of rivalry which now develops. The strength of the aggressive impulses will certainly depend on the vigor of the phallic activity.

Moreover, the masochistic turn taken by the child will prove the more intense, the more powerfully it is nourished from the source of her aggressions. The analyses of female patients in whom the castration complex is very strong show unmistakably how dangerous to them the passive attitude is—on account of its masochistic connection—and how bloodthirsty and murderous are the revengeful actions the child conceives against the mother. This is especially the case when the mother actually is or is fantasied to be pregnant, or when she has already given birth to another child. This attitude introduces into masochism its moral element, the strength of which will increase with the strength of the aggressive tendencies.

We see then what perils surround the little girl in this phase:

1. Libidinal-masochistic dangers from the anticipated fulfillment of her wishes by her father.

2. Dangers from the threatened loss of her newly chosen love object, through frustration at her father's hands.

3. Dangers from the narcissistic mortification of her ego libido through her discovery of her lack of a penis.

In these great perils the libido turns back, as I have said, to its former object, and naturally the readiness and eagerness with which it turns are in proportion to the strength of the earlier ties. It is, so to speak, a retrogression to experiences once enjoyed. By this I mean that to the early infantile ambivalent conflicts are now added the aggressive impulses arising out of the rivalry connected with the oedipus complex, as well as a more highly organized sense of guilt.

The economic advantage of this renewed turning toward the mother lies in the liberation from the sense of guilt; but I think its most important function is the protection of the little girl from the threatened loss of her love object. "If my father does not want me and such a blow is dealt to my self-love, who will love me now if not my mother?"

We have a superabundance of analytic material which demonstrates this bisexual oscillation between father and mother and its outcome in neurosis, heterosexuality, or inversion. We see the libido swinging between the poles of two magnets, between attraction and repulsion. The chances of wish fulfillment represent the *attraction* by one pole, while frustration, anxiety, and the mobilization of the sense of guilt represent *repulsion* by the other pole. The same is true of the other magnet. And one of the worst results of the oscillation is an arrest between the two in a state of persisting narcissism. There are certain cases of blocking of affect and especially certain narcissistic clinical pictures which we cannot place in the category of any of the known forms of neurosis and which represent an arrest of this sort in the swing of the libidinal pendulum. Should the analytic transference produce a more noticeable oscillation, the obsessional neurosis will then become manifest, the ambivalent swing of which had so far been concealed by the blocking of affect.

In the cases of homosexuality which I analyzed there was a longer or shorter phase of indecision, which proves that we have to do not merely with a simple fixation to the mother as the first love object but with a complicated process of retrogression. The ultimate decision in favor of the maternal magnet depends, of course, upon the old forces of attraction, but also on the conditions of repulsion from the other magnet, i.e., on frustration, anxiety, and guilt reactions.

The retrogression to the mother having been begun, there still remains something to be done in order to give the process the character of a full inversion. Above all the motives which had once induced the little girl to follow the biological summons to her father must be annulled. Thus, the sexual gratification derived from masturbation, which the mother formerly forbade, must not only be no longer forbidden by her; she must actively concur in it. The frustrations of the past must be compensated for by a subsequent sanctioning no less of 'the original passive than of the later, active experience. This sanctioning of the activity (which in the past was impossible) may be said to make up for the interruption of the phallic activity. The form now taken by the little girl's active attitude in relation to the maternal object depends on the phase of development within which the homosexual object relation unfolds. Or, to put it more accurately, it depends on which is the *predominant* phase, for closer observation shows that there is a reactivation of *all* phases in which the mother has played a part, i.e., of every phase of development

passed through in early childhood. As a rule, the phallic tendencies are the most pressing and they cause the subject's relation
to other women to assume a masculine form, implying a denial
of her lack of a penis. They may even dominate the whole homosexual picture and produce a definite—in fact the most striking—
homosexual type.[2] Women of this type deny their lack of a penis
and make their female love object confirm their masculinity and
endorse their phallic masturbation in the sense indicated above.
It is now of minor importance whether the intention be to stress
the femininity of the other woman or whether the affirmation of
the penis be meant to apply to both subject and object, the latter
assuming alternately the masculine and the feminine role. These
are two subspecies of the same basic type. Again, such factors
as the magnitude of the contribution of the old rivalry (especially
where displacement from the mother to a sister, or anything
analogous to this, has early taken place); the quantity of the masochistic or the sadistic components, i.e., the predominance of aggressive tendencies or of guilt reactions; the playing of a more
passive or more active part—all these are really only details in the
problem of feminine homosexuality as a whole.

I have said that the phallic-masculine form of homosexuality
is the most striking, but behind it there always hide far deeper
tendencies. I even have the impression that this masculine form
sometimes represents a façade erected to conceal the more infantile, yet predominant tendencies. In the majority of the cases
which I have analyzed the subject was impelled by the strength
of her pregenital instincts to a far-reaching, frank surrender of
her masculine attitude. Consciously or unconsciously, the perversion was governed by the mother-child relation enacted on pregenital levels, in the deep furrows of fixation belonging to the
prephallic phases. On her retrogressive path the subject had taken

---

[2] The case of feminine homosexuality published by Freud (1920b) would
also come into the category of this "masculine" type, even though the patient's
original attitude was entirely feminine and the wish for masculinity made
its appearance only when she identified herself subsequently with the father
whom she had once loved. The two cases of feminine homosexuality described
by Fenichel (1931b) display the same psychic mechanisms as Freud's case. In
them also we find a "masculine" identification with the father as a reaction
to the disappointments suffered.

with her from the phallic phase the wish for activity, and fulfilled this wish in the homosexual relation as her most highly prized form of gratification. We often hear little children say: "When you are little and I am big. . . ." This idea is realized in the double role always enacted in such relations, the child doing to the mother everything which the mother once did to her. This sanctioning of activity and permission to masturbate constitute a motive common to all forms of homosexuality. In the phallic situation the mortification inflicted by the mother is compensated for by a kind of affirmation of the little girl's possession of the penis; similarly, in this new edition of the mother-child relation the pregenital frustration must also be annulled, and this is what largely happens in the activities from which homosexuals derive their gratification. In *Three Essays on the Theory of Sexuality* (1905a) Freud emphasized the special preference accorded to the mucous membrane of the mouth in the practices of inverted women, and Jones (1927) found the source of the disposition to homosexuality in women in the oral-sadistic phase. The hypothesis of this dispositional factor seems to me to be fully confirmed in all my cases. Further, I can state with complete certainty that in every one of these there was a specially strong reaction to the castration complex; in all of them we discovered the oedipus complex in its entirety, with peculiarly powerful aggressive reactions.

The retrogression to the mother-child attitude was invariably introduced by the wish for that child which the subject formerly desired in exchange for the penis and which was denied to her. One of the sources from which inversion draws its strength is the little girl's reaction to the fact: "My mother has the baby and not I." The element of cruelty in this reaction follows lines already laid down by the patient's disposition, and only finds discharge, in a complicated manner, in the subject's relation to her own child. This was shown beyond any doubt in the dream material of the patient whose case I have quoted.

Seeing how deep and complex is the mother-child relation we need not wonder that the longing for the mother takes on the character of a fantasy of the mother's womb. In the first case quoted this grandiose conjunction of the longing for the mother with the death wish toward her was apparent; it forms a contribution to the subject of mother fixation and the dread of death.

I cannot leave this theme without briefly discussing a question which at this point suggests itself. Is it really necessary to explain in so roundabout a way the little girl's fixation on her maternal love object? Would it not be simpler to speak of a primal fixation and to look for its cause in constitutional factors? I approached the material under discussion without any preconceptions and yet, in the cases of feminine homosexuality which I analyzed, I found none in which the light or shade cast by the father upon this primal relation did not play an important and essential part.

In the last years, it is true, I think that in certain cases I have at times observed something which suggested that the oedipus complex had played no part, or almost none, and that the libido had always known but *one* object, the mother. But these were quite special cases, in which the whole neurosis had the character of general psychic infantilism with diffuse anxieties and perversions, and it proved impossible to extricate the transference from an adhesiveness full of anxiety which obstinately resisted correction.

In view of Freud's publication (1931) it would be a profitable piece of clinical work to collect certain obscure clinical pictures which may perhaps be explained by the primary mother fixation. Besides the cases of infantilism mentioned above, certain forms of hysteria will without doubt also come into this category, forms in which it is so hard to wean the patient from the "epinosic gain" because this visibly repeats the early infantile situation of the child whom the mother tends and cares for.

To go back to my subject: we must still consider the question of the point at which a girl takes the definitive move in the direction of homosexuality. We know that, in girls, the infantile period of sexual development terminates less abruptly and radically than in boys. The change of love object takes place gradually and it seems that not until puberty is the die cast, not only in respect of the choice of an object but also as regards the subject's readiness to adopt the passive attitude.

We find that in the latency period girls are much more dependent on the mother than are boys. Perhaps this has some connection with the girl's dread of losing her love object, as I have already tried to show, and further with the nature of the process of sublimation, which, in girls, takes place more by way of tender object relations, whereas in boys it manifests itself rather in an active attitude toward the outside world.

It seems, however, that in girls a stronger sublimation, directed more toward the outside world, occurs at puberty in the "thrust toward activity," which I have described above. This bears witness that the feminine-passive attitude is not attained definitively in the infantile phase. I believe that it is general and normal for girls to go through an active, boyish period at puberty. It is from this that they derive their best energies for sublimation and for the formation of their personality, and I think I shall be right if I venture to introduce a variation into the dictum of Richard Wagner: "A girl who was not something of a boy in her youth will turn into a *vacca domestica* in later years." Of course this period of activity harbors the familiar great dangers of the "masculinity complex" and its neurotic consequences. If it is true that the ultimate change of object likewise takes place at puberty, the swing toward activity will also involve fresh dangers for the heterosexual attitude, and the "masculine tendencies" of puberty, too, will make their contribution to homosexuality.

Lastly, I must mention the final struggles which occur at puberty in the *mastering* of the oedipus complex. In the work of Freud's which I referred to earlier we have a classical instance of feminine homosexuality arising at puberty in consequence of the difficulties connected with the oedipus complex. I must, however, avow once more that in all the cases observed by me personally the foundation stone of the later inversion had already been laid in the first period of infancy.

14

Motherhood and Sexuality

(1933)

Sexual inhibition, in men and women alike, to the best of our knowledge takes its origin in the castration complex and the oedipus complex. As we use the term here, "sexual inhibition" designates a state of blocking in the obtainment of sexual gratification: a partial or complete inability to love, unaccompanied however by neurotic symptoms. The inhibition has many forms and degrees of intensity. It may present itself as a total inability to gratify the sexual impulse, an inability even to feel any conscious sexual urgency or longing; or the inhibition may be less severe, so that there may be response and gratification, but this only under certain restrictive conditions, as for example in many men who require an inferiority of some sort in the object of their sexual wishes.

To discuss the various forms of sexual frigidity in women would take us beyond the limits set for this report. In general it may be said that the unconscious determinants of frigidity correspond to those of impotence in men. Frigidity, like impotence, also originates in the development of the castration complex and the oedipus complex. Its most frequent cause is a protest against

From a course of lectures on "The Psychic Development of Women," delivered at the Vienna Psychoanalytic Institute, Summer, 1932. First published in the *Psychoanalytic Quarterly*, 2:476-488, 1933.

the assumption of the passive feminine role—in other words, the masculinity complex.

I am inclined to ascribe the widespread distribution of frigidity to the masochistic elements in the female libido. Fear of masochistic gratification, and the possibility of obtaining sublimated gratification from motherhood, often deflect female sexuality from normal forms of gratification (Deutsch, 1930b). Granting this assumption, motherhood would have to be regarded as antagonistic to sexual gratification, a view which ill agrees with other conclusions based on other authentic observations. Nevertheless, from the analyses of neurotic women and girls we have learned of the intimate association between the neurotic repudiation of the female erotic response and impaired capacity for maternity. It is, indeed, a matter of frequent observation that sterility and frigidity have the same roots, and we have often had the satisfactory experience of observing, as the result of analysis, the appearance of a ready consent to conception and a restoration of the previously impaired sexual response. Curiously enough, the latter often develops subsequently to the former.

However, there is not always so intimate an association between motherhood and a positive sexual response. There are various possible grades of detachment of the one from the other, which may lead to conditions in the love life that can be described as neurotic. This is a parallel to the already-mentioned split in the love life of men who disregard chaste and pure women as sexual objects and are sexually aroused only by notorious low-class women. Freud (1910-1918) described this type of reaction and its variations, and showed how it is determined by the oedipus complex. Of the antithetical pair, "mother" and "prostitute," the mother is rejected as taboo, and only the prostitute is accepted. Analysis reveals that this separation maintained in the conscious mind is abrogated in the deeper layers of the unconscious. For there was a time—marked by the boy's discovery of sexual secrets—when the mother herself was depreciated and accused of unfaithfulness.

This split in the love life of men has its parallel in the love life of women, but with this difference: the woman's own ego takes the place of the man's object. The woman is herself "mother" or "prostitute," and the whole inner conflict represents the struggle between the two tendencies, which appear to be contrary, but which, ultimately, in this case too converge in the single idea of the unworthy mother.

The formulation of this unconscious thought runs somewhat as follows: Since I have discovered my mother's role as a sexual object, I can only think of her as a base and besmirched creature. If I am like my mother—that is, if I identify myself with her—I am as base and soiled as she. I am quite as much a prostitute.

From the compulsion to identify herself with the mother as well as to diverge from her by acquiring the opposite tendency (i.e., the desire to be different from the mother) there result numerous possibilities in the psychic structure.

Let us start with the preoedipal relationship and its significance for the girl's later life. Following Freud's account, we may speak of an identification with the *active* mother, which as yet had no relation to the oedipus complex. In this identification the child tries herself out in the role of mother, and displaces her own childish role onto another object, perhaps a younger child in the family, or a doll, or an adult who is willing to assume the role in play. In such play the child makes others suffer or enjoy what she has suffered or enjoyed at the hands of her mother; or she betrays her unfulfilled wishes by imputing to the fantasied child things that were refused her by her mother. If the libido remains attached to the original active and passive roles of the mother-child relationship, this play will be continued into later life under the guise of homosexuality. In the analyses of homosexual women, the preoedipal libidinal components appear repeatedly; nevertheless, one discovers as a rule (this is true at least for my cases) that the women showing such an obdurate mother attachment had developed a regular, perhaps even an unusually strong oedipus complex in childhood. Indeed, it is usually the difficulties arising out of the oedipus complex that force the little girl to retreat to the preoedipal mother relationship.

This is not the place for a further discussion of female homosexuality (see Chapter 13). I merely wish to draw attention to the fact that it is one way for the preoedipal mother relationship to secure its continued existence. Even in this relationship, as mentioned above, it is possible to discover the father's role in the libidinal economy, but in the last analysis the situation is independent of the man; and in libidinal relationships only the roles of mother and child are taken into account, without reference to men. There are various causes and various results of such a repudiation of men.

Numerous possible ways of identifying with the mother are to be found. In analytic work we are most apt to encounter the identification that leads to the normal feminine attitude. The little girl wants to be loved by the father just as her mother is, and like the mother, she wants to have a child by the father (passive identification). This wish can be realized in later life, provided she succeeds in exchanging her infantile object, her father, for another man. Otherwise, she runs into neurotic disturbances, among which we must reckon, along with others, difficulties of conception, of pregnancy and of labor. Instead of a *successful* identification with her mother, the little girl develops a spiteful rivalry, which may result in a grave sense of guilt. Weighed down by this, she renounces the maternal role once and for all, and replaces it with symptoms which betray the wish and the reason for its nonfulfillment. In still another possible development, the mother identification is maintained, the idea of having a child is acceptable, and only the part of the man as a sexual partner is denied. The girl wants to be a mother and to have a child, but quite by herself, by immaculate conception or parthenogenesis. I have described this type of wish fantasy elsewhere (1925), but at that time I understood only one of its components, the one due to the masculinity complex. Its formula is: "I have a child all my own. I am its mother and father. I neither need nor desire any man for the conception of my child." As I tried to show, this fantasy contains the fulfillment of various wishes, and betrays the influence of the oedipus complex in many ways; among others, it serves to relieve the sense of guilt by denying the father's share in the child's origin. But the *most important* component is expressed in the formula: "What a man can do, I can," which directly replaces the missing penis by another enlargement of the body-ego, namely, by the self-conceived child.

But what I originally neglected when dealing with this fantasy, I now want to make good, for it belongs to the theme of mother-child relationship. From this point of view, the fantasy is another variety of the mother-child relationship that is expressed in homosexuality. It excludes the troublesome man, and in identification, the active role as originally played with dolls is carried on in relation to the self-created fantasy child. Moreover, the original high evaluation of the mother is thereby revived. The fantasy serves as the mother's expiation. It is a counterpart of the prostitution fantasy and a variant of the part of the family romance which might be stated: "I am not my mother's child, for my mother doesn't do such things." Neither does the mother "do such things" in the parthenogenetic fantasy; she has not only borne the child herself, but conceived it by herself—whereas, according to the family romance, the mother has borne no children at all. The parthenogenetic fantasy is an expression of the longing both in boys and girls, which has given rise to the myth of immaculate conception. For the woman it is a matter of identification with the immaculate mother, whose maternity is perpetuated in her ego, with a denial of sexuality, just as she has denied sexuality to her own mother. This, then, is another way for the woman to assent to motherhood while denying sexuality. She may succeed in doing this in a variety of ways.

The first way is indicated by the preoedipal mother-child relationship; the maternal libido, which is firmly lodged in a mother identification, reaches out to an individual of the same sex, and the man's role in the libidinal economy is reduced to zero.

The second possible way depends on the marked masochistic tendencies, so dominant in the female libido. They may attain such great satisfaction from motherhood—from the role of a *mater dolorosa*—that, due to this gratification, direct sexual satisfaction becomes insignificant (see Deutsch, 1930b).

The third form of asexual motherhood is the parthenogenetic, in its various versions. Paradoxical as it may seem, this structure, too, is closely related to masochism—paradoxical, because the masculinity complex is admittedly very important in its determination. I have observed, however, that when the child conceives her mother's sexual experience as something very masochistic, she also develops a strong tendency to deny this experience. It is usually the child's marked sadistic components that account for such a conception of coitus. The mother, according to this conception, endures great suffering, and her inferior position is regarded as an extreme degradation. Now there are two possibilities: either the identification with the mother will be rejected, or the mother's role as sexual object will be denied (by the above-described mechanism), and the child will identify herself with the asexual mother. If the little girl's passive-feminine wish has a marked masochistic stamp, sexuality will be rejected in apprehension of the fulfillment of her dangerous masochistic wish, but the wish for the asexual parthenogenetically produced child will be retained.

We encounter this split between motherhood and sexuality quite as often in the neuroses as in the life patterns. We find it in the phenomenon discussed at the beginning of this article, where both trends are present in one and the same individual, but existing quite separately with no possibility of symbiosis. Either of these components may completely dominate the conscious life, while the other remains hidden in the unconscious until brought to consciousness by analysis. The genius of a great artist was able to perceive with an intuitive flash what the painstaking effort of analysis has disclosed. In his book *Two Women,* Balzac gives a masterful description of these two opposing tendencies in the female psyche. Two women relate their experiences to each other in letters. They represent contrary types, but each discovers deep within her the hidden longing for something else, for the opposite. The longing is in itself evidence of the fact that the something else is present, even though in a rudimentary form, and repressed. It would seem, indeed, that in this case, Balzac had made use of a favorite literary mechanism—the personification of two opposing psychic reactions. The two women represent, in fact, the opposing tendencies of *one woman.* Opposing tendencies are characteristic of the feminine mind and belong, as a matter of fact, to the normal psyche. Only a marked preponderance of the one or the other leads to complications and neurotic difficulties.

The Baroness Louise de Macumère is the courtesan type, the devotee of love, whose only aim in life is the pursuit of passion, the enjoyment of intense erotic experiences. Her friend, Renée de l'Estorade, on the other hand, is completely given over to her motherhood, even in her relations with her husband. Louise writes: "We are both of us women, I a most blissful love goddess, you the happiest of mothers" . . . "Nothing can be compared to the delights of love" . . . "You, my dear friend, must describe for me the joys of motherhood, so that I may partake of motherhood through you."

And yet, even in the midst of her ecstasy in love relationships, a voice within cries out: "A childless woman is a monstrosity; we are born to be mothers." . . . "I, too, want to be able to sacrifice myself, and I am often absorbed these days in gloomy thoughts—will there never be a little one to call me mother?"

However, this flicker of motherhood is extinguished in the flame of passionate love, and Louise is consumed in this fire without ever having fulfilled her womanhood—in the sense of becoming a mother.

The motherly Madame de l'Estorade writes on the other hand: "My one real happiness (and how precious that was!) lay in my certainty that I had given renewed life to this poor man, even before I had borne him a child!" (i.e., motherhood even in her love relations with her husband).

Desire for children and motherhood completely filled this woman's emotional life. In her repudiation of sexuality she admitted no other feeling beyond motherhood. And yet she writes to her erotic friend: "I had to renounce the pleasures of love and passionate joys for which I long and can only experience through you, the nocturnal meeting on the starlit balcony, the passionate yearning and unbridled effusions of love."

Thus the longing for the enjoyments of love lurks within the virtuous Renée just as the longing for motherhood lurks within the erotic Louise. She even betrays to us that a vigorous protest and hate against the unborn and newborn child can arise in spite of her self-sacrificing motherhood, a hate whose origin lies in the renunciation of erotic satisfaction, in a curtailment of the ego's expectation of erotic fulfillment. The maternal Madame de l'Estorade holds her child on her lap and writes her frivolous friend: "Marriage has brought me motherhood, and so I am happy, too." But a little later: "Everyone talks about the joy of being a mother! I alone can not feel it; I am almost ashamed to confess to you my total lack of feeling." . . . "I should like to know at just what point this joy of motherhood puts in its appearance. Good-bye, my happy friend, through whom I relive and enjoy those rapturous delights of love, jealousy at a wayward glance, the secret whisper in the ear." . . .

In a word, one is the mother longing for passion, the other the devotee of love who longs for motherhood. No clinical example could describe the phenomenon of cleavage between motherhood and erotism in a more lucid or gripping way than Balzac's portrayal of these two opposite and complementary types. I do not know the sources of Madame de l'Estorade's unbending motherhood—whether it springs from identification with the preoedipal mother, or with the later mother whose sexuality she attempts to deny. But I can speak more definitely about my own patients. They were more radical in repressing sexuality and in splitting off their maternal feelings. Madame de l'Estorade, even though clearly sexually anesthetic, has nevertheless borne a family and has satisfied her maternal feelings on her real and living children. The women under discussion are incapable even of this solution. They transfer their maternal feelings to objects other than their own children—to other women's children or to adults to whom they extend their maternal protection. Many choose a profession or work which offers an outlet for their maternal feelings.

One of my patients was a German midwife. She had chosen this work (which was very unusual for one of her social class) in order to keep on having children—many, many children—and the weaker they were and the more in need of protection, the more she liked them. Her own fear of childbirth played an important role for her; she had to leave the situation of danger to the other woman before she could identify herself with the mother in possession of a child. She was a highly qualified and well-trained midwife, and capable of unlimited self-sacrifice in her work. She came into analysis because of certain strange difficulties in the line of duty. "A patient is in labor" was a battle cry for her, to which she responded like the Germans of old with great fervor (at least inwardly). The agonies of childbirth as seen in other women aroused a curious mixture of feelings of anxiety and pleasure in her. The moment of the child's birth, when she could take it over and give it its first attention, was an ecstatic experience for her. No work was too hard for her; she could stand sleepless nights without fatigue. What she could not endure was the knowledge that a labor was going on when she could not be present; it was intolerable to her to have to miss a delivery. Since it was physically impossible for her to be on hand at every birth in a maternity hospital, she developed a state of excitement and exhaustion which brought her to analysis.

The symptoms in themselves are explanatory. Her profession was intended to free her from an oppressive sense of guilt in relation to her mother: out of her original fantasies of killing her mother and the newborn child arose her urge to rescue lives. Death and birth are closely associated in her childhood fantasies. As a child she certainly heard about pain and danger at the times of her mother's numerous deliveries. This was responsible also for her extremely masochistic conception of the female role in the sexual act. Her own masochistic wishes had manifested themselves during puberty in very sanguinary fantasies of violation. So great a danger for her ego lay in the fulfillment of these fantasies that she completely renounced her sexuality, and she could give expression to her maternal feelings only in the manner described. In her choice of work, then, she was serving two masters: her sense of guilt, and her masochism; she satisfied the latter by means of identification. I have in my possession a photograph of her with eight newborn babies in her arms—an ideal representation of motherhood.

In analysis I have come to know many professional women who were able to satisfy very warm and intense maternal feelings in their work, but who were prevented from having children of their own by a repudiation of their mothers' sexuality together with their own.

I should like to cite one of my own cases as an example of motherhood gone astray. Balzac's Louise as a patient would probably have resembled my case, a woman who sought treatment for nymphomania. From her fifteenth year on, she had given herself to any youth on hand; she was always unhappy and unsatisfied, but curiously enough, despite her puritanical upbringing, quite impenitent. Only extracts from her history can be cited here. The patient was twice forced into a respectable, middle-class marriage by friends who wanted to save her from a prostitute's life. Both marriages were, of course, unsuccessful. She had never had children. She was incapable of conceiving, and did not want children. The words "motherhood" and "motherliness" aroused her abhorrence and disgust, and this spread to all words ending in "hood" or "liness." An absolutely unmotherly woman, one would say. And yet—to betray at the outset the key to her long analysis—in her instinctual life she was nothing else but mother. All the youths to whom she gave herself represented her three younger brothers: she was always wanting to give her brothers something; she used to try taking them into her arms when they were little in the hope of attaining a genital union with them; in this she identified herself with her mother, from whom, at the same time, she took away the children.

In this case one can put the responsibility for the whole neurotic picture on the developmental processes of the preoedipal phase and an overstrong primary mother attachment. She was the only child for six long years—an extremely petted and pampered girl. Then she had to live through three of her mother's pregnancies in quick succession, and the withdrawal of her mother's love in favor of the newborn children. At these times she was always told the fiction of the child growing under the heart, and she was filled with bitter disappointment. The relationship between the little boys and her mother had in her mind a libidinal-sexual character; the mother-child unity (the child in the womb or at the breast) in which she in her childhood jealousy had wanted to play both roles, should accordingly be genitally satisfied in later life. She remained frigid because her fantasies excluded sexuality, and her feelings of guilt were kept in apparent abeyance, because by virtue of her maternal devotion she could deny her hostility toward the youngsters and thereby relieve her sense of guilt.

This case points to various psychic situations in which motherhood either completely denies sexuality, or uses it for its own ends (as in this case) to the detriment of sexual satisfaction; or sexuality may be accepted, but only under conditions which set aside and repudiate motherhood, as mentioned at the beginning of this paper; or, contrariwise, these very conditions must serve to satisfy the demands of motherhood. This may be expressed in the object choice—for example, in the acceptance exclusively of boyish, helpless men as love objects.

As an illustration I may cite another case from literature which made a great impression on me. It is taken from the book, *Aunt Tula,* by the well-known Spanish author, Miguel de Unamuno. Aunt Tula is obsessed with motherhood. Her whole relation to the world is maternal—and nothing but maternal. She regards anything that approaches sensuality or the erotic as despicable or ugly; but to the act of reproduction in another woman she gives the kind of attentive care that a farmer bestows on his crops, or a gardener on his flowers. Yet, it is only the product, the fruit that ripened under her watchful care, which she appropriates as her own, and to which she devotes herself in complete absorption. In this way she gains mental possession of a life which someone else has brought forth in pain. Aunt Tula is the psychological twin sister of our German midwife—only she is still more ruthless in the asexuality of her motherhood. She retains a lifelong hold on the children some other woman has borne for her, and—again more thoroughly consistent than the midwife—she cruelly lets the woman die after she has exhausted her function of childbearing. She even makes a child of the man: she kills his erotic attachment to her, and with iron determination steers him to another woman.

The author has described the complete severance of motherhood from erotism with fine poetical skill and power. One might very well ask how it is possible for a man to obtain such insight into the innermost depths of a woman's psyche.

Aunt Tula lets her sister marry the man whom she herself loves and by whom she is beloved. She arranges the marriage, urges them to have a child, and then takes complete charge of it. She drives her weak sister on from one childbirth to another until the sister dies from exhaustion and leaves the children to the care of Aunt Tula, their spiritual mother. Aunt Tula lives in her brother-in-law's house as the mother of his children and directs his sexual passion onto the servant, the "debased sexual object," who, in turn, is let slowly die after she has repeatedly borne children for Aunt Tula. Aunt Tula lays stress on her role as spiritual mother, and never lets the children imagine for a moment that she—the spiritual mother—conceived them in her body and gave them birth. The consciousness of the corporeal mother must always be present in the home, lest the pure, true motherhood of Aunt Tula be stained with a suspicion of physical participation. Occasionally the repressed longing breaks through, and Aunt Tula leaves the village, where she lives with her widowed brother-in-law, for the noisy city. "There is no real purity in the country. Purity develops only where people herd together in a dirty jumble of houses, where they can isolate themselves better. The city is a cloister of lonely people. But in the country the land brings everybody together, the earth on which nearly everyone lies down to sleep. And as for the animals—they are the ancient serpents of paradise. Back to the city!" But of the man who desires her she says, "He is still very childish in many ways. How may she bring him to be one of her children?"

Once again the unspiritual longing breaks the bonds of her spiritual motherhood. "She took her little nephew who was whining with hunger and shut herself in a room with him. Then she drew out one of her shriveled, virginal breasts—it was flushed and trembling as in a fever, shaken as it was by the heavy pounding of her heart—and she pushed the nipple into the baby's soft pink mouth, but his whining only grew the worse as his pale lips sucked on the tremulous desiccated nipple."

Aunt Tula's refusal to admit that she ever had a father who was co-responsible for her conception is masterfully drawn, and it agrees closely with our analytic knowledge. In her mind the really great and beloved father is Don Primitivo, her mother's brother and foster father. It is clearly brought out how Aunt Tula in her fantasy life had wanted to keep her mother's purity intact, just as she preserves her own, and that her relationship to the children is a repetition of her reaction in her relationship to her own mother. It is easy, therefore, for us to understand the following comments which Aunt Tula makes to her sister about Don Primitivo. "Always still and quiet with hardly a spoken word for us, he consecrated our life to the cult of the Holy Virgin, the Mother of God, and at the same time to the cult of our own mother and grandmother, his sister and mother respectively. He gave us a mother with a rosary, and you he taught how to be a mother." The fantasy of the mother's immaculate conception, of motherhood without a father, can be clearly recognized here—as a matter of fact the book describes Aunt Tula's memories of her childhood games with dolls which already contained the essence of the subsequent developments in this direction. One could continue thus to quote the entire book, which is to be warmly recommended to psychoanalytic readers.

15

The Psychology of Manic-Depressive States, with Particular Reference to Chronic Hypomania

(1933)

THE pioneer work of Freud, Abraham, Rado, and others has provided considerable insight into the processes of melancholia. A clinical picture of this condition having been achieved, it was natural to see what conclusions could be drawn from it and applied to manic states. However, as Freud himself pointed out, we have not yet found a satisfactory explanation of the mechanism by which melancholia is relieved by mania. We know, of course, that the manic-depressive psychoses offer a broad spectrum of variations, and that in the course of melancholia the so-called "manic triumph" may be entirely absent. We also know cases in which the typical succession of contrasting states, melancholia-mania, disappears, either through the absence of one or the other state, or through the interpolation of states in which the symptoms do not entirely correspond to either condition (mixed states).

Paper presented at the Twelfth International Psycho-Analytical Congress, Wiesbaden, 1932. First published as "Psychologie der manisch-depressiven Zustände insbesondere der chronischen Hypomanie" in the *Internationale Zeitschrift für Psychoanalyse*, 19:358-371, 1933.

In the analytic treatment of cyclic psychoses we find certain processes corresponding to these mixed states and I believe that by observing them we can achieve a better understanding of the manic state itself.

Rado (1927), in particular, has given an impressive description of a preliminary stage of melancholic depression in which the aggression of the narcissistically wounded ego is directed in accusation and protest against its surroundings. The depression then appears as the conclusion of an aggressive struggle against the outer world, which culminates in the aggression being turned against the self. The contrite ego gives itself up to masochistic expiation and self-punishment. After satisfying the punitive demands of the superego, it can then pass over into the "triumphal freedom of mania," as described by Freud.

But there are cases, by no means so simple and illuminating, where the rebellious attitude does not pass over into depression, but reappears periodically, or finds immediate discharge in a manic state. We are also uncertain as to the mechanism whereby, in certain cases, the mania is not preceded by any depression. Here we see nothing of the harsh discipline of the superego, over which the manic ego should triumph, nothing of the inner conflict, and nothing of the self-punishment which we assumed to be the prerequisites of the manic liberation.

Over whom, in such cases, does the manic ego triumph? How is the triumphant unity between ego and superego established without any previous depression? And how can we explain the state of euphoria solely on the basis of the successful shift of power within the psychic organization, in line with Freud's explanation?

I had an opportunity of studying a case of cyclic psychosis during an intensive analytic treatment, in which my understanding of the clinical picture of this disorder was considerably facilitated by a lively transference. In the course of a lengthy treatment there was a periodic recurrence, as described by Rado, of states of intensely aggressive rebellion, which then passed over directly into a manic state, without the intervention of any noticeable depression. On closer observation, this woman patient gave evidence of a distinctly paranoiac character in her gestures of rebellion. She felt that she was being persecuted and ill-treated by me, that I did not love her; she reacted to my supposedly negative attitude toward her by furious aggression of a paranoid kind. I have the impression that this paranoiac element is present in all cases in which aggressive phases appear as constituent elements of the manic-depressive picture. As in the case I am describing, the aggression can be considered as a reaction to disappointment. The aggression provokes a reaction in the ego, but this cannot find an outlet in the formation of compulsive characterological reactions, as described by Abraham (1924) for the "free interval" of cyclic psychosis. This type of patient can, as mine did, fend off for a time the feeling of guilt resulting from her own aggressive attitude, by projecting the blame for this hatred and ill-treatment onto the outer world. She could then consider her own angry and hate-laden affects purely as a response to this ill-treatment. The economic advantage of such behavior lies in the alleviation of guilt feelings, and hence achieves a release from the inner tension. The ego can then proceed to develop the most intense activity against the outer world in order to ward off its apparent attacks.

I was able to observe the mastery displayed by my patient in dealing with any of the actual transference situations which were calculated to arouse her feelings of guilt. To give one example: when it appeared necessary for me to forego payment for the analysis, my patient, instead of being grateful, was overwhelmed by a flood of recollections of minor incidents that had occurred during the analysis, and which she was able to twist to suit her purposes with psychotic blindness. She maintained, for instance, that her analysis, and her whole future, had already been ruined by a telephone conversation which had curtailed her session by a few minutes. I had done this because of my deep antipathy for her. By casting the blame on me she was able to keep herself free from guilt and therefore also free from depression.

During the analysis I did, in fact, observe a few short-lived fits of gloom, which were so covered up by the rebellious state that one could not fail to consider the latter to be the defense mechanism against the superego and a lapse into melancholia.

Theoretically speaking, there were at the time several possible outcomes to this state of rebellion: the projective defense mechanism might become stabilized and the patient's illness would then, as we know, have passed over into a typical paranoia. In point of fact the analytic situation was for a while very dangerous, to the extent that I had the impression that a paranoia would develop in the course of treatment, so to say, under my very eyes.

Alternatively, the superego might prove stronger than the defense mechanism. The aggression would then inevitably be turned against the ego, and the period of rebellion would give way to melancholic remorse, as described by Rado.

But this patient's illness took another course. After a variable period of rebellion a very short, slightly depressive phase of tranquillity would supervene, during which she suffered from minor anxiety states and was tormented by countless anxiety dreams.

The patient would then embark on erotic relationships with men, in order to prove to me how easily she could dispense with my love. But at the same time she would become exceptionally active in soliciting my love, overwhelming me with flowers and other presents, and claiming that she had only just discovered how much love and kindness I had expended on her, and so forth. Out of this there developed the typical excited restlessness of the manic state in which—in my opinion—the apparently mature object relationships really represent a narcissistic delirium: "See how I am loved and admired by everyone!" It seems to me particularly important to stress the fact that the very situations which, in her former aggressive phase, had been used by the patient to demonstrate my dislike for her, now served to prove me a loving angel of redemption. Everything in herself that she had previously considered inferior—largely, she maintained, through my fault—now appeared to her to be especially admirable.

With this patient, penis envy in all its forms played an important part. Her whole life was, so to say, the symptomatic expression of penis envy and all that goes with it. Her occupation, her marriage, maternity, her love affairs—all were pressed into the service of this sole surviving feeling. The oral envy concealed behind the penis envy was laid bare in the course of analysis, and explained the nature of the various forms by which her manic excitation was expressed. For instance, her ceaseless flow of words, which prevented anyone else from speaking, was an active expression not only of oral satisfaction, but also of aggression: of "cutting someone short." In this symptom and in most of her others the determinants of both the oral and genital disorders were to be found.

The analytic case history of the patient was otherwise so banal that there is no necessity to record it in detail. I will therefore select only such concrete material as is relevant to my concept of mania.

The patient had two brothers, one two years older and the other two years younger than herself. Penis envy was therefore encouraged from both sides. When she was four years old, a sister was born. It was easy to recall the fits of rage and envy occasioned by the mother's feeding of her youngest child. On the other hand, she disregarded the anatomical deficiencies of the little sister, since her affective, envious interest was wholly directed to the newcomer's oral possession of the mother's breast. This was all the more remarkable in that the patient was, at the time of the sister's birth, passing through a phase of intensive genital exploration.

Through this displacement of her interest onto the oral process, she could not only appear to be uninterested in her sister's genitals, and therefore blind to her own penis deficiency, but could also deny her own genital injury. This behavior was repeated in her later childhood with regard to her other sister, older by eight years, to whose body she had paid more attention, since she had for a long time slept and bathed and shared her life with her. Nevertheless she maintained stubbornly that she had never seen her sister's genitals.

It became evident that the displacement of envy onto the oral level and the linking of oral and genital frustration had already occurred with reference to the younger brother, who had been favored both with the mother's breast and with male genitals. She was unable to console herself with the fact that she too had been breast-fed, as her mother had assured her, since only one frustration was thereby made good. This information from her mother seems to have provided a motive both for furious aggression against the mother and for a denial of her own inadequacy. Already in early childhood the patient had shown, in character traits and in a number of displacements, that she was trying to deny the injury she had not been able to surmount.

One dream that occurred in analysis during her manic phase is a good illustration of her conflict: my son—the object of her wildest jealousy—had two pipes in his mouth and with a friendly gesture offered her one for her own use. The meaning of the dream is self-evident: she need not regret her loss, since she obtains what she wishes (from the brother).

The patient's manic activities indicate, just as clearly as the dream, her intention to deny the injury and deprivation she believed she had suffered earlier, and to proclaim loudly that everyone loved her, and that her remarkable ability was recognized by the world, thereby justifying her in loving the object world. But this love lacked the true stamp of a genuinely positive object relationship, since it served only to shout down her desire for hatred and revenge.

Just as projection in the rebellious phase was motivated by the need to present her own aggression, with all its consequences of object loss and risk of punishment, as coming from the outer world, so the pursuance of the same tactics in the manic state enabled her to avoid aggression, since the compensation for the injuries and sufferings she had undergone was undertaken in the outer world. This grandiose denial made it unnecessary to hate the world and thus to accept punishment for this hatred. Here again there was an economic advantage in securing freedom from guilt.

The positive advantage of this tendentious coloring of reality in mania: "The world loves me and I possess everything," was gradually exhausted. The euphoric clamor grew weaker and weaker and after every such phase the patient relapsed into a fresh and, for her environment, painful period of rebellion.

It was interesting to note that analytic therapy attacked first the manic condition. It could be seen how the patient tried laboriously to set the apparatus of denial once more in action, but she was no longer capable of doing so, and then abandoned the attempt with the recognition: "It isn't really like that." She also revealed to me that in fact, in her heart of hearts, she had never really believed in all these wonders, and was always burdened, during the manic condition, by a depressive feeling that "there was something behind it all." It was obviously the same anxiety that had previously been hidden by aggression, then demonstrated in dreams, and finally shouted down during the mania.

In the further course of analysis the aggression became weaker, as did the projective mechanism. It rebounded against the professional reaction of the analyst, who had to maintain a total, or at least outward, calm and interpret the situation analytically, instead of responding to the patient's furious affects by the expected and deliberately provoked expression of ill-will that came from others in her environment. Slowly, under the influence of analysis, her noisy aggression was transformed into an anxiety-laden gloom. Instead of a period of rebellion, there arose a melancholic depression, full of self-reproach for her former aggression against me. Here too the analysis had interpreted the defense mechanism and laid bare the depression hidden behind it.

I should like to adduce a further case in support of the theoretical considerations to follow. It is a case that is completely atypical in the clinical picture of the manic-depressive disorder, but it can contribute much to the understanding of the problem under discussion.

It concerns a woman patient who for years had suffered periodically from severe depressions, which necessitated hospitalization under close supervision for fear of suicide. The medical picture was suddenly modified to a remarkable degree. The new condition corresponded to a typical paranoia, with one very concrete, so to say, central delusion around which the other persecutory fantasies were grouped. The diary of this patient came by chance into my hands, and provided some highly interesting material.

During one of the patient's melancholic phases her husband died of an intermittent illness. This event appeared to have made no impression on the patient. Entries in the diary were, indeed, lacking during the period of her deepest depression, though they covered the period when the state of gloom was breaking up, but the attitude of self-reproach was still evident. Even before the death of the husband these entries showed the typical melancholic self-accusations, that she did not love her husband sufficiently, that she was not worthy of him, and so forth. It was most surprising that her husband's death, contrary to all expectation, only temporarily augmented the burden of this self-reproach. The explanation lies in the diary. After a short while the idea appears in the entries that her husband was not dead. Wicked people were trying to keep him away from the patient, because they knew how much he loved and respected her. The patient noted how the husband was able to inform her by secret signs that he was still alive and that he had to conceal himself for fear of these people, and this was why he was thought to be dead. The patient now developed a typical paranoid system, in which she lived through the most complicated situations, all involving a secret life with her dead but, to her, living husband.

After some months we found entries in the diary that bore witness to the persistence of the paranoid fantasies: they continued to relate to the husband, but with the difference that the loving protector had now become an increasingly cruel persecutor. The world was full of secret indications that pointed to the husband's continued existence, but now he was trying to terrify the patient in every possible way, to stir up her enemies against her, and so forth. It is striking to note how in these entries the persecutor becomes ever harsher and more relentless. During this phase the entries stopped.

I feel justified in considering this case of the transformation of the melancholic position into the paranoiac as an ego defense mechanism at a moment of extreme danger. Further identification with the dead man could only and inevitably have entailed the total annihilation of the ego. Fortunately the patient's ego obviously had at its disposal sufficient strength to shake off this dangerous identification and nullify the introjective process. It seems that this could only have been possible on one specific condition. The husband's actual death had diminished the patient's own aggression against him, so that her positive elements could come into play. In this projection she still remained tied to the object, but the ego experience of her own more positive attitude was attributed to the object, so that she could then accept love and tenderness from it in the outer world. The aggressive forces were later to prove to be the more powerful, but were still attributed to the object. As the paranoia developed, the patient was able to accept, as coming from the outside, all the aggression that, during her melancholia, had been acted out by inner forces in her inner life.

In this strange metamorphosis of the clinical picture we see how the patient was able, at the moment of greatest danger, to secure release from inner tension through projection. We can assume that the first stimulus to this modification arose from the narcissistically involved ego, which functioned as a signal of alarm in order to secure liberation from a fatal identification with the husband. We may also consider that the actual death of the object reduced the aggression and so led to a gentler disposition of the psychic organization.

This case demonstrates in particular that the attempt to resolve a psychic conflict by projection corresponds to a weaker state of ambivalence than in the process of introjection in melancholia. We saw that the reduction of ambivalence in this conflict was due to the indulgent, protective behavior of the object in the outer world. This behavior of the object was unchanged until an upsurge of aggression in the patient's own affective position transformed the protective friend into a persecuting enemy.

One gets the impression that a similar process occurred in the first-mentioned patient, even if the analogy appears, at first sight, to be rather far-fetched. In this case the ego appeared to be already provided with a sufficiently strong defense mechanism to be able to protect itself against the process of melancholic introjection, even though predisposed in that direction by a deep oral regression.

The rebellious behavior of my manic patient and the projection of her own aggression onto the outer world—during the analysis, onto me—can be considered as a lively struggle against the imminent danger of a deep depression.

This exhausts the analogy between the two patients. We have seen them both using projection, in the one case as a means of emerging from a depression, and in the other as a shield against falling *into* a depression.

Some years ago I was able to observe a case of severe melancholic depression, with suicide attempts, where a similar period of projected rebellion followed the end of the melancholic phase. In this patient the process of recovery made use of projection to enable the ego to establish a normal relationship to the outer world. She endeavored, through a specific defense mechanism, to correct her distorted relationship to the outer world by giving such a positive coloring to reality that she was able to deny any injury, and replace aggressive acts by noisy expressions of love, and all narcissistic wounds by a shrill emphasis on satisfaction.

I believe that this mechanism of denial underlies all mania. It has the same role in manic-depressive disorders as reaction formation in obsessions, projection in paranoia and phobias, and introjection in melancholia. It is an attempt to resolve an inner conflict, an attempt which should serve, in its complicated fashion, to deny the aggression of the id and thus forestall the harshness of the superego.

If this theory as to the nature of the manic mechanism should prove true, we should be able to make a slight addition to Freud's (1917) discovery of the nature of the "manic triumph" as the end phase of melancholia.

The mere fact of the continuation of such an entirely pathological process, as mania is, indicates that the conflict is not over, but has taken on another form. In the melancholic process all psychic activity is taken over by the superego and the ego appears to submit passively. It may then fall a victim to the uninhibited cruelty of the superego and must suffer the final consequence of aggression, that is, death (suicide). If this is not the case, we may be justified in assuming that the lifesaving protective mechanism in the ego economy is mobilized to protect it against such cruelty and to set a limit to aggression. It is not too much to say that this protective mechanism becomes available to the ego from two sides. On the one side the all too harsh superego is corrupted, in Alexander's sense of the word, by the suffering and can therefore relax its harshness; on the other side, within the narcissistic libido of the ego, there are those positive forces which we have already found in the instinct of self-preservation. If the pressure from the superego relaxes, then these forces can find expression. Instead of suffering passively, the ego emerges in a state of active defense and betrays its activity in various forms that now constitute the modified picture of the illness.

In my view, mania is a similar form of activity undertaken by the now unburdened ego in which the potential energy of the melancholic process, instead of remaining anchored in the inner world, is transformed into kinetic energy in the outer world. The activity of the manic ego rests on a modification, through denial, of the outer world. The aggression of the id becomes therefore unnecessary, the aggression being also subjected to the process of denial.

As a contrast to the "manic triumph" and to acute mania, we have the so-called "chronic hypomania."

Up till now we have confined ourselves to clinical states, in which the pathological factors were clear. It remains an open question as to how far we can apply our observation to the so-called "chronic hypomania."

I was able to observe one woman analytically over a considerable period. Her personality seemed indeed strange, from the psychological viewpoint, until its inner workings were disclosed in the course of analysis. All the misfortunes with which her life had been richly laden passed over her without a trace: she reacted to every mischance with philosophic superiority and by emphasis on all the values that remained to her in life. One could not call this apathy, since she was noted for her effervescent temperament, always starting new friendships and new love affairs, always studying something new, and with success, yet everything around her seemed pale and colorless. In spite of her exuberant activity, there was something lifeless and cold in all her liveliness.

I had frequent opportunities of observing her lack of concern over her outward fate. During this period she was deserted both by husband and lover, lost a large part of her fortune, suffered the tragic fate of many mothers, when her son, to whom she clung, grew up and abandoned her in favor of another woman. Finally she experienced a narcissistic **wound** when I informed her that she could not become an analyst. Nothing in all this could disturb her euphoria; she immediately found a way out, sometimes by depreciating what she had just lost, sometimes by the establishment of new substitute values that nipped in the bud any reaction to loss, by denying its existence. The final effect was always: "I have not really lost anything."

I was able to see quite clearly, in this patient as well, how the whole mechanism of denial had started in connection with the birth of a brother, with the denial that she had suffered any loss by not having a penis.

In this connection her conduct had been so peculiar that it had become almost a family legend. As a child, after a period of furious aggression against her little brother, she entered a new phase: she maintained that everything that she knew might be denied to her, was already hers. This developed over a period into a veritable pseudologia, in which she related all manner of fantastic stories, designed to show the extent of her possessions. Thus she once maintained, during her religious instruction, that God had given her Mount Ararat, and that she had built a little house there for her doll.

In later years she achieved a certain compromise with reality; although she still adapted it to suit her purpose, which was to assure a permanent denial of any deprivation and of her own aggression, she gave up constructing her fabricated stories. The neurotic element in the permanent effort at denial became apparent to her only in the course of analysis. It was also possible to uncover the strong oral component behind her penis envy.

This case of chronic hypomania also provided obvious support for the belief that the manic defense mechanism of denial represents an attempted solution by the ego that can be traced back to the narcissistic wound in the phallic phase of development.

I do not wish to be misunderstood: I am not maintaining that the etiology of mania has anything to do with it. On the contrary, I consider that all manic states are genetically linked with melancholia and look on the melancholic provocation as a prerequisite to the mobilization of the defensive processes in the ego, the most outstanding of which, and the most typical in the case of mania, is the mechanism of denial. It is only this latter that I associate with the phallic phase, in so far as analytic observation has shown us that it is precisely in this phase of libidinal development that the narcissistic ego disposes of the means of defense against injury and anxiety and the castration complex.

The process of denial in mania relates both to the outer world and to the promptings of the id, and is shown to be successful in both cases. Since it leads to control of aggression it can also be considered a fortunate solution with regard to the demands of the superego. In many cases the process can be initiated only after the harshness of the superego has been overcome by melancholic suffering (manic triumph); in other cases it is able, at periodic intervals, temporarily to repress the depressive-aggressive impulses. Sometimes this protective mechanism is able so to nip in the bud all melancholia, that it never makes an appearance: this continuous activity of the defense mechanism is displayed in chronic hypomania. We are shown that we are dealing with a defense mechanism by a surplus, an excess of expenditure, an exaggeration and restlessness. If we look more closely at the real nature of the values created by this manic industry, we note the hollowness of their success in comparison with the energy expended, how the love relationships lack warmth, in spite of their apparent passion, how sterile the performance in spite of continuous productivity. This results from the monopolization of psychic energy in service of the goal we have described: the silencing of the narcissistic wound, of aggression, and guilt reactions. In all these areas mania achieves its purpose.

A few further remarks are called for with regard to identification in mania. Nunberg (1932), in his *Principles of Psychoanalysis*, maintains that identification is not found in cases of mania. I believe that this is true of serious manic states, in the so-called *mania gravis*. In the cases I have analyzed identification played an important part. They were mostly of bisexual character. I remember in this connection an interesting observation by B. Lewin (1933) whose acutely manic patient experienced the triumphant coitus in both identifications. I have myself observed cases in which the manic process was inaugurated by a successful and positive identification.

One patient who suffered from periodic depressions had to

interrupt her analysis shortly before its termination as a result of
my departure. After a short depressive phase, in which she was,
however, consciously angry with me, there supervened for the
first time in the course of her illness a manic condition. She went
abroad, enjoyed somewhat stormily the pleasures of life, traveled
under an assumed name ("French"), and related an entirely
imaginary life story to the many acquaintances that she readily
acquired. When she returned, it appeared in analysis that all the
details she had related were compatible with *my* life, and that the
name "French" actually represented a variant of "Deutsch." This
patient was able to ward off the melancholic introjection by
accepting the aggressive character of the identification and
identifying with me in all the characteristics and possessions that
she supposed she would lose. In this way she was able to deny
her loss and remain free from aggression.

In both cases that have been mentioned here, the patient with
the diary, and the patient with the cyclic psychosis, I have tried
to show how in the course of the illness the ego attempted in
various ways to settle its inner conflicts. In the case of the patient
with the diary, the melancholic process was relieved by a paranoia.
The activity was made evident by the nature of the projection.
The second patient also made use of projection for a while, until
another, more favorable mechanism of solution came into operation, namely, mania.

In the analysis of the manic patient, as in the case I have
described as chronic hypomania, the threads of analysis led back
to childhood situations, in which the denial of the anatomical
distinction between the sexes played an important part. This
denial is, as we know from the analysis of both men and women,
a constituent of the castration complex. (See A. Angel's article
[1934] on optimism.)

In both manic patients this denial had contributed to their
character formation and had finally become a protective weapon
against the narcissistic injury inflicted by the outer world and
also against their own aggression and thus, indirectly, against
the demands of the superego.

There remain two questions: one concerns the origin of chronic
hypomania; the other is why, in some cases of cyclic psychosis, a

mania develops while in others it does not. These questions cannot, in my opinion, be answered solely by the disposition of the libido. According to my own experience and that of others, I am convinced of the oral disposition of the clinical picture, more particularly in consideration of its genetic identity with melancholia. The motivating factor in the manic condition lies, however, in the management of the narcissistic forms of the ego and makes use of the active energy that the ego has been able to build up in childhood, during the phallic phase of overcoming anxiety by a denial of castration.

16

Don Quixote and Don Quixotism

(1937)

If I were to treat the epos of Don Quixote as if it were the clinical history of a mental patient, I should preface it with the following anamnesis. Alonzo Quixano, a petty noble of the Spanish province of La Mancha, became enamored, late in life, of Aldonza Lorenzo, a peasant girl of Toboso. In this love relationship our good man showed himself no great hero. In the twelve years during which his heart was filled to overflowing with love's longing, Alonzo ventured scarcely four times to gaze upon the face of his beloved, and on each of these occasions appeared so overcome with apprehension and embarrassment that any sort of active courtship on his part was quite out of the question. All the more did his fantasy become inflamed and mirror before him the most valiant and forthright proofs of his masculinity as a substitute for his obviously severe disturbance of potency.

Alonzo's scanty life history nevertheless reveals that his very choice of love object might explain a good many of his difficulties. The good maid of Toboso was a country Brünhilde, of whom the chronicle narrates that she had "a voice loud enough for three, and in hurling the iron bar she was the equal of the strongest fellow in the place."

Read at the Thirteenth International Psycho-Analytical Congress, Lucerne, August 28, 1934, and published first in the *Psychoanalytic Quarterly*, 6:215-222. 1937.

Our hero, on the other hand, was no Siegfried. His libidinal make-up is revealed by this brief extract from his past history: a passive-feminine individual, impotent probably all his life, in whom the preclimacterium[1] obviously stimulated sexual desire but at the same time gave rise to a fresh access of passive feminine strivings. Alonzo displays in his love episode the typical behavior of a boy in early adolescence. In his later disorder so much of the material stems directly from puberty, so often is the great earnestness of his actions a replica of boyhood games, that despite the violent gusts of regression which sweep his emotional life, it is puberty, never wholly transcended and still an active force, that represents the *Leitmotif* of his existence.

Disillusioned, mortified, humiliated, Alonzo withdraws from life in a riot of inferiority feelings, and gradually, in the course of days and nights undoubtedly fraught with anxiety and depression, his real personality vanishes. In fantasy, that activity which causes reality to disappear, there is born in place of the mortal Alonzo the immortal Don Quixote.

All the threads which once linked Alonzo with the material world are severed. Aldonza is abandoned, but as analogue to her actual semblance there comes into being the resplendent Princess Dulcinea del Toboso, the most perfect creature in the world. It is to be supposed that through the preceding twelve years of ill-starred love, the overvaluation and idealization of the loved one had been slowly increasing at the expense of our hero's own ego. Dulcinea thus becomes part of the great edifice of narcissistic compensation in which Don Quixote's immortality has its being.

With the relinquishing of the *real* object there takes place a repression of all instinctual drives. "Have you ever seen knights errant eating?"—so runs the question, the negative reply to which symbolizes the entire ascetic habitus of Don Quixote. Nothing that is "human, all too human" is allowed to touch him. Love for and fidelity to Dulcinea stand guard over sexuality and make possible its complete repression. Even the most primitive anal

[1] Don Quixote was fifty years of age at the time.

needs are subjected to this asceticism—definite evidence of which is discoverable in a number of tragicomic situations.

All cathexes, from the most primitive instinctual drives to the energies which bring the ego into contact with reality, are withdrawn and become agglomerated within the ego into a single narcissistic force. It would seem that the first step therein was an overcompensation for the severe frustration of his love life, and that the phase of severe introversion served to minimize, through fantasy, the various deprivations which the external world on the one hand, and his inhibited masculinity on the other, had imposed upon him. His narcissistic needs could obviously not be satisfied by any merely rowdy activity, nor by his quite considerable intelligence. For gradually his fantasy forsakes the real world of objects, and the excessive accumulation of undisposable narcissistic libido throws him back far into his infantile past. The severely humiliated and deflated ego succumbs in favor of a newly arisen ego ideal, and does this so completely that the tension between ego and ego ideal which is necessary to self-criticism disappears. It now is possible for Don Quixote to enjoy the untrammeled possession of all the powers and attributes which his ego ideal demands of him.

There is no doubt that in connection with this impoverishment of the ego in the interest of the ego ideal, reality testing likewise undergoes impairment. For clearly the critical faculty which originates in the tension between ego and ego ideal has a particularly important share in the process which we call reality testing. Only the socialized ego ideal, that which seeks in the world of reality for possibilities of identification and measures itself in accordance with the standards of the external world, will be able to contribute its share to reality testing. An ego ideal which owes its existence to the withdrawal of object libido to such an extent as in Don Quixote is beyond any adaptation to reality.

Scarcely any other epic in history has understood with such magnificent intuition, or depicted as has Cervantes in his *Don Quixote,* the tragedy of the narcissistically conditioned "world catastrophe."[2]

2 See Freud (1911). What in the case of Cervantes the intuition of the poet had created, in the case of Freud the genius of the scientific observer had

With the loss of the object world, Don Quixote retreats through identification into the age of chivalry, an age not only past and gone but devaluated by counterfeit idealization. We understand that behind the historical past there is concealed an individual one.

When Don Quixote returns to reality from his lengthy journey through the realms of fantasy, this reality has already undergone a process of reconstruction. It is now identical with the world with which Don Quixote has become acquainted through the medium of books. In his renewal of his boyhood the fifty-year-old has lost himself so completely in the events and experiences of the age of chivalry that for him this has become the present-day world. He has made the brave heroes of that time his ideal which he substitutes for his earlier ego.

In consequence of the dissolution of the world of reality, Don Quixote finds no longer open the path of retreat from his fanciful playing at knight-errantry, or from the entire imaginary world of magic which ordinarily the boy abandons in favor of reality. Instead, our hero in his madness betakes himself into the depths of a still longer forgotten past, into the practice of the magic whereby the young child, like the savage, is himself able to cast a spell over the things of the material world and himself believes in this enchantment. Does not Don Quixote's lunacy remind one of the infant in his play, to whom the horsie which he has made himself out of paper seems perhaps more real than the real one? Is not Don Quixote's faith in his ego ideal perhaps comparable to the megalomanic self-importance of the child?

With what intuitive genius the creator of Don Quixote has recognized the genesis of this delusional structure is apparent from the following situations:

Twice in the course of his madness Don Quixote renounces his delusional system. One of these occasions is when Sancho

---

discovered. The delusions of the paranoiac Schreber and the immortal, creatively conceived fantasies of Don Quixote spring from the same origins in the unconscious. Epos and delusional systems alike build upon the ruins of the world of reality which has been abandoned, a more satisfying world of fantasy and delusion.

Panza, with deliberate braggadocio, promises to produce Dulcinea for him in actual fact. In his expectation of the fantasied loved one there awaken lively feelings toward her who once was Aldonza. What narcissistic magic has accomplished is removed from under this spell by the power of object love. The longing for the real object breaks through his madness, and with eyes from which illusion has been stripped, Don Quixote gazes on the spot in the woods where he was to have experienced Dulcinea's enchantment and wishes for the presence of the real Aldonza. What he actually saw, however, was only a strange and ugly wench whom Sancho Panza had foisted upon him.

On a second occasion it is actually experiencing the proximity of death that shatters the delusion of narcissistic immortality.

Don Quixote, in his narcissistic arrogance, esteemed himself immortal, and in this delusion had the courage of the young child who defies danger because it has no meaning for him. The realization of approaching death, the reconciliation with the inevitable, effects the return of Don Quixote to reality, so that his death becomes one of the most moving scenes in literature.

There remains little space at my disposal to consider Don Quixote's inseparable shadow, Sancho Panza.

The tragic Don Quixote is fully comprehensible only in the light of the comic Sancho Panza. If Don Quixote lives in the purified ego idealism of his madness, Sancho Panza forms a bridge to reality as a split-off part of Don Quixote, a fraction adapted to reality, and instinct-accepting rather than instinct-denying. The arid asceticism of Don Quixote would have long since driven him to the point of death, indeed, had not the assertion of robust motherly instinct on the part of Sancho Panza accompanied his path. In clinical terminology Sancho Panza is a case of "induced insanity." Sancho Panza's role as the embodiment of Don Quixote's instinct and reality acceptance consists, in fact, in his identification with Don Quixote's madness, thus endowing it with some reality value. He it is who takes care of Don Quixote's bodily needs. Through his own gluttony he forces Don Quixote to oral gratification of a reality sort, and through his ludicrous interest in anal functions he betrays his solicitude about the excretory activities of his master. Above all, however, he creates a bridge with reality by *believing* in Don Quixote's delusions, even though this belief—thus further emphasizing Sancho Panza's adaptation to reality—is confined to such parts only of these delusions as promise to bring him, Sancho Panza, some actual advantage. Of all the doublets which literature and plastic art have used to represent antitheses in man that together form a unity, this of the ascetic Don Quixote and the primitively instinct-ridden Sancho Panza is perhaps the most plastic.

Had Don Quixote, moreover, been able to impose his ego ideal upon a sufficiently large number of Sancho Panzas, he would have become, instead of a fool, a hero and a leader. For this, however, it would have been necessary for him to find room— alongside his exalted ascetic ideal—for instinctual gratification also, especially for the instincts of aggression. That he was unable to do this distinguishes the Don Quixote of the epos from those of political history of all epochs.

Of considerable significance is the aesthetic-affective impression with which the world responds to Cervantes' immortal epos. The "Donquixotesques"—to borrow a word from Unamuno—see in Don Quixote the wondrous prototype of a hero striving for the fulfillment of his ideal. They attribute to him the greatness and the truth which is so sadly lacking in the crude world of reality. This reality, under which they themselves suffer, seems to them shadowlike and grey, in comparison with the ego ideal which they harbor within them. For them, that which is ludicrous and in the nature of caricature in Don Quixote does not reside in him but in the crude world of reality which is incapable of sensing higher things, idealities, except in the form of windmills, illusions and fantasms.[3] The demand which these idealists make upon reality—that it shall adjust itself to their narcissistic ego

---

[3] See Freud (1905b, p. 232 footnote): "Don Quixote is originally a purely comic figure, a big child; the phantasies from his books of chivalry have gone to his head. It is well known that to begin with the author intended nothing else of him and that his creation gradually grew far beyond its creator's first intentions. But after the author had equipped this ridiculous figure with the deepest wisdom and the noblest purposes and had made him into the symbolic representative of an idealism which believes in the realization of its aims and takes duties seriously and takes promises literally, this figure ceased to have a comic effect."

ideal, instead, vice versa, of subordinating the latter to the demands of reality—this is the eternal quixotism of the human spirit. It is in poets, artists, and in fanatics that it is particularly well developed.

For those adjusted to reality, however, the pleasure derived from the aesthetic enjoyment of this epos lies in an altogether different direction. Their reaction is of the same order as the opinion of those critics who believe they see in Don Quixote the final disposition, by means of ridicule, of a past which has in any case lost its value. Historically considered, what is here meant is a historical past which has been desecrated by caricature; analytically regarded, however, it is a matter of the past in the psychic development of the individual. Are not, indeed, the idealistic demands which the ego imposes on itself in eternal conflict with instinct-asserting tendencies and with the necessity for adaptation to reality? Those who are adjusted to reality and accept rather than deny their instincts enjoy a pleasing triumph in seeing the ascetic ego ideal robbed of value by its caricature. This devaluation, however, refers equally to the infantile past in which the child believed himself the possessor of every perfection, and to the past in which the later ego ideal was formed on the pattern of the most perfect of all beings, the father. Is not this the world of the child, in which he believes in a godlike father, revealed as delusive as soon as the child discovers in the struggle with his own sexual drives the sexuality of the father, and therewith gives up his idealization of him? In this interpretation Don Quixote is an anachronistic caricature of the father, the father of the nonsexual period of the child, during which the father, asserting his own instincts, enforces asceticism upon the child.

Every disillusionment with and depreciation of the father flows, as we know, into the great stream of castration wishes which are directed against him. And so it is not surprising that even the outward semblance of Don Quixote should be like a symbol in a dream, in which the lean and lanky figure represents the castrated phallus.

But even in Don Quixote's antithesis, Sancho Panza, I see the ridiculous castrated father figure, a father of that later period in which the paternal demands upon the son are no longer of an ideal nature but require of him a practical adaptation to reality. In boyhood, characterized as it is by idealism, the father is usually endowed with the features of the plethoric, fat, harmless, impotent Philistine.

But does not this father have at his side the mother—the mother who is ever receptive to those ideals alone whereby, identifying herself uncritically with him, she holds firmly to a belief in his greatness, yet who at the same time, thanks to her maternal instinct, never loses sight of crude, practical reality? The strongly emphasized oral character of Sancho Panza, the fat, greedy, nurturing principle in the epos, the faithful fellow who in touchingly maternal manner takes care of Don Quixote's excretory functions, seems to me to be likewise a tenderly humorous ridiculing of the mother.

Suum cuique: to the Don Quixotesques, Don Quixote's idealistic struggle against a world consisting of windmills; to the realist, the depreciatory triumph of caricature; and to both a bit of pleasurable mastery of the infantile past! It is this that is the immortality of Don Quixote.

17

Absence of Grief

(1937)

*In publishing this paper I am fulfilling the wish of my beloved
friend, Dorian Feigenbaum. It is a tragic coincidence that my
last interchange of ideas with him was largely concerned with
the problem of death and with mourning. In his last letters to
me he pressed me repeatedly to have this paper, incomplete
as it is, published. At that time we had no suspicion that this
man, so full of the joy of life, so deeply and actively interested
in everything intellectual, would himself become so soon an
object of mourning to all those who knew and loved him.*

Mourning as a process is a concept introduced by Freud (1917)
who considers it a normal function of bereaved individuals, by
which the libido invested in the lost love object is gradually
withdrawn and redirected toward living people and problems.

It is well recognized that the work of mourning does not
always follow a normal course. It may be excessively intense,
even violent, or the process may be unduly prolonged to the
point of chronicity when the clinical picture suggests melancholia.

First published in the *Psychoanalytic Quarterly*, 6:12-22, 1937.

If the work of mourning is excessive or delayed, one might expect to find that the binding force of the positive ties to the lost object had been very great. My experience corroborates Freud's finding that the degree of persisting ambivalence is a more important factor than the intensity of the positive ties. In other words, the more rigorous the earlier attempts to overcome inimical impulses toward the now lost object, the greater will be the difficulties encountered in the retreat from that ultimately achieved position.

Psychoanalytic findings indicate that guilt feelings toward the lost object, as well as ambivalence, may disturb the normal course of mourning. In such cases, the reaction to death is greatly intensified, assuming a brooding, neurotically compulsive, even melancholic character. Indeed the reaction may be so extreme as to culminate in suicide.

Psychoanalytic observation of neurotic patients frequently reveals a state of severe anxiety replacing the normal process of mourning. This is interpreted as a regressive process and constitutes another variation of the normal course of mourning.

It is not my purpose to dwell at length upon any of the above-mentioned reactions. Instead, I wish to present observations from cases in which the reaction to the loss of a beloved object is the antithesis of these—a complete absence of the manifestations of mourning. My convictions are: first, that the death of a beloved person must produce reactive expression of feeling in the normal course of events; second, that omission of such reactive responses is to be considered just as much a variation from the normal as excess in time or intensity; and third, that unmanifested grief will be found expressed to the full in some way or other.

Before proceeding to my cases I wish to recall to your minds the phenomenon of indifference which children so frequently display following the death of a loved person. Two explanations have been given for this so-called heartless behavior: intellectual inability to grasp the reality of death, and inadequate formation of object relationship. I believe that neither of these explanations has exclusive validity. Should an intellectual concept of death be lacking, the fact of separation must still provoke some type of reaction. It is also true that although the capacity for an ultimate type of object relationship does not exist, some stage of object relationship has been achieved. My hypothesis is that the ego of the child is not sufficiently developed to bear the strain of the work of mourning and that it therefore utilizes some mechanism of narcissistic self-protection to circumvent the process.

This mechanism, whose nature we are unable to define more clearly, may be a derivative of the early infantile anxiety which we know as the small child's reaction to separation from the protecting and loving person. The children of whom we are to speak, however, were already of a sufficiently advanced age when the loss occurred that suffering and grief were to be expected in place of anxiety. If grief should threaten the integrity of the ego, or, in other words, if the ego should be too weak to undertake the elaborate function of mourning, two courses are possible: first, that of infantile regression expressed as anxiety, and second, the mobilization of defensive forces intended to protect the ego from anxiety and other psychic dangers. The most extreme expression of this defense mechanism is the omission of affect. It is of great interest that observers of children note that the ego is rent asunder in those children who do not employ the usual defenses, and who mourn as an adult does. Under certain circumstances an analogous reaction occurs in adults, and the ego takes recourse to similar defense mechanisms. The observations serve to show that under certain conditions forces of defense must be set in operation to protect a vitally threatened ego, when the painful load exceeds a threshold limit. Whether these defense mechanisms are called into operation depends upon the opposition of two forces: the relative strengths of the onrushing affects and of the ego in meeting the storm. If the intensity of the affects is too great, or if the ego is relatively weak, the aid of defensive and rejecting mechanisms is invoked. In the first instance quantitative considerations are of greater importance; in the second, special circumstances render the ego incapable of working through the mourning process. This might be the case, for example, should the ego at the time of the loss be subjected to intense cathexis on some other account. For instance, the ego

might be in a state of exhaustion by virtue of some painful occur-
rence just preceding the loss or, conversely, be engrossed in some
narcissistically satisfying situation. In brief, if the free energies
of the ego have been reduced by previous withdrawals for other
interests, the residual energy is unable to cope with the exigent
demands of mourning.

We speak then of a relative weakness of the adult ego induced
through experiences, as compared with the child's ego which is
weak by virtue of the stage of its development. We assume,
therefore, that a particular constellation within the ego is
responsible for the absence of a grief reaction; on the one hand
the relative inadequacy of the free and unoccupied portion of
the ego, and on the other hand a protective mechanism proceeding from the narcissistic cathexis of the ego.

But all considerations of the nature of the forces which
prevent affect are hypothetical and lead into the dark realms
of speculation. The questions—whether the psychic apparatus
can really remain permanently free from expressions of suffering,
and what is the further fate of the omitted grief—may be
better answered by direct clinical methods.

Among my patients there have been several who had previously experienced a great loss and who exhibited this default
of affect. I should like to present their stories briefly.

Case 1. The first case is that of a young man of nineteen. Until
the death of his mother, when he was five years old, this patient
had been a very much petted youngster with an affectionate and
undisturbed attachment to his mother, and with no special
neurotic difficulties. When she died, he showed no grief whatsoever. Within the family this apparently "heartless" behavior
was never forgotten. After his mother's death he went to live
with his grandmother where he continued to be a thriving,
healthy child.

His analysis revealed no special conflicts in his early childhood which could explain his affective behavior. He could
remember from his early years having been angry with his mother
for leaving him, but this anger did not exceed the normal
ambivalent reaction common to children under similar circum-

stances. The young man brought no other material which could throw light on the unemotional behavior of his childhood. His later life, however, revealed certain features which indicated the fate of the rejected affect. Two characteristics of his behavior were particularly striking: he complained of depression which had first appeared without apparent cause during puberty and which had recurred with no comprehensible motivation, and he was struck by the fact that he could break off friendships, and love relationships, with amazing ease, without feeling any regret or pain. He was, moreover, aware of no emotional disturbance so long as the relationships lasted.

These facts rendered comprehensible the fate of the repressed affect in childhood which interested us. Lack of emotion repeatedly recurred in analogous situations, and the rejected affect was held in reserve for subsequent appearance as "unmotivated depressions." The service performed by the postulated defense mechanism was purely in the interest of the helpless, little ego and contented itself with a displacement in time, and a dynamic distribution of the mourning.

Case 2. A thirty-year-old man came into analysis for the treatment of severe neurotic organic symptoms[1] of purely hysterical character and, in addition, a compulsive weeping which occurred from time to time without adequate provocation. He was already grown up when his very dearly loved mother died. When the news of her death reached him, in a distant university city, he departed at once for the funeral but found himself incapable of any emotion whatsoever, either on the journey or at the funeral. He was possessed by a tormenting indifference despite all his efforts to bring forth some feeling. He forced himself to recall the most treasured memories of his mother, of her goodness and devotion, but was quite unable to provoke the suffering which he wanted to feel. Subsequently he could not free himself from the tormenting self-reproach of not having mourned, and often he reviewed the memory of his beloved mother in the hope that he might weep.

[1] This case has been previously described as an example of conversion hysteria (Chapter 3).

The mother's death came at a time in the patient's life when he was suffering from severe neurotic difficulties: inadequate potency, difficulties in studying, and insufficient activity in all situations. The analysis revealed that he was having severe inner conflicts in relation to his mother. His strong infantile attachment to her had led to an identification with her which had provided the motive for his passive attitude in life. The remarkable reaction to his mother's death was conditioned by several factors. In his childhood there had been a period of intense hate for the mother which was revived in puberty. His conscious excessive affection for his mother, his dependence upon her, and his identification with her in a feminine attitude were the neurotic outcome of this relationship.

In this case, it was particularly clear that the real death had mobilized the most infantile reaction, "she has left me," with all its accompanying anger. The hate impulses which had arisen in a similar situation of disappointment in his childhood were revived and, instead of an inner awareness of grief, there resulted a feeling of coldness and indifference due to the interference of the aggressive impulse.

But the fate of the omitted grief is the question of chief interest for us in the analytic history of this patient. His feeling of guilt toward his mother, which betrayed itself even in conscious self-reproaches, found abundant gratification in severe organic symptoms through which the patient in his identification with his mother repeated her illness year after year.[2] The compulsive weeping was the subsequent expression of the affect which had been isolated from the concept—"the death of mother." Freud in "The History of an Infantile Neurosis" (1918) describes a similar fate for an inhibited expression of grief. The patient relates that he felt no suffering on hearing the news of his sister's death. The omitted suffering, however, found its substitute in another emotional expression which was quite incomprehensible, even to the patient himself. Several months after his sister's death he made a trip to the region where she had died. There he sought out the grave of a well-known poet whom he

[2] Fenichel (1931b) speaks of a "repression" in intense grief "wherein perhaps the mechanism of identification with the lost (dead) object plays a role."

greatly admired, and shed bitter tears upon it. This was a reaction quite foreign to him. He understood, when he remembered that his father used to compare his sister's poems to those of this poet.

The situation in which the affect of Freud's patient broke through to expression had direct bonds of association with the factors which had originally been repressed. In my patient the compulsive affect had been completely isolated from the original situation.

The identification with the mother which was such a preponderant factor in the libidinal economy of our patient was perhaps the most important motive for the refusal of the ego to grieve, because the process of mourning was in great danger of passing over into a state of melancholia which might effect a completion of the identity with the dead mother through suicide. When the analysis succeeded in bringing the patient into the situation of omitted affect, the danger of suicide became very actual. So we see that, in this neurotic individual there developed in addition to the existing pathological emotional conflict, a process of defense serving as protection to the severely threatened ego.

Case 3. A man in his early thirties without apparent neurotic difficulties came into analysis for nontherapeutic reasons. He showed complete blocking of affect without the slightest insight. In his limitless narcissism he viewed his lack of emotion as "extraordinary control." He had no love relationships, no friendships, no real interests of any sort. To all kinds of experiences he showed the same dull and apathetic reaction. There was no endeavor and no disappointment. For the fact that he had so little success in life he always found well-functioning mechanisms of comfort from which, paradoxically enough, he always derived narcissistic satisfaction. There were no reactions of grief at the loss of individuals near to him, no unfriendly feelings, and no aggressive impulses.

This patient's mother had died when he was five years old. He reacted to her death without any feeling. In his later life, he had repressed not only the memory of his mother but also of everything else preceding her death.

From the meager childhood material brought out in the slow, difficult analytic work, one could discover only negative and aggressive attitudes toward his mother, especially during the forgotten period, which were obviously related to the birth of a younger brother. The only reaction of longing for his dead mother betrayed itself in a fantasy, which persisted through several years of his childhood. In the fantasy he left his bedroom door open in the hope that a large dog would come to him, be very kind to him, and fulfill all his wishes. Associated with this fantasy was a vivid childhood memory of a bitch which had left her puppies alone and helpless, because she had died shortly after their birth.

Apart from this one revealing fantasy there was no trace of longing or mourning for his mother. The ego's efforts of rejection had succeeded too well and had involved the entire emotional life. The economic advantage of the defense had had a disadvantageous effect. With the tendency to block out unendurable emotions, the baby was, so to speak, thrown out with the bath water, for positive happy experiences as well were sacrificed in the complete paralysis. The condition for the permanent suppression of *one* group of affects was the death of the *entire* emotional life.

Case 4. This was a middle-aged woman without symptoms but with a curious disturbance in her emotional life. She was capable of the most affectionate friendships and love relationships, but only in situations where they could not be realized. She had the potentiality for positive and negative feelings but only under conditions which subjected her and her love objects to disappointment. In order not to complicate the presentation I shall confine myself to describing the phenomena pertinent to our problem. For no apparent reason the patient wept bitterly at the beginning of every analytic hour. The weeping, not obsessional in character, was quite without content. In actual situations which should produce sadness she showed strikingly "controlled," emotionless behavior. Under analytic observation the mechanism of her emotional reactions gradually became clear. A direct emotional reaction was impossible. Everything was experienced in a complicated way by means of displacements, identifications, and projections in the manner of the "primary processes," described by Freud in *The Interpretation of Dreams*. For example: the patient was highly educated and had a definite psychological gift. She was very much interested in the psychic life of others, made a study of it, and used to bring detailed reports of her observations. On investigation one discovered that what she had observed in the experience of another individual did not really pertain to him but represented a projection of her own unconscious fantasies and reactions. The true connection was not recognized for want of a conscious emotional reaction.

She found vicarious emotional expression through identification, especially with the sad experiences of others. The patient was capable of suffering a severe depression because something unpleasant happened to somebody else. She reacted with the most intensive sorrow and sympathy, particularly in cases of illness and death affecting her circle of friends. In this form of experience we could trace the displacement of her own rejected affects.

I am inclined to regard this type of emotional disturbance as schizoid and have the impression that it is a not infrequent type of reaction, which in its milder form usually passes unnoticed.

In the analysis of our patient one could discover how the displaced emotional discharges were related to early unresolved experiences. The original grievous experience was not a death but a loss in the divorce of her parents.

It gradually became clear that she had actually sought out the situations in which she had an opportunity to share the unhappiness of others, and that she even felt a certain envy because the misfortune had happened to another and not to herself. In such instances one is inclined to think only of masochistic tendencies as responsible. Certainly the gratification of masochism must play a role.

Observation of this patient, however, directed my attention in another direction. I believe that every unresolved grief is given expression in some form or other. For the present I limit the application of this *striving for realization* to mourning and am convinced that the unresolved process of mourning as described by Freud (1917) must in some way be expressed in full. This striving to live out the emotion may be so strong as to have an effect analogous to the mechanism which we see in criminal behavior from feelings of guilt (Freud, 1923), where a crime is committed to satisfy unconscious guilt feelings, which preceded the crime instead of following it. Analogous is the situation in which suppressed affect following a loss seeks realization subsequently. We must assume that the urge to realization succeeds under the impetus of an unconscious source of affect-energy exactly as in the case of the criminal who is at the mercy of his guilt feelings. I suspect that many life stories which seem to be due to a masochistic attitude are simply the result of such strivings for the realization of unresolved affects. Our last-mentioned patient was a particularly clear example of this assumption.

The process of mourning as reaction to the real loss of a loved person *must be carried to completion*. As long as the early libidinal or aggressive attachments persist, the painful affect continues to flourish, and vice versa, the attachments are unresolved as long as the affective process of mourning has not been accomplished.

Whatever the motive for the exclusion of the affect—its unendurability because of the ego's weakness, as in children, its submission to other claims on the ego, especially through narcissistic cathexis, as in my first case, or its absence because of a previously existing conflict with the lost object; whatever the form of its expression—in clearly pathological or in disguised form, displaced, transformed, hysteriform, obsessional, or schizoid—in each instance, the quantity of the painful reaction intended for the neglected direct mourning must be mastered.

I have already postulated a regulator, the nature of which is not clear to me. I have thought that an inner awareness of inability to master emotion, that is, the awareness by the ego of its inadequacy, was the motive power for the rejection of the emotion or, as the case may be, for its displacement.

In any case the expediency of the flight from the suffering of grief is but a temporary gain, because, as we have seen, the necessity to mourn persists in the psychic apparatus. The law of the conservation of energy seems to have its parallel in psychic events. Every individual has at his disposal a certain quantity of emotional energy. The way in which emotional impulses are assimilated and discharged differs in each individual and plays its part in the formation of the personality.

Probably the inner rejection of painful experience is always active, especially in childhood. One might assume that the very general tendency to "unmotivated" depressions is the subsequent expression of emotional reactions which were once withheld and have since remained in latent readiness for discharge.

18

Folie à Deux

(1937)

W<small>E</small> understand by *folie à deux,* in the strictest sense of the term, the transference of delusional ideas from a person psychically ill to another person psychically healthy, who then accepts the delusional system of the ill person and assimilates it into the content of his own consciousness. It is not yet completely clear to us what enters into the psychological genesis of the induction, in addition to dispositional factors, close companionship, and all the other factors through which *folie à deux* is known to arise. The deeper psychological mechanisms which result in the psychic dependence on and identification with the primarily diseased person must still be subjected to analysis in every case.

In addition to the individual adoption of the psychic contents by one person from another, we also find the process as a mass phenomenon, where entire groups of psychically healthy people are carried away by psychically diseased members of the group: world reformers and paranoiacs, for example. Indeed, great national and religious movements of history and social revolutions have had, in addition to their reality motives, psycho-

First published as "Über das induzierte Irresein (folie à deux)" in the *Internationale Zeitschrift für Psychoanalyse,* 23:470-478, 1937; in English in the *Psychoanalytic Quarterly,* 7:307-318, 1938.

logical determinants which come very close to the pathological processes of *folie à deux*.

In this presentation, I have limited myself exclusively to clinical observations and have chosen, from among a number of cases, a few in which I shall make a special attempt to clarify the differences between hysterical and psychotic forms of *folie à deux*.

I

Many years ago, while associated with the Viennese Psychiatric Clinic, I published a summary of a number of cases of *folie à deux* (1918), and I shall take from this publication one case which affected a group of three members of the same family:

In 1918 there was admitted to the Psychiatric Clinic in Vienna a family, consisting of a mother, a daughter, and a son, all suffering from the same symptom complex. The husband, father of the children, had gone to the front in 1915. Since 1916 there had been no news of him. According to a notification, not completely verified, he had been killed. The uncertainty and the anxiety about the fate of her husband, to whom she was very devoted, had aroused great turmoil and severe depression in the wife. These reactions were also manifested by her two children, with whom she had a particularly tender relationship.

For several months the woman had declared obstinately that her husband was alive and would soon come home. He had, she said, a position in the Swedish Consulate from which she received frequent written communications; moreover, an aristocratic rich family was taking care of her, was preparing a villa for her, and would buy her a car. She had connections with all the state authorities through this family, was plentifully supplied with food, and was about to move into a very elegant apartment prepared for her by the wealthy family in their own house. Her husband was to enjoy all this wealth after his return. A son of the wealthy family was to marry her daughter; a glorious future spread before her own son. The patient's two children shared in every detail their mother's delusions. Her relatives recognized these assertions as delusional, and had the three persons brought to the clinic.

Here was an exceptionally vivid pseudologia phantastica in triplicate, the elaboration of a *folie à trois* in which each could gratify his own wishes. As soon as one member of the family was ready to correct an error, another introduced his ideas, and perpetuated a cycle. During the treatment of all three I observed that if I succeeded in correcting the ideas of one patient, he or she very soon tended to allow himself to be deluded again, but only in certain directions. The son, for example, abandoned the fantasy of a rich marriage for his sister, but not the fantasy in which he was to attain the "great position" of his father. The same was true of the others who shared the delusion.

II

A seventeen-year-old girl came for psychoanalytic treatment with a diagnosis of incipient schizophrenia. Her father said that the girl had always been peculiar, preoccupied, and unsociable. Her mother had died when the child was ten years old. He had then, without assistance, assumed the task of her upbringing, and was very seldom separated from her. In the course of the last year he had made the acquaintance of a young woman and had revealed to his daughter his intention of marrying. The daughter had welcomed this proposal with great pleasure and had become very much attached to her future stepmother. After the marriage had taken place, the girl began to withdraw more and more from reality and to show changes in her personality. She sat motionless for hours at a time, laughed frequently without ascribable cause, lost contact with other people, and often gave vent to violent outbursts of anger, especially against her father.

The preceding summer the family had spent their vacation in a small Tyrolean village, where they had had a summer house years before. This was the first time the father had gone there since the death of his wife. In the little village there had lived for many years a psychotic man, who asserted that he was the Archduke Rudolph, the former heir to the Austrian throne who had died tragically while still a young man. Among the villagers in Austria there arose from time to time the rumor that the Archduke Rudolph had not died and that he would one day come back. The delusion of the paranoiac was founded on this rumor.

The girl now began to abandon her muteness, allied herself with the mentally sick man, declared that she was completely convinced he was the Archduke Rudolph, and that she would now devote her life to helping him establish his claims. No argument had any effect on her, and the doctors consulted advised that she be committed to an institution.

During a six-months' analysis I brought the patient to the point where she gave up the delusional idea, but I had, nevertheless, the impression that she was schizophrenic. Her father did not agree with this diagnosis, asserted that the patient was cured, and interrupted the treatment. I heard accidentally that the delusional idea did not reappear, but that the patient remained in a stuporous state.

We are interested here only in the psychological basis of her induced delusional idea. The analysis led directly to a "family romance"[1] that the patient had created during her childhood. In the Tyrolean village where she usually spent her vacations as a child, there was an ancient castle belonging to an aristocratic family. In her childhood the patient had created a fantasy, elaborated in the typical manner, that she was the daughter of this family. The analytic interpretation of such a "family romance" is known to psychoanalysts and need not be discussed here in detail. It was a reaction to her infantile disappointment in her love for her father. On returning to this scene of her childhood some years later, desertion by her father, through his

[1] The term "family romance," as used by Freud, is the name for fantasies of different and manifold content, that are related to one another by their invariable connection with the descent of the person imagining them. The commonest content of the "family romance" is: "I am not my parents' child"; sometimes, "not my father's (or mother's) child." This negative statement is then followed by a positive one, in answer to the question: "Whose child am I, then?" There are two typical, repeatedly recurring versions. The commoner is: "I am of higher birth." The other: "I am of lower birth," is rarer.

The "family romance" is an extremely common fantasy, and scarcely a single child does not experience it in one form or another. The motives for such fantasies are many and various. The provocation is always a disappointment, and the fantasy serves to compensate the child for deprivations he has suffered. See Freud (1909a) and Deutsch (1930a).

marriage, had become a cruel reality. The patient sought at first to find solace in her stepmother's love, but again disappointed, she withdrew entirely into introversion and was already in a completely autistic state when she came to the summer place. The memories associated with the place revived the old fantasy of the "family romance." The earlier fantasy of childhood had been warm with object relationships, although in an introverted form. Later, this fantasy had also perished in the *Weltuntergang* of her emotional life. Under the circumstances, and in the familiar setting, traces of the childhood fantasy were repetitively revived, but now in a psychotic manner. What had formerly been fantasy and had perished, was now rebuilt in the outer world as a delusion. The mechanism was not the suggestive influence exerted by the mentally sick man, nor an identification with him. The identification related merely to the delusional creation and lay in the fact that the content of his delusion was so close to her original fantasy. The analytic interpretation of the adopted delusion reads: "If it is true that one can be the disowned child of high-born parents and have a justifiable claim to a throne, then it is also true that I am unjustly disowned and have a right to the old castle of my former daydreams."

This case shows a particular mechanism of the induction of a delusional idea which is completely independent of the inducing object, and has as a foundation an already-existing psychic situation.

III

The third case is a *folie à deux* between a mother and daughter. There was no psychoanalytic treatment in this case. The material is taken from a case history in this country which was kept over a period of twelve years by a very conscientious social worker. This social worker was a particularly clever, intuitive, warmhearted person, fortunately untouched by any knowledge of psychoanalysis or psychological terminology. This lack of knowledge makes the case history especially objective and valuable.

The social worker took charge of the child when she was ten, after the death of the child's father in an accident. The mother obviously had paranoia, but dissimulated so cleverly that she was never institutionalized. Since she took excellent care of the child, there was never any necessity during the twelve years for separating the mother from her daughter.

The mother's delusion was that enemies wanted to separate her from her daughter; she had to save the child from danger and return to the home of her own childhood, to her mother in Holland. Her entire life was built around this plan to return to Holland with her daughter. Enemies prevented her from accomplishing this, the scheme of her enemies being worked out in a typically paranoid way. She gave lack of money as the reason for the postponement of her trip. Whenever she did collect the necessary amount, she made the excuse that she could not leave until she had made some arrangements about her husband's grave and provided for its future care. She obviously had an additional delusion which did not permit her to leave America—that is to say, her husband.

She lived in perpetual worry that people, men and women, would take her child away and prevent her daughter from going with her to Holland. *De facto* this meant: destroy the erotic bond between her and her daughter. The twofold course of her homosexuality is interesting. The enemies were women, above all, social workers. The actual danger to the daughter, however, lay in men. Her chief anxiety centered upon a married man with many children, with whom her daughter was having a love affair. But it was his *mother* who was using the love affair to take her daughter away from her. The daughter had had in fact a love affair with this man but she soon broke the relationship for the sake of her mother and morality.

The daughter might be seen at times—especially after a quarrel with her mother—in a half-dazed condition, introverted, wandering around the streets of the city, searching for the married, tabooed man. She always returned to her mother in deep remorse, to resume the delusional plan for the journey and to try everything to make their departure possible, but also to prevent it, following the pattern of her mother's delusional idea. Finally she became engaged to a younger man, but put off her marriage for four years because she could not bring herself to frustrate by her marriage her mother's delusional obsession. At times she gave the impression that she was only making concessions to her mother's delusion under the pressure of a severe feeling of guilt toward her. Again she would accept her mother's delusion as reality—especially after any particularly strong impulse toward freeing herself from her mother.

The case history showed that the mother had left her husband in America when the child was two, and had lived in Holland with the child for four years. Obviously, she had the wish even then to separate the child from her father in order to possess her completely—probably as a repetition of an earlier bond with her own mother. One observes that she returned to her husband, and that after his death she elaborated an ambivalence conflict in a delusional manner, gave her homosexual bond with her daughter the *content* of a persecutory delusion, and then, in an endless split, sought to separate the child from her dead father, represented specifically in this case by his grave in America and by the married man with whom the daughter was in love.

I am acquainted with the mother only from the case history. The daughter I know personally. She told me that she spent her childhood very happily with her mother in Holland. She could not remember whether she ever thought about her father, but recollected well that when she came to America as a six-year-old girl, she was the first to recognize him at the dock, "as if he had always been with me."

She had often seen her mother vex her father with her notions. He frequently took up his hat to leave, and the patient was afraid that he would desert her mother, but he remained with her, "just as I do now." This identification with her father in relation to her mother was expressed by her at other times. Particularly clear was her assertion that she knew, if she left the man to whom she was engaged and went away with her mother, that she would always sit and fantasy how lovely it would be to go to him, to have his child. She already had the feeling that she preferred fantasy to reality. "I must not reproach myself with having deserted my mother."

There is a certain similarity between the psychological processes in this case and the one preceding it, namely: the delusional creation of the mother and the fantasy life of the daughter go in the same direction. In this case, however, over a period of twelve years, the mother did not succeed in drawing her daughter completely into the sphere of her delusion. The daughter's object relationships were not destroyed, as they were in the preceding case. On the one hand, the sublimation of her positive homosexual strivings through her relationship with the social worker, on the other, a continual attempt to realize a heterosexual relationship, saved her from the psychotic induction. What still bound her to her mother, however, and did not permit her any release from the influence of her mother's delusion, was the fact that her mother's delusion and her own repressed fantasy life, her hysteria, had a similar content. The fact that the mother's delusion corresponded to the oedipal fantasies of the girl resulted in a morbid bond, with the danger that in time, because of the girl's neurotic dependence, a psychotic *folie à deux* might arise.

IV

Two sisters attracted psychiatric attention after an attempt at double suicide by gas. The elder died soon afterward; the younger, who lived, was able to undergo a thorough psychoanalytic exploration.

The two sisters lived together after the death of their parents. The elder by fifteen years took the place of a mother with the younger; both were tenderly devoted to one another. The elder was always "peculiar," unsociable, suspicious, seclusive. For financial reasons the younger had to take a position as housekeeper for a widower in another city and she married her employer. She was "contented" in her marriage and had two children but never felt any real warmth of emotion for her husband or the children. Her connection with her sister was strikingly loose; she did not visit her for years and wrote her seldom.

It was only when she received news of her sister's severe illness that she decided to visit her. She asserted that as she was on the staircase to her sister's home, she heard voices calling: "There comes the second one. Now they will sleep together again. She will help her." She thought to herself, "My poor sister, how she must suffer here!" When her sister related to her her old persecutory system, the younger sister never doubted its truth for a moment. They spent a couple of miserable weeks together and then decided to die together.

It is possible that the assertion of the rescued sister that she had perceived the persecutions *first,* before she saw her sister, was a falsification of memory and that the process of projection took place only after it was induced by the elder. This seems to me to make very little difference.

She had come to her sister's home full of timid feelings of anxious tension. The old homosexual, very ambivalent bond to her sister expressed itself in these feelings. It is possible that the hate, which she attempted to discharge on the staircase, was already projected at this point, like the fear of homosexuality, which betrayed itself in the content of the "voices." It is probable, however, that only later did she take over from her sister the paranoid process which she could use well in the service of her own defense.

The epilogue—joint suicide—confirms our suspicion as to the genesis of "induced madness." Since the hate they felt for one another could not be absorbed by projection into the persecutors outside themselves, they murdered one another under the guise of committing joint suicide.

Such paranoid pairs of siblings of the same sex are the most frequently encountered phenomena in *folie à deux.* As etiology, one thinks of constitutional predisposition in two individuals, separated from the rest of the world, living closely together, in which the more active infects the more passive with his ideas.

I believe, on the contrary, that this close living together, apart from others, is from the beginning an *expression* of those unconscious bonds which later bring *both* parties to similar delusional ideas. That the one who is more active in the delusion eventually imposes it on the other is probable.

In these cases I have described various forms of *folie à deux;* in the first case, a common pseudologia phantastica in the sense of joint, conscious and unconscious wish fulfillment in three members of a family. The basis of the shared illness was the libidinal relationship of the three persons to one another and their joint reaction to the loss of a person to whom all three stood in an affective relationship. In the second case, we saw a schizophrenic process of identification, free from any object relationship to the inducing object. It was possible, however, to discover behind the delusional idea the remnants of old libidinal bonds. In the third case there was a parallel process between the delusional ideas of one psychotic person and the fantasy life of a neurotic person, and we found in this identity the link to the induction. In the fourth case we have a true paranoid *folie à deux,* in which the psychotic distortion of reality of two individuals did not arise from one sister's influencing the other, but from the fact that both already possessed in common repressed psychic contents which broke out earlier in one and later in the other.

A brief theoretical discussion of these clinical observations still remains. I do not want to enter into a discussion of the problem of projection and the meaning of delusional ideas as a "process of restitution" in Freud's sense (1924). I want only, in connection with the problem of *folie à deux,* to indicate the presence of a deeper psychological process, which certainly functions in *folie à deux* in psychotic form.

The tendency to consider an inner psychic process as perception operates regularly within us. A typical example of this in normal life is the dream. During the process of dreaming the happenings of the dream have the character of perceptions, and often retain this character, without modification, for a time after awakening.

It is a complicated developmental process to be able to distinguish inner content from perception. The simplest criterion is: perception is that which others accept as perception. A contact with the surrounding world is indispensable in applying this criterion. A psychotic individual has not only given up the differentiation of the inner world from the world of reality, but he has given up the need for confirmation from the latter by destroying the bridge between himself and other objects. The ego then takes its delusion for reality and professes it as truth.

It can also happen, however, that a slight adaptation to reality prevents the outbreak of the delusion. In this process the ego only gradually frees itself from the cathexes, and makes a boundary autistically between itself and the surrounding world, without the ability to achieve the psychotic "restitution process" in the delusional creation. In this case, however, an affirmative gesture from the surrounding world, a confirmation, an encouragement, is enough to induce the development of the delusion. What then appears to us as suggestion or induction is only the making active of an inner content already there, an encouragement to a projection already latent.

Freud (1911) considers the delusional ideas of the psychically ill person a "rebuilding of the vanished object world." I believe that induction plays an important role in this process. In *folie à deux* in psychotics, the *common delusion appears to be an important part of an attempt to rescue the object* through identification with it, or its delusional system. This was shown particularly clearly in the example of the two paranoid sisters.

I am not attempting here to explain the difference between hysterical suggestion and schizophrenic induction. Common to both, however, is: first, that neither in suggestion nor in induction is anything adopted by the subject which is alien to his ego; and second, that the person affected by the suggestion, as well as the person affected by the induction, attempts through identification to come closer to the object, or to find again a lost object. The phenomena of *folie à deux* described above can also be found in a psychic state so universally human that its character of "normality" cannot be denied—"being in love." I shall leave this problem to a paper devoted to it alone.

In conclusion, I should like to return to the starting point of my remarks: that processes such as we have seen here in individuals can also affect large groups of men, entire nations and generations. We must, however, distinguish here as with individuals between hysterical, libidinally determined mass influences, and schizophrenic ideas held in common; likewise between mass liberations of instincts under the guise of ideals, and paranoid projections, etc. Many things have their place in these *folies en masse* and the approval or disapproval of the surrounding world is often the sole criterion as to whether a particular action is deemed a heroic deed or an act of madness.

19

A Discussion of Certain Forms of Resistance

(1939)

THE subject of defense mechanisms, first introduced by Freud in *Inhibitions, Symptoms and Anxiety* (1926), received a further expansion and clarification in Anna Freud's *The Ego and the Mechanisms of Defense* (1936). This publication directed our attention to problems worthy of further study, and it will certainly continue to influence not only our understanding of psychological processes but probably also our technical approach in treatment of patients.

The analyst has an opportunity to study the mechanisms of defense during the therapeutic process. On the one hand, they largely determine the patient's personality; on the other, they appear in the form of resistances which the analytic procedure itself mobilizes. In this case they will have a particular character appropriate to each form of neurosis and to each analytic situation.

It is not always clear why in certain individuals one type of defense stands in the foreground and in others another type, and why, although other forms of defense are simultaneously

Read before the Fourteenth International Psycho-Analytical Congress, Marienbad, 1936, and first published in the *International Journal of Psycho-Analysis*, 20:72-83, 1939.

present, the analytic situation is predominantly colored by some particular defensive tendency.

For the present discussion I have chosen three typical forms of defense encountered in analysis:

1. The "intellectual" or "intellectualizing" defenses. The positive function of these forces appears in the process of "working through" of the analytic material.

2. Defenses expressed by "turning to reality." In their function of protecting the ego from unbearable affects and impulses they may take various forms. I shall discuss two of those often encountered in the psychoanalytic procedure.

(a) The more passive form of "rationalization" in which reality testing is the guiding spirit.

(b) The direct, active turning toward "external reality," usually in a rational, well-controlled manner.

The "acting out" during analysis is the more neurotic, irrational expression of flight from the analytic situation into the external world.

3. Defenses manifested by "turning inward" to "internal reality." The essential of this form of defense is the increase of self-observation and of intuitive capacity.

I

The meaning of "intellectual defenses" may be formulated shortly as follows. In place of positive efforts to help in the process of intellectually working over the material, the patient seeks to force his analysis in that one direction alone and to substitute for analytic *experiencing* either an ostensibly affirmative "understanding" or a negative criticism.

If, then, we run through our "intellectualizing" patients in our mind, my impression is that we shall find the following types:

(a) Highly intellectual individuals of a genuinely sublimated sort who are able to place the good weapons at their command more or less extensively at the service of their resistances. Against this method of defense by the patient we have no *direct* means of attack. Although at one time the sublimation was a help to the defensive forces, it has in the course of time acquired mental elements (such as perceptual contents, talents, etc.) which contain material foreign to the analysis.

(b) Obsessional neurotics, whose intellectual resistances are well known to us in the form of direct "reaction formations" and "isolations."

(c) Patients with blocked or disturbed affects, who, having repressed the affective side of their life, have retained the intellectual side as the sole means of expressing their mental personality.

Analysis has been shown to be especially difficult in the case of these three types of resistance, for the patients obtain from their defense a "secondary gain" of narcissistic satisfaction and have so much the less reason for renouncing this mode of defense.

More amenable to analytic treatment are those intellectual resistances whose role as a process of defense reveals itself in two directions: (1) when they themselves are already affected by neurotic disturbance; (2) when they constantly reappear in the analytic treatment at the point at which an objectionable instinctual impulse or an unwelcome affect threatens to present itself. The usual technique of the analyst, which consists either in not entering into intellectual argumentation at all or in seeking to invalidate the defense by pointing out its narcissistic tendencies, is here completely useless.

An approach to the resistance from the side hostile to the ego, that is, from the side where what is being warded off is situated, is frequently found to be quite inadequate. This is not to be wondered at, since the difficulty consists precisely in the ability of the ego to master promptly by intellectual means the warded-off material and thus to effect a reinforced resistance to it. We must therefore make a direct attack on the defensive process itself; but we can be successful in this only if we have thoroughly grasped the nature of that process.

The analysis of a defensive process is possible only under one condition: there must be a weak spot in it somewhere, so that it gradually takes on the character of a symptom, or so that in some form it comes into conflict with the remainder of the ego.

It may also happen that the defensive process takes on a very complicated character, being carried out in several steps, and that what is pathological and unsuccessful in the patient is to be sought precisely in that place where everything appears to be functioning well and to the advantage of the ego.

Let me illustrate this by an example. A forty-five-year-old man in a prominent and responsible position was sent for an analytic exploration of his peculiar state. Whether he was suffering from a neurosis or not was still uncertain. For several months he and his friends had observed that his mental abilities had been losing ground. It was a question of a progressive weakening of his powers of mental retention. This became so noticeable that suspicions of the beginning of a general paralysis were aroused. Although the physical findings were negative throughout, the presence of some organic disease of the brain still seemed most probable. The patient himself said that he felt his intellectual defect very intensely, but that he had the impression that the disturbance of his powers of retention existed in isolation from the remainder of his mental faculties. He was working with especial ease and increased interest on some scientific problems and hoped soon to be able to publish the results. This claim could not be diagnosed as a tendency to paralytic ideas of grandeur, for the patient was already a prominent publicist.

During the treatment I observed that the patient was very eager to interest me in material belonging to his past and produced present-day material only in so far as it concerned his erotic life. As soon as he approached his professional or scientific interests he would avoid the subject with the excuse that it was not worth while and that he knew that patients spoke about professional and scientific matters chiefly in order to avoid the more important affective ones. For the patient knew a great deal about analysis and the theory of its technique.

The analyst often finds himself forced to give up the technical routine of analysis and to let himself be guided by intuition. It was easier to do so in this case precisely because my patient's difficulties lay in the intellectual sphere. I insisted the more energetically on dealing with the intellectual side as the patient had really been sent for diagnostic purposes and there could be no question of a long analysis. I soon discovered that his loss of retentive powers related only to scientific matters, and principally to what he had just read. To obtain a clearer picture of his mental life I asked him to bring me his latest manuscripts and to discuss with me the problems contained in them. I will give you a short résumé of the results of a couple of weeks' investigation. For some years the patient had had a very intense friendship with another man whose great scientific talents had always greatly impressed him. The fields of interest of the two friends, while closely related, did not create a situation of rivalry. The friend was a pure theoretician, while my patient took a more practical interest in the field of education. But owing to certain professional circumstances my patient too was forced more into the theoretical field. His latent homosexual aggressiveness against his friend and his burning envy of him underwent repression, and my patient now discovered the following complicated method of defense. Through identification on the one hand and an aggressive "taking away" on the other, he appropriated the thoughts of his friend. These thoughts were known to him in part from his friend's publications and in part from private discussions. In order to deny, however, the unconscious plagiarism, he forgot everything which he had read or had heard from his friend; and he extended this mode of behavior to other fields of activity. This disturbance of mental retentiveness, which has the same structure as a parapraxis such as forgetting a word, is a very interesting phenomenon.

But in my patient the process of defense did not stop at the disturbance of his retentive powers. A careful examination of his theoretical productions showed that his unconscious plagiarism referred not only to his thoughts but to his creative efforts. His scientific work turned out to be an ingenious piecing together of ideas which his friend had already put in writing. The disturbance of his retentiveness served only as a preliminary step to this plagiarism, which could be successful only because he had "forgotten" what his friend had already said.

The discovery of this complicated process did not take place at the point which was felt to be pathological, i.e., in the patient's weakness of memory, but in the activity which had been taken for a successful sublimation, i.e., in his apparently undisturbed scientific achievements.

The patient was very much shaken by this discovery, for the

process had been completely unconscious to him. I myself saw in this situation yet one more example of those paradoxes with which analysis has to struggle. In general we refuse to take an interest in the patient's case in so far as it regards his purely intellectual preoccupations, and consider it as a resistance when he seeks to guide the analysis in this direction. In matters of the intellect we are interested in his disturbances only in so far as they hide an inhibition or a symptom. His sublimations, so long as they are successful, lie outside our interests.

The patient whom we have been discussing should be a warning to us. For it often happens that what was regarded as a successful sublimation turns out to be an unsuccessful defensive process; and—as in this case—it may be only because the apparently successful activity seeks to creep behind a wall of resistance that the analyst's attention is attracted toward it. In psychoanalysis there are no hard and fast rules.

In the analytic unraveling of an intellectual defensive process of this kind it seems to become clear that the defense itself conforms in its structure to a neurotic symptom, that is, that there are contained in it not only an ascetic trend directed against the instinctual danger, but also an affirmative and gratificatory one, though in this case it is quite unconscious.

I should like to give another example to illustrate what I have been saying. An especially intelligent woman came to me for analysis on account of professional difficulties; these consisted in a purely intellectual inhibition of her scientific abilities. Her principal resistance showed itself in the constant efforts she made to give her analysis a didactic, intellectual character. But in the end, with the help of the transference, the analysis was successfully converted into an emotional experience and led to a good therapeutic result.

After her analysis, the patient provided an interesting epilogue to it. She declared that she had not the slightest recollection of the material which had come up during her analysis. This was all the more strange in a patient who had so thoroughly worked over her analysis on intellectual lines. In addition, she believed that her own efforts as an analyst were less successful than they might have been, because she was too much inclined to carry the analysis onto the intellectual plane.

The situation, which became quite clear in the analysis, was that since her childhood she had had to struggle against an especially strong sexual curiosity and against active tendencies to make sexual investigations. This curiosity was opposed by strong external and internal prohibitions. The rejected strivings were continued in the sublimated form of her intellectual proclivities —the defense thus received its specific character from the nature of that which had been warded off.

Analysis had indeed helped the patient to revive and deal with the sexual investigations hidden behind the defense; at the same time, however, my opposition to any "intellectualizing" on her part, which had the effect of a prohibition, repeated the prohibiting attitude of her very ascetic childhood environment. After the analysis—in deferred obedience—we see the old process being repeated. She renounced "knowledge" exactly like the child who apparently accepts sexual enlightenment only promptly to repress it once again.

But the fact that she sought to "intellectualize" with her own analysands originated in another unconscious motive. This "intellectualizing" was not only a sublimation of her infantile sexual curiosity, but also represented an identification with her father. She followed the same profession as he and was interested in the same kind of scientific work. Before her analytic treatment she had come to grief over this process of identification because of the fact that she was a girl and found her activities hampered by the anatomical difference.

Anna Freud regards the tendency to intellectualization in puberty as an effort of the ego to master the instincts with the aid of thought processes. According to my view, this form of defense appears only in those young people in whom *specific* instinctual tendencies in early childhood have already prepared a defensive process of this kind, and in such a manner that that process can cover a gratification of instinct. In the case of our patient it was sexual curiosity and everything connected with it which was indirectly gratified by the "intellectualization."

But to a defensive process of this type, formed early in life, there must be added, according to my observations, a later factor before this form of defense can be established and fixated. In the case under discussion this factor was the patient's identification with her father. I believe that it is these later factors which are decisive for the further development of the intellectualizing tendencies of puberty.

At this point I should like to make an observation which is not directly connected with my theme, but offers a contribution to the problem of the influence of affective factors on retentive memory.

It is considered to be an established fact that the presbyophrenic phenomena of defects of memory are of an organic nature and show themselves purely in the intellectual sphere. In this connection I have been following up for some time a fact which came to my notice by chance. This is that the frequently increased ability of the presenile to recall memories from their more distant past does not appear to confine itself to conscious material. Childhood experiences, and fantasies, which have been excluded from consciousness all through life, often spring up spontaneously with great plasticity. My patient's old grandmother, a very puritanical and sexually repressed woman, acknowledged her sympathy for analysis when she recalled, in her seventieth year, oedipal fantasies and sexual experiences which she had forgotten all her life. My further observations appear to show that there is an early stage of presbyophrenia, in which material which has up till then been unconscious is remembered as well.

I am inclined to suppose that this process originates when the ego, in renouncing sexual wishes, can also give up those inhibitions and resistances which it had built up against dangers that now no longer exist. Although this theory may be wrong, the observation underlying it is certainly true.

II

Closely related to the "intellectualizing" form of those defensive processes which express themselves as a resistance is another form—that of "rationalization" and turning to reality.

I assume that in a patient with this sort of defensive processes what has happened is that he has successfully disposed of his entire anxiety in regard to his internal situations by avoiding them. He has simply fled from the gloomy world of his mental life into reality; and he proceeds to utilize reality as a defense against the analytic evocation of the ghosts which he has successfully dispelled. In consequence he hastens to translate the interpretations in analysis into the language of material reality. Thus figures of speech, symbols, and psychic reality are alien to him even when he does accept them intellectually and understands them. In his analysis he sometimes gives the impression of being stupid, sometimes of making fun of the treatment. But one soon discovers that it is a question of resistance and that he is making use of a form of defense which has freed him from anxiety on former occasions.

Here is an example of what I mean. A well-educated man who was pursuing active studies in the natural sciences had turned his attention to experimentation with great keenness and would accept as "science" only that which could be objectively demonstrated—was written in black on white, as it were. Science was to him a collocation of facts. Hypotheses, problems, and everything that is not directly demonstrable, he called "poetry but not science," and declared that he would have nothing to do with such matters.

He rejected analytic interpretations as "not demonstrable," and sought to invalidate his transference experience through argumentation. In this way he often succeeded in struggling successfully against his anxiety states, for quite a long while; but in the end they overpowered him and made the treatment possible.

The patient was the last child in the family. He was born two months after the death of his father. There was a great deal of filial feeling in his family circle and he was extremely envious of his older brothers and sisters because they had known, and been loved by, his father. He entertained fantasies full of longing and —encouraged by his nurse—hoped some day to see his father as a ghost. Yet later this expectation was transferred into a fear. His energetic mother freed him from the influence of this nurse and the patient found consolation and help in his mother's as-

surance that there were no such things as ghosts, that no one
had ever seen one yet, and that death was decay and irrevocable
annihilation.

Now we can understand, I think, the sources from which his
turning to reality sprang and his denial of things which were not
"materially" demonstrable.

This patient's attitude was determined by a quite individually
colored prehistory. But exactly the same reactions and defensive
processes can, as observation shows, also be turned against the
ghosts which dwell within the subject and which threaten to return.

Another patient of mine exhibited a still more "realistic" mode
of behavior. He concerned himself only with things which were
useful, was interested in culture only because, after all, one had
to "do what the others did," and let himself be analyzed because
afterward he could make more money and better his position.

In the analysis he showed himself unable to link his mental
phenomena with a verbally conscious comprehension of them, as
will be seen from his attitude to his dreams and their interpretation. He dreamed that a strikingly beautiful youth was revealed
on closer inspection to be a hateful hairy ape with frightfully
long arms. His associations pointed very clearly to his conflict
over masturbation as well as to the identity of the ape with his
own person. He understood and accepted this interpretation, yet
the next day he repudiated it because he had seen in the mirror
that he was not hairy at all and the measurement of his arms
showed that they were much shorter than the ape's—consequently
he could not be the ape.

After the interpretation of another dream, in which I was able
to show him his negative transference as revealed in the identification of myself with a deceitful old fruit seller, he inquired of
common acquaintances about my honesty, so as to prove to himself and to me that my interpretation possessed no reality value
whatsoever.

This patient, too, had—as his analysis showed—learned early
on in life to set up against his internal anxieties a reality which
was innocuous because he could record and check up on it.

There was in him no trace of a Don Quixote who, carried along by the force of his illusions, of the unreal, would translate them into his life. Much rather was he a Sancho Panza; for he gave everything which was unreal, fantastic, or spiritual, the character of the crudely real. Reality gave him protection and enabled him to obtain satisfactions which were not prohibited.

We assume that this type of defense as we observe it in our patient had originated in that period in which the anxiety of the child was directed to the external world and in which the testing of reality had at the same time the effect of freeing him from anxiety, like a game in which the father, disguised as a wolf, cries out in order to quiet the mounting anxiety of the child: "But look, that's not a wolf, it's Papa." Hence it appears as if reality testing and adaptation to reality originate not only under the pressure of necessity but also as a consequence of their function in freeing from anxiety.

This method, already prepared in childhood, for gaining freedom from anxiety seems to me to be especially operative in the prepubertal stage before the onset of the genital trends. From analytic experience I have the impression that it serves chiefly for defense against the newly mobilized activity of fantasies and that it represents a defense form which is more complete and more ominous than "intellectualization." While in the latter case the function of affect and fantasy is replaced by intellect, in the former the thinking process itself is limited and the fear of fantasies is transferred to the fear of thinking.

A typical example is the gifted twelve-year-old boy, with his head full of fantastic plans for the future, who suddenly exclaims that he wants first of all to prove, as a common worker in a factory, which of his chemical and physical ideas can be realized. This boy is a youthful forerunner of a certain kind of specialists who are to be found as group products in some civilized societies. My first patient, in his clearly neurotic structure, is a prototype of such a group. I think we may expect to find certain civilizations which are deeply imbued with this particular form of defense against anxiety. I believe that too forcible an education on lines of reality strongly reinforces this defense mechanism. This was the case with my last patient cited above.

From the point of view of the technical art of the analyst there arise here great difficulties. For, so long as he has not shattered the "reality values" of the patient, his efforts are almost hopeless, and in doing so he is going contrary to the analytic task of making the patient adapted to reality. I shall postpone the discussion of defenses expressed in "acting out." They are manifold, can be observed in many analyses; to bring clarity and cohesiveness to various forms in which they appear calls for a separate publication.

III

In complete contrast to the "realization" type, there is another type of patient whose characteristic is an especial intuition for his own internal process, a striking gift for "internal perception." So far as I know them, this kind of patient comes as a candidate for training in analysis and gives the impression of having a particular psychological aptitude for the profession of analyst.

Closer observation shows, however, that this acuteness of "internal perception," which strikes us as a talent, is in fact a defensive process. We find that the patient (or candidate) lives in a severe anxiety state, which has neither a phobic nor yet a "free-floating" character. It gives the impression, rather, of a state of rigidity from panic. The main way in which the internal anxiety finds expression is in numerous anxiety dreams of a persecutory character. The patient works brilliantly in the first phase of the analysis, sees and understands things which are usually unconscious, and takes away from the analyst every possibility of intervention in his analysis. This activity which is forcibly directed onto his internal life goes along with a markedly passive attitude toward the real world about him. These patients are more or less adapted to reality, but they do not exert much will power and allow themselves to be dominated by men and circumstances.

Their internal perception is gradually revealed as a sharpened self-observation with the aim of defending against internal dangers. They are like a timid listener in the dark who perceives sounds more clearly. One of these patients actually told me that he observed himself so exactly "so as not to go insane." This introspection always becomes intensified when the transference becomes stronger and the understanding collaboration of the analyst more dangerous. Gradually this defense becomes unsatisfactory and the anxiety takes on more and more a transference character. In one case it was transformed into a paranoid attitude to the analyst. One could observe *in statu nascendi* the process of transformation from "internal perception" to the "hostile observer" in the external world. Whether this is a question of the reinforcement and breaking through of repressed instinctual tendencies, which provoke by an anxiety signal the defending forces of self-observation, or whether it is primarily a matter of an increased activity of the ego or superego, remains at present an open question.

This process certainly has analogies with hypochondria and depersonalization (in Schilder's sense), in which also an attempt is made to objectify and master rejected mental contents by means of self-observation.

The line of demarcation between the positive and the pathological functioning of such an "intuitive" attitude is not clear-cut. Where this attitude takes on more and more the character of a resistance in the analysis we are led on the one hand to think of the familiar clairvoyance of the schizophrenic, and on the other to take into consideration the possibility of a preliminary stage of a paranoid process.

I have, for the present, set up three forms of "internal perception":

1. A purely positive achievement on the part of the observing portion of the ego without pathological reaction, which is therefore not an object of direct analytical treatment, even when it is used as a defense.

2. An endophobia, i.e., a phobia of the internal part of the self, in which the strengthened introspection affords freedom from anxiety but with internal restrictions.

3. Paranoia turned against the inner self, in which the introspecting ego is felt as something strange and so plays the part of persecutor. The comprehension of this type leads directly to the problem of depersonalization and other forms of schizoid reaction, but is not the theme of my paper.

I have attempted to show how a specific way of reacting of the ego, which began as a defense mechanism, can either become an immovable and positive possession of the mental apparatus, or merely form a thin veil over the subject's neurotic fears—a veil which must be drawn away by analysis in order to allow what it conceals to be dealt with.

I have brought forward a few types to show that something that has hitherto been of positive value in the ego can be made to serve a negative purpose during the analysis and that it must be destroyed by the process of analysis; but that this should be done only if there is a possibility of creating a better economy in the mental life of the individual. Whether such a possibility exists or not is a question which analytic experience and tact alone can decide.

20

Some Forms of Emotional Disturbance and Their Relationship to Schizophrenia

(1942)

PSYCHOANALYTIC observations of a few types of emotional disturbances are presented in this paper, and a series of cases reported in which the individual's emotional relationship to the outside world and to his own ego appears impoverished or absent. Such disturbances of the emotional life take various forms. For example, there are the individuals who are not aware of their lack of normal affective bonds and responses, but whose emotional disturbance is perceived either only by those around them or is first detected in analytic treatment; and there are those who complain of their emotional defect and are keenly distressed by the disturbance in their inner experiences. Among the latter, the disturbance may be transitory and fleeting; it may recur from time to time but only in connection with certain specific situations and experiences; or it may persist and form a continuous, distressing symptom. In addition, the emotional disturbance may be perceived as existing in the personality or it may be

This publication is a combination of a paper published in the *Internationale Zeitschrift für Psychoanalyse*, 20:323-335, 1934, under the title "Über einen Typus der Pseudoaffektivität ('als ob')" and of a lecture given at the Chicago meeting of the American Psychoanalytic Society, 1938. It was first published in the *Psychoanalytic Quarterly*, 11:301-321, 1942.

projected onto the outside world. In the one case the patient says, "I am changed. I feel nothing. Everything seems unreal to me." In the other, he complains that the world seems strange, objects shadowy, human beings and events theatrical and unreal. Those forms of the disturbance in which the individual himself is conscious of his defect and complains of it belong to the picture of "depersonalization." This disturbance has been described by many authors. In the analytic literature the reader is especially referred to the studies of Oberndorf (1934, 1935), Schilder (1939), and Bergler and Eidelberg (1935).

Most of the psychoanalytic observations in this paper deal with conditions bearing a close relationship to depersonalization but differing from it in that they were not perceived as disturbances by the patient himself. To this special type of personality I have given the name, "as if." I must emphasize that this name has nothing to do with Vaihinger's system of "fictions" and the philosophy of "As If." My only reason for using so unoriginal a label for the type of person I wish to present is that every attempt to understand the way of feeling and manner of life of this type forces on the observer the inescapable impression that the individual's whole relationship to life has something about it which is lacking in genuineness and yet outwardly runs along "as if" it were complete. Even the layman sooner or later inquires, after meeting such an "as if" patient: what *is* wrong with him, or her? Outwardly the person seems normal. There is nothing to suggest any kind of disorder, behavior is not unusual, intellectual abilities appear unimpaired, emotional expressions are well ordered and appropriate. But despite all this, something intangible and indefinable obtrudes between the person and his fellows and invariably gives rise to the question, "What is wrong?"

A clever and experienced man, a patient of mine, met another of my patients, a girl of the "as if" type, at a social gathering. He spent part of his next analytic hour telling me how stimulating, amusing, attractive, and interesting she was, but ended his eulogy with, "But something is wrong with her." He could not explain what he meant.

When I submitted the paintings of the same girl to an authority for his criticism and evaluation, I was told that the drawings showed much skill and talent but there was also something disturbing in them which this man attributed to an inner restraint, an inhibition which he thought could surely be removed. Toward the end of the patient's not too successful analysis, she entered this critic's school for further instruction in painting and, after a time, I received a report in which her teacher spoke in glowing terms of her talent. Several months later I received a less enthusiastic report. Yes, the girl was talented, her teacher had been impressed by the speed with which she had adopted his technique and manner of artistic perception, but, he had frankly to admit, there was an intangible something about her which he had never before encountered, and he ended with the usual question, "What is wrong?" He added that the girl had gone to another teacher, who used a quite different teaching approach, and that she had oriented herself to the new theory and technique with striking ease and speed.

The first impression these people make is of complete normality. They are intellectually intact, gifted, and bring great understanding to intellectual and emotional problems; but when they pursue their not infrequent impulses to creative work they construct, in form, a good piece of work but it is always a spasmodic, if skilled, repetition of a prototype without the slightest trace of originality. On closer observation, the same thing is seen in their affective relationships to the environment. These relationships are usually intense and bear all the earmarks of friendship, love, sympathy, and understanding; but even the layman soon perceives something strange and raises the question he cannot answer. To the analyst it is soon clear that all these relationships are devoid of any trace of warmth, that all the expressions of emotion are formal, that all inner experience is completely excluded. It is like the performance of an actor who is technically well trained but who lacks the necessary spark to make his impersonations true to life.

Thus the essential characteristic of the person I wish to describe is that outwardly he conducts his life as if he possessed a complete and sensitive emotional capacity. To him there is no difference between his empty forms and what others actually experience. Without going deeper into the matter I wish at this point to state that this condition is not identical with the coldness of repressed individuals in whom there is usually a highly differentiated emotional life hidden behind a wall, the loss of affect being either manifest or cloaked by overcompensations. In the one there is flight from reality or a defense against the realization of forbidden instinctual drives; in the other, a seeking of external reality in an effort to avoid an anxiety-laden fantasy. Psychoanalysis discloses that in the "as if" individual it is no longer an act of repression but a real loss of object cathexis. The apparently normal relationship to the world corresponds to a child's imitativeness and is the expression of identification with the environment, a mimicry which results in an ostensibly good adaptation to the world of reality despite the absence of object cathexis.

Further consequences of such a relation to life are a completely passive attitude to the environment with a highly plastic readiness to pick up signals from the outer world and to mold oneself and one's behavior accordingly. The identification with what other people are thinking and feeling is the expression of this passive plasticity and renders the person capable of the greatest fidelity and the basest perfidy. Any object will do as a bridge for identification. At first the love, friendship, and attachment of an "as if" person have something very rewarding for the partner. If it is a woman, she seems to be the quintessence of feminine devotion, an impression which is particularly imparted by her passivity and readiness for identification. Soon, however, the lack of real warmth brings such an emptiness and dullness to the emotional atmosphere that the man as a rule precipitously breaks off the relationship. In spite of the adhesiveness which the "as if" person brings to every relationship, when he is thus abandoned he displays either a rush of affective reactions which are "as if" and thus spurious, or a frank absence of affectivity. At the very first opportunity the former object is exchanged for a new one and the process is repeated.

The same emptiness and the same lack of individuality which are so evident in the emotional life appear also in the moral structure. Completely without character, wholly unprincipled, in the literal meaning of the term, the morals of the "as if" individuals, their ideals, their convictions are simply reflections of another person, good or bad. Attaching themselves with great ease to social, ethical, and religious groups, they seek, by adhering to a group, to give content and reality to their inner emptiness and establish the validity of their existence by identification. Overenthusiastic adherence to one philosophy can be quickly and completely replaced by another contradictory one without the slightest trace of inward transformation—simply as a result of some accidental regrouping of the circle of acquaintances or the like.

A second characteristic of such patients is their suggestibility, quite understandable from what has already been said. Like the capacity for identification, this suggestibility, too, is unlike that of the hysteric for whom object cathexis is a necessary condition; in the "as if" individual the suggestibility must be ascribed to passivity and automatonlike identification. Many initial criminal acts, attributed to an erotic bondage, are due instead to a passive readiness to be influenced.

Another characteristic of the "as if" personality is that aggressive tendencies are almost completely masked by passivity, lending an air of negative goodness, of mild amiability which, however, is readily convertible to evil.

One of these patients, a woman, and the only child of one of the oldest noble families in Europe, had been brought up in an unusual atmosphere. With the excuse of official duties, and quite in accordance with tradition, the parents delegated the care and training of their child to strangers. On certain specified days of the week she was brought before her parents for "control." At these meetings there was a formal check of her educational achievements, and the new program and other directions were given her preceptors. Then after a cool, ceremonious dismissal, the child was returned to her quarters. She received no warmth and no tenderness from her parents, nor did punishment come directly from them. This virtual separation from her parents had come soon after her birth. Perhaps the most inauspicious component of her parents' conduct, which granted the child only a very niggardly bit of warmth, was the fact—and this was reinforced by the whole program of her education—that their sheer *existence* was strongly emphasized, and the patient was drilled in love, honor, and obedience toward them without ever feeling these emotions directly and realistically.

In this atmosphere, so lacking in feeling on the part of the parents, the development of a satisfactory emotional life could scarcely be expected in the child. One would expect, however, that other persons in the environment would take the place of the parents. Her situation would then have been that of a child brought up in a foster home. In such children we find that the emotional ties to their own parents are transferred to the parent substitutes in relationship to whom the oedipus complex develops with greater difficulty perhaps but with no significant modifications.

This patient, in accordance with ceremonial tradition, always had three nurses, each of whom wanted to stand first in the eyes of the parents and each of whom continually sought the favor of the child. They were, moreover, frequently changed. Throughout her whole childhood there was no one person who loved her and who could have served as a significant love object for her.

As soon as she was able to conceptualize, the patient immersed herself intensively in fantasies about the parents. She attributed to them divine powers through which she was provided with things unattainable to ordinary mortals. Everything she absorbed from stories and legends she elaborated into the myth about her parents. No longing for love was ever expressed in these fantasies; they all had the aim of providing a narcissistic gain. Every meeting with the real parents separated them further from the heroes of her imagination. In this manner there was formed in the child a parental myth, a fantasmic shadow of an oedipus situation which remained an empty form so far as real persons and emotions were concerned. Not only did reality which denied her parent relationships lead to narcissistic regression into fantasy, but this process gained further impetus from the absence of any substitutive object-libidinous relationships. The frequent change of nurses and governesses and the fact that these persons were themselves subjected to strict discipline, acted on orders, and used all available measures to make the child conform to the demands of reality, measures in which a pseudo tenderness was consciously used as a means to attain didactic ends, precluded this possibility. The child was trained very early to cleanliness and strict table manners, and the violent outbreaks of anger and rage to which she was subject in early childhood were successfully brought under control, giving way to an absolutely pliant obedience. Much of this disciplinary control was attained by appeal to the parents so that everything the child did which was obedient and proper she referred to the wish or command of the mythical father and mother.

When she entered a convent school at the age of eight, she was completely fixed in the "as if" state in which she entered analysis. Superficially, there was no difference between her life and that of the average convent pupil. She had the customary attachment to a nun in imitation of her group of girls. She had the most tender friendships which were wholly without significance to her. She went devoutly through the forms of religion without the slightest trace of belief, and underwent seduction into masturbation with quasi feelings of guilt—simply to be like her comrades.

In time, the myth of the parents faded and disappeared without new fantasies to take its place. It disappeared as her parents became clearer to her as real persons and she devaluated them. Narcissistic fantasies gave way to real experiences in which, however, she could participate only through identification.

Analysis disclosed that the success of her early training in suppressing instinctual drives was only apparent. It had something of the "trained act" in it and, like the performance of the circus animal, was bound to the presence of a ringmaster. If denial of an instinct was demanded, the patient complied, but when an otherwise inclined object gave permission for the satisfaction of a drive, she could respond quite without inhibition, though with little gratification. The only result of the training was that the drive never came into conflict with the external world. In this respect she behaved like a child in that stage of development in which his instinctual drives are curbed only by immediate external authority. Thus it happened that for a time the patient fell into bad company, in unbelievable contrast to her home environment and early training. She got drunk in low dives, participated in all kinds of sexual perversions, and felt just as comfortable in this underworld as in the pietistic sect, the artistic group, or the political movement in which she was later successively a participant.

She never had occasion to complain of lack of affect for she was never conscious of it. The patient's relationship to her parents was strong enough to enable her to make them heroes of her fantasy, but for the creation of a warm dynamic oedipus constellation capable of shaping a healthy future psychic life in both a positive and a negative sense the necessary conditions were obviously lacking. It is not enough that the parents are simply there and provide food for fantasy. The child must *really* be seduced to a certain extent by the libidinous activity of the parents in order to develop a normal emotional life, must experience the warmth of a mother's body as well as all those unconscious seductive acts of the loving mother as she cares for his bodily needs. He must play with the father and have sufficient intimacy with him to sense the father's masculinity in order that instinctual impulses enter the stream of the oedipus constellation.

This patient's myth bore some similarity to the fantasy which Freud called the "family romance"[1] in which, however, the libidinal relation to the parents though repressed is very powerful. By repudiating the real parents, it is possible partly to avoid strong emotional conflicts from forbidden wishes, feelings of guilt, etc. The real objects have been repressed, but in analysis they can be uncovered with their full libidinal cathexis.

But for our patient there was never a living warm emotional relationship to the parents or to anyone else. Whether after weak attempts at object cathexis the child returned to narcissism by a process of regression or never succeeded in establishing a real object relation as the result of being unloved is, for all practical purposes, irrelevant.

The same deficiency which interfered with the development of the emotional life was also operative in the formation of the superego. The shadowy structure of the oedipus complex was

[1] See Chapter 18, footnote 1.

gradually given up without ever having come to an integrated and unified superego formation. One gains the impression that the prerequisites for such a development also lie in strong oedipal object cathexes.

It is not to be denied that at a very early age some inner prohibitions are present which are the precursors of the superego and are intimately dependent on external objects. Identification with the parents in the resolution of the oedipus complex brings about the integration of these elements. Where this is absent, as it was in our patient, the identifications remain vacillating and transitory. The representatives which go to make up the conscience remain in the external world and instead of the development of inner morals there appears a persistent identification with external objects. In childhood, educational influences exerted an inhibitory effect on the instinctual life, particularly on the aggressions. In later life, in the absence of an adequate superego, she shifts the responsibility for her behavior to objects in the external world with whom she identifies herself. The passivity of this patient as the expression of her submission to the will of another seems to be the final transformation of her aggressive tendencies.

As the result of this weak superego structure, there is little contact between the ego and the superego, and the scene of all conflicts remains external, like the child for whom everything can proceed without friction if he but obey. Both the persistent identification and the passive submission are expressions of the patient's complete adaptation to the current environment, and impart the shadowy quality to the patient's personality. The value of this link to reality is questionable because the identification always takes place with only a part of the environment. If this part of the environment comes into conflict with the rest, naturally the patient is involved. Thus it can come about that the individual can be seduced into asocial or criminal acts by a change in his identifications, and it may well be that some of the asocial are recruited from the group of "as if" personalities who are adapted to reality in this restricted way.

Analysis of this patient revealed a genuine infantilism, that is, an arrest at a definite stage in the development of the emotional life and character formation. In addition to particularly unfavorable environmental influences, it should be noted that the patient came from a very old family overrun with psychotics and invalid psychopaths.

Another woman patient had a father who had a mental illness and a mother who was neurotic. She remembered her father only as "a man with a black beard," and she tried to explain as something very fascinating and wonderful, his absences as he was moved to and from a sanitarium and an isolated room at home, always under nursing care. Thus she built a myth around her father, replacing him in fantasy by a mysterious man, whom she later called an "Indian" and with whom she had all sorts of experiences, each of which served to make her a superhuman being. The prototype for the Indian was the father's male nurse, whom the little girl saw mysteriously disappearing into her father's room. The education and upbringing of the child were relegated to nurses, but despite this she succeeded in establishing a strongly libidinous attachment to the very abnormal mother. Her later relationships had elements of object-libidinal attitudes, sometimes warmer, especially in homosexual directions, but never sufficiently to change their "as if" quality. The failure to develop an adequate object cathexis was, in this patient, related to the birth of her brother toward whom she developed an unusually aggressive envy. Comparisons of genitalia led the little girl to scrutinize her body for hours on end in a mirror. Later this narcissistic activity was gradually sublimated. At first she tried to model parts of her body in clay in order to facilitate her mirror studies. In the course of years she developed great skill in modeling and was for a brief time under the tutelage of a sculptress. Unconsciously, it was the fantasy of displaying repeatedly her body to the world. In later years she created only large, very voluptuous, matronly female figures. These proved to be weak attempts to recreate the mother she had lost in childhood to her brother. Ultimately she abandoned sculpture for music simply because she believed her teacher failed to appreciate her sufficiently.

Most conspicuous in her childhood was a monkeylike imitation of her brother with whom she was for years completely identified, not in fantasy but by acting out. Disastrously for both, the brother quite early betrayed unmistakable signs of a psychosis which culminated in a catatonic excitement. The sister imitated all her brother's bizarre activities and lived with him in a world of fantasy. Only her partial object-libidinal cathexis and a displacement of the process from the brother and identification with more normal objects saved her from being institutionalized. I was inclined at first to regard her condition as the result of an identification with her psychotic brother; only later did I recognize that the etiology of her condition lay deeper.

I believe this patient is similar to the first despite the differences in their development. In the second, it seems that a disappointment shattered the strong relationship with the mother, that the mysterious absence of the father made it impossible for the little girl to find in him a substitute when her relationship to her mother was shaken, and that further relationships to objects remained at the stage of identification. By such identification she averted her intense hatred of her brother and transformed her aggression toward him into an obedient passivity in which she submissively identified herself with him. She developed no other object relationships. Her superego suffered the same fate as that of the first patient. The myth of the father and the very early devaluation of the mother prevented integration of her superego and left her dependent on persons in the external world.

A third patient, a pretty, temperamental woman of thirty-five with many intellectual and artistic talents, came to analysis because she was "tired" after a long series of adventures. It soon became clear that, as the result of a certain combination of circumstances, her interest in psychoanalysis was actually an interest in the analyst, especially in her profession. While she frequently spoke of her tremendous interest in child psychology and in Freud's theory and read widely on these subjects, her understanding of them was extraordinarily superficial and her interest entirely unreal. More careful observation disclosed that this was true not only for all her intellectual interests but for everything she did or had ever done. It was surprising to recognize in this woman, who was so indefatigably active, a condition so closely related to the pseudo affectivity of the "as if" patient. All her experiences too were based on identifications, though her identifications were not so straightforward as were those of the other type of patient which is, one might say, more monogamous and adheres to but one person or one group at a time, while this patient had so many concurrent identifications —or symbolic representations of identifications—that her conduct appeared erratic. She was, in fact, considered "crazy" by those who knew her. Her friends, however, had no notion that her apparently rich life concealed a severe lack of affect. She had come to me because of a wish to change her character, that is, to create more peace and harmony in her life by identifying herself with a "particularly solid" professional personality.

After six months the analysis appeared to be unusually successful. The patient learned to understand many things about herself and lost her eccentricities. She determined to become an analyst and when this was denied her, she collapsed. She was completely lacking in affect and complained, "I am so empty! My God, I am so empty! I have no feelings." It transpired that prior to analysis she had got into serious financial difficulties by breaking off various friendships and love relationships and had realized that she would soon have to work. It was with this intention that she came to analysis. Her plan was to become an analyst by identification with her analyst. When this proved impossible, this seemingly very able and active woman changed into a completely passive person. From time to time she had extraordinarily violent fits of childish weeping or outbursts of rage, flung herself on the floor, and kicked and screamed. Gradually, she developed a progressive lack of affect. She became completely negativistic and met all interpretations with, "I don't understand what you mean by that."

At two points in this patient's development she had suffered severe trauma. Her father was an alcoholic, and the patient often witnessed his brutal mistreatment of the mother. She sided vehemently with the latter and, when she was only seven, had fantasies in which she rescued her mother from her misery and built a little white cottage for her. She saved every penny and worked hard in school to attain this aim, only to discover that her mother was not merely a passive victim of her husband but took pleasure in being brutalized. The consequent devaluation of her mother not only deprived her of her only object of love but also arrested the development of a feminine ego ideal of an independent, adequate personality. She spent the rest of her life trying to make up for this lack by creating a whole series of identifications, in the same way as the "as if" patients.

Deprived of tenderness and affection in her childhood, her instincts remained crudely primitive. She vacillated between giving these instincts free rein and holding them in check. She acted out prostitution fantasies, indulged in a variety of sexual perversions, often giving the impression of hypomania. She emerged from these debauches by identification with some conventional person and achieved by this means a kind of sublimation, the form dependent on the particular object. This resulted in a frequent shifting of her occupation and interests. So long as it was possible for her either to retain such a relationship or to allow herself the gratification of very primitive drives she was not aware of her lack of affect.

The following cases of emotional disturbances bear close similarity with the "as if" group but differ in certain respects.

A seventeen-year-old boy of unusual intellectual ability came for analysis because of manifest homosexuality and a conscious lack of feeling. This lack of emotion included his homosexual objects, about whom he created all sorts of perverse fantasies. He was obsessionally scrupulous, modest, exact, and reliable. He was passively oral and anal in his homosexuality. The analysis was extremely rich in material but progressed in an emotional vacuum. While the transference was frequently represented in his dreams and fantasies, it never became a conscious, emotional experience.

One day I gave him a ticket to a series of lectures in which I was taking part. He went to my lecture and had severe anxiety on the stairs leading to the lecture hall. By thus mobilizing his anxiety in the transference, the analysis began to progress.

An only child from a highly cultured environment, with a father who was strict and ambitious and a mother who dedicated her life to this handsome and talented son, he nevertheless suffered the fate of affective deficiency. The fact that he grew up in an atmosphere in which he never needed to seek for love, that he was overwhelmed with tenderness without having to make any effort to obtain it paralyzed his own active strivings for tenderness. He remained bound to primitive instinctual impulses, and because there were few infantile anxieties which were not warded off with scrupulous care, there was no motive in him to build up defense mechanisms.

He underwent the trauma of the depreciation of his ego ideal when he discovered that his admired father was uncultivated and limited. This realization threatened to depreciate his own value, for he was like his father, bore his name, and heard his resemblance to him repeatedly stressed by his mother. Through rigidity and strictness, in ethical and intellectual demands, he strove to become better than the self which was identified with the father. In contrast to the previous patients, he did not identify himself with a series of objects. Instead of having emotional relationships to people, he was split into two identifications: one with his beloved mother and the other with his father. The first was feminine and sexualized; the second was overcompensatory, rigid, and narcissistic.

Unlike the "as if" patients, he complained of lack of feeling. He completely lacked the tender emotions which would have given warmth to his emotional life. He had no relation to any woman, and his friendships with men were either purely intellectual or crudely sexual. The feelings he had were of a character he would not let himself express. These were very primitive aggressions, the wildest, most infantile sexual drives, which were rejected with the declaration, "I feel nothing at all." In one way he told the truth; he was really lacking in any permissible feelings, that is, in the tender, sublimated emotions.

The tendency to identification is characteristic also of this type of affective disturbance. Even though this patient did not completely sink his personality in a series of identifications, the strongest section of his ego, his intellect, lacked originality. Everything he wrote and said in scientific matters showed great formal talent but when he tried to produce something original it usually turned out to be a repetition of ideas which he had once grasped with particular clarity. The tendency to multiple identifications occurred on the intellectual level.

Another patient of this group, a thirty-year-old married woman who came from a family in which there were many psychotics, complained about lack of emotion. In spite of good intelligence and perfect reality testing, she led a sham existence and she was always just what was suggested to her by the environment. It became clear that she could experience nothing except a completely passive readiness to split into an endless number of identifications. This condition had set in acutely after an operation in her childhood for which she had been given no psychological preparation. On recovery from the anesthesia she asked if she were really herself, and then developed a state of depersonalization which lasted a year and turned into passive suggestibility which concealed a crippling anxiety.

Common to all these cases is a deep disturbance of the process of sublimation which results both in a failure to synthesize the various infantile identifications into a single, integrated personality, and in an imperfect, one-sided, purely intellectual sublimation of the instinctual strivings. While critical judgment and the intellectual powers may be excellent, the emotional and moral part of the personality is lacking.

The etiology of such conditions is related, first, to a devaluation of the object serving as a model for the development of the child's personality. This devaluation may have a firm foundation in reality or be traceable, for example, to shock at discovery of parental coitus at a period of development when the child is engaged in his last struggles against masturbation and needs support in his efforts toward sublimation. Or, as in the case of the boy described above, the successful sublimation may be interfered with by a sexualization of the relationship to an object who should serve the child as a model for his ego ideal, in this instance, a grossly sexual identification with his mother.

Another cause of this kind of emotional disturbance is insufficient stimulus for the sublimation of the emotions, as the result either of being given too little tenderness, or too much.

Infantile anxiety may suffer a similar fate. Too harsh or too indulgent treatment may contribute to failure in the economic formation of defense mechanisms resulting in remarkable passivity of the ego. It will be recalled that in the case of the boy reported, an attack of anxiety not only mobilized the transference but also opened the way to his recovery.

The question must be raised as to how the tendency of "as if" personalities to identification with current love objects differs from the same tendency in hysteria. The great difference between the latter and the "as if" disturbance lies in the fact that the objects with which the hysterics identify themselves are the objects of powerful libidinal cathexes. Hysterical repression of affect brings freedom from anxiety and so represents a way out of the conflict. In "as if" patients, an early deficiency in the development of affect reduces the inner conflict, the effect of which is an impoverishment of the total personality which does not occur in hysteria.

The patients described here might make one suspect that we are dealing with something like the blocking of affect seen especially in narcissistic individuals who have developed loss of feeling through repression. The great fundamental difference, however, is that the "as if" personality tries to simulate affective experience, whereas the individual with a blocking of affect does not. In the analysis of the latter it can always be shown that the once-developed object relationships and aggressive feelings have undergone repression and are not at the disposal of the conscious personality. The repressed, affectively toned segment of the personality is gradually uncovered during the analysis, and it is sometimes possible to make the buried part of the emotional life available to the ego.

For example, one patient had completely repressed the memory of his mother who died when he was four, and with whom, it was clear, the greater part of his emotions had been involved.

Under the influence of a very weak but nonetheless effective transference, isolated memories gradually emerged. At first these had a negative character and denied all tenderness. During analysis this patient showed also another form of emotional disturbance, namely, depersonalization. Before analysis his self-satisfaction had been unshaken. He defended himself against the transference with all his power. In the analytic hours, when clear signs of a transference *in statu nascendi* were perceptible, the patient would complain of sudden feelings of strangeness. It was clear that in him the depersonalization corresponded to the perception of a change in cathexis. It remained a question whether this was due to a new libidinal stream emerging from repression, or to a suppression of feelings connected with transference. The inner conflict in such an instance of repression of affect has little similarity to that of an "as if" patient. The analogy rests only on the affective impoverishment in both.

The narcissism and the poverty of object relationships so characteristic for an "as if" person bring to consideration the relationship of this defect to a psychosis. The fact that reality testing is fully maintained removes this condition from our conception of psychosis.

Narcissistic identification as a preliminary stage to object cathexis, and introjection of the object after its loss, are among the most important discoveries of Freud and Abraham. The psychological structure of melancholia offers us the classical example of this process. In melancholia, the object of identification has been psychologically internalized, and a tyrannical superego carries on the conflict with the incorporated object in complete independence of the external world. In "as if" patients, the objects are kept external and all conflicts are acted out in relation to them. Conflict with the superego is thus avoided because in every gesture and in every act the "as if" ego subordinates itself through identification to the wishes and commands of an authority which has never been introjected.

From the beginning, both the personal impression given by the patients themselves and the psychotic disposition in the family, especially in the first two analytically observed cases, make one suspect a schizophrenic process. The tracing of the severe psychic disturbance directly back to the developments of early childhood seems to me completely justified, and whether this speaks against the diagnosis of a schizophrenic process must, for the time being, be left undecided. My observations of schizophrenic patients have given me the impression that the schizophrenic process goes through an "as if" phase before it builds up the delusional form. A twenty-two-year-old schizophrenic girl came to me after a catatonic attack, oriented for time and place but full of delusional ideas. Until the onset of the confusional state she had led an existence almost indistinguishable from "as if" patients. Her bond to objects with whom she identified herself, and who were always outstanding women, was extremely intense. As a result of rapid shifting of these relationships, she changed her place of residence, her studies, and her interests in an almost manic fashion. Her last identification had led her from the home of a well-established American family to a Communistic cell in Berlin. A sudden desertion by her object led her from Berlin to Paris where she was manifestly paranoid and gradually developed a severe confusion. Treatment restored her to her original state, but despite warnings, her family decided to break off the analysis. The girl was not able to summon enough affect to protest. One day she bought a dog and told me that now everything would be all right; she would imitate the dog and then she would know how she should act. Identification was retained but was no longer limited to human objects; it included animals, inanimate objects, concepts, and symbols, and it was this lack of selectivity which gave the process its delusional character. It was the loss of the capacity for identification with human objects which made possible the erection of a new, delusional world.

Another schizophrenic patient for years had had a recurrent dream in which in great pain and torment she sought her mother but could not find her because she was always faced with an endless crowd of women, each of whom looked like her mother, and she could not tell the right one. This dream reminded me of the stereotyped, recurrent mother figures in the sculpture of the second "as if" patient.

Freud (1923) speaks of "multiple personality" as the result of a process in which numerous identifications lead to a disruption of the ego. This may result in manifest psychopathology, or the conflicts between the different identifications can assume a form which need not necessarily be designated as pathological. Freud refers to a purely inner process of ego formation, and this does not apply to the "as if" identifications with objects in the outer world. However, the same psychological process will also in the "as if" personality on one occasion have a more "normal" resolution and on another a pathological outcome which may be more or less severe.

Anna Freud (1936) points out that the type of pseudo affectivity observed in "as if" patients is often found in puberty. I believe that the depreciation of the primary objects (also typical of puberty) who served as models for the ego ideal plays an important role in both. Anna Freud describes this type of behavior in puberty as incurring the suspicion of psychosis. I believe that the reflections which I have presented here will also serve for puberty. At one time the process will lie within the bounds of the "normal" and at another it bears the seeds of a pathological condition. The type justifies the designation "schizoid," whether or not schizophrenia later develops.

Whether the emotional disturbances described in this paper imply a "schizophrenic disposition" or constitute rudimentary symptoms of schizophrenia is not clear to me. These patients represent variants in the series of abnormal distorted personalities. They do not belong among the commonly accepted forms of neurosis, and they are too well adjusted to reality to be called psychotic. While psychoanalysis seldom succeeds, the practical results of treatment can be very far-reaching, particularly if a strong identification with the analyst can be utilized as an active and constructive influence. In so far as they are accessible to analysis, one may be able to learn much in the field of ego psychology, especially with regard to disturbances of affect, and, perhaps, make contributions to the problem of the "schizoid" which is still so obscure.

In the great delusional formations of the psychoses we see primitive and archaic drives returning from the depths of the unconscious in a dramatic manner. Regression takes place because the ego has failed. We speak of this as a "weakness of the ego" and assume that the reasons for this failure are psychological, constitutional, or organic. Psychoanalysis can investigate the first of these, especially in prepsychotic conditions to which these cases belong.

21

Some Psychoanalytic Observations on Surgery

(1942)

First of all, I would like to point out that the observations to be presented in this discussion of psychic reactions to surgical operations did not arise from an experimental, planned collection of specific data designed to answer a well-defined and carefully delimited question; on the contrary, in large measure the material to be discussed has come from looking back over long years of psychoanalytic experience and collecting and reconstructing observations which originally were not intended to answer the questions included here.[1]

The percentage of analytic patients who have had operations before they come to analysis is extraordinarily high. Operations during the period of analytic treatment are, on the other hand, rather rare. There has, consequently, been some, but not much, opportunity for direct observation of the immediate psychic effect of surgical attack on the body. As a rule, the psychoanalytic reliving of an operation which occurred perhaps years before is intense and vivid and the reconstruction of the psychic reac-

First published in *Psychosomatic Medicine*, 4:105-115, 1942.

[1] The only psychoanalytic work known to me on the present theme is the thorough study of Karl A. Menninger, "Polysurgery and Polysurgic Addiction" (1934).

tions at the time of the operation is especially reliable, first, because memories of the operation always reappear in those analytic situations for which there is an emotional associative link, and, secondly, because the analytic procedure itself is very often experienced psychologically as an operation and, as a result, mobilizes all the psychic attitudes which accompanied the real operation in the past.

The question of psychic reactions to surgical procedures can be divided into the following problems:

1. The psychology of the individual and his neurosis, as well as the psychic situation which precedes an anticipated operation.

2. The actual meaning of the operation per se; that is, the threat of danger, the amount of suffering to be expected, the chances of cure, and so forth. In these, the patient's relationship to the diseased organ and the significance of that organ for him in reality and symbolically are of particular importance. The act of the operation, it may be added, can be divided into two parts, each of which has a specific and different meaning: (a) the anesthesia, and (b) the bloody, surgical attack itself.

3. The postoperative reaction.

4. Last, but not least, the patient's emotional relationship to the surgeon.

Obviously, it is difficult to discuss these points separately since they overlap and are closely interrelated.

The first and most important problem which meets us is the behavior of the patient before the operation, for we know that his later fate, that is, the postoperative reaction, is dependent upon this, and this problem, *eo ipso,* belongs to the larger problem of anxiety. Observation shows that the factor of greatest importance for the successful conquest of operation anxiety and its results is the amount of preoperative preparation; that is, whether the operation was performed as an emergency without the patient having a chance to prepare himself or whether the more propitious situation held and the patient had an opportunity for a longer or shorter time of inner preparation. In the first case we have to expect a psychic shock reaction in the patient and its influence on the postoperative situation. The conditions developed in such a shock reaction are very closely related to the so-called traumatic neuroses, which usually are called forth by serious accidents, unexpected attacks, train wrecks, and other situations of sudden and unheralded invasions of danger. Let us rather speak here of "fright neurosis," traumatic neurosis being a larger and more complicated conception. Symptoms developed in such a condition are those of general irritability, sleeplessness, anxiety dreams and nightmares, attacks of anxiety with cardiac and respiratory distress, with vasomotor and secretory disturbances, etc. The physiological symptoms accompanying the state of anxiety are particularly unwelcome to the surgeon and interfere with the patient's postoperative recovery. It is my impression—and it was not difficult to verify this by questioning surgeons—that the more acutely indicated the operation and the more unprepared the patient, the greater is the possibility of this reaction appearing during the postoperative period. This observation agrees with Freud's (1920a) theory of shock as a result of an unanticipated danger in which the psychic life is overwhelmed by sudden great excitement in response to a flood of abrupt, new stimuli without the possibility of mobilizing an inner struggle for defense. On the other hand, anxiety about a danger expected to be encountered after a certain period of time is a signal for the psyche to form defense reactions, which then weaken the shock and have an ameliorating influence. The more prepared the patient for the operation, therefore, the less is the chance of an anxiety reaction following it. I will return to these reactions later. Here, however, I would like to point out an important detail: it is not the freedom from anxiety or its presence before an operation which gives the favorable prognosis, but the inner assimilation of the *anxiety signal* which arises in the patient who expects an operation; its goal is the building up of inner defenses. You may see patients who have lived in fear for weeks before an operation and are completely free from anxiety after it, and you may see others who, being prepared for the operation, were apparently free from all fear beforehand and subsequently develop severe and dangerous anxiety states.

To understand what is meant by the inner assimilation of the anxiety signal we must first understand what it is the person to be operated upon fears. In the first place, his fear is objective;

it is, naturally, dependent upon the real danger brought by the operation. The opening of a small abscess on a finger is certainly not so perilous as a complicated abdominal operation, whose actual danger is known to the patient. We frequently find, however, that the patient's fear reaction is not at all commensurate with the actual motive. We often even see the paradoxical situation in which the greater the real danger the smaller the conscious fear reaction, and we can change our question to: what inner dangers are so mobilized by the external threat of the operation that the anxiety takes on an entirely individual character which is dependent upon the pre-existing psychic situation?

Let us keep to reality. The patient is threatened by two things. The first is an injury, which may include even the loss of a part of his own body, a piece of his bodily ego to which he is emotionally attached. The second danger which threatens the patient is the loss of his life. No matter how much confidence he may have in the present state of surgical knowledge and skill, he has the feeling—which is based on reality—of a threat to his life.

As was briefly mentioned before, this twofold danger, and the anxiety which goes with it, is, for the most part, divided into the two operative situations, the narcosis and the action on the organ. Any loss of consciousness, such as fainting, hysterical and epileptic attacks, narcoleptic sleep, and, on occasion, as is shown by certain neurotic sleep disturbances, even normal sleep itself, may be the representative of a going away from life, that is, of death. Many patients say that every time they recover from such a state of unconsciousness, particularly from general anesthesia, they have the exhilarating feeling of having returned to life. No wonder then that the fear of death, mobilized by the expectation of an operation, is connected first of all with narcosis anxiety.

The second anxiety reaction, that related to the diseased organ, is directly connected with the anxiety formation which we call fear of castration. The relation which the two forms of anxiety bear to one another is greatly dependent upon the patient's past development and his working out of the normal anxieties of childhood. The first normal infantile anxiety state, as we all know, is usually the expression of the fear of separation, or, to state it more simply, the fear of being alone, of being abandoned by the mother or her substitute. I consider this anxiety to be the first manifestation of what later appears as the fear of death. The second form of infantile anxiety is that of being punished, and the most powerful form of this fear of punishment, which is never really definitely and finally solved in human beings, centers around the sexual organ and is called "fear of castration" or "castration anxiety." As a historical residue of this fear, there remains the anxiety about all the constituent parts of the body, and we find it later again in all sorts of organic cathexes, in symptoms, anxieties, and hypochondrias. An organ which has been diseased for a long time has, by very virtue of this fact, centered the psychic energies on itself and therefore has assumed a special role in the inner economy of anxiety distribution. It is this role which will determine whether or not and how intensively the threat to the organ brought by an operation will mobilize the old fears of castration.

Still other elements complicate the situation. In chronic disease not only are psychic forces concentrated dynamically on the organ but the latter is also connected with various fantasies. Its location in the body, its role in limiting the freedom of the patient by bringing sickness, its symptoms, which may appear in sudden attacks, give rise to various cathexes; indeed, certain types of neurotic disposition even assign various roles to the diseased organ. A hysteric, for example, will certainly tend to use the diseased organ as a bridge for identification with other objects. An obsessional neurotic or a melancholic will use the organic disease for the purpose of loading and unloading the feeling of guilt. Frequently the organ even has an extremely personified significance; it then becomes the most loved part of the whole body, a second, beloved little self, and takes on, so to speak, the cathexis of an object solicitously loved and carefully tended. In some patients it assumes the guise of a cruel punishment, and I have had under my own observation two cases of paranoid reactions after operations in which the excised organ became a persecutor in the external world.

We must also not forget that specific psychic determinants have been connected with the diseased organ before the disorder set in and that the lesions may even be the result of such psychic attitudes and not their cause. Such organ cathexes can be general in character or more individual in their implication. In all individuals certain parts of the body mobilize quite definite modes of reaction. The threatened loss of sight or hearing will provoke a multitude of emotions, not only as a consequence of the importance of these organs but also as the result of the abundance of their psychological associations. Voyeuristic interests and prohibitions against looking, listening, and not wanting to hear, controlling the environment by seeing and hearing and the danger of losing this control, all these are only a few examples of the various possibilities determining the importance of the involved organs. In addition, the position of various parts of the body—above or below, inner or outer—will be of great general significance psychologically. The individual significance of the organ before and after the disease also enters the picture, and it, too, can be extremely varied.

This brief survey of well-known facts was intended only to remind you that the patient's relation to the organ which is to be operated upon is extremely complex and that postoperative reactions, whether they be normal or pathological, are dependent upon these relationships.

Analytic theory has established an identity between the fear of castration and the fear of death. In this paper I have separated the manifestations of the fear of death from those connected with dread of the loss of an organ. The total psychic situation existent at the time of an operation determines whether the subsequent reaction will have more the character of anticipation of an irrevocable annihilation through death or correspond rather to the fear of castration.

I have been much impressed by certain of my analytic observations concerning the import of previous operations. I have noted, for example, that operations performed in childhood leave indelible traces on the psychic life of the individual.[2] Memories or affective reaction to the original operation return again and

[2] K. Menninger (1934) refers to a case of circumcision of a three-year-old boy which had a powerful reactivation of horror and fright connected with this operation twenty-five years later in attacks of depression.

again in certain situations. The reaction to an operation later in life corresponds often in form and essence to that of the first. In analysis I observed a very impressive case of such an influence from an operation in childhood on later reactions. A thirty-year-old patient had decided to undergo a harmless orthopedic operation on her knee. Shortly before the operation she developed pain in her ear and dizziness. At the same time she suffered severe attacks of anxiety from which she had been free for several months as a result of the analysis. Examination of the ear was negative. The psychogenesis of the complaints lay in the reactivation of the associative link between the expected operation and a mastoid operation in her fourth year—the only operation which she had had in the past.

The child's reaction, on the other hand, depends upon his psychic situation at the time of the operation. If he is struggling with infantile masturbation, he will interpret every surgical act involving his body, whether bloody or not, as an attack and a punishment and will react to later situations in the same way as he did to the first and regard them as assaults. Consequently, he will protest furiously against the attack and in some way or another against the environment connected with the operation. I have observed that even the best-tempered and mildest people will have increased aggressive tendencies in the period preceding an anticipated operation or after it.

Another child may take his punishment passively because of the pressure of his sense of guilt, and he will repeat this attitude later. Many prolonged convalescences and many depressions are connected with this surrender to the punishing forces.

A different situation arises when the child is operated on at a time when his anxieties are bound up, because of external or internal experiences, with the real or emotional loss of a love object. For example, the first operative experience of one of my patients occurred when he had not yet recovered from the privation he experienced from his mother's going away on a trip, and the entire operative experience was felt as being separated from his mother, from the world, and from life.

Still another situation, and the most common, arises when the child is burdened not only with a sense of guilt because of forbidden masturbation but also by death wishes against some person near to him. The expectation that his own death will result from this attitude is a powerful factor in both the early and the late fears of operation. If we remember the infantile conception of death as a disappearance and a staying away, it will be clear why the loss of consciousness in narcosis is synonymous with entering death.

The adult's attitude to the expected operation, thus, is in large measure determined by the experiences of his childhood and in this an operation during his early years will play an important role; but aside from this, his early development, that is, his psychic disposition, will also determine his reactions to an operation and give them an individual character. Common to most if not all patients is the fact that the expectation of an operation mobilizes a large amount of aggression, whose motives and fate likewise have an individual character.[3] And common probably to all patients facing operation is the expectation of a great event, whose content has a more or less feminine or masculine cast, which is not always identical with the actual, anatomical sex of the patient. As is to be expected, however, in the overwhelming majority of cases, for women the operation will become a delivery, with all the fears and anxieties pertaining to the birth of a child. In men, on the other hand, castration stands in the center of the experience. As a result, in women the anxiety will have a character identical to that of the fear of delivery and will, like this, be quite dependent upon the fate of the patient's relationship to her own mother. Reactions to death wishes against the mother, particularly against the pregnant and life-giving mother, guilty feelings resulting from the impulse to murder the child already born or in fantasy expected to be born of the mother, may accompany the narcotic sleep and will give content to the anxieties and related symptoms which precede and follow the general anesthesia. An unsuccessfully resolved relation to the mother contains a still greater, deeper danger. The increased tie to the mother which develops under the pressure of anxiety and the burden of the feeling of guilt, can receive a new regressive

[3] E. Lindemann (1941) also observed in his patients the strengthening of aggressive impulses.

thrust in the moment of the danger from an operation. The masochistic turning of the aggressions against the person's own self then brings about the ominous state of clinging to the suffering and to the postoperative symptoms. An early infantile longing for the mother, mobilized by the operation, then gives rise to oral and mother's womb fantasies, whose content is so closely related to the death wish that one frequently is misled into ascribing them to the "death instinct." Going to sleep under the narcosis often represents the realization not only of the fear of death but also of the wish for death.

I had a chance to observe in analysis a case of insomnia which developed after a successful gall bladder operation. The patient told me that before the operation she was relatively healthy and free from anxiety. For certain reasons she decided to be operated on for a chronic, long-standing gall bladder disturbance. No anxiety reaction of any sort could be observed before the operation. In analysis she remembered that she had had a similar condition of sleeplessness after the birth of her only child fifteen years before. It was learned that she always had had the feeling that she never could be the mother of a child. During the first five years of her marriage she constantly expected to become pregnant, but the first conception occurred only after this time. During her pregnancy she never could realize that she actually was expecting a child, and she was tormented by a fear that her child might die very soon after its birth. She refused to accept any narcotic during her delivery to minimize the pains, pretending that she did not want to miss the first appearance of the child, but, *de facto,* she was afraid that something would happen to her child while she was asleep. In the insomnia which followed the birth she continued this fearful watching over the child. She developed no anxiety before her operation, but during the postoperative period her sleeplessness expressed the fear: "If I go to sleep, death will carry me off." Her operation was for her another delivery situation with the mobilization of the same anxieties, connected especially with narcosis, which she could not evade this time.

The menace of death implicit in the operation may be thought of as suicide. When this occurs, two diametrically opposed reactions may appear during the postoperative period: a state of euphoria, such as is often observed after unsuccessful suicidal attempts, or even a manic condition, may set in and the patient feel like one reborn; or else a deep depression and an unwillingness to be cured may develop, another frequent reaction to unsuccessful suicide.

I once observed a psychically healthy woman who, after the marriage of her only daughter, decided to have an operation for an old, chronic renal calculus. She felt that now she was alone and free she should begin a new life with new energy and. for this reason she wanted to get rid of her old trouble, which had necessarily limited her activities. She showed no fear of the approaching operation and her behavior was absolutely normal. The operation was very successful, but her convalescence was prolonged; she was more and more depressed and finally decided to seek analytic help. The entire depression was explained retrospectively by the first dream she remembered on awakening from the anesthesia, and the dream was as follows:

It was a beautiful sunny landscape. Her Aunt Anna, radiant, young, beautiful, and dressed in a white summery hat and a light dress, embraced her tenderly and said, "It's splendid that everything is finished."

In the dream the patient herself felt weak, exhausted, and depressed. This Aunt Anna had played an important part in the patient's life as a mother substitute. She had once been a famous beauty, and the patient was named Anna after her, her parents expecting that she would grow up to be as beautiful as her namesake. As a young girl, she had been distressed by comparisons with her aunt and, considering her obligation to become a beauty as a burden, had finally taken up a very serious profession out of an already neurotic fear that she would disappoint her parents in their expectations. Aunt Anna had died after an operation when she was still relatively young. In her dream the patient identified herself with her aunt and in this way fulfilled two mutually contradictory wishes: Aunt Anna, and with her the patient, died as the result of an operation, but at the same time

Aunt Anna's death was denied and the patient returned to life, radiant and young like the admired Aunt Anna of her childhood. In the analysis it developed that the patient was deeply, but not consciously, unhappy about the marriage of her daughter. She saw no hope of any more real joy in life, and the conscious wish to become more active by having an operation was accompanied by a death wish. Her whole attitude toward the operation was very ambivalent, and the dream was a perfect representation of this ambivalence.

Further observations have shown that this patient's dream might almost be called typical. I have a large collection of postoperative dreams which express the wish for life and the longing for death in this double form. If the patient is naïve or particularly religious, these contradictory wishes often appear in the shape of angels and devils, the former as representatives of life and the second of death.

Naturally, the reactions will always depend upon the state of the patient immediately before the operation.

In all the observations I am reporting here I have excluded those cases in which severe loss of blood, toxicity, exhaustion, undernourishment, suppuration, or other organic conditions before or after operation may be regarded as provocators of the psychic reactions. Psychiatric case histories include patients in whom relatively insignificant operations were followed by manic conditions, depressions, melancholias, and so forth. And in contrast to this, psychoses have been seen to benefit from operations; in fact, for a time some were tempted to suspect a link between melancholia and diseases of the gall bladder after a number of cases were seen to improve appreciably as a direct response to a gall bladder operation. This scientific error was a repetition of a very ancient concept concerning the relation between gall and depression of mood which persists today in the residue of the name applied to the illness, "melancholia" ("black bile"). Soon, however, everyone had to agree that the observed cure was due to the unspecific effect of the operation. Later it was noted that in many psychiatric patients, especially in depressions, the operation and the suffering it entails could be experienced as a punishment and thus bring enormous relief. A hypomanic patient whom

I analyzed had her first severe manic attack after an operation for chronic appendicitis. Her manic reaction arose from the meaning which the organ had had for her for years. It had hindered her activities in life; she herself had given it the role of a guardian with commands and prohibitions. The operation freed her from her dictator, and she experienced the manic triumph, known to us all.

The use that may be made of an operation in the fantasy life is particularly clear in hysterical patients. I should like to illustrate this statement by an example.

Many years ago an analyst from another country wrote me that he was sending a fifteen-year-old girl for analysis and that she was suffering from an obviously hysterical stomach complaint. The arrangements were made in June, and the girl was to come to me in September. In September, instead of the patient, a letter arrived telling me that her condition had grown worse during the summer and her doctors had found it necessary to perform an exploratory laparotomy, which had shown nothing. After that the patient had been in bed for weeks. Her condition was serious; she was weak as the result of continual vomiting; and she was severely depressed. Later she improved somewhat and came to me for analysis. She told me in her first analytic hour about the operation and that as she was coming out of the general anesthesia she asked for something to drink. The nurse gave her a cold drink to wash out her mouth but ordered her not to swallow any. The patient went to sleep, still very thirsty, and dreamed that a big, blond woman wearing glasses gave her a drink and said, "Drink, my child." This woman was the analyst as she pictured her in her fantasy to whom she was to go for analysis. I understood this dream as a simple wish fulfillment in which I, in contrast to the wicked nurse, gave her a drink. Only one thing was obscure: since she gave me the role of fulfilling her wishes, why didn't she come for analysis as soon as possible? The patient herself was not conscious of her motives, just as she was not aware of why she provoked her operation. Analysis revealed that all her intestinal troubles, her frequent X-ray examinations, her eating ceremonials were for the purpose of determining whether or not something were growing in her body and her restrictions in eating were aimed at hindering this growth. She had chosen the operation rather than analysis because another of her masochistic fantasies was that a woman would tie her up and force her to become pregnant by introducing a fluid into her body through her mouth. The analyst who sent her to me had told her that I had recently had a child myself and would know how to make her into a real woman. Another determinant of her dream was the fact that the blond, heavy woman who appeared in it was the midwife of the little village in which she had spent her childhood. She began her resistance to the analysis with this postoperative dream and would have preferred to die from the operation—which had disappointed her because nothing had been found inside her body—rather than accept the analysis and its aim. Surgeons naturally are not acquainted with such complicated psychological processes, and if the analyst had not intervened the patient would have been operated on again, as she demanded.

Every analyst will see in my patient's dreams and attitude an interplay between pregnancy and birth fantasies on the one hand and the castration complex on the other. This close amphimixis is typical for pubescent girls and in rare cases has an analogy in boys. A large percentage of all appendectomies performed on girls during the puberty period serve psychogenic purposes similar to those observed in this patient. With greater distance from puberty the castration complex in girls fades more and more in the content of operations and is absorbed in stronger, deeper, specifically feminine anxieties. This brings us back to the death-castration problem in operations.

I have pointed out that the narcosis and the sex of the patient play an important role in determining the predominance of the one or the other reaction. I might call special attention to the fact that in contrast to general anesthesia, spinal anesthesia seems to exhibit many more castration elements. This difference is of great practical importance, for the effect of death wishes and the fear of death will produce other symptoms than will that of the castration complex. For a long time I have been interested in observing how closely linked in the fantasies of women are birth, the creator of life, and death, the annihilator of life. Every situation of delivery, whether it be in reality or in fantasy, brings with it the reinforcement of the old relationship to the mother with all the interplay of the mobilized aggression, the feeling of guilt, the masochistic reaction, and the dangerous reunion with the mother. This constellation plays a much greater role in the normal psychic life and in the neuroses of women than the castration complex. That we meet the latter so frequently rests upon its role as a defender against the greater, bloodier, and more annihilating dangers of femininity.

The material gained from the study of the problem of operations has reinforced my critical evaluation of the concept of the female castration complex. Karen Horney once made the remark that our concept of feminine psychology, especially of the female castration complex, is too masculine in its orientation. While my interpretation of the whole problem is very different from that of Karen Horney, I believe, however, that the role which is ascribed to "penis envy" in female psychology still needs some reorientation. The greater anxieties and the reactions connected with them which can be seen in surgical patients, for instance, refer predominantly to purely feminine processes in which, in contrast to men, the castration complex plays a less important role. In women fear of delivery stands in the dynamic position held by the fear of castration in men. This anxiety has a double content: it is the talion anxiety in which the destructive impulses once directed toward the mother are turned against the self, and it hides the deep longing for the mother, whose realization already lies at the threshold of death.

I will not deny that castration anxiety also makes its appearance. It is probably possible to approach the problem statistically. My observation that the kind of narcosis, on the one hand, and the organ operated upon, on the other, determine the form in which the anxiety is expressed can surely be proven numerically. It would seem that operations on important inner organs, especially on the genital organs, like the general narcosis, tend to bring more death anxieties in their wake and that operations on peripheral organs and spinal or local anesthesia result in more castration anxiety.

To illustrate my differentiation between the reaction to general anesthesia, on the one hand, and to spinal anesthesia, on the other, I should like to present the following case history.[4]

The patient was admitted to the Psychiatric Department of the Massachusetts General Hospital because of the psychic symptoms she developed after a hysterectomy.

She was admitted to the hospital because of weakness of her legs, bending over of her trunk, and because of an impulse to throw herself through a window. These symptoms came on gradually following a hysterectomy and perineorrhaphy. Total hysterectomy was performed under ether narcosis and perineor- rhaphy some time later under spinal anesthesia. She did well following the operation and was discharged two weeks later. After she returned home she was restless and developed her symptoms. The symptoms in the legs and the pain in her back were con- sidered to be psychological, the more so since the case history gave evidence that she had already suffered similar symptoms several years ago which had disappeared following the birth of her second child. Some years later, after a period of conflict with her husband, she had a nervous breakdown, lost the use of her legs, but recovered immediately after the adoption of a child. Twice during the years of her marriage she had shown symptoms of pseudocyesis. Once she maintained the fantasy of being preg- nant for nine months and went to the hospital for delivery, where she gave birth to gas and bloody fluid but no child. Her whole life history showed that she had two ways of ending her symptoms of paralysis of the legs, irritability, and depression: by giving birth to a child or adopting a child, or by creating preg- nancy by fantasy.

A short excerpt of the recent case history is the following: The patient was aware of her deep dependency on her mother. Sixteen years previous to our patient's own operation, her mother was operated on for cancer of the uterus and died as a result of the operation, on the morning on which the patient herself had a thyroidectomy. In connection with the mother's death the patient says she wished she "could have gone with mother because she

[4] The case history was taken in an absolutely objective manner by Dr. B. Bandler. I have taken only a small excerpt from it, which, however, is quoted almost verbatim.

has nothing to live for." After her mother's death she dreamed every night that her mother held her hand. The fact that the patient had an operation on the same day as the mother causes one to suspect hysteria, and the symptoms, as described by the patient, evidently had a hysterical character. She felt "something snap in her throat." The doctor said it was imaginary, but the imagination gradually materialized into a lump in her neck. She was told of her mother's death just before the operation, which apparently resulted in her being on the danger list for five days after the thyroidectomy. After her mother's death she wept a great deal until the birth of her child one year later, when "life again appeared livable."

Some months prior to her hysterectomy she was told about the need of an operation but she was not at all bothered, even when she knew that she had a tumor in her uterus. "My mother died of cancer of the uterus. It was a tumor she started with, but she had also other organs operated on, her gall bladder and others. That didn't bother me. If it is only a tumor in the uterus they would get at it." She energetically and absolutely denied any feeling of danger from this operation, but she began to develop anxiety when hearing about ether narcosis. "The doctor told me at the time of my thyroid operation that I had two leaking heart valves and that makes me be afraid of ether." Evidently the fear of having a cancer like her mother was repressed, but the fear came out in an indirect association with her mother's death, namely, that she heard on the day of the mother's death that her own heart was not good; and now she concentrated all her anxieties on this fact alone and on ether narcosis, denying any fear of cancer or of the operation itself. She had no recollections of going under ether except gradually falling asleep. Two days after the operation the first thing she remembered having heard were carollers singing "Come All Ye Faithful." The singing was real, but the patient thought she was dead and being welcomed into heaven. A little poetry included in her case history shows her ideas about heaven.

> Dear God, you will know my mother
> By the beauty of her smile?

Wilt Thou say to her I'm coming home
In just a little while?

After her hysterectomy, besides the weakness of her legs mentioned, she developed a psychic state which is identical with one
she suffered after her thyroidectomy and mother's death. This was
described as: "I could not speak for a couple of days. I went to
pieces. I lost faith of myself. I did not cry. I had a ravenous appetite. I was around the house with nothing to do and I kept eating
as though there was no end to me. I haven't slept. I was up at
night and would sit in the living room. I didn't seem to have
control. When I would go to get up I felt I wanted to go out
the window. I wanted to hear glass crash. They held me. I felt
like somebody who had lost the mind." A similar state developed
after her recent operation, which was a mixture of manic and
depressive features. She pretended to feel wonderful, had no
pains and no complaints. By and by she was more depressed. She
said she had nothing to live for. She was a crippled old lady. She
stopped going out, going to church, and didn't want to see her
family and her friends. She developed again a ravenous appetite.
She swelled up and started again to develop some symptoms of
pseudopregnancy.

In the hospital her mood changes were of circular form with
quick changes of happy manic feeling of "marvelous" to suicidal
ideas, especially of jumping through the window.

I want to tell you some of her dreams after her operation. She
reported: A tall man is there. He says, "She is married and has
nine children." "No, only three," says the patient in the dream.
In reality she had three children and her mother had nine
children. She repeatedly tried to convince her environment that
she had no anxiety about the operation, but further investigation
shows that she brought with her a letter for her husband which
he was to read after her death, and in it she gave directions
for her funeral and named the people who were to be her pall-
bearers. Now in her depressions she contemplated suicide. Two
topics prevail in her case history: loving recollections about her
mother and complaints about her husband. She told of her
mother's wish when she was dying that the patient die too. After

her mother's death she felt that eventually she would get cancer of the womb, be operated on, and would die. The dream material in the first weeks after the operation represented longing for the mother and birth situations, either symbolically or in manifest dreams. With increasing depression the dream material was more and more filled with the mother-daughter relation; sometimes her mother was suffering, operated on, dying, sometimes the patient herself, sometimes her daughter. I want to mention at this point that the patient's relationship to her daughter was an absolute copy of her relationship to her own mother. She even told the doctor that her daughter had a lump on her neck and would probably have to have an operation, a thyroidectomy. She reinforced this relationship whenever her relation to her husband was severed, especially the sexual part. Another time she stated that her mother told her before her death not to have more children. She felt bad and thought her mother had no right to tell her that and very soon became pregnant with her second child. The first five months of pregnancy she did not know about it because her periods continued, and she consulted a doctor because of her weight loss, which she felt was due to her having cancer as her mother did. It is interesting that her attempt to deny the dependency on her mother expressed itself in getting more children and in creating pseudopregnancies.

During her stay on the ward her behavior was a mixture of hysterical excitements and manic-depressive features. Her hysterical tendencies expressed themselves also in conversion symptoms connected with her back and her legs. These symptoms were directly referred to her spinal anesthesia, and the patient expressed her anger against this part of the operation, especially against the doctors. The associations connected with this part of her symptoms and reactions had nothing to do with her mother but were connected with an operation of her father and her brother, who once was operated on with spinal anesthesia, and she heard that if he had not died from his diabetes both legs would have been cut off as the result of the operation. Also, her husband had had a spinal anesthesia in connection with a hernia operation, which then made him stop the sexual relationship with the patient. Probably the patient suspected that the operation made him impotent. It is interesting how the two consecutive operations, one with general narcosis and the other with spinal anesthesia, mobilized two groups of reactions. The first, the general narcosis, was associated with birth and death. The reality situation was her mother's death in hysterectomy, which has given a powerful motive for identification. The spinal anesthesia provoked reactions which we consider to be the expression of her castration complex in which her identification with men who have been operated on is due to their castration.

Not all patients who are operated on have these impressive reality situations for their two forms of identification. The reality of the situations in the above history has given us the opportunity to understand the patient's reactions, even with the simple method of a direct clinical investigation. In the cases known to me psychoanalytically, absolutely the same reactions could be observed without the reality situations of mother's death or father's or brother's and husband's operations under spinal anesthesia. Whatever the operation was, abdominal or on organs with less cathexis than the abdominal ones, the ether narcosis itself, the sleeping act, the surrender to cruel and dubious treatment, has provoked the identification with the mother who gives birth to a child and the mother who is dying. The ravenous eating of this patient and her real or fantasied pregnancies were the expression of a deep longing for the mother-baby relationship, once in the form of an oral longing with ravenous eating, once directly in pregnancy. The realization of this wish in real or pseudopregnancy was an energetic flight from death and avoiding the reunion with the mother by giving life to a child, that is, becoming a mother herself. This motif of reunion appeared again and again in her dreams and suicidal tendencies in the form of dark, deeply rooted mother's womb fantasies.

Let us return to the case history. After leaving the hospital the patient continued to see the psychiatrist. When he left, she became quite restless and saw various other departments in the hospital during the next two months, complaining about vague abdominal distress, and made arrangements with the surgical department for a gall bladder operation. She had definite attacks of gall bladder colic with mild jaundice, sufficient to make it seem imperative to remove the gall bladder before the operation might have to be done in a state of dangerous emergency. The patient seemed rather cheerful at the prospect of the operation and toyed with the idea that maybe she would not recover and again in a somewhat playful manner spoke about getting everything ready in case she should die. I would remind you that before her hysterectomy she said that she was not at all afraid of the operation because she was to have only a uterus operation and not, like her mother, the dangerous gall bladder operation too. Her anticipation of death, according to the report, seemed not serious; it was rather a matter of a playing with a danger. According to my opinion, it was rather a wish for a reunion with the mother, a real, dangerous suicidal attitude.

A psychiatrist saw her a few hours before the operation, and she seemed unusually confident and without any trace of fear. After the operation she remained in a state of curious unresponsiveness for three days and reported later that this whole period could hardly be remembered by her. When she finally became communicative, she told the psychiatrist that she had only one dream. In this dream her mother seemed to appear and seemed to be friendly with her, and seemed to say, "I'm glad you have come." There was a marked degree of happiness in this dream. After the night in which she had this dream she felt "like her old self again," had a rapid physical recovery, and felt very well on the sixteenth day, when she left the hospital. She had expected her husband to come but he was detained. She wanted the psychiatrist to have an interview with her husband to make it quite clear to him that he had to permit her sister, I suppose as a mother substitute, to stay with her from now on, the sister to whom he had forbidden the house some time ago. Personally, I think that the patient will have more operations or make a suicidal attempt.

You will have noticed that in this paper the psychic reactions of men to surgical procedures have received less consideration than have those of women. This inequality has come about because I do not possess as many data about men and must give you more of a general impression.

302 CLINICAL PAPERS

I have already mentioned that in men, as is to be expected,[5] the castration complex stands in the center of the anxieties. In the dreams and in the associations to operations experienced by men or expected by them, fighting with a man or a group of men very frequently appears. The patient actively defends himself against being overcome. When passive tendencies predominate in the man, the act of operation can be experienced as a delivery, just as it is in women. In general, the relationship to the surgeon as a father or brother figure seems to determine the man's manner of experiencing the operation. The sex of the surgeon, who is usually a man, plays a greater role in male patients than it does in female, and I have often been astonished at how many fantasies of being raped and the libidinous-masochistic elements of the operation remain in the background in women patients (which does not deny the existence of sadomasochistic fantasies centering about the surgeon).

I once observed a man who had had a woman surgeon perform a harmless operation on his finger when he was a child and who had been left with an inextinguishable resentment against all women.

At the beginning of this paper I mentioned that anxiety is an important signal for the psychic organism to mobilize and create defense mechanisms for the assimilation of that anxiety. During the period of preparing for an operation the fear of death is combated in two ways, the same two ways used, to a certain extent, by all mankind in attempting to free itself from this fear. There is, first, a strong emphasis on the positive relation to life, which lets man forget his future death, and, second, an inner preparation for and acceptance of death. The poor patient, whom we might call a candidate for death, strengthens his ties to this life while he is waiting for his operation by asking for more love and attention from those around him, by making increased demands upon members of his family, by loving and trusting his surgeon. The necessary acceptance of possible death is expressed even in his conscious actions; he, for instance, draws up his will

[5] Menninger (1934) gives interesting illustrations for the different relationships of the castration complex to surgery. It is no coincidence that almost all the cases he cites in this connection are men.

and arranges his affairs. I have been deeply impressed by my observations of this reaction, and I have the impression that this process of accepting possible death leaves traces which do not always disappear after the person has returned to life from beyond the operation.

I should like to say a few words about the dream life of the patient who undergoes an operation. Earlier in the paper I compared the condition seen in surgical patients to a traumatic neurosis. A very interesting difference exists between the two. We know from experience and from the literature that the traumatic situation is usually repeated in the dream life in a remarkable manner. According to Freud, this recurrence of the original situation constitutes a subsequent abreaction through repetition. In the many dreams I have observed in postoperative patients, I have never seen such a direct repetition of the traumatic experience. If the dream contains direct references to the operation, as may occur frequently during analysis, the dreamer usually appears in the active role; that is, he himself performs an operation or carries out an act against another person which through association leads back to the operation once experienced. This dream is typical for men. The person against whom the patient acts in such a dream is usually one of authority, a father figure; he frees himself from anxiety by reversing the situation.

An interesting dream mechanism after operations portrays the dreamer himself as bleeding, not at the site of the operative wound but from a totally different part of the body. For example, after genital operations in men and women there are frequent dreams of bleeding from the upper parts of the body, especially from the mouth or the nose (see Lindemann, 1941).

The psychology of the surgeon would be a chapter in itself. We are often inclined to blame him for his unfamiliarity with psychological processes. We see how many operations are staged by patients out of neurotic motives, and we would like to see the surgeon an ally combating these motives with us rather than accepting them. We must not forget, however, that psychological tendencies have a direct influence on the body and that the indications for an operation seen by the surgeon and accepted by him constitute an already established, objective organic fact. Often we psychiatrists are absolutely helpless when we are approached for advice. In spite of the fact that in the patient I discussed in detail the psychiatrist understood all the psychic determinants, he could not decide to give a contraindication for the surgical procedure and so perhaps endanger the patient's life. As long as so much remains unclear about psychosomatic events we must not blame either the surgeon or ourselves for errors. The surgeon gives his indications for an operation on the basis of organic findings, and it is certainly a delusion to expect him to comprehend the unconscious psychic life of the patient and to be influenced by it; he should, however, be expected to take the psychological situation into account in childhood, and a very energetic warning should be given conservative doctors. If surgeons only knew how much damage is done, for example, by a circumcision performed as a hygienic measure during the early years of childhood, they would feel like so many Herods. Modern pediatricians are beginning to take the state of infantile anxiety into account before deciding on any operation which is not absolutely necessary.

And the surgeon's own psychic make-up would form another chapter. To illustrate it briefly, I should like to relate the following, absolutely true anecdote:

One early summer morning many years ago, the inhabitants of a small German university town—I think it was Würzburg—made the horrifying discovery that all the dogs which had been running loose during the night in a certain part of the city had lost their tails. They learned that the medical students had attended a drinking bout that night and that when they left the party one young man had had the highly humorous inspiration to cut off the tails of the dogs. Later he became one of the most famous surgeons in the world.

22

The Psychiatric Component in Gynecology
(1950)

UNTIL recently the interest of the psychiatrist in gynecological illnesses and in the reproductive functions of women was limited to the major psychopathological disturbances which sometimes accompany them. These are in part due to organic causes such as the exhaustive psychoses in toxemia, and states of confusion and febrile deliria in the puerperium. On the other hand, the increased psychological demands and emotional adaptations required in the course of normal organic processes may precipitate psychic illnesses hitherto latent but to which the individual was predisposed, such as manic-depressive psychosis or schizophrenia.

The psychiatrist was further attracted to the gynecologist's domain by certain obscure problems in which no organic changes could be determined to account for the subjective complaints. It was found that the psychiatrist was more competent to deal with these cases, and so the responsibility for them fell to him. However, the conscientious psychiatrist could not legitimately accept this task unless the gynecologist presented him with fully documented evidence of the lack of organic findings. The progressive collaboration between the two branches often gave rise to the

First published in *Progress in Gynecology*, 2:207-217, 1950.

problem of priority. Some authors have claimed that much mental illness is caused by gynecological disturbances and that deliverance from the latter would also eliminate the psychic illness. Others maintain that in many cases the influence of the psychic components on the organic structure is the determining factor, and consequently feel that the psychotherapeutic approach is first indicated.

Gradually we have learned that real competence evolves only from close collaboration: the psychiatrist has come to recognize that the absence of demonstrable organic changes in the so-called "functional" illnesses does not exclude the possibility of somatic disorder. What today belongs in his field may tomorrow pass into the hands of the gynecologist; psychotherapeutic measures may be more successfully replaced by injections. The organically minded gynecologist, on the other hand, has learned that even in cases with organic changes the etiological factor and the motivation of persistent symptoms might have to be sought for in the psyche.

However this may be, we are witnessing tremendous progress in both fields—progress which brings both disciplines closer and closer together: the more refined and profound our understanding, the more the dichotomy, somatic or psychic, vanishes. Of all the existing psychological methods of research psychoanalysis seems the most adequate to bring psychology into close relation with biological or physiological processes. The foundation of this science is the study of instincts; by this very fact psychoanalysis is allied to biology.

Progress in endocrinology and our increasing knowledge concerning the influence of nerve stimuli upon hormonal secretion have brought the importance of psychological events into the ken of the gynecologist. All fundamental biological events of maturation and reproduction—menstruation, pregnancy, birth, postnatal events, climacteric—are to a high degree dependent on the chemical actions and interactions of various endocrine glands. Gynecological diseases and interferences in reproductive functions are in a great number of cases the result of either organic or functional disturbances of the endocrine system.

It is now common knowledge that the harmonious integration of the chemical (hormonal) phenomena of the endocrine system is dependent upon the coordinating effect of the central and peripheral nervous systems. Nerve influences on the endocrine functions of a depressive or exciting character may come from the central zones (hypothalamus, pituitary) or pass through medullosympathetic pathways; stimulation or inhibition of the parasympathetic nerves may result in liberation or withholding of certain chemical products, and vascular alterations may be a response to nerve influences, etc.

Briefly, the definite role played by the endocrine system in gynecology is responsible for the fact that emotional irritations, communicated through the complex avenues of the sympathetic-parasympathetic system, are many times the etiological factors in gynecological diseases, particularly in the functional disorders.

The recognition of these factors may be of the greatest importance for the therapeutic help which the patient expects from the physician, be he a gynecologist or a psychiatrist. The harmonious collaboration between both—often a *sine qua non*—depends on the amount of knowledge one specialist has in the field of the other, because only scientific acceptance and mutual respect create successful collaboration. As a result of this collaboration we have gained in recent years much understanding of one of the most important phenomena of female sexual functions: menstruation. Great progress has been made in our knowledge concerning the physiological process of menstruation. We know what is going on organically in the sexual development of the girl at puberty. We are impressed by the exactness of these physiological functions, their dependency on certain predetermined sequences of hormonal interaction, and by the importance of strictly determined quantitative factors. Too much or not enough of one specific secretion, such as estrogen in relation to progesterone, at a definite moment may disturb the whole course of the menstrual cycle, confuse its periodicity, and bring about a surplus or a lack of menstrual flow, resulting in irregularities of menstruation, oligomenorrhea, amenorrhea, hypermenorrhea, or polymenorrhea, and various other forms of menstrual disturbances well known to the gynecologist.

Each of these disturbances has its empirically suggested endocrinological pathology, each an indicated therapy. Even if the theoretical conclusions and the therapy are still in the experimental stage, the road to be followed for diagnostic and therapeutic goals is determined.

Simultaneously with this progress in endocrinology we began to understand that menstruation—this *par excellence* "biological event"—is to a high degree influenced by psychological factors. The interplay of physiological hormonal functions and psychological reactions, the cyclic course of the somatic process, etc., make menstruation one of the most interesting of psychosomatic problems.

Numerous psychological observations have brought conclusive evidence that each particular type of menstrual disturbance has a definite psychological etiology and may be treated psychologically with success. These psychological elements appear to the experienced psychiatrist as specific for each type of disturbance as the hormonal processes do to the endocrinologist.

Our psychoanalytic observations on puberty in girls have taught us a great deal about the psychological factors which accompany the first appearance of menstruation. This powerful biological event of sexual maturation can be completely diverted from its normal course by psychological influences.

The following case has been selected from many because it exemplifies particularly clearly the coexistence of somatic disorder and decisive psychological forces.

An eighteen-year-old girl sought psychoanalytic treatment because she was suffering from certain, for this age typical, neurotic inhibitions. She was shy, tormented by feelings of inferiority, found almost no contact with other girls, and felt herself undesired by men. When away from her parents' home, she had a feeling of isolation and anxiety. Forced by family circumstances, she lived all by herself in a strange city where her fears grew into phobic anxieties (claustrophobia, agoraphobia). The history of her sexual development was not unusual. Her menstruation started in her thirteenth year. The bleeding surprised her on a skiing trip among female and male friends. She thought that at the time of her first menstruation she was still a healthy girl without neurotic difficulties. The night after the appearance of menstruation she spent in a cold, unheated cabin, where the young people slept close together under a common blanket. She could not sleep and shivered all night. She felt her menstruation was very inconvenient and was happy that it stopped completely the next morning, after having lasted for only one day. Such incomplete menstruations are not infrequent during puberty, and it often takes a certain time before the menstrual cycles in a young woman reach a more or less constant length. This patient had then ceased to menstruate for five years, i.e., until she came under psychoanalytic treatment for her anxiety neurosis. For her amenorrhea she herself had a theory. She thought that she had caught cold that night and thus had lost her capacity to menstruate. She had for some time been under gynecological treatment; as a result of various examinations she had received medicines and a few injections; she also once had some genital bleeding during these treatments which afterward stopped. As she had a low metabolic rate (-25) she had taken thyroid for several years. It was my intention first to treat her anxiety neurosis and afterward to leave the treatment of the amenorrhea to a gynecologist. But it never came to that, because after a few weeks of analysis menstruation reappeared and became regular every thirty days. Whatever her endocrine disorder was, psychic observation disclosed that the amenorrhea and the whole anxiety neurosis had started with an anxiety attack that night at the cabin; the attack which the patient herself and her relatives considered to be a "cold with shivers." This anxiety was, so to speak, a puberty warning, because the situation at night in the cabin confronted the patient for the first time with certain observations and dangers of seduction. This warning was so powerful that its influence was felt by the arrest of the phenomenon of sexual maturity—menstruation—until the moment when psychic treatment and the relation to the analyst gave her shelter and security. The fact that menstruation ceased again during a four months' interruption of the analytic treatment vouches for the psychogenesis of the disturbance. Since the patient had gone for summer vacations to her family and home town where the previous somatic examinations had been made, I asked her to obtain the former reports and to undergo an endocrinological examination. The patient resented my advice and accused me of doubting the psychogenesis, and thus also the success of the treatment; she demonstrated her emotional reaction with a new amenorrhea. Later she apparently was really cured of her neurosis and of the menstrual disturbances. In spite of the obvious psychogenesis of the symptoms and the therapeutic success, I am convinced that the patient was endocrinologically unbalanced and that probably the motor behind the symptom was to be sought in some organically disturbed function. The whole habitus of the patient corresponded to hypothyroidism. Her basal metabolic rate was depressed, and she responded well to thyroid treatment, even though this did not influence her amenorrhea. Whether subsequent endocrine treatment would have had the same therapeutic effect as the psychological is difficult to decide.

The realization that psychological factors can express themselves in various menstrual disturbances also in the mature life of the woman is becoming more and more widespread. Even some severe cases of menorrhagia renitent to organic treatment have proved to react with great success to psychotherapy (Fremont-Smith and Meigs, 1948).

One of the most disturbing symptoms of menstruation—dysmenorrhea—still lacks an explanation on both sides, the psychological and the organic. All efforts to trace dysmenorrhea to disordered uterine contractability, vascular alterations, or endocrine disturbances prove inadequate.

In order to explain the psychological factors, psychoanalytic observations offer the best and perhaps the only recourse. Of course, they lack—as in all deep psychology—objective demonstrability. Therefore, each observation must be considered only a working hypothesis that can be accepted as true only after it has been substantiated by further observation. In the study of psychological determinants of different organic symptoms, we repeatedly meet the same methodological mistake, namely, that generalizations are given as explanations but the specific implications of the symptoms are omitted. The stereotype references to "anxiety," "wish," "environment," actually offer very little to the understanding of the symptom and only prove that there is a willingness to accept psychogenic factors.

The résumé of my study of dysmenorrhea patients states:

Women suffering from dysmenorrhea assume *a priori* the attitude toward menstruation that all occurrences in the female genital region are an orgy of painful suffering. The physical discomfort of menstruation mobilizes and substantiates this assumption. Often a feeling of oppression and even fear of death accompany the pain.

The physical discomfort which a normal woman accepts as a matter of course evokes in these patients a kind of shock reaction. The significance of menstruation as a normal physiological process escapes them and it appears as a painful experience which cannot be avoided. The premenstrual phases of each consecutive menstruation are associated with an increasing anxiety and with the anticipation of something terrible soon to happen. Women suffering from dysmenorrhea are also for the most part hypersensitive to pain and if they are slightly injured, the sight of their own blood arouses terror.

Analytic observation permits the conclusion that deeper psychological mechanisms are responsible for the suffering of pain during menstruation. In general it is obvious that the psychological process of menstruation is capable of disrupting the relative emotional equilibrium by overburdening the psychic apparatus and of playing the role of *agent provocateur* for unconscious latent tendencies. Here can be seen the apparent paradox: that women who suffer from dysmenorrhea are hypersensitive to pain but at the same time have strongly masochistic tendencies. This paradoxical state of affairs, even in overtly perverted masochists, is well known to observers.

A clinical example of the foregoing was supplied by one of my patients, who provided a theoretical explanation of her suffering in the form of a rationalization. In this explanation was the clue to the psychological riddle: she stated that the sexual processes produce poison which is eliminated from the woman's body through menstruation. This generally popular poison theory of menstruation was strengthened in the case of the particular patient and was the expression of definite anxiety-laden ideas. The abundance of poison she interpreted as the result of her sexual guilt, and the pain which accompanied menstruation served for "purification" of the body and expiation of sins. Burning sensations all over the body, headaches, and nausea served to prove to this patient that a purification process affected not only the genital region but her whole personality. Since the pain, serving as a punishment and so as an outlet of guilty feelings, also has a function of relief in the psychic economy, freedom from suffering can have unexpected and undesired results. One of these patients reacted to the psychotherapeutic release from suffering in this way: she transferred the masochistic need from her own body into the outside world and through her behavior provoked situations of suffering dangerous for her.

Another patient, after the disappearance of dysmenorrhea, manifested another symptom—headache—which sometimes accompanies menstruation but which she had not suffered before. In some patients it was possible to observe how the need for suffering was gratified in a less dramatic form through the building of a passive, pliable personality prone to resignation.

Of course, only through further experience with a greater number of individual cases can we come to the conclusion that these observations are typical and valid.

Occasionally there are menstrual disorders in which the organic etiology is not clear but into which we are able to gain some psychological insight. For example, the rare condition of cyclic extrauterine bleeding—"vicarious menstruation"—is of very obscure etiology.

The bleeding in this condition is usually transferred to a part of the body (nose, chin, etc.) removed as far as possible from the genitals. I have had occasion to observe a case in which the bleeding and the localization could be fully clarified by psychological insight. The psychoanalytic treatment of this patient started when she was twenty-two years old. At this time she suffered from amenorrhea and her history was as follows:

At the age of fifteen she had one normal menstruation; later she suffered from irregular bleedings under the skin of one ear lobe, to which she always reacted with the most violent hypochondriacal anxieties. Each time she imagined that she had cancer and would inevitably die as a result of the bleeding ulcer under her ear lobe. Her case was diagnosed as one of vicarious menstruation; all attempts of gynecologists to restore the normal menstrual cycle failed. Later, the bleedings under the ear lobe ceased, but she failed to menstruate for many years.

In the course of her psychoanalytic treatment, the patient developed fantasies in which the vagina was avoided as an organ and everything connected with femininity was centered in her back. She complained of pains in her back at almost periodic intervals, and their psychological origin was evident from the analysis. One day the patient was informed by a telegram that her sister had given birth to a child. The following day she complained of terrible pains in her back and told me that she could feel a lump there. I sent her to a gynecologist, who found that an operation was indicated. Later he told me that he had discovered something he had never seen before in all his practice: biopsy revealed a large number of blood-filled cysts in the tissues around the vertebrae, and the consistency of the blood showed them to be of both old and new formation. There was no doubt that they were vicarious menstruations that, in conformity with the patient's fantasies, had avoided the genitals and were localized in her back. It is quite possible, however, that certain physiological factors had intensified and influenced her fantasy life, as is always the case in the formation of a psychosomatic symptom.

In our patient, the psychological components of the bleeding ear lobe symptom were easily ascertainable. Even in her early childhood the patient used in her struggle against masturbation the device of "plucking" her ear as a diversion from the genitals. It is true that the ear lobes are used for this purpose mostly by boys; girls favor the hair, fingernails, etc., but it is impossible to formulate any general rule on this point.

It is noteworthy that with her menstruation, the patient resorted to the same organ that she had chosen during her childhood as a substitute for her genitals—the ear. Of course, the organic process remains here obscure and hypothetical.

An important psychic element in various cases of menstrual disturbance is the conscious and unconscious attitude of the woman toward pregnancy. Amenorrhea can appear as the expression of the wish for a child or it can be an attempt to escape the feminine destiny. Here previous warning against schematization is important. For example, in cases of hysteria, amenorrhea is often associated with other organic manifestations and the whole complex of symptoms can be explained as a conversion of pregnancy fantasies. The conversion can appear in a single function (for example, hysterical vomiting), or it can be manifested in the whole physical picture of pregnancy.

In cases of anorexia nervosa, amenorrhea is the expression of a much more complicated psychic situation. The entire personality of the patient is completely different from that of the hysterical patient. In anorexia nervosa, the sexual ideas, including pregnancy fantasies, are shifted from the genitals to eating and are deeply connected with prohibitions and commands regarding food. This attitude has more of an obsessive-neurotic character and is especially clear in cases where abstinence from food (anorexia nervosa) alternates with a strong compulsion to eat. These patients often gain and lose up to 100 pounds, but throughout the changes in physical weight, amenorrhea persists. In both conditions, the same psychic attitude toward menstruation obtains.

Another interesting and not fully explained psychosomatic process is pseudocyesis. This condition includes various types. There are cases in which the organic, endocrine process constitutes the cause: for example, a persistent corpus luteum may be manifested by signs of pregnancy (pseudopregnancy). The hypothesis that certain disorders in the endocrine system and an abnormal state in hormonal functions provoke objective changes in the uterus, breasts, etc., identical to those of real pregnancy, has been proved experimentally.

My personal observations on a number of cases were made largely on patients who came for psychiatric help only at the end of the condition with reactive neurotic symptoms (mostly depressive in character). I succeeded in gaining insight into the psychic process; as to the somatic, it was not possible to obtain a clear explanation, as a collaboration with the gynecologist was impossible in these cases seen *post factum*.

In two cases which recently came to my attention the diagnosis of pregnancy had been made by two reliable gynecologists. Objective changes of the uterus in keeping with the third month of pregnancy could be found. The urine test was not made because the diagnosis was beyond any doubt. Both women failed to undergo any further examinations, thus preventing the correction of the wrong diagnosis, a characteristic behavior in many cases of pseudocyesis. Upon the wrong diagnosis, taken as solid evidence, they built up the fantasied pregnancy. In both women their pregnancy developed into an obvious conversion symptom, in the one up to the seventh month, in the other up to the ninth. One demonstrated a tremendous increase in adipose tissue, the other an accumulation of gas in her intestines which seemed to give the appearance of pregnancy to her abdomen. There is no doubt that in these cases the organic condition inaugurated a psychological process. Other cases of pseudocyesis proceed without any objective changes and often occur in women in whom the organic situation precludes pregnancy. Here the whole process seems to be purely psychological and to have the character of a conversion symptom.

In cases like the two mentioned above one question remains open: Was the psychological factor, perhaps, the primary one, and were the organic changes only a secondary result of emotional influences on the functions of the endocrine apparatus?

The female reproductive function is composed of several physiological acts, each of which is accompanied by certain psychological reactions which either hamper or further the physiological functions. Even the first act of reproduction—fecundation, the success of which determines the woman's fertility—is the result of definite and complicated physiological processes. With the great advance in endocrinology the gynecologist is more and more frequently in a position to explain sterility on the basis of defective functioning of one or more hormonal factors.

The entire hormonal activity that prepares for fecundation is probably constantly influenced by emotional elements. When we refer to "psychogenic difficulties" of conception, we mean that the given woman's inability to conceive has psychic causes which have disturbed some part of the complicated physiological machine. Sometimes difficulties of conception resulting from psychic factors can appear directly in the mechanical aspect of sexual intercourse (e.g., vaginismus or muscular motions in the vagina preventing the phallus from entering). Usually, however, psychogenic sterility stems from more hidden and complicated interactions.

There is no direct and objective evidence for this hypothesis, but reliable observations show that a large number of cases of sterility fail to respond to purposeful organic therapy and that often relatively sterile women conceive with the help of psychic influences in spite of the negative results of hormonal therapy and apparently unchanged organic condition.

This favorable psychic influence can be brought about in different ways: sometimes only by changing the external conditions, sometimes by a lengthy and complicated psychotherapeutic procedure.

According to my observations, the change of external conditions is of any influence only if it contains specific elements which have the power to overcome the inhibitions and anxieties interfering with conception. For example, a financially settled way of life, the founding of a protected home, will be of consequence only where previously the uncertainty of life had increased the inner, pre-existing anxiety in the given woman and contributed in this way to her sterility.

In another woman the renunciation of a profession can express a greater readiness for motherhood and—as often observed—be followed by pregnancy. But I have also seen women who have conceived only after having diverted their tense and continuous expectation of impregnation through professional, social, or scientific tasks, or the adoption of a child. Paradoxically, a change of living conditions to the worse, even to the painful, brings fulfillment of pregnancy to many women. Evidently, expiation of old guilt feelings through suffering and sacrifice may sometimes relieve inner tensions.

Many gynecologists who treat sterility by physical methods admit the part played by psychic influences, but insist that these are only secondary. In many cases, however, the opposite is true. Physical treatment may actually play the part of liberating punishment, and it is this factor that is often of primary importance in achieving successful results.

The same psychic factors may interfere only in later phases of the reproductive function without disturbing its first phase, fecundation. In such cases the energy of the germ plasm proves stronger than the counteracting psychic tendencies. In various symptoms of pregnancy, especially in one of its most typical, vomiting, the psychological factor is generally recognized.

The advances of endocrinology have taught us that a large percentage of spontaneous abortions, miscarriages, and premature deliveries are caused by general endocrine imbalance. The uterine contractions then occurring are the end result of a process that can be traced back to a disturbance of the hormonal supply, but that can doubtless also be inaugurated, provoked, or intensified by emotional factors.

If we consider many cases of infertility as psychogenic, this question still remains to be answered: how is the physical result brought about, where does the psychic factor intervene in order to assert itself in this way? The priority of the organic as against the psychic case has not yet been clearly established. Does a definite hormonal disturbance create a predisposition for certain psychic reactions, paving a way for them, or do psychic elements provoke a hormonal disturbance through the detour of the autonomic nervous system? The important practical question for the psychiatrist is: to what extent can a somatic manifestation be cured by psychotherapeutic intervention?

The collaboration between the gynecologist and the psychiatrist must be improved. At the moment it should be guided by the most important principle of medical science: *non nocere*. The psychiatrist must have the courage to hand over to the gynecologist the right of treatment at the proper moment, thus giving up his own therapeutic ideal of healing the patient psychically, whenever the gynecologist is capable of eliminating an important defect more quickly. The gynecologist, on the other hand, should give up his surgical treatment whenever he learns from the psychiatrist that the operation, if not absolutely indicated, may have bad psychic results. Another example demonstrating the need of collaboration is this: personal observations in many cases have taught me that the recording of the time of ovulation by the woman for contraceptive reasons is helpful, but that the recording for purposes of conception rather diminishes than increases the capacity to conceive. The subordination of sexual relations to the wish to conceive, the timing of coitus, the anxious watching for orgasm, are factors which increase tensions and anxieties that may be in many cases the psychological reason for sterility. In these cases the timing of copulation according to the best moment of the cycle may cause a paradoxical reaction.

It must be admitted that we have not yet achieved clear insight into where and how these two particular branches—gynecology and psychiatry—overlap, or how their coordination can be best achieved so as to contribute to the progress of research and to the welfare of the patient. The results of endocrine research are often ambiguous, and psychological observations are not well suited to objective schematic presentation and to final conclusions. The common denominator which includes both factors, the psychological and the somatic, can be found only by means of conscientious and objective observations clarifying the process by which psychic stimuli influence the endocrine system and the chemical actions by way of the central and autonomous nervous systems.

23

The Impostor: Contribution to Ego Psychology of a Type of Psychopath

(1955)

For psychoanalytic research in the field of psychopathy, the year 1925 constitutes a historical milestone, as it was then that Aichhorn published his book, *Wayward Youth*, and Abraham his paper, "The History of a Swindler." Whereas Aichhorn drew his knowledge from many years of observation and from the therapy of numerous cases, Abraham based his psychoanalytic findings on the study of one psychopath of a certain type. Abraham's paper has remained one of the classics of psychoanalytic literature. Following his example, I consider it especially valuable to single out from the many varieties of psychopathic personality one particular type and to attempt to understand him. The type I have chosen is the impostor. I will restrict myself to the un-dramatic kind of impostor and leave the others—more fascinating ones—to a later publication.

About twenty years ago, the head of a large agency for the treatment of juvenile delinquents persuaded me to interest my-self in a fourteen-year-old boy and, if possible, to lead him into analysis. The boy came from an exceedingly respectable family.

The 1955 A. A. Brill Memorial Lecture. First published in the *Psycho-analytic Quarterly*, 24:483-505, 1955.

319

His father, a business magnate, was a well-known philanthropist to whom the agency was indebted for major financial assistance. A typical American businessman, he was entirely committed to the financial aspects of life. His sincerity and altruism gave him a dignity which everyone respected. He never pretended to be something he was not, and his business acumen was accompanied by a great sense of social responsibility. Son of a poor Lutheran clergyman, the manners and morals of his pious father were engrained in his character.

This father's hard work, perseverance, and—judging from his reputation—his "financial genius" had made him one of the richest men in the community. He loved to stress the fact that he was a "self-made man," and it was his great ambition to leave his flourishing business to his sons for further expansion. At home he was a tyrant who made everyone tremble and subject to his command. His wife was a simple woman from a poor family, not very beautiful, not gifted with any sort of talent. He had simply married an obedient bed companion and housewife, let her share his material goods and, in part, his social prominence, and supported various members of her family.

Jimmy, the patient, was born late in the marriage. At his birth, his older brother was eleven, the next ten years old. The mother, always anxious, but warmhearted and tender, devoted herself completely to her youngest child. She indulged him endlessly, her chief interest being to please him. All his wishes were fulfilled and his every expression of displeasure was a command to provide new pleasures. In such an atmosphere, narcissism and passivity were bound to flourish. These were the foundations, the powerful predisposing factors for the boy's further development. The growing brothers abetted the mother's coddling, and for them the little boy was a darling toy to whom everything was given without expecting anything in return.

The father did not concern himself with the boy during the first three or four years of his life. In those days Jimmy escaped the paternal tyranny, and the older brothers' battle against the despot took place outside the little boy's sphere of living. As the two older boys entered adolescence, this battle became more intense and ended in full rebellion. The younger brother, an introverted, artistically inclined boy, exchanged home for boarding school; the older, mechanically gifted, soon became independent and left the family.

The father was not a man to accept defeat. He simply renounced the older sons and with his boundless energy turned to his youngest, thus transferring the boy from his mother's care into his own. He partially retired from business but continued the pursuit of his financial and philanthropic activities from home. Jimmy, then four years old, spent the major part of the day with his father, and heard his conversations with visitors who were all in a subordinate position to his father and in many cases financially dependent on him. The father became to him a giant, and the boy reacted to his father's efforts to make him active and aggressive and to arouse intellectual interests in him with some anxiety, yet with positive signs of compliance. A strong unity developed, and the process of the boy's identification with his father, which the latter had mobilized, was in full flower.

When Jimmy was seven, his father became the victim of a serious chronic illness resulting in five years of invalidism, during which time he lived at home in a wing removed from the central part of the house. Whether this illness was pulmonary tuberculosis or lung abscess never became clear. The boy saw very little of his father and the most vivid memory of this sickness was his father's malodorous sputum. According to Jimmy's report, his father remained alive only to spit and to smell bad.

Around this time a change took place in Jimmy. He developed a condition which appears to have been a genuine depression. He stopped playing, ate little, and took no interest in anything. Then—in a striking way—he became very aggressive, tyrannized his mother, and attempted to dominate his brothers. His first truancy was to run away to a nearby woods and refuse to come home. He created for himself a world of fantasy and described in a pseudological fashion his heroic deeds and the unusual events in which he had played a prominent role. These pseudologies, typical for his age, may well have been the precursors of Jimmy's future actions. While his mother—"for the sake of peace" and not to disturb the sick father—continued giving in to him in

everything, his brothers now ridiculed him and relegated him
to the role of a "little nobody."

In the course of the next few years, Jimmy had some difficulties
in school. Though he was intelligent and learned quickly, he
found it hard to accept discipline, made no real friends, was
malicious and aggressive without developing any worth-while
activity—"a sissy"—as he characterized himself. Since the father's
name carried weight in the community, Jimmy felt with partial
justification that nothing could happen to him, his father's son.
He was not yet guilty of asocial acts, not even childish stealing.

When he was twelve years old, his once beloved father died.
Jimmy did not feel any grief. His reaction was manifested in
increased narcissistic demands, the devaluation of all authority,
and in a kind of aggressive triumph: "I am free—I can do whatever I want." Soon afterward, his asocial acts began to occur.

Before we discuss his pathology, let us say a few words about
this boy's relationship to his father, which suffered such a sudden
break. In this alliance with his father, which began in his fifth
year, the spoiled, passive little boy became in part the father's
appendage. Identification with the powerful father created a
situation in which the ego was simultaneously weakened and
strengthened. When he had been in competition with the father,
he was forced to feel small and weak, but when he accepted as a
criterion of his own value his father's verdict: "You are my
wonderful boy," and his plans for the future: "You will be my
successor," then Jimmy's self-conception and ego image resembled
his marvelous father, and his narcissism—originally cultivated by
his mother—received new powers from his relationship with his
father. In his seventh or eighth year Jimmy lost this "wonderful"
father (not yet by death, but by devaluation), and his *own* conception of himself as a "wonderful boy" suffered a heavy blow.

The events of later years give more understanding of what
took place in this period which was so fateful for him. As mentioned before, I first saw Jimmy when he was fourteen years old.

I was determined to resist accepting Jimmy for treatment. I
had never had any experience in treating juvenile delinquents,
associating such cases with Aichhorn and his school, which I con-

sidered outside my sphere. I yielded, however, to the pressure of the boy's mother, whom I knew and respected, and to the pleas of the heads of the social agency. Because of the uncertainty of my approach and in contrast to my usual habit, I made notes of Jimmy's behavior. They contain the results of four to six interviews. At the time they seemed somewhat sterile to me and yet, regarding them in the light of later insights, they are extraordinarily illuminating. The interviews took place in 1935.

Jimmy was a typical young psychopath. He was increasingly unable to submit to the discipline of school. There was a repetitive pattern in his pathological acting out. At first he ingratiated himself by doing quite well; after a time he became insolent and rebellious toward his superiors, seduced his friends to break discipline, tried to impress them by the extravagance of his financial expenditures, and started quarrels and fights only to escape in a cowardly fashion under the ridicule of his companions. He forged checks with his mother's or older brother's signatures and disrupted the school and the neighborhood by his misdeeds. Every attempt to bring about his adaptation by changing schools ended in truancy. Toward me he behaved very arrogantly. With an obvious lack of respect he stated that he had not come of his own accord. He claimed nothing was wrong with him; that it was "the others" who would benefit by treatment.

He admitted he had again run away from school, and that this had been bad for him, and insisted that his trouble started when he began to "grow very fast." He wanted to remain a little boy; when he was little he was his father's pet. His father used to say, "Just wait until you are grown-up: *we* [father and he] will show the world."

Jimmy complained that the boys laughed at him; but "You know," he said, "I can defend myself." Sometimes he was sincere and admitted that essentially he was helpless and weak: "You know, they never took me seriously at home. For my big brothers I was sort of a puppet, a joke. I was always a kid whose ideas did not count and whose performance was laughable."

School was like home. He had difficulties because not to learn meant showing them, "I can do what I want, and do not have to obey." He forgot everything he learned, so "Why learn," he asked, "if I forget it?" He told me that his father had cursed his brothers: "I will show them," he had said, "they will end up in the gutter without my help." But to his father, Jimmy was different: father based all his hopes on him. When he was a little boy he felt that nothing could happen to him because his father was very powerful. Everything was subject to his father and together they were allies against all hostile influences. His father's sickness changed all this. The big promise, "We will show them," could not be redeemed. The brothers were now stronger than he. They ridiculed him and he was waiting to be grown up; then he would show them!

In school it was always the same story. The teachers and especially the headmasters were "no good." They pretended to be something they were not. Of course he did not wish to obey them. He knew at least as much as they did, but they refused to acknowledge it. The boys were no good. Some might have been but they were led on by the others. And all this was instigated from "above," because "they" knew that he would not let himself be put upon.

In this short period of observation I learned that Jimmy was infuriated by not being acknowledged as someone special; some of his complaints had an uncanny, paranoid character.

During our meetings, Jimmy played the undaunted hero, but with no trace of any emotion. One got an impression of great affective emptiness in him. All his asocial acts were his means of showing that he was something special. Stealing, debts were ways of obtaining money for the purpose, one might say, of buying narcissistic gratifications. He rebelled against all authority and devalued it. The moment he perceived that the methods he employed no longer sustained his prestige, his displeasure quickly mounted and drove him away.

With me he was overbearing, arrogant, cocksure. One day he came with the question: "Are you a Freudian?" He then proceeded, most unintelligently, to lecture me about analysis with catchwords he had picked up, or remarks based on titles he had seen. For instance: "That thing about civilization is particularly idiotic"; or "The old man [meaning Freud] isn't even a doctor." When I tried to point out to him that, after all, he did not know anything, and that I believed he talked so big because he was afraid, he stopped coming; as usual, a truant.

He presented such a typical picture of a juvenile delinquent that I felt concern about his future, wondering whether he would eventually become a criminal. His lack of affect, inability to form human relationships, and paranoid ideas led me to consider the possibility of an incipient schizophrenia.

I did not see Jimmy for eight years, but remained in contact with several people close to him. Some of the news about him was reassuring. He nevertheless confronted those around him with one problem after another. These were truancies in a more adult sense. He accepted positions which he did not keep, responsibilities he failed to meet. He made promises and broke them, with serious consequences to himself and to others. He accepted financial commitments, but neglected them so that they ended in failure. He provoked situations ominous not only for himself but also for those whom he had lured into these situations with false promises which to him, however, were real. Up to the time he came of age, his misdeeds were regarded as youthful indiscretions by the executors of the family estate. At twenty-one, he assumed that he was now financially independent and had already made financial commitments in the most extravagant ventures, when, to his fury, he was placed under legal guardianship.

With his customary bravado, Jimmy volunteered for military service during the war. He reported for duty on his new, shiny motorcycle. Soon he was the center of admiration among his comrades. Neither he nor they had any doubt that he would become one of the heroes of the war. He had, after all, volunteered to protect his fatherland, and his grandiose spending, his hints at connections with military authorities left no doubt that he was someone quite special. In this atmosphere he thrived until one day the news came that a commanding officer, noted for his severity, was to attend inspection. Jimmy had sufficient orientation in reality to realize that one cannot fool military authorities. The "hero" turned into a truant. But in military life that was not so easy. One does not desert, as one does in civilian life under the auspices of an approving family. On the contrary, one is punished for such actions, and Jimmy could never tolerate punishment. He had an attack of anxiety—which was genuine—and a delusional state—which was not. He was declared to be sick, taken to a hospital, and from there sent home.

The anxiety had been real, and his fear frightened him. His dream of being a hero was shattered. It is quite possible that under more favorable circumstances Jimmy, like so many other heroes of wars and revolutions, might have made his pathology serve a glorious career. Now he remembered that years ago a woman had predicted just this kind of fear, and he came straight to me for help.

He was in analysis so-called, although it was actually more a supportive therapy, for eight years. The success of this treatment, while limited, was nevertheless important for him. During that period I witnessed many episodes in his pathological acting out, and gained some insight into its nature. What kept him in treatment, however, was his anxiety which had increased since the war episode. It was evident that the defensive function of his acting out had been sufficiently threatened by reality that it was no longer adequate to hold internal dangers in check.

During the eight years which had elapsed since my first contact with Jimmy, he had been put through high school and prep school by the combined efforts of tutors, teachers, advisors, the head of the child guidance clinic, and his financial managers. They had even succeeded in having him admitted to a college where he stayed half a year. His intelligence and ability to grasp things quickly had, of course, been a help, but further than this he could not go. His narcissism did not permit him to be one of many; his self-love could be nourished only by feeling that he was unique. This desire for "uniqueness" did not, however, make him a lonely, schizoid personality. He was oriented toward reality which to him was a stage on which he was destined to play the leading role with the rest of humanity as an admiring audience. There were for him no human relationships, no emotional ties which did not have narcissistic gratification as their goal. His contact with reality was maintained, but it was not object libido which formed the bridge to it. He was always active and he surrounded himself with people; he sent out "pseudopodia," but only to retract them laden with gifts from the outside world.

After Jimmy left college, it was necessary to find him a job, to settle him in some field of work. All attempts at this of course failed. As in his school days, he could not tolerate authority and had no capacity for sustained effort. Success had to be immediate; he had to play the leading role from the start. He decided to become a gentleman farmer. A farm was purchased for him and he worked zealously on the plans for the farm. The preliminary work was done, the livestock was in the barn, and Jimmy even behaved as a socially responsible person. He created several positions at the farm for his former cronies; the fact that they knew as little about farming as he did was to him beside the point. His adaptation to reality had come to its end, and the enterprise was doomed to failure. Jimmy, however, acquired an elegant country outfit, saw to it that his clothing was saturated with barnyard smells, dyed his hair and eyebrows blond, and appeared among a group of former acquaintances in a New York restaurant as a "country gentleman." His farm project was soon involved in various difficulties, and his protégés deserted him; he was in debt, and financial ruin seemed imminent, when his guardians came to his rescue and he was saved by his fortune.

In another episode Jimmy was a great writer. Here his pseudo contact with others was even more intense. He presided over a kind of literary salon where intellectuals gathered about his fireplace, with Jimmy in the center. Short stories were his specialty for, of course, he lacked the capacity for prolonged, patient creativity. He knew how to make life so very pleasant for his literary admirers that they remained within his circle. He had even drawn several well-known writers into his orbit. He already visualized himself as a great writer, and brought a sample of his productivity for me to read. When I seemed somewhat critical (his writing was pretentious and quite without originality) he was furious and told me that I simply did not understand modern literature.

He soon gave up his literary career to become a movie producer. He made connections with men in the industry and spent considerable sums of money, but the result was always the same.

At one time he became an inventor and even succeeded in inventing a few small things. It was fascinating to watch the great ado over these little inventions and how he used them to appear a genius to himself and to others. He had calling cards printed with the identification "inventor" on them, and set up a laboratory to work out his discoveries. This time he chose as his collaborator an experienced physicist, and within a short period succeeded in making this man believe that Jimmy was a genius. With uncanny skill he created an atmosphere in which the physicist was convinced that his own achievements were inspired by Jimmy, the genius. His pretense that he was a genius was often so persuasive that others were taken in for a short time. Jimmy's self-esteem was so inflated by these reactions from his environment that occasionally he was able to achieve things which to some degree justified the admiration which he himself had generated.

In the course of his treatment I succeeded in getting Jimmy through college. His success in temporarily impressing his teachers as an outstanding student of philosophy was almost a farce. Actually he knew little beyond the titles and the blurbs on the jackets of the books; but on this basis he was able to engage for hours in polemics, and it was some time before he was found out. In these activities Jimmy did not impress us as a real impostor. His transformations from a pseudo impostor into a real one were only transitory. For instance, he made certain connections by using the name of the above-mentioned collaborator; another time he altered his name in such a way that it was almost identical with the name of a celebrity in a particular field. He was not an extravagant impostor; his pretenses were always close to reality but were nevertheless a sham.

For purposes of comparison, it may serve to summarize briefly the stories of impostors who are closely related to the type described. They differ only in the stability of their chosen roles. A fascinating example is the well-known case of Ferdinand Demara, which was much discussed several years ago (McCarthy, 1952). After running away from home, Demara became, in turn, a teacher of psychology, a monk, a soldier, a sailor, a deputy sheriff, a psychiatrist and a surgeon—always under another man's name. With almost incredible cleverness and skill he obtained each time the credentials of an expert, and made use of knowledge acquired *ad hoc* so brilliantly that he was able to perpetrate his hoaxes with complete success. It was always "by accident," never through mistakes he had made, that he was exposed as an impostor. In his own estimation, he was a man of genius for whom it was not necessary to acquire academic knowledge through prolonged studies, but who was able to achieve anything, thanks to his innate genius.

Reading his life history, one sees that he was perpetually in pursuit of an identity which would do justice to his narcissistic conception of himself in terms of "I am a genius," and which at the same time would serve to deny his own identity. This denial of his own identity appears to me to be the chief motive for his actions, as is true in the case of other impostors. In the course of his masquerading, Demara did much capable work and could bask in the sunshine of his successes. His parents had wanted to finance his way through college and medical school but he was never interested in a conventional way of life. When interviewed by reporters he acknowledged his enormous ambition and his need to take "short cuts." He declared that he would like for a change to use his own name but that he could not because of all that had happened. Whenever Demara resumes his activities, one may presume it will be possible only under a usurped name or not at all. His statement that he cannot use his own name—however rational it may sound—is nevertheless the expression of a deeper motive.

Another famous impostor of recent years is the "physicist" Hewitt, who, under the name of Dr. Derry, began teaching theoretical physics, mathematics, and electrical engineering in numerous universities with great success, without ever having finished high school (Brean, 1954). Like Jimmy, he sometimes used his own name, but again like Jimmy, under false colors. He impersonated two different actual doctors of philosophy in physics, masqueraded as a nationally known man, and took responsible positions under various names. He had been unmasked twice, yet tried again to achieve success under still another physicist's name.

In Hewitt's life history there are many analogies to Jimmy's history. Hewitt's need for admiration was as great as Jimmy's, and the narcissistic motive behind his masquerading was equally evident. At the beginning of his career as an impostor, Hewitt was somewhat unsure of himself, but when he found himself being admired, his personality unfolded its full capacities. He was able to create for himself an atmosphere of power and prestige. When he felt that his masquerading was becoming too dangerous, he abandoned his project, changed his name, and embarked on another masquerade which became a new source of narcissistic satisfaction. Sometimes he was presented with an opportunity to work under his own name, as he was a gifted and really brilliant man who could have had a successful career. Such offers he always turned down: he could work only under another name, in an atmosphere of tension, in the precarious situation of imminent exposure. Like Jimmy, he regarded himself as a genius and courted situations in which he would be exposed as the counterpart of a genius—a liar, an impostor.

Demara, Hewitt, and Jimmy appear to be victims of the same pathological process of the ego—only the level of their functioning is different.

Demara changed the objects of his identifications perhaps because he was driven by fear of impending unmasking. The objects whose names he temporarily bore corresponded to his high ego ideal, and he was able to maintain himself on the high level of the men he impersonated. His manifold talents and his intelligence were outstanding, his capacity for sublimation was but little impaired. It was not lack of ability, but psychopathology which made him an impostor.

Hewitt had a much more consolidated ego ideal. His interests were from the beginning oriented toward physics, his talent in this direction even made him a child prodigy; his path was marked out. But he rejected any success which he could realistically achieve through work and perseverance under his own name, and preferred *pretending* under the mask of a stranger's name. The objects of his identification were physicists of repute, men who already were what he would have liked to become. In this as in the other cases, I consider the incapacity to accept the demands imposed by the discipline of study, and the lack of perseverance, to be a secondary motive for becoming an impostor.

Jimmy, in his striving for an ego ideal, appears to us like a caricature of Demara and Hewitt. In contrast to them he was unable to find objects for successful identification because his limited capacity for sublimation and his lack of talent made this impossible for him. He was able to satisfy his fantasies of grandeur only in naïve acting out, pretending that he was *really* in accordance with his ego ideal. On closer examination I was struck by the resemblance of his acting out to the performance of girls in prepuberty. "Various identifications, which later in puberty can be explained as defense mechanisms, and which one meets in schizoid personalities as expressions of a pathologic emotional condition, prove on closer inspection to have a completely specific character in prepuberty. They remind us strongly of the play of small children, and seem to be an 'acting out' of those transitory, conscious wishes that express the idea, 'That's what I want to be like.' It is noteworthy that this acting out has a concrete and real character, different from mere fantasying" (Deutsch, 1944).

Jimmy too acted out his transitory ideals which never became fully established. Compared with Greenacre's (1945) "psychopathic patients," Jimmy's ideals did not have the character of magic grandeur, and were not so unattached to reality. Quite the contrary. Jimmy always turned to external reality to gratify his narcissistic needs. His emptiness and the lack of individuality in his emotional life and moral structure remind us furthermore of the "as if" personalities (Chapter 20). In contrast to these, Jimmy's ego did not dissolve in numerous identifications with external objects. He sought, on the contrary, to impose on others belief in his greatness, and in this he often succeeded. His only identifications were with objects which corresponded to his ego ideal—just like the impostor Hewitt, only on a more infantile level. Another difference is that the "as if" patients are not aware of their disturbance, whereas Jimmy, while firmly pretending that he *was* what he pretended to be, asked me again and again, sometimes in despair: "Who am I? Can *you* tell me that?"

In spite of these individual differences between the various types, I believe that all impostors have this in common: they assume the identities of other men not because they themselves lack the ability for achievement, but because they have to hide under a strange name to materialize a more or less reality-adapted fantasy. It seems to me that the ego of the impostor, as expressed in his own true name, is devaluated, guilt-laden. Hence he must usurp the name of an individual who fulfills the requirements of his own magnificent ego ideal. Later we shall see that Jimmy's fear of being unmasked as an impostor increased when he began to be successful under his own name and figure.

As his treatment proceeded, Jimmy's fears increased as his acting out lessened. With this change of behavior he entered a new phase in his therapy: the phase of anxiety. It was this phase which revealed more of the nature of the process. But this does not mean that the phase of acting out was free of anxiety. It was anxiety that brought him to me, and anxiety kept him with me. In time, his increasing anxieties assumed a more hypochondriacal character. He examined his body, his pulse, etc., and wanted to be certain that a physician could be reached. It was not difficult to assume that a man whose personality was limited by an unsuccessful identification with his father repeated his father's disease in hypochondriacal symptoms.

By and by Jimmy gave up his grotesque acting out and his behavior became increasingly realistic. First, he founded an institute for inventions. This project was still in accordance with his fantasy of being a great inventor. Because he had associated himself with a friend who, despite his naïve belief in Jimmy, was genuinely gifted scientifically and had already achieved recognition, and because of the considerable sums of money available, Jimmy gradually worked his way toward acquiring a going concern. Here, for the first time in his life, he functioned well and enjoyed a certain solid respect. He limited his acting out to founding a colony for artists in which he acted the role of a "brilliant connoisseur of art"; also he set up for himself some sort of an "altar" at home. He married a girl with an infantile personality who blindly believed in his "genius" and adored him. When she began to have doubts, he simply sent her away and threatened her with divorce. Love he never experienced; even from his children he expected gratifications for his narcissism and he hated them when they failed him in this respect.

The condition which now confronted us seemed paradoxical: the more effectively he functioned in reality, the more anxiety he developed. In the days when he had really been a swindler, he never feared exposure. Now that he worked more honestly and pretended less, he was tortured by the fear that his deceit might be discovered. He felt like an impostor in his new role: that of doing honest work. Obviously he remained an impostor after all, and in his very real personal success he now had an inner perception of his inferiority. In the beginning, we had had the suspicion that Jimmy always feared his own inferiority, and that he was hiding his anxiety behind a bloated ego ideal. It could now be better understood why he inquired after his identity, why he had the depersonalized feeling, "Who am I really?" In this he reminds us of those more or less neurotic individuals who, having achieved success, experience like Jimmy the painful sensation: "I am an impostor," stemming from the same inner motivation.

Jimmy's anxieties gradually acquired a phobic character. His professional activities were impeded by a fear of leaving town and of being too far from home. This evidently represented a counterphobic mechanism against his earlier running away.

Thus we may speak of a certain success in his treatment which was never a psychoanalysis. In my forty years of practice I have never seen a patient as little capable of transference as Jimmy. He and I sometimes talked of "hot-air therapy," for I called his grandiose acting out, "hot air," until it was greatly devalued. At the same time I appealed to his narcissism by showing him what he could really achieve. In this way we continued for eight years. About two years ago I passed him on to a colleague who is continuing the therapy.

Reviewing Jimmy's pathological behavior chronologically, the connection between his preadolescent delinquency and his later acting out becomes clear. By the phrase he used when he came to see me as a fourteen-year-old, "I became grown up too fast," he meant to say that he did not yet feel capable of playing the role his father had assigned to him for a time when he would be grown up. His high ego ideal, cultivated by the father, and an identification with the "great father" did not permit him— despite a certain degree of insight—to wait for the process of growing up to take place. He demanded that the world treat him not according to his achievements but according to his exalted ego ideal. The refusal of his environment to do so was an attack on himself, on his grandeur, on his ego ideal. This feeling that hostile elements were aligned against him grew at times into paranoid reactions. He responded to these insults in a way which brought him to the borderline of real criminal behavior; but when he began to feel that he was defeated, he ran away.

Perhaps if he had had enough aggression at his disposal, he would have continued his career as a criminal. An appeal to his conscience was fruitless, as, after all, he considered himself to be a victim and his actions as self-defense. Maybe this is true of all juvenile delinquents. Social injustice and a desire to avenge oneself for it is often given as a reason for delinquent behavior. In Jimmy's case such a rationalization could not be used.

His passivity led him in another direction. Instead of fighting for his narcissistic "rights," he found less dangerous and more regressive methods of asserting his ego ideal. What he was not, he could become by "pretending." Only when this was made impossible for him—first through external reality (the army), then through his treatment—was he overwhelmed by anxiety and feelings of inferiority, and one could then realize the defensive function of his pathological behavior.

We suspect that Demara and Hewitt, the other two impostors mentioned, were also hiding such an ego through identification with someone else's ego, by means of what might be called a "non-ego ego." In these cases of a more solidly constructed imposture, the inner anxiety is partly projected to the outside, and the impostor lives in perpetual fear of discovery. Jimmy did not fear such discovery, for he had not assumed another's name. What threatened him was that if his "pretending" were to be unmasked, he would be laughed at, as he was once ridiculed by his brothers and later by his schoolmates. He developed real anxiety only when he gave up "pretending" so that both he and others were confronted with his "true" ego.

Let us consider the causes of Jimmy's pathology. Greenacre (1945)—in agreement with other writers—finds etiological factors in the emotional deprivation of psychopaths and delinquents. Her emphasis rests on the combination of both indulgence and severity on the part of the parental figures; this is in accordance with Wilhelm Reich's (1933) conception of the character structure of the psychopath. The emotional climate of Jimmy's childhood was different, but evidently no less disastrous. Whereas Greenacre's patient was emotionally deprived, Jimmy was overloaded with maternal love. I knew the mother very well, and I know that she was one of those masochistic mothers who, loving and warmhearted, completely surrender themselves for the benefit of others. She was a masochistic victim not only of the despotic father, but also of her children, especially Jimmy. Her last child's every wish was granted. Any active striving he had was paralyzed through premature compliance; every need for wooing and giving was smothered by the mother's loving initiative in meeting his demands.

I believe that the emotional "overfeeding" of a child is capable of producing very much the same results as emotional frustration. It contributes to an increase of infantile narcissism, makes adaptation to reality and relationships to objects more difficult. It creates intolerance of frustration, weakens the ego's ability to develop constructive defenses, and is in large measure responsible for passivity.

Jimmy's relationship with his father was very well suited to strengthen the predisposition created by the mother. The powerful, despotic personality of the father contributed to Jimmy's passivity, and the father's narcissism prepared the ground for Jimmy's later, fateful identification with him.

These attitudes of the parents created a predisposition for the pathological development of the boy. But it was a traumatic experience which activated this predisposition. The father's sickness and isolation caused an abrupt interruption of the normal maturing process of Jimmy's ego. The frustration stemming from the fact that Jimmy was no longer able to feel himself to be part of a great father crippled his ego which was not yet strong enough to endure the brutal attack of separation. The enforced awareness of his self as being distinct from that of his father was anachronistic in his development. The normal process of identification had not yet reached that degree of maturity from which further development would have been possible.

Simultaneously with the separation from his father came the devaluation of that "powerful" figure. Consequently, the character of his identification also underwent a change. What had so far strengthened his ego was no longer available. With the devaluation of the father, a shadow fell across his own identified ego. The fact that the traumatic event occurred in the latter part of latency was decisive for Jimmy's psychopathology. As we know, this period is of utmost importance for the maturation of the ego apparatus, for the establishment of a less rigid superego, and for the capacity to cope with reality. In a normal, gradual development of a boy in latency, not harmed by trauma, Jimmy would have transferred his identification with the father onto other suitable objects. Eventually his ego would have been ready to assimilate the identifications into the self, and to achieve a reliable degree of inner stability. His ambivalent sexual relationship to the father would have yielded to tender love, and a path toward reality and toward the formation of constant object relationships would have been made.

The pathogenic force of this trauma was due to two factors: first, its suddenness; second, its daily repetition during the four years that preceded his father's death. As a result, regressive forces in the ego replaced progress in development, and the whole process of sublimation was impaired.[1] The boy was incapable of goal-oriented endeavor, because he was unable to postpone reaching an attempted goal. The fact that his relationship to the father never became desexualized was revealed in his masturbatory fantasies of a passive-feminine-masochistic character and

[1] There are psychopaths endowed with great capacities for sublimation and creativeness, although their ego functioning is gravely impaired.

in his fears of homosexuality. His relationship to his mother became submerged in his identification with her as his father's debased sexual object. The manifestations of this identification could be traced back from his recent masturbatory fantasies to that period of his childhood in which he had been enuretic (Michaels, 1955).

It is interesting to observe pathology in what is commonly agreed to be "normal." The world is crowded with "as if" personalities, and even more so with impostors and pretenders. Ever since I became interested in the impostor, he pursues me everywhere. I find him among my friends and acquaintances, as well as in myself. Little Nancy, a fine three-and-a-half-year-old daughter of one of my friends, goes around with an air of dignity, holding her hands together tightly. Asked about this attitude she explains: "I am Nancy's guardian angel, and I'm taking care of little Nancy." Her father asked her about the angel's name. "Nancy" was the proud answer of this little impostor.

Having referred to "normal impostors," I should clarify my conception of the term "impostor." The pathological impostor endeavors to eliminate the friction between his pathologically exaggerated ego ideal and the other, devaluated, inferior, guilt-laden part of his ego, in a manner which is characteristic for him: he behaves as if his ego ideal were identical with himself; and he expects everyone else to acknowledge this status. If the inner voice of his devaluated ego on the one hand, and the reactions of the outside world on the other hand, remind him of the unreality of his ego ideal, he still clings to this narcissistic position. He desperately tries—through pretending and under cover of someone else's name—to maintain his ego ideal, to force it upon the world, so to speak.

A similar conflict, though in a milder form, seems to exist also in the normal personality. In the complex development of a "normal" individual, there are certain irregularities, and only seldom can a successful harmony be attained. Perhaps the identity between the ego ideal and the self is achieved only by saints, geniuses, or psychotics. As one's ego ideal can never be completely gratified from *within*, we direct our demands to the external world, *pretending* (like Jimmy) *that we actually are what we would like to be.* Very often we encounter paranoid reactions in normal personalities, which result from the fact that their environment has refused to accept an imposture of this sort.

Both history and belletristic literature are rich in impostors. Thomas Mann's story (1954) about the impostor Felix Krull shows the most profound understanding of this type. It is amazing to consider how the psychological genius of a writer is able to grasp intuitively insights at which we arrive laboriously through clinical empiricism. The passivity, the narcissistic ego ideal, the devaluation of the father's authority, and the complicated processes of identification of the impostor Felix Krull are very well understood by Mann; and even the profound similarity between the shabby Krull and the wealthy, distinguished prince whose name and existence Krull, the impostor, takes over, is well understood by the writer.

I wish to close by repeating what I stated at the beginning. The case here discussed represents only a certain type of psychopath. I believe that such an individual typological approach to the large problem of psychopathy may prove very fruitful.

24

Psychoanalytic Therapy in the Light of Follow-up

(1959)

In the course of years we have learned a lot about the theoretical aspects of psychoanalytic therapy. This knowledge should enable us in each individual case to judge when an analysis is finished, and whether the therapeutic result is in agreement with our theoretical demands. Certain doubts had always accompanied our overvaluation of analytic therapy, but not until Freud's "Analysis Terminable and Interminable" was published (1937) were we able to set definite criteria regarding the limitations of psychoanalysis as a therapeutic method.

There are two ways in which to evaluate the therapeutic successes in analysis: (1) the statistical reports as submitted by Alexander (1937), Knight (1941), Jones (1936) and others, and (2) individual observation. In my efforts to arrive at statistical data on the basis of my personal experience with 250 to 300 analyzed patients plus a great number of control cases, I came to the conclusion that it is very difficult to speak of therapeutic results in general terms. From what point of view should the analyst classify his success? By the loss of the symptom? By the ability

First published in the *Journal of the American Psychoanalytic Association*, 7:445-458, 1959.

to adapt to reality? Or by the degree of harmony achieved in the patient's personality (ego)?

I consider the method of individual observation the more reliable of the two. The analytic literature is rich in case histories, in reports of failures and successes, and in theoretical interpretations. There is, however, an evident lack of information about the postanalytic psychic state of patients whose treatment has been successfully terminated. At this point the method of direct observation is no longer available. We have learned certain general facts, such as that the patient will for a time continue the analytic process by self-analysis, and that the remnants of incompletely resolved transference may reappear and cause difficulties, etc.

To these generalizations I may add some observations made on patients in shorter and longer periods following a successful analysis.

In many cases, patients whose excellent result of analysis is acknowledged by themselves and by those around them experience shortly after the end of treatment, without external provocation, a recurrence of their old neurosis. They declare in despair that "everything is like it was before analysis." More often the unexpected negative reaction takes the form of a more or less severe depression. The patient has opposing attitudes toward the results of his analysis. *Realistically* he is aware of the changes which took place in him and expresses his astonishment over the recurrence of his neurosis, but this rational attitude is counteracted by deeply rooted residues of his infantile past. In contrast to his analytic achievement, he had expected and trusted that something very special would be bestowed on him by the omnipotent analyst and through his own painful experience. During the whole process of analysis he preserved (disregarding the analyst's effort to dispel it) the infantile belief that he would emerge from the procedure not simply as a more mature *he*, but as his own ego ideal. Disappointed in this, he reacts with a kind of undoing of the analytic success, not by a new repression but by a repetition or restoration of his preanalytic way of neurotic gratification. Since the whole process is inaugurated by the separation from the analyst, the depressive reaction is the most common one. Fortunately, this attitude is a transitory phenomenon, for the more mature state soon takes over and directs the patient toward reality.

Another postanalytic phenomenon which we observe with certain astonishment is the *pseudo amnesia* for the events of analysis. The patients claim that the content of their memories of a long, successful analysis can be expressed in "two sentences." They simply do not remember more. This is not the result of afterrepression, because the analytic material is preserved in the preconscious, and can be revived at any time when the patient finds himself again in analysis. I assume that this peculiar phenomenon is a result of a change in cathexis. During analysis cathexis is shifted from the outer world onto the intrapsychic experience of the analytic situation. The emotional reliving of the infantile conflicts in the transference creates a climate in which the psychic reality is stronger than the external one. The dynamic change which has taken place in the patient at the end of analysis, his turning from the internal process to external reality, constitutes the experience of two different worlds. Now the cathexis is directed toward external reality, and the world of analysis is pale, unreal, without content.

It is characteristic that this pseudo amnesia occurs less frequently and intensely in persons for whom the analysis was strongly intellectualized. The emotional experience was already associated with intellectual conceptions during analysis and is in this form preserved in memory.

Another factor which makes the experience of analysis easier to remember after its termination is the acting out during the treatment. Through this acting out the analytic material evidently acquires a more realistic meaning and is now obtainable. A woman patient of Freud's reported to me that she could not remember anything from her analysis. Especially the oedipal character of transference had totally escaped her memory. But she retained the recollection of an episode which happened outside the analytic room and which convinced her of this transference. She remembered that once she left the analytic session very excited—she did not know why. She stopped in front of a store window and experienced a tormenting thought: "What is poor Frau Professor going to do in *this* case?" This event remained vivid in her memory, likewise every detail of the objects in the window, but what occurred before in the analytic session was forgotten.

A good opportunity for observing postanalytic attitudes is a second analysis with another analyst. We here take into consideration cases whose first analysis was terminated with "success," but for whom another analysis seemed indicated after a longer or shorter interval. It would be worth while to make an extensive study of the differences encountered in second analyses. What alterations of the ego occurred in the first analysis? Which kind of resistances were resolved and which appear again? How does the second transference situation influence the residua of the first one, and vice versa? What specific factors mobilized the new neurotic difficulties, etc.?

I am restricting myself to the most evident and superficial manifestations. One of the surprising statements of these patients often is: "*This* was never in my first analysis," disregarding the fact that this very material—according to the report of the first analyst—constituted one of the central problems of the previous analysis. And vice versa: problems which were never manifested in the first analysis are now produced with the feeling, "that was already analyzed." This kind of positive and negative *fausse reconnaissance* is, according to my experience, not simply the expression of unresolved residua of transference or a sign of after-repressions.

Harmless as these postanalytic events may be, they evoke serious considerations. They seem to indicate that even after a suc-cessful analysis in which amnesias and resistances were conquered and the patient's ego went through the laborious operation of "working through," the process of assimilation is not fully achieved.

This achievement does not depend on the skill of the analyst, on the resolution of the infantile conflicts, nor on the quality of the psychological insight, and above all—not on the duration of the treatment. This fact poses the question whether the ego of the neurotic personality is—or can be made—capable of assimilating effectively the newly acquired psychic energies ("Where id was, there shall ego be"). Perhaps the study of defense mechanisms and the enriched knowledge of the ego will contribute to a better orientation in this direction.

The therapeutic efficiency of analysis has to be evaluated in regard to the degree of immunity it has provided and to the duration of the success. From this point of view I consider the insight I was able to obtain into the psychic condition of two successfully analyzed patients after nearly thirty years as extremely valuable. The presentation of these follow-ups is facilitated by the fact that these two cases have been published previously to some extent, so that the subsequent developments can be added to the published material. I should like to review these case histories briefly. The first case is published in the first part of the present volume.[1]

The patient, a girl in her twenties, had made a long journey to Vienna to seek help in psychoanalytic treatment. She was beautiful, cultured, and rich. Shortly before, she had made a serious but unsuccessful attempt at suicide with a revolver. The scar of the wound was visible on her temple. The motive for her suicidal attempt had never been clear to her before analysis.

Her main complaint was that "something in her" prevented her from gratifying her intense intellectual ambitions and her desire to study and to take up a profession. When still quite young she became engaged to a man with whom she had a tender love relationship for several years. But she did not feel "fulfilled" in this relationship. In her view, her fiancé loved too much "the woman" in her, and left the intellectual tendencies on which she laid so much stress completely unsatisfied.

On one of her travels the patient made the acquaintance of an elderly married man of high intellectual attainments, in an important diplomatic position. An intellectual friendship developed, at first without erotic elements, but this gradually changed into a passionate love relationship. She broke off her engagement, her

---

[1] Chapter 2, "Hysterical Fate Neurosis." This case has also a certain historical importance. In the development of our teaching methods, it was the first case presented in weekly reports for the candidates of the Vienna Psychoanalytic Institute in 1928-29. (These reports were made by the instructor.)

beloved separated from his wife, and an apparently happy period set in.

Then a strange incident brought clouds into their relationship. The lover was called away to his wife's sickbed. During his absence she went on a short trip, on which she met a young man to whom she gave herself physically—without any erotic feeling, compulsively. She became pregnant, and an immediate marriage was decided on. Gradually, however, she altered her decision, interrupted her pregnancy by abortion and returned to her lover with a remorseful confession of her guilt. Her relationship to him became as tender as before, he divorced his wife, and the date of the wedding was settled. And then—in the middle of these preparations—the patient attempted suicide.

In her description of this love, the patient contrasted it with her first affair. The second relationship was intellectually satisfying and a source of great happiness because her lover, himself very intelligent, had so high an opinion of her intellectual attainments. In contrast to her first lover, he made considerable intellectual and moral demands on her. But, strangely enough, it was just these demands which she herself so deeply wished for that became the cause of her unhappiness. She went through nights of agony, tortured by a feeling of her own inadequacy and inferiority. The nearer she came to the fulfillment of her desires, the deeper this shadow descended on her, driving her eventually to attempt suicide just before the wedding—without motivation, as it seemed both to herself and to others.

In her first interview she had told me that the attempt had had nothing to do with her love. What had driven her to despair was her feeling of inferiority. For years she had tried to win independence by study and work, but despite her manifold talents all her efforts were in vain. In despair she used to say, "Why is it that I alone cannot do what every woman in my country manages so naturally?"

The case history of this patient is filled with fascinating episodes of neurotic acting out, which justify the diagnosis of fate neurosis. Let us review very shortly her past history. Her childhood followed the typical development of a young girl. She loved her father and possessed strongly negative, hostile feelings against her mother, who was "stupid, uneducated, and above all slavishly devoted to father." In short, she had a typical oedipal attitude, which had been intensified after the birth of a brother by the typical reaction of disappointment—the mother and not she had borne the child.

As one would expect, the birth of the brother and the powerful provocation of penis envy were the source of her inferiority feelings and her inhibitions. Her jealousy and aggression toward the brother evoked guilt reactions, which contributed their part to prevent her from competition with him in later life. We now see her paralyzed by feelings of inferiority due to this competition and on the other hand repudiating her own femininity: "I refuse to play the part my mother played—to be passively and slavishly devoted to my father." Alongside this conscious revolt, however, arose an unconscious submission to the father from which she was never able to free herself.

In her neurotic hesitation between the conscious protest and the unconscious masochistic need, she was unable to find a solution. The man who at the end became the leading figure in her life was an active, imposing figure like her father. In contrast to him, he did not involve her in the humiliating role which her mother played, but put her on a pedestal and made the same demands on her which she always made on herself; that is, to be different from her mother: intellectual, learned, professional. But her old inhibitions again made the fulfillment of these demands impossible. In the inner awareness of her old guilt feelings toward the brother, but above all of her deeply rooted masochistic attachment to her father, she was panicky at the thought that she might be unable to meet her lover's intellectual and moral demands. Unmotivated as her attempt to commit suicide may seem, she preferred to die rather than to adopt toward her lover the masochistic attitude of her mother to which she was compulsively driven.

The analytic treatment of this patient ended with complete success. At its termination she was ready to accept her love for the man from whom she had run away. Indeed, the patient's choice of object remained determined by her father relationship, but as a result of her analysis the anachronistic effect of the previous taboo and the old guilt reactions were removed and she was evidently free from the previously insoluble inner conflict. As one would expect, her wish for a child, previously acted out neurotically and destructively, could now be realized.

The analysis also proved successful in another direction: the neurotic inhibition and renunciation of any ambitious goal subsided. With my active help she started her education during analysis, and finished her treatment simultaneously with her graduation from high school, which opened to her the doors of higher learning.

Before the patient left I asked for her permission to publish her case history. I presented her with the manuscript and asked her to correct whatever she thought was incorrect. She was in complete agreement with the content and we parted. I did not hear from her for more than twenty-five years. When a patient is silent following a successful analysis, it is usually considered as good news.

Apparently it was not her wish but a coincidence that brought us together again. I anticipated meeting her with foreboding: although I considered her one of my best therapeutic results, I have learned to expect surprises in analysis, and I had very much in mind Freud's saying, "We have no means of predicting what will happen later to a patient who has been cured" (1937).

Here is what I found: she was still as beautiful as she had been years ago. She told me that after the analysis she returned to her lover, freely and lovingly. His sick wife died and the patient could marry him without any complications standing in their way. After years of a perfectly happy marriage a son was born—a wonderful boy, as she had always seen him in her dreams. However, what seemed to her the most important achievement was the fact that she had finished her college education with highest honors and had become a well-known physicist who had already made recognized contributions in this field.

According to her report, her husband was extremely proud of her: he himself achieved fame in a different field. Due to political developments, she occasionally had to be the breadwinner of the family—as was the case at present.

She told me that she adored her child. Asked why she had

waited so long to have the child (she must have been about forty years old when he was born), she replied with some hesitation that she first wanted to bring her studies to a successful completion.

Toward me she showed a certain condescending benevolence, as to a good, old aunt. When I pointed out how successful her analysis had been, she said, again with a benevolent smile: "You have helped me a great deal, but analysis gave me nothing. I don't believe in analysis at all—it is a hoax—all bunk—purely constructions of your own mind. . . ."

Let us reconstruct the patient's hostile attitude toward analysis on the basis of her past history. (1) With her narcissistic personality she will certainly dislike being confronted with the neurotic past. The publication of the case history—even with her consent—may greatly increase the feeling of narcissistic offense. (2) Her husband is not favorably inclined toward analysis. (3) We may assume that the old hostility and devaluating attitude toward her mother are still present despite a thorough analysis of the negative transference. She expresses this devaluation by displacement from my role as woman and mother into the sphere in which she herself feels secure: in the professional life where she achieved so much (as physicist) and I so little ("nothing") (as analyst). These explanations may be correct, but they leave us unsatisfied. Perhaps an insight into the character of the analytic success will enlighten us.

What has the analysis done for this patient? (1) Utilizing her latent intellectual capacity, it led her to a successful sublimation. This was achieved through the lessening of her guilt feelings toward the brother and through the favorable influence on her inferiority feelings. (2) The oedipus conflict has been settled in the most successful way; she could permit herself to love and marry the man whom she had chosen under the definite influence of the oedipus complex. She could experience the death of her rival without guilt feelings, and was able to realize her wish for a child.

And yet, it is obvious that something could not be settled. In my deliberations about this case I proceeded from the start of the analysis. The patient came to me following a serious attempt at suicide. She was loved by the man of her choice, she was victorious against her rival—and yet she had to run away—preferring death! She has given us in this analysis sufficient information regarding her reasons for wishing to die: prior to her analysis she had felt condemned to repeat the degrading masochistic destiny of her mother. Her narcissism chose death rather than such a future.

What made her free from this destiny in the analysis? It was the great, now liberated capacity for sublimation, and largely also her identification with the female analyst. It was her ego that underwent a successful transformation. She was now able to develop defensive mechanisms previously not at her disposal. Her capacity for accomplishments in her work could now be used as a defensive power toward the infantile form of her femininity, the masochistic part of which was not and could not be mastered completely in analysis. A glance at her postanalytic life shows that she was able to take the role of a wife and mother only when she felt secure in the other role, that of an active career woman. To her, femininity was and is the degradation to the passive, slavish role of her mother. She can accept the reality of her marriage and her motherhood only on her own terms: by opposing defensively her femininity with work and intellectual life.

As I mentioned in the beginning, I consider this patient to be an excellent therapeutic result, but I am aware that her psychic harmony can be achieved only with the help of her newly acquired defenses. These defenses are the result of constructive sublimation; they are ego syntonic. Their function is also to supply the patient with narcissistic gratifications. As long as the patient can enjoy the services of these defensive powers, she is not in danger of a neurotic illness.

I do not consider the masochistic element of this patient's personality as a danger. She finds in her social and other activities sufficient outlet in a form acceptable to her. She also had shown evidence of great strength in all the tragic events of her life, provoked partly by political changes in her country. But she will react neurotically to any stronger blow to the narcissistic gratification she derives from her active, sublimated endeavors.

I would call that blow a "specific trauma." The patient's neurotic feeling of inferiority centered, as we previously learned, around her relationship to her brother. Analysis led her, through her pathological reactions to the birth of this brother and the effects of penis envy, to a success, but it evidently failed to free her from the primary narcissistic injury of the phallic past.

I speculate that her declaration, "Analysis gave me *nothing*," expresses her unconscious dictum that analysis did not change the biological fact. This may become the focus of new neurotic problems when the compensations refuse their services.

The second patient, whom I saw twenty-seven years after analysis, had a quite different postanalytic relationship to me than the first one. I was informed about all the important events in her life; she sent me photographs of her children and asked my advice whenever she needed it. She was a very sick young girl when she was seeking analytic help about twenty-nine years ago. Her main problem was gynecological: she suffered, prior to her analysis, from amenorrhea and vicarious menstruation for seven years.[2]

At the age of thirteen the patient had one normal menstruation; later she had irregular bleedings under the skin of one ear lobe, to which she always reacted with hypochondriac anxieties. She imagined that she had cancer and would inevitably die. All attempts of gynecologists to restore the normal menstrual cycle failed.

In the course of her analytic treatment the bleeding changed its localization. First she complained about pains in her back at periodic intervals; later she would feel a lump in this region. The gynecologist found a tumor and an operation was performed. The biopsy revealed a large number of cysts filled with blood, and its consistency made the diagnosis of vicarious menstruation certain. Apart from the menstrual problem the patient suffered from depression, headaches, various conversion symptoms, and stubborn constipation.

According to the family history, her father was one of the richest farmers in her country. He had a very active, impressive

2 This case history was published in the first volume of *The Psychology of Women* (Deutsch, 1944).

personality, and was a leader in his field and in social endeavors. The mother, a strong, active woman, ruled the family. She had many children, and there were already grown-up sisters when the patient was born. When she was six years old, the last children were born—twin brothers.

The mother's interest in children was not limited to her own. She encouraged her employees to produce large families, and when her older daughters married there was always someone pregnant or giving birth and a new generation of children filled the estate. The patient reacted to these events with horror and fantasies. Even in childhood she started to avoid her genitals, and her masturbation was displaced to the ear lobe. During puberty she resorted to the same region as a substitute for her genitals, and the menstruation was also diverted to bleeding in the ear lobe.

It will be easily understood that her chronic constipation was in accordance with an anal pregnancy fantasy.

After one year of analysis the patient began to menstruate regularly, her constipation subsided, and she became free of depressions. With the end of analysis she fell in love and married. It was a successful marriage and she was free of neurotic symptoms. She gave birth to several children in quick succession and always proved herself an excellent, understanding mother.

After an interval of twenty-seven years I received a letter containing complaints for the first time. The patient had not menstruated for the past two months and her family doctor considered this an early menopause. She reacted with depression, anxiety, and constipation. "It is scary," she wrote, "to realize that one has lost all normal functions of elimination, that drugs don't help. . . ." Her condition grew worse during the next months. She was suffering from depressions and was occasionally unable to move her legs. The symptoms were exactly like those which she had had twenty-nine years ago.

She now wrote very often and communicated to me a series of dreams: they were anxiety-laden and their content usually represented loss of a baby. Birth and death appeared in the same form as years ago, before and during analysis. "All is almost a pattern by now—like an old, old record," she wrote. "Why must I again live over this dreary past when I understand all so well?" "Then I began to have repeated dreams about that twelve- to thirteen-year-old period full of horror about menstruating, with the feeling I am an outcast, homeless, lost in childhood scenes. . . ." In another enlightening letter, she wrote: "This winter it was Nancy [her oldest daughter] who upset me. She is approaching adolescence rather rapidly physically, but has remained entirely the little girl in her activities. At one of the events of Nancy's graduation I had to leave the auditorium. I felt I could not possibly go through with it. This old dizzy feeling with lightness in my head and neck came in waves."

At my request the patient came for some weeks of treatment. Again in the analytic situation she remembered fully her previous analysis. There was no evidence of afterrepression.[3] An extremely interesting detail of her neurotic upset came to light. Nancy's graduation about which the patient spoke in her letter was only a screen for the first appearance of Nancy's menstruation which "graduated" her for womanhood. By identification with her daughter, the patient's adult ego regressed to its status in puberty and reacted to the trauma of climacterium in the same manner as to the trauma of puberty.

Let us make a brief survey of this case. We have seen how the patient's neurosis found its expression in physiological processes. Her first menstruation, as part of the whole problem of reproduction, provoked anxiety and flight from the painful, mysterious events which she had observed as a child in her environment. Through analysis the physiological processes could be liberated from the regressive psychic forces. With psychic maturation the patient's fear of motherhood changed into a desire for it, and she could follow the traditional pattern of women in her family: having more and more children! She could remain healthy as long as she could make use of her formerly neurotically distorted

---

[3] Freud, in "Postscript to the Analysis of a Phobia in a Five-Year-Old Boy" (1922), reports that Little Hans had appeared at his office after twenty years. He had apparently become a healthy man who showed no obsessive symptoms or anxieties. There was complete amnesia for the treatment he had undergone as a child and he could not identify at all the classic material of his treatment which Freud had published. Freud considered this phenomenon an afterrepression.

physiological functions in a normal, active manner. However, when the menopause confronted her with the fact that her active functions as a woman must come to an end, the regressive forces were revived and created neurotic difficulties similar to those in her puberty. The achievement of the analysis could not withstand the biological assault and proved reversible.

I should like to inform you that the first patient's achievement and success are increasing and her narcissistic gratification is at its peak. But if we observe her activities we may recognize residua of her previous "acting out" on a level accepted socially and admired by all around her. As to our second patient, letters received from her lately indicate that things are going well and that she seems to reach joyfully the last step toward maturity in her grandmotherhood. Optimistically, we may say that after all, every woman has difficulties in her menopause, and it is characteristic that regressive currents lead even the relatively healthy one back into puberty.

My insight into these two cases taught me that the therapeutic success in both has been dependent upon certain conditions. In the first case, it was necessary that the efficiency of the patient's ego defenses, increased through analysis, should remain unimpaired in their function. For the second patient, the essential condition was that the biological functions through which she expressed her psychic conflicts should be in accordance with the solution she found through the analysis; that is, to exchange the horrors of motherhood for the wish and its gratifications.

Such individually varying conditions hold true for analytic therapy in general. What we conquer are only parts of psychogenesis: expressions of conflicts, developmental failures. We do not eliminate the original sources of neurosis; we only help to achieve better ability to change neurotic frustrations into valid compensations. The dependence of psychic harmony on certain conditions makes immunity unattainable. Freud's "Analysis Terminable and Interminable" brought for those of us who nourished unlimited therapeutic ambitions both disappointment and relief.

25

Lord Jim *and Depression*

(1959)

I BELIEVE that the real strength and uniqueness of Edward Bibring's analytical work was in his clinical acumen and his unusual intuition. These qualities made him for a whole generation of younger analysts a beloved teacher for whom they are grieving deeply.

In a brief, time-limited way I want to attempt a clinical approach to Bibring's paper on "The Mechanism of Depression" (1953). I shall restrict my remarks and my clinical illustration to the process of restitution in the state of depression, which seems to me to be a very important part of Bibring's paper.

Let me for a moment go back in time. In the late 20s (or early 30s) I once met Edward Bibring at a social gathering (as we often had in the old times in Vienna). We were both enchanted by a book which by chance we had read simultaneously. It was Joseph Conrad's *Lord Jim,* which I think had just then appeared in German translation and was not yet well known. From a long, enjoyable conversation I remember only one detail: we came to the conclusion that whereas guilt feelings (superego) played a great role in this deeply psychological novel, the most important problem was what we then referred to as *narcissism* and what

---

Read at the Edward Bibring Memorial Meeting held on April 14, 1959, at the Boston Medical Library.

today we describe as an "ego-psychological problem" or the "problem of ego state."

I do not know how often in our later contacts we returned to the literary phenomenon Joseph Conrad, but in 1955 when the Boston Society honored my husband and me by the celebration of our anniversary, Edward Bibring announced his paper on Joseph Conrad. I understood this to be a very personal gift to me, a reference to our earlier conversations. I hope that his paper, which Bibring was not able to finish at that time, is in his files.

A few years earlier (1953) Bibring's paper on "The Mechanism of Depression" was published. Perhaps one can dare to speculate that Bibring's clinical interest in his depressed patients and his absorption with Conrad, respectively Lord Jim, found their combined expression in this paper. This assumption may explain why I attempt to use *Lord Jim* as a clinical example of Bibring's theoretical statements.

Jim (later Lord Jim) was a fine, English "clear-cut" boy from a parsonage, good-looking, medium intelligent, rather on the stupid side. Since his age after some years of pilgrimage is quoted as "four and twenty," he must have been in late adolescence when a certain tragic event occurred. Until then he was doing good, efficient work as a junior officer on a ship engaged in various enterprises in the Far Eastern Seas. In this period of life he was what may be called "well adjusted." We might never have known him if the catastrophe had not occurred. Only after this event Conrad tells us that behind his everyday façade Jim's life was filled with glorious thoughts: they were full of valorous deeds and imaginary achievements. "They were the best parts of his life, its secret truth, its hidden reality. They had a gorgeous virility, they passed before him with a heroic tread, they carried his soul away with them, making it drunk with the divine philter of an unbounded confidence in itself. There was nothing he could not face. He saw himself saving people from sinking ships, swimming through a surf with a line; he confronted savages on tropical shores, in a small boat upon the ocean he kept up the hearts of despairing men—always an example of devotion to duty, and as unflinching as a hero in a book."

Jim went. "He left his earthly failings behind him and there was a totally new set of conditions for his imaginations." "He had to deal with another sort of reality and here he had achieved greatness. He captured much honors and an Arcadian happiness. The legend gifted him with supernatural powers. The natives proclaimed him Tuan—God—Lord."

But even here in this complete isolation from the world of his past, the "visitors" from outside reappear; the isolation breaks down and so does the narcissistic splendor. Some harmless words which he regards as allusions to his failure, to the *Patna,* bring about a total collapse of this new world and his death.

Jim's attempts at restitution were along the lines of Bibring's ideas: "The depression subsides when the ego recovers from the narcissistic shock by regaining its self-esteem with the help of various recovery mechanisms." Jim's mechanism of isolation did not fulfill this task. All the new supplies of narcissistic gratification could not keep away the memory of his failure.

Conrad's novel is not a clinical study; it affords a deep insight into the human soul.

I think that Bibring's theoretical conception of depression—and particularly his views on the methods of restitution—express not only the analyst's insight into pathological processes of his patients; they can also be applied to depressive states of mind with which all normal human beings are afflicted. Bibring says, "Everything that lowers the self-esteem without changing the narcissistically important aims represents a condition of depression."

We do not like to change our narcissistic aims, and our self-esteem is always under attack from the "visitors" from inside—hence "conflicts within our ego and the resulting tensions are always present."

Bibring's paper is an important contribution to the ego-psychological aspects of depression. It is also a contribution to normal ego psychology.

26

Frigidity in Women

(1960)

B<small>Y</small> adding some remarks to this discussion, I am abusing the
privilege of the Chairman, who is supposed to be an organizer
and not a contributor.

After I published the two volumes on *The Psychology of
Women* (1944, 1945), I felt that I had exhausted my knowledge
on the topic. Twenty-five years of analytic experience were
deposited in these books, and I was prepared never to return to
the problem of femininity.

But like Faust, I could not get rid of the ghosts I had called up.
Letters from sexually disturbed women and from men disturbed
by women's disturbances followed. I was kept busy with the
problem by many consultations, by the newly aroused interest of
gynecologists, by brief therapies, etc. These experiences afforded
me an opportunity to gain a rich macroscopic view of the psychopathology of women, a valuable review of psychic events
which I had previously seen in the microscope of analysis.

In that period of my professional work I was shocked by the
number of frigid women and bitterly disappointed in the results

---

Chairman's Introduction to the Panel on "Frigidity in Women," held at the
Fall Meeting of American Psychoanalytic Association, New York, 1960. For a
report of the Panel, see Moore (1961).

of psychoanalytic treatment of frigidity. I have seen cases in which the most severe neurotic illness was helped by psychoanalysis without in the least influencing the same patient's frigidity. I have seen very sick women, even psychotic women, who experienced an intense vaginal orgasm, and women relatively free of neurosis who had never had this experience. I have seen aggressive, masculine, demanding, and efficient women, for whom the vaginal orgasm was an absolute condition of the sexual act, and loving, maternal, giving, and happy women, for whom the vaginal orgasm was *terra incognita*. Many women had not the slightest doubts that their sexual needs were fully gratified in intercourse; yet vaginal orgasm was not included in their conception of gratification.

According to our analytic experience, frigidity is rooted in the individual life history of a woman. There are many conditions which have to be fulfilled before a woman reaches her orgastic capacity:

1. Influences of pregenital and preoedipal development have to be conquered;

2. oedipal problems have to be solved;

3. bisexuality has to be resolved;

4. object relationships have to be based on postambivalent affective positions.

5. The main source of sexual inhibition, feminine masochism, has to be in full control, etc.

In short: every single disturbance in development can become a source of frigidity.

In addition, perhaps the most troublesome invasion into the sphere of sexual gratification comes from the reproductive functions, and from the psychological meaning of coitus as the first act of these functions.

We know the danger of motherhood for the security and solidity of the ego; we know the conflicts between the narcissistic forces and the object-directed forces of reproduction. I suspect that even intercourse mobilizes the struggle between the narcissistic elements of self-preservation and the demands of reproduction. Therese Benedek (1960) describes very clearly the dangers for the ego resulting from the sexual act. She sees in frigidity a defense against these "dangers"; I wholeheartedly agree with this idea.

In summary: considering the numerous conditions under which a woman can reach vaginal orgasm, one is compelled to ask: what kind of sexual organ is this vagina, when the simple, most primitive function of the female *homo sapiens* is so terribly complicated? This question brings another one to mind. Is the vagina really the organ created by nature, and developed phylogenetically, for the sexual function we assume and demand of it?

My long preoccupation with the problem under discussion, various influences of analytic and nonanalytic literature, and above all the lasting impression of Freud's ideas brings me via a detour to the old conviction—shared with many—that the female sexual organs consist of two parts with a definite division of function: the clitoris is the sexual organ, the vagina primarily the organ of reproduction. All waves of sexual excitement, often very strong and urgent in women, flow into the clitoris, and only subsequent, more or less successful, communication of this excitement to the vagina secondarily incorporates this organ into the sphere of sexual experience. Originally the vagina was endowed with the dynamic forces of reproduction. The erotization of the vagina is a job performed by way of the clitoris and by the active intervention of man's sexual organ.

This central role of the clitoris is not merely the result of masturbation, but is a biological destiny. The muscular apparatus of the vagina is in the service of reproduction and may or may not become involved in the orgastic activity.

In this dualistic conception of the female sexual apparatus, I am ready to reverse the burning question: "Why are women frigid?" into "Why or how are some women endowed with vaginal orgasm?"

After many years of experience it seems that one must return to Freud's conception (1932):

"The sexual frigidity of women . . . is still a phenomenon which is insufficiently understood. Sometimes it is psychogenic, and, if so, it is accessible to influence; but in other cases one is led to assume that it is constitutionally conditioned or even partly caused by an anatomical factor." And I would add, "and a physiological one."

We are well acquainted with the process of sexualization of the vagina during the sexual act and of the biological hormonal forces participating in this process. But I remind you that the typical function of the vagina during intercourse is passive-receptive. The movements have the character of sucking in and relaxing. The rhythm of these movements is adjusted to the rhythm of the male partner.

In a great number of women—I would say in the majority of them—the orgastic function does not culminate in the sphincterlike orgastic activity of the vagina, but is brought to a happy end in a mild, slow relaxation with complete gratification. I assume that this form is the typical and the most feminine one.

To challenge the vaginal orgastic experience familiar to quite a number of women would be irrational. This fact does not change my belief that the activity—any activity—of the vagina is essentially supplied by forces of reproduction. Biological research seems to confirm this assumption.

Psychological factors accompany both spheres of vaginal activity, the sexual and the reproductive one. We must postulate that both processes are sharing not only the organ but also the emotional cathexis. This duality of function seems to bear the greatest part of responsibility for vaginal frigidity. We learned from many observations that the original sexual organ of the woman, the clitoris, is the receiver of castration fears. The vagina is the receiver of the deepest anxiety, i.e., of death, which accompanies motherhood and is mobilized in pregnancy and delivery. It is this anxiety which seems to prevent sexual responses in the vaginal part of the female organ.

There is a widely held opinion that frigidity is increasing. When we restrict the term "frigidity" to the lack of a certain form of vaginal activity and accept the more passive-receptive way of gratification for women, I think that we shall find that frigidity is in fact not as common as we assume. What has increased are demands for a form of sexual gratification which is not fully in harmony with the constitutional destiny of the organ. The insistence on the active participation of women in coitus aims directly at the function of the vagina. Women's aspirations to social equality do not sufficiently explain the obsessive demand for vaginal activity.

The evidence of increased passivity in men and of masculine activity in women is to a high degree an explanation of the intolerance of both sexes regarding vaginal insufficiency. We can even speak of "sexual ambition," which may rather inhibit the normal function of the vagina by expectations of great performances called "vaginal orgasm."

The following may illustrate this point. In the last years my practice consisted mainly of male patients in a ratio of 7:2. I expected this would free me from the sometimes annoying problem of frigidity, but unfortunately many of my male patients are very preoccupied with the frigidity of their sexual partners. And so I can observe how one of the few opportunities of human beings to forget the miseries and conflicts of life in an ecstatic experience changes into a *folie à deux,* which runs: "has she, will she have or not?" and "have I, will I have?" The watchfulness and fearful observation and desperate expectation of vaginal orgasm take the place of orgastic oblivion.

Perhaps we are living in a specific stage of an evolutionary development of female sexuality. The vagina may become independent of developmental interferences, and the social equality of sexes will reflect the possession of a solid, reliable active organ.

27

Acting Out in the Transference

(1963)

PHYLLIS GREENACRE defines "acting out" in analysis as "memory expressed in active behavior, without the usual sort of recall in verbal and visual imagery." Acting out, however, is not restricted to analysis. To some extent, we all are actors-out, because nobody is free of regressive trends, repressed strivings, burdens of more or less conscious fantasies, etc.

Artists are able to create in acting out their work of art, neurotics of every type and degree are using their symptoms to act out: hysterics in conversion symptoms, and often very dramatic twilight states; obsessionals in their ceremonies; psychotics in hallucinations and delusions; delinquents in their asocial behavior. In one word: everybody's "old memories seem to have found their resting place in action tendencies" (Greenacre).

Psychoanalytic practice gives us the best opportunity to observe the process of acting out *in statu nascendi,* to see its start, its functions, and very often the conditions under which it is arrested. One is able to understand what the patient expresses

---

Contribution to a discussion of the paper by P. Greenacre on this subject. Both papers were first published as part of the "Symposium on a Developmental Approach to Problems of Acting Out" in the *Journal of the American Academy of Child Psychiatry,* 2:1-175, 1963.

through his actions, and also to see what *specific* situations of analysis are provoking, reinforcing, or interrupting the acting out. Greenacre assumes a definite predisposition to acting out, generally and more specifically, in a group of patients she had under her analytic observation.

First of all, let us not forget that every patient brings into analysis his own personal predisposition which constitutes the roots and the form of his neurosis. As far as my experience goes every patient in analysis will, under certain psychological conditions, act out more or less intensively. The dispositional factors of *his neurosis* will give to his acting out a specific character.

Greenacre's paper is focused mainly on acting out inside the analytic situation. When we take the word *acting* in a motoric sense (as the word demands, and she is using it), there is very little room for *motoric* expressions in the analytic situation per se. Coming late or early, doing some chores such as fixing the window, moving the table, etc., certainly do not provide a sufficiently strong push toward activity. It happened once in my practice that a patient acted out his furious mood, and broke my wall with his fist; and another patient in a state of panic lost her bladder control on the couch. But these are rare and single events.

Inside the analytic locality there are only two ways of acting: (1) by actions of the body (see Felix Deutsch's "Thus Speaks the Body" [1950], "Analytic Posturology" [1952] and Zeligs's "Acting In" [1957, 1961]); and (2) by verbalization. We can define acting out inside the analytic situation as expression of revived emotions projected onto the analyst and communicated verbally to him.

Greenacre presented a group of patients who verbalize very strongly and actively, but their expressions of wild transference emotions still stay in the realm of verbal communication. In my opinion, we can speak of acting out proper only when a patient leaves the seclusion of the analytic room, and carries out the transference situation in the outside world, disregarding whether the place of action is nearby, for example, the patient's own family home, or in the Far East, as it happened with one of my patients during his analysis. As long as the emotional center of the activities is connected with analysis, we can speak of "acting out."

We consider intensification of transference a resistance phenomenon against the recovery of memories. But transference, on the other hand, is the most important source of information, the most convincing part of the revival of the past. One can even ascribe to transference a certain degree of catharsis which may contribute more or less to the therapeutic efforts of analysis. Acting out during analysis is always a part of transference and one can say that every transference, even a mild one, is a form of acting out—let us say, "pre-acting." It takes the character of real acting out when the emotional cathexis of transference has reached a certain point of intensity.

The emotional forces of transference belong to various developmental periods of the past; they may represent primitive impulses of genital and pregenital character, or they may be repetitions of more consolidated emotional experiences.

We assume that, in a workable analytic situation, the ego of the patient does not participate fully in the regressive process, and has the power of "editing" the tendencies to repeat. Various situations may arise: in one, the impulsive elements of transference take over the field of analytic procedure, and the ego is not able to develop a rational control. Massive acting out, as in Greenacre's cases, will be the result. In another situation, the more effective ego will meet the impact of transference rationally and reinforce the therapeutic alliance with the analyst to analyze the transference.

Another possibility is that the controlling capacity of the ego will make attempts not only to rationalize the transference actions, but also to give it a pseudo-rational character. An example is the patient who energetically protested the "new edition" of his feelings for the analyst. He insisted on the realistic character of this love, courted the analyst with flowers, presents, theater tickets, etc. He became furious when the analyst rejected the courtship, and the analysis was on the brink of collapse. The analyst, in an act of professional despair, pretended to be at last convinced of the reality of his love, and asked the patient whether he thought that she should start divorce proceedings with her husband—whereupon the patient jumped from the couch and exclaimed: "That would be poison." Evidently somewhere in his preconscious, the patient was aware of the anachronism of his emotions.

But there also exists a danger on, so to say, the other side of the analytic situation. The transference may stay in the honeymoon stage of peaceful collaboration; the patient produces innumerable memories, finds connections, and works "through" the material. By and by, analysis passes on into the dangerous sphere of "intellectualization" and the situation collapses.

The progress of analysis fluctuates according to the interplay of these two factors: the recovery of memories, and the emotional experience of transference. The tension of these emotional experiences may rise very high and the patient is forced to look for outlets for these pent-up feelings—and he is doing that by "acting out."

As to Greenacre's patients, they represent a special group with a definite genesis. But I do not think that vicissitudes of the oral stage are always the reason for increased tendencies to act out. I also doubt that the primitive intolerance to frustration is always the culprit responsible for acting out. The atmosphere of the analytic situation is such that it may easily become a breeding place for various acting-out forces! Expectation and frustration, forced passivity, isolation from the outside world, onesidedness of the relation between the patient and the analyst, anonymity and secrecy of the latter, mobilization of latent emotions, etc.—all that plus the neurotic disposition are the provoking forces.

An excellent source of information comes from cases which acted out before analytic treatment and stopped the acting soon after the start of analysis; also from cases which acted out during an intermission or after interruption. During analysis, the "acting-out" patients are either runners-away from a danger or stowaways in search of gratification missed in the analytic situation.

This symposium brought a wealth of observations on children and adolescents, as well as interesting theoretical contributions dealing with the problem of "acting out." To the clinical material presented by Greenacre, I would like to add some of my own experiences with "acting-out" patients. I shall start with the one Greenacre mentioned in her paper.

"Fate Neurosis" is the case history of a young, beautiful, talented, attractive, and even intellectually outstanding girl (see Chapter 2). Her life before analytic treatment consisted in a compulsive pattern in which it was not difficult to recognize the roots of the oedipal past. Love affairs with married men in the typical triangle situation, craving for gratification, provoking situations, and running away were her way of living. Every fresh experience had the quality of the previous one and the same unsuccessful end. The oedipal pattern of her acting out was evident, the secondary elaboration being simple and direct. Even the imaginary child of the little girl's fantasy was re-enacted by a nonsensical provocation of an illegitimate pregnancy.

A paradoxical situation arose in her acting out: when the man she loved was putting an end to the triangle by divorcing his wife and preparing for marriage with the patient, she made a serious attempt of suicide; after recovery, she came to analysis.

When you look into the case history you will see another pattern repeated in her verbalized, not acted-out desires. She had a sincere and burning wish to study; she was endowed with manifold talents; she had financial resources to engage in a professional and scientific training; but all her efforts in this direction came to grief, owing to an inhibition and feelings of inadequacy. She said in despair: "Why is it that I alone cannot do what every woman in my environment manages so easily and naturally?"

If we remind ourselves that this girl had a brother, born when she was four years old, that this brother not only was better equipped somatically than she was, but that he also took her place as father's favorite, we will be able to understand the compulsivity of her acting out. We see that this acting out is not a simple projection of an oedipal conflict. The jealousy and aggressiveness toward the little brother had evoked guilt reactions in her and the superego prevented her from entering into competition with him. She was using the unresolved oedipal conflict in a compulsive way to cover another one which she had solved by an unconscious act of sacrifice to fate by complete resignation.

This act of resignation was triumphant; it interfered successfully with her capacity to sublimation.

In this case, we see that the acting out which impresses us as simple repetition of the conflicting inner situation represents an effort to cover another unresolved conflict, a defensive measure achieved under pressure of guilty feelings.

Discussing this case of fate neurosis, Greenacre saw the "dispositional factor in the preconscious genital stimulation, with habitual masturbation without discharge." I am very eager to accept this proposition. The traumatic situation which the patient was re-enacting was experienced in the period of strong genital masturbatory impulses, especially increased by the birth of a brother. But I doubt that this disposition would have been sufficient to produce the acting out without the intervention of the superego as described above.

This patient stopped acting out after a short period of analysis. Why? After the preliminary steps toward therapeutic alliance, I actively reinforced this alliance. My emphasis was not so much on her acting out, but on her inhibition of *acting*. I helped her to overcome this inhibition, supported her in finding teachers, passing examinations, and getting her full education in the field in which she had shown an unusual talent. She is now a famous person in her chosen field. This was indeed a very unorthodox approach on the part of the analyst, but I knew that this was the only way to prevent the next wave of acting out, perhaps even a suicide, and, above all, to make the analytic treatment work. Such a mechanism of utilizing one conflict-laden sector of the unconscious against another as defense and protection was observed by Spiegel (1954) in his acting-out patients.

In her paper on "General Problems of Acting Out" (1950), Greenacre mentioned a certain type of patient with poor ego structure, shallow transference capacity, and great tendency to acting out. I am acquainted with quite a number of patients with very infantile personality, very narcissistic, and not able to establish a real object relationship. Their instinctual development is anchored in the pregenital and preoedipal period. These patients, outside and in the transference, dramatically act out emotions which they never experienced before, and, when in analysis with men, fake seducingly oedipal situations.

I would like to give a very short report on Nora, who, like the case of fate neurosis, acted out before analysis, stopped during analysis, but started again in a more ominous way after the interruption of analysis necessitated by my departure. It is a case of a sixteen-year-old girl of an aristocratic and socially prominent Hungarian family.

She was educated in a convent, completed her schooling in an exclusive institution, and was to be introduced to society. But instead of taking over the role of a fine lady, she started to act out in a nearly delinquent way, mixed with the wayward youth of the town, and continuously provoked public opinion. In analysis, all the acting out stopped like magic. She created an extremely positive transference, and analysis was progressing.

She was a typical oversized adolescent rebeller, with a furious anger against her demanding and devaluated mother. She was young and susceptible, and it was not difficult to rebuild a more respectable ego ideal by identification with the analyst. My leaving Vienna necessitated the interruption of her analysis after one year of treatment. I left her in the hands of a colleague, whom we all considered the best in working with adolescents.

When I returned, after some months, she was already back with her family in Hungary, after a period of wild acting out in Vienna and an abortion of pregnancy from an unknown man. I do not think it necessary to show you how the disappointment, the desertion by the once lost and newly found mother destroyed the still unconsolidated equilibrium, and provoked the revengeful acting out even more forcefully than before.

Whereas the two cases described above were actors-out outside the analytic situation, I want to mention now two cases whose acting out was purely the result of the analytic situation.

One is that of a highly cultivated, gifted woman in an important position with great responsibilities. She came to Vienna for "impressions," insights, etc. Her goal was very serious. We did not have at that time a properly organized Institute, and the patient, very respectable in her profession, was accepted for didactic orientation for a few months of analysis. The analysis was, so to say, going, but the anxiety connected with transference was overwhelming. Her behavior was very childish, she cried often, trembled, her whole attitude was in contrast to her real personality. On week ends she used to travel, and I sensed that something was going on in those free days that was not reported to me. She left analysis very thankful, she learned a lot and planned to come back.

Some years later a friend of mine, an analyst in Switzerland, mentioned her name in a conversation. The fact was discovered that, on her week-end trips, she had been in analytic treatment with him. He had known that she had some professional contact with me, but he did not know that it was called analysis. This was an acting out *par excellence* of a situation in which the patient, endangered by the infantile and dependent form of transference, hurried under the guise of learning more into the protection of a man, and a better opportunity to reinforce her ego by a masculine identification.

Another patient was a very mature, active, independent woman who never demonstrated any tendency to act out. She wanted to get acquainted with analysis for professional reasons—she was a social worker—and presented no real neurotic difficulties. During her treatment, I left for a vacation and we agreed to meet again in two months. She went on a little trip to Western Europe and came back refreshed and ready to work. There was no sign of anger or depression, but she confessed that she was depressed immediately after the interruption, and that she had the crazy idea to travel under the false name "French" (a variation on "Deutsch" [German]) and that she introduced herself on many occasions as an analyst from Vienna, wife of a physician, and mother of a little boy. She herself was not married. Her rationalization was that I was better known in the countries she traveled in, and that it was a kind of expediency to travel under disguise. It was not difficult to convince her that she reacted to the separation depressively, and that the identification with her analyst was a helpful way to get rid of depression.

I could present many cases and many variations of acting out as expressions of transference. I have already mentioned that the atmosphere of the analytic situation and the forces inherent in the transference can be made responsible for various forms of acting out.

After this indirect discussion of Greenacre's paper, I now turn to the interesting group of her cases with "massive acting out." I looked back for similar cases and found three patients whose attitudes correspond exactly with the description given by Greenacre. An abusive, hostile, demanding attitude toward the analyst is not unfamiliar to us, but Greenacre's cases are especially characterized by the intensity and periodicity in their behavior, and by the fact that they restrict their activity to the analytic hour and to verbalization—they do not carry their acting out to the external world.

One of these three patients was an alcoholic who drank periodically. In his alcohol-free periods, he was a man of very high ethical and intellectual standards, a distinguished personality, and an excellent father and husband. In his drinking bouts, he was a destructive, dangerous man. Oddly enough, he usually restricted his destructiveness to his immediate environment where he shattered to pieces everything breakable, beat his wife who adored him and whom he loved. In those days, he behaved like a wild animal.

In the so-called analysis, he developed an excellent positive transference, gave up drinking, but soon demonstrated "massive transference attacks," exactly like Greenacre's patients. These attacks were periodic and continued throughout the treatment. He then gave up drinking and left after one and a half years in excellent condition. However, after some months of well-functioning, he started to drink again, deteriorated completely, and committed suicide (in "self-defense") when the police came to take him in custody.

His alcoholic bouts were *de facto* attacks of anxiety and the pleasure of intoxication was relief from anxiety and release of aggression. His transference behavior was a substitute for his dipsomaniac attacks, and there is no doubt that the provocation which he could not tolerate was, like in Greenacre's patients, the lack of response on the part of the analyst.

Another patient was a morphine addict. He, too, stopped his addiction for the love of the analyst, but developed periodically a behavior of anger and abuse similar to Greenacre's patients. During the period between the attacks, he was a mild, rather submissive, depressive person. He was to some degree accessible to analysis. After some months of complete abstinence, he declared that he could no longer tolerate analytic treatment and left. He started again to take morphine and later committed suicide in the hospital where he was admitted.

The third patient was a young nurse who came from America to Vienna because of "hysterical fits." She was free of her "fits" during the first months of analysis, but she did not impress me as hysteric. In the analytic hours, especially at the time of menstruation, she demonstrated a mounting tension. Usually a benign and inhibited person, during that time she abused, cursed, degraded the analyst and the treatment. Her companion reported to me that in those days she behaved "peculiarly" after her analytic hour, and I had the suspicion of *petit mal* attacks. Her fits reappeared and were diagnosed as epileptic. I think that her transference behavior was an equivalent of her epileptic attacks.

Describing her patients Greenacre used the term "this kind of acting-out addiction." My two patients *were* addicts and their acting out was a substitute for their addiction now related to transference. Perhaps the accumulation of anxiety and aggressiveness, mobilized by transference, creates in these patients increasing tension which has to be discharged in periodic attacks, in analogy to the dipsomaniac states of my alcoholic patient or to the seizures of the epileptic girl.

When I review all the years of my analytic practice, I come to the conclusion that there is hardly a case which, during the long analytic treatment, did not seek in reality outlets for aroused and frustrated emotions, inhibited activity, and, above all, compensations for narcissistic deprivation.

I am aware of a great omission in my discussion. The most important part of Greenacre's paper is, as she emphasized, the "genetic approach." I must confess that I am a little bit lost: are the ideas expressed in this approach based on direct observations of infants, or on information from the child's environment, or on analytic reconstructions?

In my discussion I was able to offer you only simple, clinical, empirical observations, a modest contribution to Greenacre's thought-provoking paper.

Bibliography

Abraham, K. (1913), A Constitutional Basis of Locomotor Anxiety. *Selected Papers of Karl Abraham.* London: Hogarth Press, 1927, pp. 235–243.
—— (1917), Ejaculatio Praecox. *Selected Papers of Karl Abraham.* London: Hogarth Press, 1927, pp. 280–298.
—— (1924), A Short Study of the Development of the Libido, Viewed in the Light of Mental Disorders. *Selected Papers of Karl Abraham.* London: Hogarth Press, 1927, pp. 418-501.
—— (1925), The History of an Impostor in the Light of Psychoanalytical Knowledge. *Clinical Papers and Essays on Psychoanalysis.* New York: Basic Books, 1955, pp. 291–305.
Aichhorn, A. (1925), *Wayward Youth.* New York: Viking Press, 1955.
Alexander, F. (1927), *The Psychoanalysis of the Total Personality.* New York & Washington: Nervous and Mental Disease Publishing Co., 1930.
—— (1937), *Institute for Psychoanalysis: Five Year Report, 1932–1937.* Chicago: Institute for Psychoanalysis, 1937.
Angel, A. (1934), Einige Bemerkungen über den Optimismus [Some Remarks on Optimism]. *Int. Z. Psychoanal.,* 20:191-199.
Benedek, T. (1960), On Frigidity. Contribution to the Panel on "Frigidity in Women." For an abstract, see Moore (1961).
Bergler, E. & Eidelberg, L. (1935), Der Mechanismus der Depersonalization [The Mechanism of Depersonalization]. *Int. Z. Psychoanal.,* 21:258-285.
Bibring, E. (1953), The Mechanism of Depression. In: *Affective Disorders,* ed. P. Greenacre. New York: International Universities Press, pp. 13-48.
Brean, H. (1954), Marvin Hewitt Ph(ony)D. *Life,* April 12.
Breuer, J. & Freud, S. (1893–1895), Studies on Hysteria. *Standard Edition,* 2:1-305. London: Hogarth Press, 1955.
Conrad, J. (1900), *Lord Jim.* London: Dent, 1948.
Deutsch, F. (1950), Thus Speaks the Body. II. A Psychosomatic Study of Vasomotor Behavior. *Acta Med. Orient.,* 9:199-215.
—— (1952), Thus Speaks the Body. III. Analytic Posturology. *Psychoanal. Quart.,* 21:338-339.
Deutsch, H. (1918), Kasuistik zum "induzierten Irresein." *Wien. klin. Wschr.,* 31:809-812.

375

—— (1920), Mutterliebsträume und Selbstmordideen. Read at the Vienna Psychoanalytic Society.

—— (1925), *Zur Psychoanalyse der weiblichen Sexualfunktionen* [*On the Psychoanalysis of the Female Sexual Functions*]. Vienna: Internationaler psychoanalytischer Verlag.

—— (1930a), Zur Genese des Familienromans [On the Genesis of Fantasies of Descent]. *Int. Z. Psychoanal.*, 16:249-253.

—— (1930b), The Significance of Masochism in the Mental Life of Women. *Int. J. Psycho-Anal.*, 11:48-60.

—— (1944), *The Psychology of Women*, Vol. 1. New York: Grune & Stratton.

—— (1945), *The Psychology of Women*, Vol. 2. New York: Grune & Stratton.

Fenichel, O. (1931a), *Hysterien und Zwangsneurosen: Psychoanalytische spezielle Neurosenlehre* [*Hysterias and Obsessional Neuroses: Special Theory of Neurosis According to Psychoanalysis*]. Vienna: Internationaler psychoanalytischer Verlag.

—— (1931b), *Perversionen, Psychosen, Charakterstörungen* [*Perversions, Psychoses, Character Disturbances*]. Vienna: Internationaler psychoanalytischer Verlag.

Fremont-Smith, M. & Meigs, J. V. (1948), Menstrual Dysfunction due to Emotional Factors. *Amer. J. Obst. & Gyn.*, 55:1037-1043.

Freud, A. (1936), *The Ego and the Mechanisms of Defense*. New York: International Universities Press, 1946.

Freud, S. (1905a), Three Essays on the Theory of Sexuality. *Standard Edition*, 7:125-243. London: Hogarth Press, 1953.

—— (1905b), Jokes and Their Relation to the Unconscious. *Standard Edition*, 8:9-236. London: Hogarth Press, 1960.

—— (1909a), Family Romances. *Standard Edition*, 9:235-241. London: Hogarth Press, 1959.

——(1909b), Analysis of a Phobia in a Five-Year-Old Boy. *Standard Edition*, 10:5-147. London: Hogarth Press, 1955.

—— (1910–1918), Contributions to the Psychology of Love. *Standard Edition*. 11:163-208. London: Hogarth Press, 1957.

—— (1911), Psycho-Analytic Notes on an Autobiographical Account of a Case of Paranoia (Dementia Paranoides). *Standard Edition*, 12:9-82. London: Hogarth Press, 1958.

—— (1917), Mourning and Melancholia. *Standard Edition*, 14:243-258. London: Hogarth Press, 1957.

—— (1918), From the History of an Infantile Neurosis. *Standard Edition*, 17:7-122. London: Hogarth Press, 1955.

—— (1920a), Beyond the Pleasure Principle. *Standard Edition*, 18:7-64. London: Hogarth Press, 1955.

—— (1920b), The Psychogenesis of a Case of Homosexuality in a Woman. *Standard Edition*, 18:145-172. London: Hogarth Press, 1955.

—— (1922), Postscript to Analysis of a Phobia in a Five-Year-Old Boy. *Standard Edition*, 10:148-149. London: Hogarth Press, 1955.

—— (1923), The Ego and the Id. *Standard Edition*, 19:12-59. London: Hogarth Press, 1961.

—— (1924), The Loss of Reality in Neurosis and Psychosis. *Standard Edition*, 19:183-187. London: Hogarth Press, 1961.

—— (1925), Some Psychical Consequences of the Anatomical Distinction be-

tween the Sexes. *Standard Edition*, 19:248-258. London: Hogarth Press, 1961.
—— (1926), Inhibitions, Symptoms and Anxiety. *Standard Edition*, 20:87-172. London: Hogarth Press, 1959.
—— (1931), Female Sexuality. *Standard Edition*, 21:225-243. London: Hogarth Press, 1961.
—— (1932), *New Introductory Lectures on Psychoanalysis*. New York: Norton, 1933.
—— (1937), Analysis Terminable and Interminable. *Collected Papers*, 5:316-357. London: Hogarth Press, 1950.
Greenacre, P. (1945), Conscience in the Psychopath. *Trauma, Growth and Personality*. New York: Norton, 1952, pp. 165–187.
—— (1950), General Problems of Acting Out. *Psychoanal. Quart.*, 19:455-467.
Jones, E. (1927), The Early Development of Female Sexuality. *Int. J. Psycho-Anal.*, 8:459-472.
—— (1936), *The London Clinic of Psycho-Analysis: Decennial Report (May 1926–May 1936)*. London: Institute of Psycho-Analysis.
Knight, R. P. (1941), Evaluation of the Results of Psychoanalytic Therapy. *Amer. J. Psychiat.*, 98:434-446.
Lewin, B. D. (1933), The Body as Phallus. *Psychoanal. Quart.*, 2:24-47.
Lindemann, E. (1941), Observations on Psychiatric Sequelae to Surgical Operations in Women. *Amer. J. Psychiat.*, 98:132-139.
McCarthy, J. (1952), The Master Impostor. *Life*, Jan. 28.
Mann, T. (1954), *Confessions of Felix Krull*. New York: Knopf, 1955.
Menninger, K. A. (1934), Polysurgery and Polysurgic Addiction. *Psychoanal. Quart.*, 3:173-199.
Michaels, J. J. (1955), *Disorders of Character*. Springfield, Ill.: Thomas.
Moore, B. E. (1961), Panel Report: Frigidity in Women. *J. Amer. Psychoanal. Assn.*, 9:571-584.
Nunberg, H. (1932), *Principles of Psychoanalysis*. New York: International Universities Press, 1955.
Oberndorf, C. P. (1934), Depersonalization in Relation to Erotization of Thought. *Int. J. Psycho-Anal.*, 15:271-295.
—— (1935), The Genesis of the Feeling of Unreality. *Int. J. Psycho-Anal.*, 16:296-306.
Rado, S. (1927), The Problem of Melancholia. *Int. J. Psycho-Anal.*, 9:420-438, 1928.
Reich, W. (1933), *Character Analysis*. New York: Orgone Institute Press.
Schilder, P. F. (1939), The Treatment of Depersonalization. *Bull. N. Y. Acad. Med.*, 15:258-272.
Spiegel, L. A. (1954), Acting Out and Defensive Instinctual Gratification. *J. Amer. Psychoanal. Assn.*, 2:107-119.
Strohmayer, W. (1925), *Die Psychopathologie des Kindesalters*. Munich: Bergmann.
Zeligs, M. A. (1957), Acting In: A Contribution to the Meaning of Some Postural Attitudes Observed during Analysis. *J. Amer. Psychoanal. Assn.*, 5:685-706.
—— (1961), The Psychology of Silence: Its Role in Transference, Counter-transference and the Psychoanalytic Process. *J. Amer. Psychoanal. Assn.*, 9:7-43.

Index

Abraham, K., 41, 116, 203, 205, 278, 319
Absences, 69
Acting out, 23, 323, 331
  and addiction, 372
  defenses and, 259
  and memory of analysis, 341
  outside analysis, 363
  preadolescent delinquency and, 333f.
  in the transference, 363-373
Activity, thrust toward, 189
Actual conflict, *see* Conflict
Actuality, attempt to direct attention to, 12
Actualizing of childhood conflicts, 11
Affect
  blocking of, 232, 250, 277
  displacement of, 26
  lack of, 274
  omission of, 228; *see also* Grief
  transformation into anxiety, 66f.
  unconscious of lack of, 269
Affectivity
  disturbances of, 262-281
  increased by introversion, 67
  pseudo, at puberty, 280
Aggression
  "against aggression," 67, 132
  in agoraphobia, 102
  against brothers and sisters, 122, 147, 149f.
  against father, 183
  against mother, 77
  danger to ego, 150
  flow of words as, 207
  and libidinal wish in hysterical seizure, 72f.
  and male coitus, 70
  in manic depression, 205, 207, 209, 211
  in melancholia, 151, 204
  in mother-child relation, 174n.

  in obsessional neurosis, significance for prognosis, 139
  overcompensation of, 82
  primitive, 275
  as reaction to surgery, 288f.
  and sense of guilt, 132
  and superego, 132, 151
  turning against self, 95, 100, 108, 151, 153
Aggressive
  death wish against rival, 102
  tendencies in "as if" personalities, 266, 270
Agoraphobia, 5, 81, 97-116, 308
  aggression in, 102
  and animal phobia, 116
  danger of death, 100f., 111
  disappearance of death anxiety, 102
  and hysteria and obsessional neuroses, 113f.
  meaning of, 102f., 114
Aichhorn, A., 319
Alexander, F., 67, 212, 339
Ambivalence, ambivalent conflict, 7, 111, 121, 133, 139, 143, 147, 243
  constitutional, 129, 138f.
  doubt as expression of, 142
  in obsessional neurosis, 122
  persisting, and mourning, 227
  primordial, 82
Amenorrhea, 307, 309ff., 349
Amnesia
  and childhood, 85
  and hysterical seizures, 69, 71
  pseudo, for events of analysis, 341
Amphimixis, 294
Anal
  disposition, 91
  game, 87
  phase, 52; development to genital, 87f.
  reactivation of infantile pleasure, 123
  relationship to mother, 94

Fantasies—*Continued*
feminine-masochistic, 99, 115
of oral impregnation, 59, 347, 350
Fixation, 4, 26, 28, 48, 144
on mother, 175
primal, and female homosexuality, 188
Flight
from grief, 235f.
into illness, 64
from men, 180
into nunnery, 118
Folie à deux, 237-247, 362
Folie à trois, 239
of prostitution, 72, 101, 191, 194, 274
in puberty, 70, 99, 101
urethral, 40
womb, 187, 290
of world destruction, 220f.
see also Masturbation, Pregnancy
Fear
of earthquakes, 103
preoperative, 284f.
of thinking, 258
of thunder, 103
see also Anxiety, Phobia
Feeding
difficulties, 62ff.
refusal of, 160, 162
Feminine attitude, 94, 189, 231
Feminine-masochistic
attitude, 58, 109
fantasies, 99, 115
Feminine-passive attitude, 41, 195, 336
Feminine sexuality, *see* Sexuality
Fenichel, O., 186n., 231n.
Fits, 62, 70f.
Fremont-Smith, M., 310
Freud, A., 179-181, 248, 254, 280
Freud, S., 11, 15, 90, 114f., 132, 143f., 180f., 186-189, 191f., 203f., 220n., 223n., 226, 231, 234f., 240n., 246f., 248, 278ff., 284, 303, 339, 346, 351n., 352, 360
Fright neurosis, 284
Frigidity, in women, 190f., 358-362
Frustration, 4, 7, 16, 20, 69, 71, 79, 92, 100, 136ff., 207
and acting out, 366
and delinquency, 336
external, 6f.

maternal, 183
of wish for child, 182

Gastric symptoms, 59
Genital
libido, repression of, 55, 58
phase (stage), 67, 87f., 114
Genitalization of organs, 62
Gluttony, 54ff.
Grandeur, fantasies of, 331
Greed, *see* Gluttony
Greenacre, P., 331, 335, 363ff.
Grief, absence of, 226-236
Groups
"as if" personality and, 266
folies in, 237, 247
Guilt (feelings, sense of), 7, 20, 22, 25, 27, 39, 49, 53, 59ff., 67, 77ff., 96, 103, 105, 114, 119f., 122f., 127f., 131ff., 170, 175, 184, 193, 198ff., 205, 231, 289, 345
and crime, 235
expiation of, and pregnancy, 316
and mourning, 227
in obsessive neurotic, 141f., 147
quasi, 268
see also Superego
Gynecology, psychiatry and, 305-318

Hate
and love, 137f., 149, 176
of mother, 168ff.
mutual, of sisters, 245
overcompensation of, 78f., 84, 113, 121, 147, 149
unconscious, 121
Hen phobia, 84-96
Hewitt, M., 329f., 334
Hoffmann, E. T. A., 94
Homosexuality, 242
conditions for break-through of, 92
cure of, 93
defense against, 87ff., 137f.
fear of own, 92, 245, 337
female, 165-189
intensified: by double identification, 144; by frustration, 92, 138
latent, 252
manifest, 84, 87ff., 274
phallic-masculine, 186
preoedipal components, 176, 192f.

Homosexuality—*Continued*
  and triangular relationship, 10, 76, 79
  unconscious, and obsessional neurosis, 143
Hormones, *see* Endocrinology
Horney, K., 295
Horse as phobic object, 84, 96
Hypermenorrhea, 307
Hypochondria, 260, 312, 332
Hypomania, 213f., 216, 274
Hypomanic states, in normal life, 155
Hypothyroidism, 310
Hysteria, hysterical, 14-73
  and agoraphobia, 109f., 113f.
  amenorrhea and, 314
  and "as if" personality, 277
  convulsions, 69ff.
  fate neurosis, 14-28, 75
  and female homosexuality, 188
  and fixation on object, 26
  and genital symbolism, 110
  and melancholia, 156
  and obsessional neurosis, 67, 133
  and surgery, 293
  and organic disease, 286
  paralysis, 43f.
  reaction formations, 99, 111
  seizures, 4, 57-73
  and sense of guilt, 67
  tonic-clonic, 107
  trance states, 57-73
  without clinical symptoms, 29
  see also Conversion hysteria

Id
  aggression of, 212f.
  and denial in mania, 215
Identification, 40, 51-54, 59f., 88, 92, 94, 100ff., 108, 114f., 144, 150, 153, 234
  in "as if" personality, 265ff.
  as attempt to rescue object, 247
  with brother, 272
  with father, 174, 254f., 321f.
  of impostors, 330f.
  in mania, 215f.
  masculine, 370
  with mother, *see* Mother
  multiple, 273, 276
  narcissistic, 148ff.

  with nonhuman objects, 279
  with other person's ego, 334
  with parents, 270, 275
  passive, 193
  prepubertal, 331
  and restitution, 356
  schizophrenic, 246
  split, 275
Identity
  denial of own, 329
  search for, 329
Immortality, narcissistic, 222
Impostor, 319-338
Impotence, 29-42, 62
Incorporation, 151, 154
Indecision, inner, 143
Induced insanity, 222
Induction, 247
Infantile
  anxiety, 46
  attitudes, 9
  conflicts, 10f.
  experience, 14
  jealousy, 25, 64
  pleasure zones, 53f.
  reactions, 63, 202
  situation, reactivation of, 24, 68, 137
  trauma, *see* Trauma
Infantilism, 188, 270
Inferiority
  feelings, 20, 22, 62, 171, 308, 333, 344ff.
  need for, 190
Inhibition
  of acting, 368
  ascetic, 54
  hysterical, 62, 68, 74
  in place of anxiety, 62, 74
  and rage, 65
  sexual, 191ff.
  see also Motor inhibition
Insomnia, and delivery, 290
Instincts, defusion of, 132f.
Instinctual danger, 49ff., 65f., 91, 102, 114f.
Intellectualization, 253ff., 366
Internalization, 152f.
Introjection, 278
  of object in melancholia, 114, 152, 154, 211f., 216

Mother—*Continued*
  longing for, and operation, 290
  unworthy, 192
Mother-child relation, and homosexuality, 171f., 186f., 194
Motherhood and sexuality, 190-202
Motility, sexualization of, 34
Motor inhibition, 34f., 37, 50, 54
Mourning, 7, 9, 226ff.
  absence of, 227ff.
  need to complete, 235
Mouth, and homosexuality, 187
Multiple personality, 279

Narcissism, narcissistic, 147, 185, 232, 271, 320ff.
  in "as if" personality, 278
  cathexis of organ, 60
  in Conrad, 353
  delirium, 206
  forms of ego, 217
  identification, 148, 278
  injuries, 6
  neuroses, 145
  object choice, 85, 92f.
  regression to, 269
  satisfaction, 250
Narcosis, 294f.
  and death, 289f.
  and operative fear, 285
Negative transference, *see* Transference
Negativism, 273
Neurosis
  actual conflict in formation of, 3-13
  anachronism of, 49, 54
  etiological factors in, 4
  infantile, 16
  postanalytic recurrence of, 340
  transformation into other form, 110, 112
  traumatic, 284
Nightmare, 34, 37
"Normal," pathology in the, 337
Nunberg, H., 215
Nymphomania, 199

Oberndorf, C. P., 263
Object
  cathexis: inadequate, 271; loss of, 265

choice: heterosexual, 88; narcissistic, 85, 92f.
  loss, 111f., 288
  oedipal, 175, 270
"Observer, hostile," 260
Obsessional
  acts, 117-133
  ideas, 134-144
  see also Ceremonial
Obsessional neurosis, 117-144, 250
  ambivalence conflict in, 122, 129f., 138f.
  and anal-sadistic phase, 113, 144
  and character traits, 140
  and change of character, 120
  and double meaning of symptom formation, 122
  and genital phase, 114
  and hysteria, 67, 83, 111ff., 133
  and organic disease, 286
  and phobia, 83, 110, 130f., 133
  and projection, 141f.
  and sadism, 132
  and sense of guilt, 96, 131-133
  and unconscious homosexuality, 143
  in women, 143f.
Oedipus complex, 46, 59, 91, 99, 111f., 121, 129, 143, 171, 175f., 188, 270
  in girls, 19f., 180f., 192
  mastering of, 189
  and parent substitutes, 267
  and sexual inhibition, 190
Oligomenorrhea, 307
Omnipotence of thought, 140f.
Onanism, 30-37, 44f., 47f., 87f., 108, 110, 120, 124-126, 169
  repressed, 43
  see also Masturbation
Oral
  aggression, 64
  envy, 63
  impregnation fantasy, 59, 347, 350
  libido, decathexis of, 164
  stage, 55, 151, 154, 366
Oral-sadistic phase, and predisposition to female homosexuality, 187
Organ
  cathexes, 286
  personification of, 286
  psychological significance of, 287
  see also Compliance

388 INDEX